To Prof. J.

Best regards

[signature]

October, 1989

MACROECONOMIC EFFECTS AND DIFFUSION OF ALTERNATIVE TECHNOLOGIES WITHIN A SOCIAL ACCOUNTING MATRIX FRAMEWORK

The World Employment Programme (WEP) was launched by the International Labour Organisation in 1969, as the ILO's main contribution to the International Development Strategy for the Second United Nations Development Decade.

The means of action adopted by the WEP have included the following:

- short-term high-level advisory missions;

- longer-term national or regional employment teams; and

- a wide-ranging research programme.

Through these activities the ILO has been able to help national decision-makers to reshape their policies and plans with the aim of eradicating mass poverty and unemployment.

A landmark in the development of the WEP was the World Employment Conference of 1976, which proclaimed inter alia that 'strategies and national development plans should include as a priority objective the promotion of employment and the satisfaction of the basic needs of each country's population'. The Declaration of Principles and Programme of Action adopted by the Conference will remain the cornerstone of WEP technical assistance and research activities during the 1980s.

This publication is the outcome of WEP project.

Macroeconomic Effects and Diffusion of Alternative Technologies within a Social Accounting Matrix Framework

The Case of Indonesia

HAIDER A. KHAN
ERIK THORBECKE

Gower

A study prepared for the International Labour Office within the framework of the World Employment Programme

Published by
Gower Publishing Company Limited
Gower House
Croft Road
Aldershot
Hants GU11 3HR
England

Gower Publishing Company
Old Post Road
Brookfield
Vermont 05036
USA

ISBN 0 566 05681X

Printed and bound in Great Britain by
Athanaeum Press Limited, Newcastle upon Tyne.

Contents

I.   INTRODUCTION   1

II. DESCRIPTION OF INDONESIAN SAM-TECH AND THE SOCIAL
     ACCOUNTING MATRIX AS A DATA AND CONCEPTUAL FRAMEWORK   9

     A.   The basis of SAM-Tech   9
     B.   Selection of dual sectors according to technological indicators   14
     C.   The Social Accounting Matrix as a data and conceptual framework
          to explore the macroeconomic effects of alternative technologies
          within SAM-Tech   17

III. ANALYSIS OF MACROECONOMIC EFFECTS OF ALTERNATIVE
     PRODUCT-CUM-TECHNOLOGIES BASED ON SAM-TECH AND OTHER
     SOURCES   53

     A.   A synopsis of other studies   53
     B.   Increasing relative importance of modern technological alternative in
          selected dualistic sectors   57
     C.   Effects on national and sectoral output and energy requirements   62
     D.   Linkages between and among traditional activities, modern activities
          and other sectors   63
     E.   Effects on factor income and employment   66
     F.   Effects on household income distribution   67
     G.   Structural path analysis methodology: transmission of economic influence
          within the SAM framework   71
          1.   Direct influence   72
          2.   Total influence   73
          3.   Global influence   74
     H.   Structural path analysis applied to Indonesian SAM-Tech   76

IV. MACROECONOMIC AND SAM ANALYSIS OF THE ENERGY SECTOR
     IN INDONESIA   89
     Introduction   89

A.   Macroeconomic analysis: energy, balance of payments and government revenue   90

B.   An analysis of the energy sector within a Social Accounting Matrix
framework   94

Appendix to Chapter IV — Consumption, production and reserves of energy
in Indonesia   111

V.   RESEARCH AND DEVELOPMENT AND DIFFUSION OF TECHNOLOGY: NEW
THEORETICAL APPROACHES AND SOME EXAMPLES FROM INDONESIA   119

    A.   Research and development (R & D) and technology   119

        1.   R & D policy in an economy-wide setting: the SAM approach   120

        2.   Studies of agricultural mechanisation research on rice and textiles   124

        3.   Current priority areas in R & D and the SAM approach   128

    B.   Diffusion of technology   132

        1.   Some microeconomic studies of technology, employment and
income distribution   133

        2.   Incorporation of microeconomic technology diffusion models
into a SAM framework at conceptual level   140

    C.   Summary   143

Appendix A to Chapter V — Description and explanation of trends in output,
employment and value added in selected dualistic and other sectors   147

Appendix B   159

VI.   SUMMARY, POLICY CONCLUSIONS AND NEW RESEARCH DIRECTIONS   161

    A.   A Social Accounting Matrix for modelling technology choice and the
energy sector in Indonesia   162

    B.   Dynamic aspects of technology choice: R & D and diffusion of technology   166

    C.   Limitations of this study   167

    D.   Some policy issues and directions for future research   170

APPENDICES   177

Appendix A - The construction of SAM-Tech: sources of information and
major assumptions   177

Appendix Table B - Social Accounting Matrix SAM-Tech, Indonesia, 1975,
transactions matrix (in billion of Rupiahs)   184

Appendix Table C - Household expenditure elasticities for Indonesia, 1975   194

Appendix Table D - Household marginal expenditure propensities for Indonesia, 1975   196

BIBLIOGRAPHY   198

INDEX   204

ILO preface

In spite of a growing body of microeconomic work on technology, there is as yet no systematic macroeconomic framework which provides a missing link between the microeconomic and macroeconomic aspects of technological decision making. Lack of such a framework has resulted in the failure of many dedicated and serious policy makers to integrate technological parameters and plans into development plans in any systematic manner.

Technology needs to be considered in a wider context of alternative policy instruments which are at the disposal of the national decision makers to achieve the objectives of output and employment growth. Furthermore, the usefulness of technology as a policy instrument for achieving employment and equity objects has intertemporal implications which are often neglected.

In this study, Professor Erik Thorbecke, H. E. Babcock Professor of Economics and Food Economics at Cornell University and Dr. Haider Khan, Assistant Professor of Economics at the Graduate School of International Studies, University of Denver develop a macroeconomic framework using a Social Accounting Matrix (SAM) of Indonesia. The authors show the superiority of this framework over an input-output matrix which does not take into account iterative effects of increased sectoral outputs on labour and other factors of production. The SAM framework enables an analysis of interrelationships between structure of production, alternative technologies, employment and income distribution of household groups and their consumption and savings behaviour.

The SAM macroeconomic framework classifies production activities according to dualistic lines, i.e. those produced with traditional labour-intensive technologies and others, with modern capital-intensive technologies. In addition to production activities, energy is also disaggregated.

The study arrives at an interesting finding that, in general, traditional technology generates more aggregate output and employment effects on the economy than the modern alternative. This finding would hold in the short run if these traditional techniques had greater backward linkages and smaller leakages through imports and savings. The study also extends ingeniously the use of the SAM framework to examine the effects of R & D on the generation and adaptation of technology; although data limitation prevented a thorough examination in the context of Indonesia. It shows that the traditional technology generates greater direct as well as indirect labour income effects than the modern technology for the same increase in output.

It is thereore concluded that at least in the case of Indonesia. commitment to high technology needs to be combined with support to more traditional techniques especially when deciding on allocation of R & D resources.

This study was financed by a generous grant from the Swedish Government to the ILO/WEP Technology and Employment Programme.

A. S. Bhalla
Chief
Technology and Employment Branch

I Introduction

The effects of technology on the economy and society, in general, are pervasive. Whereas the direct microeconomic effects of alternative technologies can easily and accurately be determined, it is much more difficult to capture and estimate the direct and indirect macroeconomic effects.

The most obvious and simplest manifestation of alternative technologies takes the form of how much and what type of employment they generate per unit of output. Likewise, the direct requirements of domestic and imported intermediate inputs (such as for different energy sources) and capital can readily be estimated for the alternative technologies which prevail. All that is needed to compute these direct microeconomic effects is a knowledge of the production functions or technical coefficients linking product outputs to inputs. Thus, for example, intermediate and primary inputs (e.g. in terms of person days of labour and investment costs) needed to process one ton of rice using the traditional handpounding method can be compared with the requirements under an alternative technology such as a small or even large rice mill. A good project analysis or feasibility study can also determine reasonably accurately the private and social benefit-cost ratios of alternative technologies. Thus, at the microeconomic level, it is relatively easy to measure the direct consequences of the choice of techniques on such variables of interest to the policy maker as employment, capital and energy requirements, and imports.

In many instances, however, the indirect effects of techniques are significantly more important than the direct effects per se. This follows, of course, from the interdependencies which prevail in an economic structure and the variety of backward and forward linkages engendered by the choice of a given technology in the

1

production of a given good. Until recently, these indirect effects were estimated with the help of an input-output framework which allowed one to compute the vector of sectoral outputs resulting from a given increase in the final demand for the product-cum-technology under consideration. The input-output methodology--although superior to a purely microeconomic approach in capturing at least some of the indirect effects--is limited. It embraces the intersectoral linkages within the production sphere exclusively. More specifically, starting with an increase in final demand for and consequent production of a given product-cum-technology (i.e. a given production activity embodying a specific technology such as, for example, rice processing in small mills) the input-output approach captures only the output effects on all other production activities (sectors) which either directly or indirectly provide inputs to the initial sector.

What the input-output methodology (strictly speaking the Leontief-inverse) does not take into account are the further consequences of increased sectoral outputs on the employment of labour and other factors of production which generates a stream of income received by these factors. In turn, this value added ends up--assuming no supply constraints (i.e. excess capacity)--[1]as income to the various socioeconomic households and other institutions in the economy allowing the latter to spend more on consumption of the various commodities produced by the production activities thereby generating additional production. By excluding the link between increased output, the factorial and household income distribution and increased consumption the I/O approach short circuits the circular flow in the economy and thereby accounts for only a part of the indirect effects generated by increased production in any of the production activities.

In the last half dozen years a more generalised approach based on the Social Accounting Matrix (SAM) framework has been formulated to capture not only the above direct and indirect effects of technology but also to analyse in detail the whole network of paths through which technological influence is transmitted within the economy. The SAM provides a useful data and conceptual framework within which the effects of alternative technologies on major macroeconomic variables and policy objectives can be explored. It provides a data and analytical system within which the interrelationships between a) the structure of production; b) the distribution of value added generated by the production activities and yielding the factorial income distribution; and c) the income distribution by socioeconomic household groups and their resulting consumption and savings behavior can be studied. In particular, the production activities can be classified according to types of commodity as well as technology and form of organization such as, for example, handpounded rice produced almost exclusively with labour in traditional household enterprises as compared to milled rice requiring mechanised techniques and a larger scale of operation in unincorporated or corporate enterprises.

In fact, the present study has two major purposes: First, to formulatea methodology to analyze and estimate the macroeconomic

2

effects of alternative technologies within a comprehensive SAM framework which incorporates the major interdependencies which exist within an economy. Secondly, this methodology is applied to the case of Indonesia to provide a better understanding of some of the macroeconomic consequences of current technological trends in that country and as an illustration of the issues the SAM approach can address. Even though in some instances we could not go as far in the quantitative analysis as we would have liked to because of the nonavailability of certain types of information and data on Indonesia, an attempt is made throughout the study to show how the SAM methodology could be used to answer a variety of questions regarding both the static and some of the dynamic macroeconomic effects of technology on the economy given adequate data.

The present study contains four major chapters in addition to a summary and conclusions part. Chapter II is devoted to a description of the Indonesian SAM which was built specifically for the present study and, in a more general sense, to the way in which the SAM can be used as a data and conceptual framework to analyse the macroeconomic effects of alternative technologies. In section II.A, the main features of SAM-Tech (the name we gave to our version of the Indonesian SAM used in the present study) are laid down. The SAM built by the Indonesian Central Bureau of Statistics (CBS) for 1975 provided the basis for SAM-Tech. The main modifications which were grafted on to the CBS SAM were 1) a different classification of production activities identifying, more specifically, six products (sectors) broken down along dualistic technological lines; and 2) a more detailed breakdown of the energy sector. The idea behind the dualistic sectors was to identify relatively homogeneous products or groups of products which could be produced either with traditional, essentially labour intensive technologies or, alternatively, with more modern and capital intensive technologies. Ultimately, the following dualistic sectors were incorporated into SAM-Tech (for each product, the traditional technology is listed first): handpounded rice vs. rice milling; farm processed tea vs. tea processing (in plants); dried and salted fish vs. canned fish; brown sugar vs. refined sugar; canning and preserving of fruits and vegetables in small firms as opposed to medium and large firms; and clove cigarettes vs. white cigarettes.[2]

The second modification consisted of a disaggregation of energy into the following six components: coal, petroleum and natural gas, gasoline and avigas, fuel oil, kerosene, and electricity, and gas.[3]

In section II.B, the rationale is provided for the selection of the twelve dualistic sectors in SAM-Tech according to a number of different technological indicators. It is argued (on the basis of an examination of the latter) that the traditional technological alternative is significantly different from the corresponding modern one in each pair of product-cum-technologies.

Section II.C discusses in some detail how the SAM can be used as a data and conceptual framework to explore the macroeconomic

3

effects of alternative technologies and presents the complete SAM-Tech. SAM-Tech consists of 78 columns and corresponding rows. It includes three endogenous accounts i.e., 1) twenty-three different factors of production representing sixteen different labour groups that are broken down according to main sector employment, paid vs. unpaid and rural vs. urban and seven types of capital including land); 2) eleven institutions which are further broken down into ten socioeconomic household groups and one group of companies; and 3) forty different production activities of which twelve are the previously mentioned dualistic sectors defined according to technological criteria. The other accounts are considered as exogenous i.e., government; the combined capital account; net indirect taxes; and, the rest of the world.

Both the transaction matrix and the corresponding matrix of average expenditure propensities (the so-called A matrix) are given and discussed. It is shown that if a certain number of conditions are met and, in particular, if there exists excess capacity which would allow prices to remain constant, the SAM framework can be used to estimate the effects of exogenous changes and injections such as an increase in the output of a given production activity (e.g. one of our dualistic sectors), government expenditures or exports on the whole system i.e. the seventy-five variables which constitute the above three endogenous accounts. This last type of simulation can be undertaken on the basis of the so-called fixed price multipliers which are derived empirically from SAM-Tech with the help of additional information on the income elasticities of demand of the various socioeconomic household groups for the different commodities (production activities) appearing in SAM-Tech. In a sense, the fixed price multiplier matrix which is presented represents a giant policy navigation table.

Chapter III is devoted to the actual analysis of the macroeconomic effects of alternative technologies mainly based on SAM-Tech. In Section III.A a brief review is undertaken of other existing studies exploring the macroeconomic effects of technology choices in Indonesia. It is shown that while many of these studies are very useful in their own right--particularly the comprehensive studies based on an input/output approach--they do not go far enough in capturing the indirect effects of technology choice by failing to incorporate explicitly the link between the impact of changes in the structure of production engendered by the new or changing technologies and the resulting household income distribution and consequent effects on final (particularly consumption) demand.

Next, in Section III.B, the tendency in Indonesia, as in many other developing countries, for medium size and large establishments to displace small scale and household and cottage establishments is scrutinized. In particular, to the extent that the latter are very likely to use a traditional technology while medium and large establishments are likely to adopt a modern technology, this above trend implies as well a corresponding displacement of the traditional technology by a more modern one at the product or sector level. The existence of this trend within the twelve dualistic sectors appearing in SAM-Tech is confirmed.

The next four sections of Chapter III (III.C-F) use the fixed price multipliers derived from SAM-Tech to explore the implications of the above trend on, respectively, national and sectoral output and energy requirements; factor income and employment; the household income distribution by socioeconomic groups; and, finally, the linkages between and among traditional activities, modern activities and other sectors. In general, it appears that the traditional technology generates greater aggregate output effects on the whole economic system than the corresponding modern technology for four of the six products constituting our dualistic sectors while in the other remaining two cases the difference was marginal. Likewise, the effects of increased production of the traditional technology has a greater impact on total employment and a much greater impact on the incomes of lower skilled workers than the corresponding modern alternative--again on the basis of pairwise comparisons of product-cum-technologies.

The final part of Chapter III is devoted to a review of the methodology underlying structural path analysis and the transmission of economic influence within the SAM framework. This methodology is applied to the Indonesian SAM-Tech to illustrate on the basis of a number of selected examples, the whole network of paths through which the impact of a change in output originating in a traditional or its corresponding modern product-cum-technology gets transmitted within the Indonesian SAM structure. In this way, the different network of paths and poles through which the influence of a traditional technological alternative gets propagated throughout the Indonesia SAM structure can be compared to the network followed by its modern counterpart again on a pairwise basis product by product for the six products in our sample of dualistic sectors. In this sense, structural path analysis can be considered a key methodology in identifying the complex mechanism through which technological influence gets transmitted within an economy.

Chapter IV is devoted to a macroeconomic analysis of the energy sector in Indonesia basing it partially on the SAM-Tech framework. It starts in Section IV.A with a short analysis of the interrelationship between the energy picture both in its national and international dimensions and the Indonesian balance of payments and government revenues.

Section IV.B which is devoted to an analysis of the energy sector within a SAM framework forms the heart of this chapter. The first finding is that the modern technological alternative for each set of products tends to be significantly more energy intensive (in terms of its direct effects) than the corresponding traditional alternative.[4] Furthermore, the total direct and indirect energy requirements for the twelve dualistic activities are computed on the basis of the relevant fixed price multipliers. This analysis is undertaken both in terms of aggregate energy requirements and disaggregated requirements for the six different energy sources (sectors) appearing in SAM-Tech. Two additional questions which are addressed in this section are, respectively, 1) estimating the likely effects on the household income distribution (by socioeconomic groups) of observed or likely changes in the pattern and structure of energy production among the six energy sectors; and 2) estimating the likely consequences of changes in the income distribution among the different socioeconomic groups on the demand for the six different energy sources. In both instances the analysis is based on using the appropriate fixed price multipliers. In general, this section demonstrates the usefulness of the SAM approach in allowing a detailed macroeconomic analysis of the interrelationship between technological choice, energy requirements, the structure of production, and the resulting household income distribution including the changing demand for different energy sources.

Chapter V consists of two main parts dealing respectively with A) the relation between research and development (R & D), on the one hand, and technology, on the other; and B) the diffusion of technology in the context of a SAM. In turn, the first part above consists of three subsections. The first one suggests a procedure for identifying and incorporating R & D as a separate production activity within a SAM. Although this procedure could not be applied to Indonesia for lack of data, it appears promising whenever such data are available. The second subsection reviews and analyses three specific areas of the Indonesian economy (i.e. sectors) on which some work has been done on the impact of R & D on the generation and adoption of technologies. The three cases embrace the development of mechanised technology (particularly in the form of small tractors in paddy production), the impact of rice research in Indonesia on productivity, and the impact of R & D in the Indonesian textile sector. The final subsection deals with an examination of the current priority areas for R & D in Indonesia and, more particularly, the present emphasis which appears to be placed on high technology among some of the ministries. It is argued that a SAM embodying alternative technologies as well as R & D information could prove to be useful in providing detailed macroeconomic estimates of the effects of different sectoral R & D allocations and technology policies on output, employment, income distribution, the balance of payments and other objectives of interest to the policymaker.

Section V.B on diffusion of technology is likewise broken down into two subsections. The first subsection reviews two important microeconomic studies of the effects of technology on employment and income distribution in the Indonesian context. In particular, the link between technology diffusion in paddy production and the resulting pattern of employment and income distribution appears very complex and significantly influenced by the prevailing institutional setting. The second subsection is devoted to an attempt to incorporate a simple evolutionary model of technical change within a SAM framework. The synthesis of this evolutionary model and the SAM framework demonstrates the potential for micro-macro linkages in the area of technology diffusion and represents a step in the direction of converting the SAM from a purely comparative

6

static framework to one capable--albeit in a limited way to handle simple dynamic processes.

Finally, Chapter VI includes a summary, policy conclusions and new research direction. Parts A and B, summarise and synthesize the major findings of the study. Part C identifies some of the limitations of the study. In particular, it is emphasized that the type of comparative static exercises undertaken in this study on the basis of SAM-Tech are only valid in the very short run assuming the existence of a current SAM reflecting accurately the underlying structure of the economy. For purposes of medium or long term planning, the SAM framework has to be complemented by a more dynamic model capable, at least partially, to determine the new set of prices and SAM coefficients endogenously. Part D completes the study by exploring some important policy issues and directions for future research.

It should be re-emphasized that the methodology underlying the present study and applied to Indonesia as a demonstration of its potential is, in principle, transferable to any country for which a SAM exists as well as complementary information on such variables as R & D and diffusion.

In a general sense the SAM framework has widespread applicability for planning. The present study provides one illustration of the usefulness of this approach--particularly in deriving the distributional consequences of a variety of policy measures and exogenous changes originating in the rest of the world. In interpreting the results of this study it is important to realise the limitations of the SAM approach as they relate to the assumptions of excess capacity and constant relative prices. Chapter VI (mainly section C) brings out these limitations and qualifies the analysis accordingly.

The Indonesian Central Bureau of Statistics with the help of a team from the Institute of Social Studies (ISS) in The Hague and Cornell University has built the most comprehensive SAM available anywhere in the world. It appears that this effort is in the process of being institutionalised. At this time the CBS with the continuing help from ISS is completing a SAM for 1980. It is important that the SAM tables be kept to date and current through both updating of existing SAMs and new ones being prepared, say, every five years. Furthermore, the gathering of additional information on such variables as sectoral capital stocks, R & D and diffusion of alternative technologies--as indicated throughout the study--would permit the SAM skeleton to be filled with flesh. In fact, a major reason for undertaking this study was to demonstrate areas of policy usefulness for the SAM methodology and encourage other researchers and policymakers to use it as well. Finally, we are very grateful to the CBS for its continuing assistance without which this project could not have been completed.

Notes

1   The realism and the implications of this assumption are dis-
    cussed subsequently.
2   It should be emphasized that within each dualistic pair,
    products are not necessarily pure substitutes. This does not
    really matter since the purpose of the exercise is to explore
    the macroeconomic consequences of changes in the output of any
    product-cum-technology activities not just the dualistic ones.
3   Further disaggregation of some of these sectors (e.g. petro-
    leum and natural gas) is desirable, but was not possible
    because of data limitations. This is discussed further in
    Chapter 4.
4   This conclusion holds only for the energy sectors broken down
    explicitly in the SAM. Some energy inputs such as biomass are
    not shown as separate productive activities in the SAM-Tech.

II Description of Indonesian SAM-Tech and the Social Accounting Matrix as a data and conceptual framework

A. The basis of SAM-Tech

The starting point of the Social Accounting Matrix (SAM) which we built to explore some of the macroeconomic implications of technology choice (which we shall call SAM-Tech, for short) was based on the sixty-two sector SAM built by the Central Bureau of Statistics for 1975 (see CBS 1982).[1]

In what follows, we describe briefly the original CBS SAM and the modifications which were made. The original CBS-SAM was expressed at purchasers' prices with separate trade and transportation margin accounts. It also distinguished between production activities and commodities. Since the same classification scheme was used for both sets of production activities and commodities, a major purpose of introducing a commodity account was to allocate net indirect taxes to the indirect tax account. Furthermore, in the original CBS-SAM a separate "imported commodities" account appeared with the domestic production activities purchasing imported inputs from the latter account.

In building SAM-Tech the following changes were made. First, by subtracting trade and transportation margins from production accounts and adding these to the "wholesale and retail trade" activity, the commodity and production accounts were consolidated into one set of accounts i.e. "production activities". This means that in SAM-Tech the production activities pay indirect taxes directly to the indirect tax account. Secondly, in the new SAM production activities purchase imported inputs directly from the rest of the world account rather than indirectly via the imported commodities account.

Since the major purpose of building SAM-Tech was to identify and distinguish some production activities according to technological criteria along dualistic lines, the major difference between the

CBS-SAM and SAM-Tech relates to the classification of production activities. Table II.1 gives the classification scheme used in SAM-Tech. The classification of factors of production and of institutions is exactly the same as that of the CBS SAM. On the other hand, twelve new production activities were identified along dualistic lines. The purpose of the so-called dualistic sectors was to distinguish alternative technologies used in the production of relatively homogeneous products. The idea was to identify products which could be produced either with traditional, essentially labour intensive technologies or, alternatively, with more modern and more capital intensive technologies. The following sectors were incorporated into SAM-Tech (for each product the traditional technology is listed first): handpounded rice vs. rice milling; farm processed tea vs. tea processing (in plants); dried and salted fish vs. canned fish; brown sugar vs. refined sugar; canning and preserving of fruits and vegetables in small firms as opposed to medium and large firms; and clove cigarettes vs. white cigarettes. Subsequently, the characteristics of these dualistic activities and the procedure which were used to estimate the production coefficients (i.e the column vectors in the SAM in terms of intermediate input requirements and distribution of value added) as well as estimating the household demand for these dualistic commodities are discussed.

The second modification which was made in the classification of production activities, as compared to that used in the CBS-SAM consisted of a somewhat more specific breakdown of energy sectors into the following groups, i.e. coal, petroleum and natural gas, gasoline and avigas, fuel oil, electricity, and gas. The other production activities, in addition to the dualistic sectors and the six energy sectors, follow essentially the same breakdown as in the CBS SAM with the already mentioned qualification that the "wholesale and retail trade" sector includes the trade and transportation margins.

Thus, it can be seen from Table II.1 that production activities are broken down into six major sets: 1) Agriculture, Forestry and Fishing which includes five sectors; 2) Mining with two sectors; 3) the Dualistic sectors with twelve activities; 4) Other Manufacturing and Processing with five sectors; 5) Energy with six sectors and 6) Services with ten sectors for a total of forty distinct production activities.

In summary, the classification scheme of SAM-Tech and the criteria upon which it is based are given in Table II.1. Factors of Production (numbering 23 groups) are broken down first according to labour type and non-labour (capital and land) type. At the second level, labour is broken down according to sector of employment, occupation and skills and further broken down according to paid vs. unpaid and rural vs. urban. In turn, the non-labour factors of production are broken down into unincorporated and incorporated, capital with the former further subdivided into land and other agricultural capital owner occupied

10

TABLE II.1: CLASSIFICATION OF SOCIAL ACCOUNTING MATRIX
(SAM-TECH) INDONESIA, 1975

Description					Code
Factors of Production	Labor	Agricultural	Paid	Rural	1
				Urban	2
			Unpaid	Rural	3
				Urban	4
		Production, Transport Equipment Operator, and Manual	Paid	Rural	5
				Urban	6
			Unpaid	Rural	7
				Urban	8
		Clerical, Sales and Services	Paid	Rural	9
				Urban	10
			Unpaid	Rural	11
				Urban	12
		Professional, Managerial and Non Civilians	Paid	Rural	13
				Urban	14
			Unpaid	Rural	15
				Urban	16
	Others	Unincorporated Capital	Land, Other Agricultural Capital		17
			Owner occupied housing		18
			Other Capital : Rural		19
			Other Capital : Urban		20
		Incorporated Capital	Domestic Private Capital		21
			Government Capital		22
			Foreign Capital		23

			Description		Code
I n s t i t u t i o n s	H o u s e h o l d s	Agricultural	Employees		24
			Operator, Land Owner 0.000 – 0.500 Ha		25
			Operator, Land Owner 0.501 – 1.000 Ha		26
			Operator, Land Owner > 1.000 Ha		27
		Non Agricultural	Rural	Lower Level; Non Agriculture Self Employed, Clerical, Retail Sales, Personal Services, and Transport & Manual Workers	28
				Non Labor Force and Unclassified Household	29
				Higher Level; Non Agriculture Self Employed, Clerical & Sales, Services, Managers, Supervisors, Technicians, Teachers and Non Civilians	30
			Urban	Lower Level; Non Agriculture Self Employed, Clerical, Retail Sales, Personal Services, and Transport & Manual Workers	31
				Non Labor Force and Unclassified Household	32
				Higher Level; Non Agriculture Self Employed, Clerical & Sales, Services, Managers, Supervisors, Technicians, Teachers and Non Civilians	33
	Companies				34

		Description	Code
PRODUCTION ACTIVITIES	**Agriculture, Forestry and Fishing**	Farm Food Crops	35
		Farm Nonfood Crops	36
		Livestock and Products	37
		Forestry and Hunting	38
		Fishery	39
	Mining	Metal Ore	40
		Other Mining	41
	Dualistic Sectors	Handpounded Rice	42
		Rice Milling	43
		Farm Processed Tea	44
		Tea Processing	45
		Dried and Salted Fish	46
		Canned Fish	47
		Brown Sugar	48
		Sugar	49
		Canning and Preserving of Fruits and Vegetables (Small)	50
		Canning and Preserving of Fruits and Vegetables (M+L)	51
		Clove Cigarettes	52
		White Cigarettes	53
	Manufacturing and Processing	Other Food, Beverages and Tobacco	54
		Wood Products and Construction	55
		Textile, Leather and Apparels	56
		Paper and Printing, Transport Equipment, Metal Products and Others	57
		Other Chemicals, Clay Products, Cement and Basic Metals	58
	Energy	Coal	59
		Petroleum and Natural Gas	60
		Gasoline and Avigas	61
		Fuel Oil (including kerosene)	62
		Electricity	63
		Gas	64
	Services	Water	65
		Wholesale and Retail Trade	66
		Restaurants	67
		Hotels and Lodging	68
		Road Transport and Railways	69
		Air, Water Transport and Communication	70
		Banking and Insurance	71
		Real Estate including Business Services	72
		Public Administration, Social and Cultural Services	73
		Personal, Household and Other Services	74
EXOGENOUS ACCOUNTS		Government	75
		Capital Account	76
		Net Indirect Taxes	77
		Rest of World	78

housing, other capital rural and urban and the latter into domestic private capital, government capital and foreign capital. Next, eleven institutions are identified i.e. ten different types of households and one aggregate group of companies. In turn, households are further broken down into agricultural/ nonagricultural. Next, agricultural households are subdivided according to the amount of land owned by the household (four groups) and nonagricultural households are broken down first according to location i.e. rural vs. urban and at the next level according to socioeconomic characteristics. Finally, in addition to the breakdown of production activities which has just been discussed, four exogenous accounts appear i.e. government, the capital account, net indirect taxes and rest of the world. The overall dimension of SAM-Tech, as can be seen from Table II.1, is in terms of 78 rows and columns.

B. Selection of dual sectors according to technological indicators

Technologies may be distinguished by using any or all of a number of criteria. Formally we may define each element of a technology set T, T (t_1, t_2,...t_n) where t_i = the ith characteristic of the technology T. Two technologies T and T' are distinct when there exist at least t_i and t_i' such that $t_i \neq t_i'$.

To operationalise the above abstract characterization, each t_i must be determined empirically and some basis for comparison of two technologies must be set up. This involves defining a set of technological indicators and then comparing them. Previous works by Bhalla (1975), Svejnar and Thorbecke (1980, 1982), and Khan (1982)[2] illustrate this approach. Among the technological indicators which have been proposed as admissible by the preceding authors are capital-labour ratio, output-capital ratio, value added per worker, value added going to capital or labour as a percentage of total value added, the ratio of skilled to unskilled workers, vintage and origin of the capital stock, and firm size.

Under ideal conditions (i.e. no data restrictions) the choice of criteria depends entirely upon the research questions being asked. As the main concern of our investigation is focused on the macroeconomic effects of traditional vs. modern techniques, the above list of criteria seems relevant. If one were interested in "appropriate" technology per se some other additional criteria might have to be considered. For example, if environmental protection were a factor in the choice of technology, then pollution characteristics of different technologies would be very relevant as distinguishing criteria.

One of the key differences between traditional and modern techniques is the degree of labour and capital-intensity. Therefore, data on capital stock as well as employment and output should be gathered and capital-labour and output-capital ratios should be computed. Unfortunately, data at the sectoral level on capital stock are not available for the Indonesian economy.[3]

The starting point in our attempt to distinguish sectors according to dualistic technological criteria was on the basis of firm sizes.[4] Surveys and censuses of manufactures exist for both small (and in some cases household and cottage industries) as well as for large and medium firms. At this stage, a few words are in order about the industrial census sources and coverage. In 1974-75 the Central Bureau of Statistics carried out the second industrial Census in Indonesia (the first one took place in 1964). It included the following sectors:

1) large manufacturing establishments (employing 100 persons and over)
2) medium manufacturing establishments (employing between 20 and 99 individuals
3) small manufacturing establishments (employing 5 to 19 individuals)
4) household and cottage establishments (less than 5 employees)
5) organised mining and extraction of petroleum and other minerals, and
6) unorganised mining and quarrying of gravel, sand, lime, salt pans, etc.

Even though a complete enumeration is claimed to have been achieved, it is doubtful that this was indeed the case because of large discrepancies between the census figures and the input/output figures. In many instances, the latter are a multiple of the corresponding census figures. The reliability of the census information seems to be inversely related with the sizes of the establishment. For large and medium firms, there is relatively more complete and more accurate information. For the small firms, information relating to value added is often suspect and is even worse at the household sector level where it is aggregated (whenever available) at the three digit level. In any case the data used to estimate the production coefficients and technological indicators of the twelve dualistic sectors in SAM-Tech came from CBS sources which were checked whenever possible for internal consistency. Thus, for a few sectors such as canning and preserving of fruits and vegetables (modern vs. traditional technology) and dried and salted fish (traditional) and canned fish (modern), the two alternative technologies seem to be correlated with firm size and were therefore based on this criterion with small and household and cottage establishments employing less than twenty persons presumed to reflect the traditional technology and medium and large establishments employing more than twenty employees presumed to reflect the modern technology.

For the other dualistic product-cum-technologies (i.e. hand-pounded rice vs. milled rice, farm processed tea vs. tea processing, and brown sugar vs. refined sugar and dried and salted fish vs. canned fish) the input/output table of 1975 provided the necessary information to estimate the intermediate input requirements and the distribution of value added between wages and non-

wage income. Unfortunately several potentially interesting agricultural sectors from a technological standpoint (e.g. rice harvesting or paddy growing) were not amenable to a dualistic breakdown because of the lack of detailed input/output type information. In manufacturing, textiles was a major omission. Here data
were available but within the two major activities under textiles,
"yarn and thread" and weaving, respectively, more than 95% of the
total production in 1975 was already carried out under the modern
technology. Hence, from a macroeconomic standpoint, the effects
of the traditional alternative is dwarfed by those of the predomi-
nant modern alternative. Another sector which would have been a
desirable candidate for a dualistic breakdown is the transportation sector--in particular, the breakdown between informal activities (e.g. becak driving) and more formal transportation activities, such as taxi and organised bus transport. However, here
again data limitation precluded such a breakdown. Appendix A
provides more information regarding the procedure used to estimate
the production coefficients (i.e. the SAM-column vectors) of the
dualistic sectors and the corresponding demand for these dualistic
products (i.e. the SAM-rows).

   The following technological indicators were used to characterise
the technology and to verify that the traditional alternative
could indeed be distinguished from the modern one for the twelve
dualistic sectors: 1) value added per worker; 2) average expenditure propensity for energy (six different types); 3) the capital
(i.e. non-labour income) share of value added; and, 4) the ratio
of paid to unpaid workers. This information is provided in Table
II.2. In addition, in col. 5 the share of total output contributed by, respectively, the traditional and modern alternative is
given for each product. It should be noted that the energy share
indicator is used as a proxy for capital-intensity in the absence
of any sectoral or subsectoral capital stock figure. Likewise,
value added going to capital as a share of total value added is
also used as some proxy of capital intensity. Lacking any detailed information about the number of skilled and unskilled
workers, the ratio between paid and unpaid workers can be considered as an index of skill intensity (assumed to be positively
correlated to other characteristics of the modern technological
alternative).

   On the basis of this limited set of indicators (which, in any
case, was the only one available) it does appear that, generally
speaking, the traditional technological alternative was significantly different from the corresponding modern one in each pair of
product-cum-technologies. The comparison between the two techniques is straightforward. For example, going down the first
column of Table II.2, all the traditional technological alternatives, with one exception, have lower value added per worker
than the corresponding modern alternative. The exception consists
of traditional canning and preserving of fruits and vegetables.
However, the other three technological indicators suggest that the
traditional technique in this sector is significantly different
from the modern (large scale) alternative.

The only other inconsistency which can be noticed in Table II.2 relates to brown sugar vs. refined sugar. Whereas three indicators are significantly higher for refined sugar than for brown sugar, somewhat surprisingly the fourth indicator, i.e. the capital share of value added is slightly higher for brown sugar than for refined sugar.

C. **The Social Accounting Matrix as a data and conceptual framework to explore the macroeconomic effects of alternative technologies within SAM-Tech**

The SAM provides a useful data and conceptual framework within which, first, technology can be incorporated; and, second, the effects of alternative technologies on major macroeconomic variables and policy objectives can be explored. It is useful at this stage to summarise briefly the essence of the SAM methodology and how it can be adapted more specifically to deal with the above two questions.[5]

Perhaps the simplest starting point in describing the SAM framework as an analytical system is to recall the interrelationship between: a) the structure of production; b) the distribution of value added generated by the production activities and yielding the factorial income distribution; and c) the income distribution by socioeconomic groups and the corresponding consumption and savings behavior of these socioeconomic groups. Figure II.1 shows this interrelationship. Of special relevance in the present context, the production activities can be classified according to types of commodity as well as technology and form of organization, such as for example, a) handpounded rice produced with almost completely labour intensive techniques usually in a family farm setting as opposed to rice being processed in modern mills using essentially capital intensive technologies within a factory setting; and b) clove cigarettes produced with relatively labour intensive techniques in typically informal enterprises as compared to white cigarettes requiring mechanised techniques and a larger scale of operation in the formal sector. Hence, within the SAM, the value added which is generated by the various production activities gets mapped into a factorial income distribution where factors are broken down according to such criteria as a) labour skills or occupations of the workers, whether the latter are paid or unpaid (self-employed) and location of employment (i.e. rural or urban areas); and, b) unincorporated and incorporated capital income, with a further breakdown into such categories as land, owner occupied housing, domestic private capital, government capital and foreign capital. This transformation from value added generated by the various production activities to the factorial income distribution is denoted by the matrix T_{13} in Figure II.1. It is through this transformation--together with input/output transaction matrix T_{33}--that the effects of alternative technologies on the system are captured (i.e. what is called the technological link in Figure II.1).

Table II.2 Technological Indicators of Dualistic Sectors, 1975.

Sectors	Value Added per Worker (000 Rupiahs) (1)	Average Expenditure Propensity for All Energy Sources (2)	Capital Share of Value Added (%) (3)	Ratio of Number of Paid to Number of Unpaid Workers (4)	Share of Output of Traditional and Modern Technology (%) (5)
A. Rice Processing					
Handpounded Rice	183	0	0	2.71	35
Milled Rice	1495	.022	54.1	45.2	65
B. Tea Processing					
Farm Processed Tea	115	.033	30.1	4.0	83
Off-farm Processing	136	.042	46.7	55.1	17
C. Sugar					
Brown Sugar	54	.005	78.4	1.7 no unpaid workers	26
Refined Sugar	1127	.059	71.3		74
D. Canning and Preserving of Fruits & Vegetables					
Traditional Small Scale	598	.010	30.7	5 no unpaid	32
Modern Large Scale	129	.016	51.0		68
E. Fish Processing					
Dried and Salted Fish	97	.002	62.1	4.3	85
Canned Fish	97	.022	96.7	213.1	15
F. Cigarettes					
Clove Cigarettes	967	.009	76.2	134.5 no unpaid workers	74
White Cigarettes	7441	.011	91.2		26

Source: col. 1 - Census Industri and Statistik Industri, CBS 1975.
col. 2 - Sum of average expenditure propensities for energy sectors (code 59-64 in SAM-Tech) in Table II.5.
col. 3 and 5 - Appendix Table B; Census Industri and Statistik Industri, CBS 1975 and Input-Output Table 1975.
col. 4 - Census Industri and Statistik Industri, CBS 1975.

Figure 1. Simplified Interrelationship among Principal SAM Accounts
(Production Activities, Factors and Institutions)*

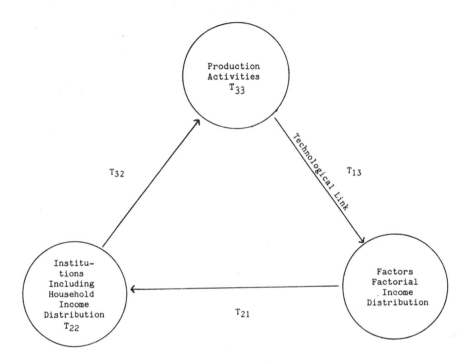

*T stands for the corresponding matrix in the simplified SAM which appears
on Table 2. Thus, for example, T_{13} refers to the matrix which appears at
the intersection of row 1 (account 1), i.e., "factors" and column 3
(account 3), i.e., "production activities".

Table II.3: Format of SAM-TECH Indonesia, 1975. (Numbers under each account represent the various sectors appearing in the SAM, e.g. 23 different factors, 10 households, etc. The complete classification is given in Table II.1.).

| | | ENDOGENOUS ACCOUNTS | | | EXOGENOUS ACCOUNTS | | | | |
| | | | Institutions | | | | | | |
RECEIPTS	Factors 1 / 23	Households 24 / 33	Companies 34	Production Activities 35 / 74	Government 75	Capital Account 76	Net Indirect Taxes 77	Rest of the World 78	Total
Factors 1 / 23				Allocation of Labor and Capital Value Added to Factors				Factor Income Received from Abroad	Total Incomes of Factors
Households 24 / 33	Allocation of Labor and Uninc Capital Income to Households	Current Transfers Among Households	Profits and Dividends Distributed to Households		Current Transfers to Households			Nonfactor Income Received from Abroad	Total Incomes of Households
Companies 34	Allocation of Inc Operating Surplus to Companies				Current Transfers to Domestic Companies				Total Incomes of Domestic Companies
Production Activities 35 / 74		Household Consumption Expenditures on Domestic Commodities		Domestic Intermediate Input Requirements	Government Current Expenditures On Domestic Commodities	Investment Expenditures on Domestic Goods		Exports	Aggregate Demand = Gross Output
Government 75		Direct Taxes	Direct Taxes on Companies	Net Indirect Taxes			Net Indirect Taxes	Net Nonfactor Incomes Received from Abroad	Total Government Receipts
Capital 76		Household Savings	Undistributed Profits After Tax		Government Current Account Surplus			Net Capital Received from Abroad	Aggregate Savings
Net Indirect Taxes 77				Net Indirect Taxes				Net Indirect Taxes on Exports	Total Indirect Taxes
Rest of the World 78	Factor Payment Abroad	Household Consumption Expenditures on Imported Goods	Nonfactor Payment Abroad	Imports of Intermediate Inputs	Government Expenditures on Imports	Imports of Capital Goods			Total Foreign Exchange Expenditures
Totals	Total Expenditures of Domestic Factors of Production	Total Expenditures of Households	Total Expenditures of Companies	Total Costs of Gross Output	Total Expenditures of Government	Aggregate Investment	Total Indirect Taxes	Total Foreign Exchange Receipts	

*The complete SAM-Tech Transaction table is given in Appendix Table B.

20

Table II.3 represents the format of the SAM-Tech which was built for Indonesia. In keeping with the characteristics of a SAM, it is a square table consisting of as many columns as rows, i.e. 78 in this specific case. The expenditures incurred by the variables into which each account has been broken down are entered in columns and the receipts are entered in the rows. Since, by definition, the sum of expenditures or outlays of a given sub-account has to be equal to the sum of the receipts of the same subaccount, the total expenditures appearing at the bottom of Table II.3 (the complete SAM-Tech transaction table is given in Appendix Table B) have to be equal to the total receipts appearing in the corresponding row. It can be seen from that table that SAM-Tech consists of three sets of endogenous accounts i.e. 1) factors numbered from 1-23 (the complete classification including the corresponding number code for the factors and other variables is given in Table II.1); 2) institutions which are further broken down into households (code nos. 24-33) and companies (34); and 3) production activities (code nos. 35-74) of which twelve activities are also called dualistic sectors defined according to techno-logical criteria. The other accounts are considered as exogenous i.e. government (75); the combined capital account (76); net indirect taxes (77); and, finally, rest of the world (78). The distinction between endogenous and exogenous accounts will be explained and rationalised shortly.

An easy way to understand the SAM is to describe the most impor-tant transformations appearing in Table II.3. Starting with the expenditure side of production activities (i.e. going down the column entitled production activities) one can identify the value added going to the different factors and the purchases of domestic intermediate inputs by the various production activities (i.e. the typical input-output transaction matrix). Next, looking at the incomes of factors (along the rows marked 1-23, we can see that the major source of factor income is in fact the value added which they receive from the production activities. In turn, reading down the columns corresponding to factors, it can be seen that labour and nonlabour incomes are allocated to households and com-panies.[6] Next, to obtain the household income distribution, one has to read along the household rows where the various sources of incomes accruing to households appear, i.e. labour and nonlabour income earned by the factors of production possessed by the house-hold, transfers received from other households, profits and divi-dends distributed by companies to households and government transfers and subsidies to households. The final transformation which might be emphasised is the consumption expenditures pattern of the various household groups on domestic goods which is the matrix appearing at the intersection of the household columns and the production rows.

As previously noted, the transaction matrix of SAM-Tech for 1975 is given in the Appendix Table B and corresponds to the format given in Table II.3. This transaction table provides the basis for the type of multiplier analysis and structural path analysis which is undertaken subsequently. Before using the SAM as a fixed coefficient conceptual framework, the underlying methodology is very briefly described next. The first step is to decide which accounts are endogenous and which are exogenous. It is assumed here that three accounts are endogenously determined i.e. factors, institutions (households and companies) and production activities, while all other accounts are exogenous (governments, capital and the rest of the world). The three endogenous accounts are the same as those depicted graphically in Figure II.1 and the corresponding SAM using the same notation as in Figure II.1 is given in Table II.4. In particular, the five non-trivial endogenous transformations are given in II.4. Thus, for example, T_{13} is the matrix which allocates the value added involving these three accounts appear in both Figure II.1 and Table generated by the various production activities into income accruing to the various factors of production and T_{33} shows the intermediate input requirements (i.e. the input-output transactions), while T_{32} reflects the expenditure pattern of the various institutions including the different household groups for the commodities (production activities) which they consume.

If a certain number of conditions are met--in particular, the existence of excess capacity which would allow prices to remain constant--the framework depicted in Table II.4 can be used to estimate the effects of exogenous changes and injections such as an increase in the output of a given production activity, government expenditures or exports on the whole system. The underlying logic, as will be seen shortly, is that exogenous changes (the x_i's) in Table II.4 determine through the SAM matrix the incomes of a) the factors (vector y_1) b) the household and companies incomes (y_2) and c) the incomes of the production activities (y_3). For analytical purposes, the transaction matrix is converted into the corresponding matrix of average expenditure propensities. These can be obtained simply by dividing a particular element in any of the endogenous accounts by the total income for the column account in which the element occurs. In fact, to be exact, the matrix of average expenditures propensities consists of two parts A_n which is the square matrix of average expenditure propensities for the endogenous accounts (in the specific instance of SAM-Tech, this is a 74 X 74 matrix), while the second part consists of the so-called leakages i.e. the proportions of each endogenous variable which leaks out as expenditure into any one of the four exogenous accounts (government, capital, net indirect taxes, and rest of the world). If this last matrix is denoted by A_1 its dimension would be the 74 endogenous columns and the four exogenous rows (i.e. in the SAM-Tech case it would embrace columns 1-74 and rows 75-78). Thus, whereas the transaction matrix is expressed in money flows the A_n and A_1 matrices are expressed as ratios with each column adding up to exactly one, as can be readily verified by looking at Table II.5 which presents these average expenditure propensities.

A few examples should suffice to illustrate the meaning of the A matrix in Table II.5: 1) Reading down the first column which gives the average expenditures propensities of the factor "agricultural paid rural workers", it can be seen that 63.2% of that factor's income is distributed to the household group headed by

Table 11.4 Simplified Schematic Social Accounting Matrix

			Expenditures				
			Endogenous Accounts			Exog.	Totals
			Institutions				
			Factors	Households and Companies	Production Activities	Sum of Other Accounts	
			1	2	3	4	5
Receipts	Endogenous Accounts	Factors — 1	0	0	T_{13}	x_1	y_1
		Institutions, i.e. Households and Companies — 2	T_{21}	T_{22}	0	x_2	y_2
		Production Activities — 3	0	T_{32}	T_{33}	x_3	y_3
	Exog	Sum of Other Accounts — 4	l_1	l_2	l_3	t	y_x
		Totals — 5	y_1	y_2	y_3	y_x	

Table II.5: Matrix of Average Expenditure Propensities, Indonesian SAM-Tech, 1975*

		Name	Factors of Production							
			Ag Paid Rural 1	Ag Paid Urban 2	Ag Unpaid Rural 3	Ag Unpaid Urban 4	Prod Paid Rural 5	Prod Paid Urban 6	Prod Unpaid Rural 7	Prod Unpaid Urban 8
Factors of production	1	Ag Paid Rural								
	2	Ag Paid Urban								
	3	Ag Unpaid Rural								
	4	Ag Unpaid Urban								
	5	Prod Paid Rural								
	6	Prod Paid Urban								
	7	Prod Unpaid Rural								
	8	Prod Unpaid Urban								
	9	Cler Paid Rural								
	10	Cler Paid Urban								
	11	Cler Unpaid Rural								
	12	Cler Unpaid Urban								
	13	Prof Paid Rural								
	14	Prof Paid Urban								
	15	Prof Unpaid Rural								
	16	Prof Unpaid Urban								
	17	Uninc Capital Land								
	18	Uninc Capital Housing								
	19	Uninc Capital Rural								
	20	Uninc Capital Urban								
	21	Inc Capital Domestic								
	22	Inc Capital Government								
	23	Inc Capital Foreign								
Institutions	24	Ag Employees	0.632	0.541	0.016	0.013	0.051	0.009	0.070	0.009
	25	Farm Size 1	0.191	0.097	0.393	0.419	0.108	0.014	0.175	0.020
	26	Farm Size 2	0.051	0.032	0.249	0.202	0.046	0.007	0.088	0.009
	27	Farm Size 3	0.032	0.029	0.302	0.247	0.028	0.007	0.062	0.011
	28	Rural Lower	0.068	0.000	0.023	0.000	0.681	0.000	0.396	0.000
	29	Rural Middle	0.011	0.000	0.009	0.000	0.034	0.000	0.023	0.000
	30	Rural Higher	0.014	0.000	0.009	0.000	0.051	0.000	0.186	0.000
	31	Urban Lower	0.000	0.134	0.000	0.069	0.000	0.878	0.000	0.696
	32	Urban Middle	0.000	0.018	0.000	0.007	0.000	0.024	0.000	0.017
	33	Urban Higher	0.000	0.148	0.000	0.043	0.000	0.061	0.000	0.239
	34	Companies	0.000	0.000	0.000	0.000	0.000	0.000	0.000	0.000
Production activities	35	Food Crop								
	36	Nonfood Crop								
	37	Livestock and Products								
	38	Forestry and Hunting								
	39	Fishery								
	40	Metal Ore Mining								
	41	Other Mining								
	42	Handpounded Rice								
	43	Milled Rice								
	44	Farm Processed Tea								
	45	Processed Tea								
	46	Dried and Salted Fish								
	47	Canned Fish								
	48	Brown Sugar								
	49	Refined Sugar								
	50	Canning (s+c)								
	51	Canning (m+l)								
	52	Kretek Cigs								
	53	White Cigs								
	54	Other Fbt								
	55	Wood and Construction								
	56	Textiles, etc								
	57	Paper, Transport, Metal, etc.								
	58	Chemical, Cement, etc								
	59	Coal Mining								
	60	Petroleum Mining, etc								
	61	Gasoline								
	62	Fuel Oil								
	63	Electricity								
	64	City Gas								
	65	Water								
	66	Trade								
	67	Restaurants								
	68	Hotel, etc								
	69	Road Transport, etc								
	70	Air Transport, etc								
	71	Banking and Insurance								
	72	Real Estate								
	73	Public Services, etc								
	74	Personal Services, etc								
M		Sum of Endogenous Accounts	1.000	1.000	1.000	1.000	1.000	1.000	1.000	1.000
Exo ac	75	Government	0.000	0.000	0.000	0.000	0.000	0.000	0.000	0.000
	76	Capital Accounts	0.000	0.000	0.000	0.000	0.000	0.000	0.000	0.000
	77	Net Indirect Taxes	0.000	0.000	0.000	0.000	0.000	0.000	0.000	0.000
	78	Rest of World	0.000	0.000	0.000	0.000	0.000	0.000	0.000	0.000
M		Sum of Exogenous Accounts	0.000	0.000	0.000	0.000	0.000	0.000	0.000	0.000
		Total	1.000	1.000	1.000	1.000	1.000	1.000	1.000	1.000

* Both the A_n and A_1 matrices are given (see text for more detail)

Table II.5: Cont

	Name	Factors of Production							
		Cler Paid Rural 9	Cler Paid Urban 10	Cler Unpaid Rural 11	Cler Unpaid Urban 12	Prof Paid Rural 13	Prof Paid Urban 14	Prof Unpaid Rural 15	Prof Unpaid Uban 16
1	Ag Paid Rural								
2	Ag Paid Urban								
3	Ag Unpaid Rural								
4	Ag Unpaid Urban								
5	Prod Paid Rural								
6	Prod Paid Urban								
7	Prod Unpaid Rural								
8	Prod Unpaid Urban								
9	Cler Paid Rural								
10	Cler Paid Urban								
11	Cler Unpaid Rural								
12	Cler Unpaid Urban								
13	Prof Paid Rural								
14	Prof Paid Urban								
15	Prof Unpaid Rural								
16	Prof Unpaid Urban								
17	Uninc Capital Land								
18	Uninc Capital Housing								
19	Uninc Capital Rural								
20	Uninc Capital Urban								
21	Inc Capital Domestic								
22	Inc Capital Government								
23	Inc Capital Foreign								
24	Ag Employees	0.060	0.003	0.062	0.006	0.073	0.001	0.055	0.002
25	Farm Size 1	0.107	0.004	0.145	0.012	0.045	0.003	0.101	0.002
26	Farm Size 2	0.042	0.001	0.063	0.003	0.029	0.001	0.038	0.002
27	Farm Size 3	0.039	0.001	0.053	0.004	0.050	0.001	0.074	0.003
28	Rural Lower	0.529	0.000	0.475	0.000	0.111	0.000	0.409	0.000
29	Rural Middle	0.032	0.000	0.027	0.000	0.074	0.000	0.032	0.000
30	Rural Higher	0.192	0.000	0.175	0.000	0.617	0.000	0.291	0.000
31	Urban Lower	0.000	0.452	0.000	0.660	0.000	0.039	0.000	0.486
32	Urban Middle	0.000	0.025	0.000	0.019	0.000	0.013	0.000	0.009
33	Urban Higher	0.000	0.514	0.000	0.295	0.000	0.941	0.000	0.497
34	Companies	0.000	0.000	0.000	0.000	0.000	0.000	0.000	0.000
35	Food Crop								
36	Nonfood Crop								
37	Livestock and Products								
38	Forestry and Hunting								
39	Fishery								
40	Metal Ore Mining								
41	Other Mining								
42	Handpounded Rice								
43	Milled Rice								
44	Farm Processed Tea								
45	Processed Tea								
46	Dried and Salted Fish								
47	Canned Fish								
48	Brown Sugar								
49	Refined Sugar								
50	Canning (s+c)								
51	Canning (m+l)								
52	Kretek Cigs								
53	White Cigs								
54	Other Fbt								
55	Wood and Construction								
56	Textiles, etc								
57	Paper, Transport, Metal, etc.								
58	Chemical, Cement, etc								
59	Coal Mining								
60	Petroleum Mining, etc								
61	Gasoline								
62	Fuel Oil								
63	Electricity								
64	City Gas								
65	Water								
66	Trade								
67	Restaurants								
68	Hotel, etc								
69	Road Transport, etc								
70	Air Transport, etc								
71	Banking and Insurance								
72	Real Estate								
73	Public Services, etc								
74	Personal Services, etc								
	Sum of Endogenous Accounts	1.000	1.000	1.000	1.000	1.000	1.000	1.000	1.000
75	Government	0.000	0.000	0.000	0.000	0.000	0.000	0.000	0.000
76	Capital Accounts	0.000	0.000	0.000	0.000	0.000	0.000	0.000	0.000
77	Net Indirect Taxes	0.000	0.000	0.000	0.000	0.000	0.000	0.000	0.000
78	Rest of World	0.000	0.000	0.000	0.000	0.000	0.000	0.000	0.000
	Sum of Exogenous Accounts	0.000	0.000	0.000	0.000	0.000	0.000	0.000	0.000
	Total	1.000	1.000	1.000	1.000	1.000	1.000	1.000	1.000

Factors of production

Institutions

Production activities

M Exoac M

	Name	Factors of Production							
		Uninc Capital Land 17	Uninc Capital Housing 18	Uninc Capital Rural 19	Uninc Capital Urban 20	Inc Capital Domestic 21	Inc Capital Government 22	Inc Capital Foreign 23	Ag Employees 24
Factors of production	1 Ag Paid Rural								
	2 Ag Paid Urban								
	3 Ag Unpaid Rural								
	4 Ag Unpaid Urban								
	5 Prod Paid Rural								
	6 Prod Paid Urban								
	7 Prod Unpaid Rural								
	8 Prod Unpaid Urban .								
	9 Cler Paid Rural								
	10 Cler Paid Urban								
	11 Cler Unpaid Rural								
	12 Cler Unpaid Urban								
	13 Prof Paid Rural								
	14 Prof Paid Urban								
	15 Prof Unpaid Rural								
	16 Prof Unpaid Urban								
	17 Uninc Capital Land								
	18 Uninc Capital Housing								
	19 Uninc Capital Rural								
	20 Uninc Capital Urban								
	21 Inc Capital Domestic								
	22 Inc Capital Government								
	23 Inc Capital Foreign								
Institutions	24 Ag Employees	0.019	0.060	0.139	0.000	0.000	0.000	0.000	0.000
	25 Farm Size 1	0.163	0.118	0.194	0.000	0.000	0.000	0.000	0.000
	26 Farm Size 2	0.216	0.072	0.086	0.000	0.000	0.000	0.000	0.000
	27 Farm Size 3	0.539	0.090	0.072	0.000	0.000	0.000	0.000	0.000
	28 Rural Lower	0.034	0.099	0.390	0.000	0.000	0.000	0.000	0.000
	29 Rural Middle	0.011	0.029	0.037	0.000	0.000	0.000	0.000	0.004
	30 Rural Higher	0.012	0.049	0.082	0.000	0.000	0.000	0.000	0.000
	31 Urban Lower	0.003	0.172	0.000	0.685	0.000	0.000	0.000	0.000
	32 Urban Middle	0.000	0.055	0.000	0.026	0.000	0.000	0.000	0.001
	33 Urban Higher	0.002	0.256	0.000	0.289	0.000	0.000	0.000	0.000
	34 Companies	0.000	0.000	0.000	0.000	1.000	0.957	0.645	0.000
Production activities	35 Food Crop								0.182
	36 Nonfood Crop								0.009
	37 Livestock and Products								0.023
	38 Forestry and Hunting								0.005
	39 Fishery								0.015
	40 Metal Ore Mining								0.000
	41 Other Mining								0.002
	42 Handpounded Rice								0.036
	43 Milled Rice								0.248
	44 Farm Processed Tea								0.003
	45 Processed Tea								0.001
	46 Dried and Salted Fish								0.013
	47 Canned Fish								0.004
	48 Brown Sugar								0.006
	49 Refined Sugar								0.012
	50 Canning (s+c)								0.000
	51 Canning (m+l)								0.000
	52 Kretek Cigs								0.046
	53 White Cigs								0.000
	54 Other Fbt								0.015
	55 Wood and Construction								0.004
	56 Textiles, etc								0.026
	57 Paper, Transport, Metal, etc.								0.020
	58 Chemical, Cement, etc								0.014
	59 Coal Mining								0.000
	60 Petroleum Mining, etc								0.000
	61 Gasoline								0.001
	62 Fuel Oil								0.003
	63 Electricity								0.002
	64 City Gas								0.000
	65 Water								0.002
	66 Trade								0.114
	67 Restaurants								0.046
	68 Hotel, etc								0.000
	69 Road Transport, etc								0.027
	70 Air Transport, etc								0.010
	71 Banking and Insurance								0.001
	72 Real Estate								0.042
	73 Public Services, etc								0.046
	74 Personal Services, etc								0.031
M Sum of Endogenous Accounts		1.000	1.000	1.000	1.000	1.000	0.957	0.645	1.013
Exoac	75 Government	0.000	0.000	0.000	0.000	0.000	0.043	0.000	0.003
	76 Capital Accounts	0.000	0.000	0.000	0.000	0.000	0.000	0.000	-0.064
	77 Net Indirect Taxes	0.000	0.000	0.000	0.000	0.000	0.000	0.000	0.000
	78 Rest of World	0.000	0.000	0.000	0.000	0.000	0.000	0.355	0.047
M Sum of Exogenous Accounts		0.000	0.000	0.000	0.000	0.000	0.043	0.355	-0.013
	Total	1.000	1.000	1.000	1.000	1.000	1.000	1.000	1.000

Table II.5: Cont

			Institutions						
	Name	Farm Size 1 25	Farm Size 2 26	Farm Size 3 27	Rural Lower 28	Rural Middle 29	Rural Higher 30	Urban Lower 31	Urban Middle 32
Factors of production	1 Ag Paid Rural								
	2 Ag Paid Urban								
	3 Ag Unpaid Rural								
	4 Ag Unpaid Urban								
	5 Prod Paid Rural								
	6 Prod Paid Urban								
	7 Prod Unpaid Rural								
	8 Prod Unpaid Urban								
	9 Cler Paid Rural								
	10 Cler Paid Urban								
	11 Cler Unpaid Rural								
	12 Cler Unpaid Urban								
	13 Prof Paid Rural								
	14 Prof Paid Urban								
	15 Prof Unpaid Rural								
	16 Prof Unpaid Urban								
	17 Uninc Capital Land								
	18 Uninc Capital Housing								
	19 Uninc Capital Rural								
	20 Uninc Capital Urban								
	21 Inc Capital Domestic								
	22 Inc Capital Government								
	23 Inc Capital Foreign								
Institutions	24 Ag Employees	0.000	0.000	0.000	0.000	0.000	0.000	0.000	0.000
	25 Farm Size 1	0.000	0.000	0.000	0.000	0.000	0.000	0.000	0.000
	26 Farm Size 2	0.000	0.000	0.000	0.000	0.000	0.000	0.000	0.000
	27 Farm Size 3	0.000	0.000	0.000	0.000	0.000	0.000	0.000	0.000
	28 Rural Lower	0.000	0.000	0.000	0.000	0.000	0.000	0.000	0.000
	29 Rural Middle	0.004	0.006	0.023	0.011	0.001	0.022	0.001	0.000
	30 Rural Higher	0.000	0.000	0.000	0.000	0.000	0.000	0.000	0.000
	31 Urban Lower	0.000	0.000	0.000	0.000	0.000	0.000	0.000	0.000
	32 Urban Middle	0.001	0.002	0.001	0.002	0.000	0.003	0.033	0.000
	33 Urban Higher	0.000	0.000	0.000	0.000	0.000	0.000	0.000	0.000
	34 Companies	0.000	0.000	0.000	0.000	0.000	0.000	0.000	0.000
Production activities	35 Food Crop	0.226	0.133	0.124	0.128	0.083	0.113	0.068	0.065
	36 Nonfood Crop	0.010	0.008	0.006	0.006	0.007	0.005	0.003	0.003
	37 Livestock and Products	0.030	0.034	0.031	0.024	0.033	0.034	0.022	0.024
	38 Forestry and Hunting	0.005	0.003	0.002	0.003	0.003	0.002	0.001	0.001
	39 Fishery	0.015	0.015	0.014	0.017	0.019	0.018	0.014	0.013
	40 Metal Ore Mining	0.000	0.000	0.000	0.000	0.000	0.000	0.000	0.000
	41 Other Mining	0.002	0.001	0.001	0.001	0.001	0.001	0.001	0.001
	42 Handpounded Rice	0.108	0.172	0.104	0.028	0.051	0.026	0.007	0.009
	43 Milled Rice	0.144	0.038	0.066	0.189	0.152	0.141	0.105	0.095
	44 Farm Processed Tea	0.004	0.003	0.002	0.002	0.004	0.002	0.001	0.001
	45 Processed Tea	0.001	0.001	0.001	0.001	0.001	0.001	0.001	0.001
	46 Dried and Salted Fish	0.014	0.013	0.012	0.015	0.018	0.017	0.012	0.011
	47 Canned Fish	0.003	0.002	0.002	0.003	0.003	0.003	0.002	0.002
	48 Brown Sugar	0.008	0.006	0.004	0.004	0.005	0.004	0.002	0.002
	49 Refined Sugar	0.011	0.011	0.012	0.011	0.011	0.011	0.008	0.007
	50 Canning (s+c)	0.000	0.000	0.000	0.000	0.000	0.000	0.000	0.000
	51 Canning (m+l)	0.000	0.000	0.000	0.000	0.000	0.000	0.000	0.000
	52 Kretek Cigs	0.042	0.029	0.020	0.027	0.012	0.008	0.018	0.012
	53 White Cigs	0.000	0.004	0.008	0.011	0.012	0.030	0.011	0.007
	54 Other Fbt	0.037	0.090	0.035	0.036	0.118	0.026	0.070	0.072
	55 Wood and Construction	0.004	0.003	0.003	0.004	0.004	0.003	0.002	0.003
	56 Textiles, etc	0.034	0.022	0.025	0.037	0.030	0.034	0.045	0.052
	57 Paper, Transport, Metal, etc.	0.015	0.014	0.016	0.029	0.036	0.046	0.030	0.052
	58 Chemical, Cement, etc	0.013	0.010	0.009	0.013	0.016	0.012	0.014	0.015
	59 Coal Mining	0.000	0.000	0.000	0.000	0.000	0.000	0.000	0.000
	60 Petroleum Mining, etc	0.000	0.000	0.000	0.000	0.000	0.000	0.000	0.000
	61 Gasoline	0.000	0.000	0.001	0.001	0.002	0.003	0.001	0.003
	62 Fuel Oil	0.002	0.002	0.001	0.002	0.002	0.002	0.003	0.002
	63 Electricity	0.002	0.001	0.001	0.002	0.002	0.004	0.008	0.012
	64 City Gas	0.000	0.000	0.000	0.000	0.000	0.000	0.000	0.000
	65 Water	0.001	0.001	0.001	0.001	0.001	0.000	0.002	0.001
	66 Trade	0.113	0.094	0.080	0.101	0.105	0.098	0.080	0.087
	67 Restaurants	0.034	0.019	0.014	0.044	0.031	0.029	0.078	0.083
	68 Hotel, etc	0.000	0.000	0.001	0.001	0.001	0.001	0.001	0.001
	69 Road Transport, etc	0.033	0.026	0.019	0.038	0.028	0.025	0.054	0.050
	70 Air Transport, etc	0.010	0.009	0.009	0.013	0.012	0.014	0.013	0.014
	71 Banking and Insurance	0.001	0.001	0.002	0.002	0.002	0.004	0.002	0.003
	72 Real Estate	0.042	0.034	0.025	0.037	0.050	0.036	0.056	0.094
	73 Public Services, etc	0.043	0.038	0.033	0.049	0.057	0.053	0.063	0.079
	74 Personal Services, etc	0.028	0.023	0.020	0.030	0.028	0.032	0.031	0.038
	Sum of Endogenous Accounts	1.040	0.872	0.729	0.927	0.943	0.863	0.865	0.916
M Exoac M	75 Government	0.004	0.006	0.018	0.004	0.005	0.007	0.017	0.008
	76 Capital Accounts	-0.081	0.093	0.225	0.018	0.001	0.076	0.061	0.001
	77 Net Indirect Taxes	0.000	0.000	0.000	0.000	0.000	0.000	0.000	0.000
	78 Rest of World	0.037	0.029	0.029	0.050	0.051	0.054	0.057	0.074
	Sum of Exogenous Accounts	-0.040	0.128	0.271	0.073	0.057	0.137	0.135	0.084
	Total	1.000	1.000	1.000	1.000	1.000	1.000	1.000	1.000

27

Table II.5: Cont

		Name	Production Activities							
			Urban Higher 33	Companies 34	Food Crop 35	Nonfood Crop 36	Livestock and Products 37	Forestry and Hunting 38	Fishery 39	Metal Ore Mining 40
Factors of production	1	Ag Paid Rural			0.125	0.116	0.028	0.039	0.094	0.000
	2	Ag Paid Urban			0.004	0.003	0.006	0.004	0.018	0.000
	3	Ag Unpaid Rural			0.351	0.070	0.090	0.073	0.081	0.000
	4	Ag Unpaid Urban			0.013	0.004	0.007	0.003	0.013	0.000
	5	Prod Paid Rural			0.000	0.002	0.000	0.006	0.001	0.124
	6	Prod Paid Urban			0.000	0.000	0.000	0.001	0.000	0.012
	7	Prod Unpaid Rural			0.001	0.000	0.000	0.008	0.000	0.000
	8	Prod Unpaid Urban			0.000	0.000	0.000	0.000	0.000	0.000
	9	Cler Paid Rural			0.000	0.003	0.002	0.004	0.001	0.026
	10	Cler Paid Urban			0.000	0.001	0.000	0.002	0.000	0.010
	11	Cler Unpaid Rural			0.000	0.000	0.003	0.001	0.001	0.000
	12	Cler Unpaid Urban			0.000	0.000	0.000	0.000	0.000	0.000
	13	Prof Paid Rural			0.000	0.005	0.000	0.002	0.000	0.003
	14	Prof Paid Urban			0.000	0.002	0.000	0.000	0.000	0.000
	15	Prof Unpaid Rural			0.001	0.000	0.000	0.000	0.000	0.000
	16	Prof Unpaid Urban			0.000	0.000	0.000	0.000	0.000	0.000
	17	Uninc Capital Land			0.400	0.386	0.511	0.298	0.543	0.000
	18	Uninc Capital Housing			0.000	0.000	0.000	0.000	0.000	0.000
	19	Uninc Capital Rural			0.000	0.000	0.000	0.000	0.000	0.000
	20	Uninc Capital Urban			0.000	0.000	0.000	0.000	0.000	0.000
	21	Inc Capital Domestic			0.001	0.017	0.018	0.217	0.057	0.000
	22	Inc Capital Government			0.007	0.071	0.003	0.022	0.003	0.179
	23	Inc Capital Foreign			0.000	0.018	0.001	0.068	0.026	0.148
Institutions	24	Ag Employees	0.000	0.000						
	25	Farm Size 1	0.000	0.000						
	26	Farm Size 2	0.000	0.000						
	27	Farm Size 3	0.000	0.000						
	28	Rural Lower	0.000	0.000						
	29	Rural Middle	0.002	0.009						
	30	Rural Higher	0.000	0.023						
	31	Urban Lower	0.000	0.000						
	32	Urban Middle	0.044	0.011						
	33	Urban Higher	0.000	0.121						
	34	Companies	0.000	0.008						
Production activities	35	Food Crop	0.056	0.000	0.022	0.000	0.008	0.000	0.000	0.000
	36	Nonfood Crop	0.002	0.000	0.000	0.152	0.002	0.000	0.000	0.000
	37	Livestock and Products	0.031	0.000	0.001	0.001	0.235	0.000	0.000	0.000
	38	Forestry and Hunting	0.000	0.000	0.000	0.001	0.000	0.054	0.004	0.000
	39	Fishery	0.012	0.000	0.000	0.000	0.000	0.000	0.000	0.000
	40	Metal Ore Mining	0.000	0.000	0.000	0.000	0.000	0.000	0.000	0.000
	41	Other Mining	0.001	0.000	0.000	0.000	0.000	0.000	0.000	0.000
	42	Handpounded Rice	0.004	0.000	0.000	0.000	0.001	0.000	0.000	0.000
	43	Milled Rice	0.062	0.000	0.000	0.000	0.008	0.000	0.001	0.000
	44	Farm Processed Tea	0.001	0.000	0.000	0.000	0.000	0.000	0.000	0.000
	45	Processed Tea	0.001	0.000	0.000	0.000	0.000	0.000	0.000	0.000
	46	Dried and Salted Fish	0.011	0.000	0.000	0.000	0.000	0.000	0.000	0.000
	47	Canned Fish	0.002	0.000	0.000	0.000	0.000	0.000	0.000	0.000
	48	Brown Sugar	0.001	0.000	0.000	0.000	0.000	0.000	0.000	0.000
	49	Refined Sugar	0.006	0.000	0.000	0.000	0.000	0.000	0.000	0.000
	50	Canning (s+c)	0.000	0.000	0.000	0.000	0.000	0.000	0.000	0.000
	51	Canning (m+l)	0.000	0.000	0.000	0.000	0.000	0.000	0.000	0.000
	52	Kretek Cigs	0.006	0.000	0.000	0.000	0.000	0.000	0.000	0.000
	53	White Cigs	0.014	0.000	0.000	0.000	0.000	0.000	0.000	0.000
	54	Other Fbt	0.054	0.000	0.000	0.000	0.002	0.000	0.009	0.000
	55	Wood and Construction	0.002	0.000	0.005	0.013	0.005	0.018	0.012	0.022
	56	Textiles, etc	0.042	0.000	0.002	0.002	0.001	0.002	0.005	0.002
	57	Paper, Transport, Metal, etc.	0.059	0.000	0.003	0.007	0.002	0.011	0.025	0.001
	58	Chemical, Cement, etc	0.011	0.000	0.009	0.008	0.001	0.000	0.000	0.000
	59	Coal Mining	0.000	0.000	0.000	0.000	0.000	0.000	0.000	0.006
	60	Petroleum Mining, etc	0.000	0.000	0.000	0.001	0.000	0.000	0.000	0.009
	61	Gasoline	0.004	0.000	0.000	0.001	0.000	0.002	0.001	0.000
	62	Fuel Oil	0.001	0.000	0.000	0.002	0.000	0.003	0.010	0.000
	63	Electricity	0.011	0.000	0.000	0.001	0.000	0.004	0.000	0.072
	64	City Gas	0.000	0.000	0.000	0.000	0.000	0.000	0.000	0.000
	65	Water	0.001	0.000	0.000	0.000	0.000	0.000	0.000	0.000
	66	Trade	0.074	0.000	0.029	0.044	0.042	0.059	0.037	0.156
	67	Restaurants	0.044	0.000	0.000	0.002	0.001	0.001	0.001	0.009
	68	Hotel, etc	0.001	0.000	0.000	0.000	0.000	0.001	0.002	0.006
	69	Road Transport, etc	0.041	0.000	0.003	0.013	0.005	0.022	0.012	0.018
	70	Air Transport, etc	0.012	0.000	0.001	0.006	0.003	0.009	0.003	0.028
	71	Banking and Insurance	0.003	0.000	0.008	0.008	0.001	0.016	0.009	0.042
	72	Real Estate	0.070	0.000	0.000	0.001	0.001	0.004	0.001	0.028
	73	Public Services, etc	0.064	0.000	0.000	0.000	0.000	0.000	0.000	0.010
	74	Personal Services, etc	0.033	0.000	0.000	0.009	0.002	0.022	0.000	0.028
M		Sum of Endogenous Accounts	0.782	0.171	0.985	0.970	0.992	0.977	0.971	0.940
Exoac	75	Government	0.024	0.375	0.000	0.000	0.000	0.000	0.000	0.000
	76	Capital Accounts	0.136	0.433	0.000	0.000	0.000	0.000	0.000	0.000
	77	Net Indirect Taxes	0.000	0.000	0.001	0.003	0.005	0.007	0.006	0.060
	78	Rest of World	0.059	0.021	0.014	0.027	0.004	0.016	0.023	0.000
M		Sum of Exogenous Accounts	0.218	0.829	0.015	0.030	0.008	0.023	0.029	0.060
		Total	1.000	1.000	1.000	1.000	1.000	1.000	1.000	1.000

	Name	Other Mining 41	Handpounded Rice 42	Milled Rice 43	Farm Proc Tea 44	Processed Tea 45	Dried and Salted Fish 46	Canned Fish 47	Brown Sugar 48
					Production Activities				
1	Ag Paid Rural	0.000	0.066	0.000	0.147	0.000	0.000	0.000	0.000
2	Ag Paid Urban	0.000	0.000	0.000	0.000	0.000	0.000	0.000	0.000
3	Ag Unpaid Rural	0.000	0.141	0.000	0.221	0.000	0.000	0.000	0.000
4	Ag Unpaid Urban	0.000	0.000	0.000	0.000	0.000	0.000	0.000	0.000
5	Prod Paid Rural	0.028	0.000	0.025	0.002	0.047	0.016	0.005	0.068
6	Prod Paid Urban	0.052	0.000	0.010	0.000	0.022	0.049	0.003	0.000
7	Prod Unpaid Rural	0.053	0.000	0.026	0.000	0.000	0.049	0.000	0.071
8	Prod Unpaid Urban	0.048	0.000	0.000	0.000	0.000	0.016	0.000	0.000
9	Cler Paid Rural	0.018	0.000	0.002	0.003	0.005	0.001	0.001	0.008
10	Cler Paid Urban	0.011	0.000	0.003	0.000	0.009	0.000	0.001	0.000
11	Cler Unpaid Rural	0.016	0.000	0.000	0.000	0.000	0.000	0.000	0.001
12	Cler Unpaid Urban	0.006	0.000	0.000	0.000	0.000	0.000	0.000	0.000
13	Prof Paid Rural	0.001	0.000	0.001	0.007	0.002	0.000	0.000	0.002
14	Prof Paid Urban	0.007	0.000	0.001	0.000	0.003	0.000	0.000	0.000
15	Prof Unpaid Rural	0.004	0.000	0.000	0.000	0.000	0.000	0.000	0.000
16	Prof Unpaid Urban	0.001	0.000	0.000	0.000	0.000	0.000	0.000	0.000
17	Uninc Capital Land	0.000	0.000	0.000	0.005	0.000	0.191	0.000	0.000
18	Uninc Capital Housing	0.000	0.000	0.000	0.000	0.000	0.000	0.000	0.000
19	Uninc Capital Rural	0.197	0.000	0.081	0.000	0.000	0.000	0.171	0.346
20	Uninc Capital Urban	0.394	0.000	0.012	0.000	0.001	0.000	0.066	0.000
21	Inc Capital Domestic	0.007	0.000	0.003	0.020	0.010	0.023	0.031	0.002
22	Inc Capital Government	0.031	0.000	0.001	0.131	0.064	0.001	0.008	0.000
23	Inc Capital Foreign	0.000	0.000	0.000	0.008	0.004	0.000	0.018	0.001
24	Ag Employees								
25	Farm Size 1								
26	Farm Size 2								
27	Farm Size 3								
28	Rural Lower								
29	Rural Middle								
30	Rural Higher								
31	Urban Lower								
32	Urban Middle								
33	Urban Higher								
34	Companies								
35	Food Crop	0.000	0.783	0.686	0.000	0.000	0.002	0.003	0.002
36	Nonfood Crop	0.000	0.000	0.000	0.294	0.475	0.000	0.000	0.398
37	Livestock and Products	0.000	0.000	0.000	0.000	0.000	0.000	0.000	0.000
38	Forestry and Hunting	0.001	0.000	0.000	0.002	0.005	0.005	0.002	0.003
39	Fishery	0.000	0.000	0.000	0.000	0.000	0.435	0.371	0.000
40	Metal Ore Mining	0.000	0.000	0.000	0.000	0.000	0.000	0.000	0.000
41	Other Mining	0.000	0.000	0.000	0.000	0.000	0.005	0.000	0.000
42	Handpounded Rice	0.000	0.000	0.019	0.000	0.000	0.000	0.000	0.000
43	Milled Rice	0.000	0.000	0.009	0.000	0.000	0.000	0.000	0.000
44	Farm Processed Tea	0.000	0.000	0.000	0.000	0.000	0.000	0.000	0.000
45	Processed Tea	0.000	0.000	0.000	0.000	0.000	0.000	0.000	0.000
46	Dried and Salted Fish	0.000	0.000	0.000	0.000	0.000	0.000	0.000	0.000
47	Canned Fish	0.000	0.000	0.000	0.000	0.000	0.000	0.001	0.000
48	Brown Sugar	0.000	0.000	0.000	0.000	0.000	0.000	0.000	0.000
49	Refined Sugar	0.000	0.000	0.000	0.000	0.000	0.000	0.000	0.000
50	Canning (s+c)	0.000	0.000	0.000	0.000	0.000	0.000	0.000	0.000
51	Canning (m+l)	0.000	0.000	0.000	0.000	0.000	0.000	0.000	0.000
52	Kretek Cigs	0.000	0.000	0.000	0.000	0.000	0.000	0.000	0.000
53	White Cigs	0.000	0.000	0.000	0.000	0.000	0.000	0.000	0.000
54	Other Fbt	0.000	0.000	0.000	0.000	0.000	0.001	0.060	0.001
55	Wood and Construction	0.047	0.002	0.001	0.005	0.004	0.015	0.005	0.005
56	Textiles, etc	0.002	0.002	0.000	0.000	0.010	0.002	0.000	0.000
57	Paper, Transport, Metal, etc.	0.014	0.000	0.006	0.004	0.021	0.002	0.008	0.008
58	Chemical, Cement, etc	0.000	0.000	0.001	0.000	0.008	0.002	0.016	0.001
59	Coal Mining	0.000	0.000	0.000	0.000	0.000	0.000	0.000	0.000
60	Petroleum Mining, etc	0.000	0.000	0.000	0.000	0.000	0.000	0.000	0.000
61	Gasoline	0.003	0.000	0.002	0.001	0.007	0.000	0.002	0.000
62	Fuel Oil	0.001	0.000	0.005	0.002	0.013	0.001	0.002	0.004
63	Electricity	0.001	0.000	0.015	0.000	0.022	0.001	0.018	0.001
64	City Gas	0.000	0.000	0.000	0.000	0.000	0.000	0.000	0.000
65	Water	0.000	0.000	0.002	0.000	0.000	0.000	0.000	0.000
66	Trade	0.011	0.005	0.027	0.121	0.187	0.150	0.144	0.044
67	Restaurants	0.002	0.000	0.001	0.002	0.004	0.002	0.001	0.001
68	Hotel, etc	0.000	0.000	0.000	0.000	0.001	0.000	0.000	0.000
69	Road Transport, etc	0.009	0.001	0.006	0.012	0.021	0.012	0.010	0.009
70	Air Transport, etc	0.001	0.000	0.001	0.001	0.014	0.004	0.005	0.002
71	Banking and Insurance	0.001	0.000	0.002	0.002	0.010	0.005	0.004	0.001
72	Real Estate	0.003	0.000	0.001	0.000	0.002	0.000	0.000	0.004
73	Public Services, etc	0.001	0.000	0.000	0.000	0.005	0.002	0.000	0.000
74	Personal Services, etc	0.004	0.000	0.001	0.008	0.005	0.001	0.001	0.012
	Sum of Endogenous Accounts	0.976	1.000	0.950	0.999	0.980	0.993	0.958	0.996
75	Government	0.000	0.000	0.000	0.000	0.000	0.000	0.000	0.000
76	Capital Accounts	0.000	0.000	0.000	0.000	0.000	0.000	0.000	0.000
77	Net Indirect Taxes	0.013	0.000	0.000	0.001	0.016	0.007	0.000	0.004
78	Rest of World	0.011	0.000	0.049	0.000	0.004	0.000	0.042	0.000
	Sum of Exogenous Accounts	0.024	0.000	0.049	0.001	0.020	0.007	0.042	0.004
	Total	1.000	1.000	1.000	1.000	1.000	1.000	1.000	1.000

Factors of production

Institutions

Production activities

Exoac M

29

	Name	Refined Sugar 49	Canning (S+C) 50	Canning (M+L) 51	Kretek Cigs 52	White Cigs 53	Other Fbt 54	Wood and Construction 55	Textiles etc 56
1	Ag Paid Rural	0.000	0.000	0.000	0.000	0.000	0.000	0.000	0.000
2	Ag Paid Urban	0.000	0.000	0.000	0.000	0.000	0.000	0.000	0.000
3	Ag Unpaid Rural	0.000	0.000	0.000	0.000	0.000	0.000	0.000	0.000
4	Ag Unpaid Urban	0.000	0.000	0.000	0.000	0.000	0.000	0.000	0.000
5	Prod Paid Rural	0.058	0.136	0.057	0.016	0.017	0.009	0.076	0.045
6	Prod Paid Urban	0.027	0.066	0.016	0.007	0.008	0.009	0.046	0.046
7	Prod Unpaid Rural	0.037	0.040	0.000	0.006	0.000	0.021	0.037	0.021
8	Prod Unpaid Urban	0.005	0.005	0.000	0.001	0.000	0.008	0.005	0.007
9	Cler Paid Rural	0.007	0.015	0.004	0.002	0.002	0.003	0.007	0.003
10	Cler Paid Urban	0.011	0.025	0.005	0.003	0.003	0.004	0.006	0.010
11	Cler Unpaid Rural	0.001	0.000	0.000	0.000	0.000	0.001	0.001	0.001
12	Cler Unpaid Urban	0.001	0.000	0.000	0.000	0.000	0.001	0.000	0.001
13	Prof Paid Rural	0.003	0.005	0.002	0.001	0.001	0.001	0.002	0.002
14	Prof Paid Urban	0.004	0.010	0.004	0.001	0.001	0.002	0.007	0.005
15	Prof Unpaid Rural	0.001	0.000	0.000	0.000	0.000	0.002	0.002	0.002
16	Prof Unpaid Urban	0.002	0.005	0.000	0.000	0.000	0.004	0.003	0.003
17	Uninc Capital Land	0.000	0.000	0.000	0.000	0.000	0.000	0.000	0.000
18	Uninc Capital Housing	0.000	0.000	0.000	0.000	0.000	0.000	0.000	0.000
19	Uninc Capital Rural	0.123	0.056	0.029	0.005	0.029	0.001	0.016	0.039
20	Uninc Capital Urban	0.118	0.056	0.029	0.005	0.024	0.121	0.018	0.062
21	Inc Capital Domestic	0.056	0.025	0.013	0.054	0.141	0.032	0.100	0.039
22	Inc Capital Government	0.060	0.000	0.014	0.001	0.002	0.071	0.025	0.011
23	Inc Capital Foreign	0.033	0.000	0.007	0.054	0.141	0.008	0.002	0.024
24	Ag Employees								
25	Farm Size 1								
26	Farm Size 2								
27	Farm Size 3								
28	Rural Lower								
29	Rural Middle								
30	Rural Higher								
31	Urban Lower								
32	Urban Middle								
33	Urban Higher								
34	Companies								
35	Food Crop	0.009	0.253	0.375	0.001	0.000	0.151	0.002	0.001
36	Nonfood Crop	0.186	0.000	0.018	0.305	0.100	0.100	0.001	0.008
37	Livestock and Products	0.000	0.000	0.000	0.000	0.000	0.007	0.000	0.012
38	Forestry and Hunting	0.002	0.000	0.000	0.000	0.000	0.001	0.043	0.000
39	Fishery	0.000	0.000	0.000	0.000	0.000	0.000	0.000	0.000
40	Metal Ore Mining	0.000	0.000	0.000	0.000	0.000	0.000	0.000	0.000
41	Other Mining	0.000	0.000	0.000	0.000	0.000	0.000	0.036	0.000
42	Handpounded Rice	0.000	0.000	0.000	0.000	0.000	0.003	0.000	0.000
43	Milled Rice	0.000	0.000	0.000	0.000	0.000	0.015	0.000	0.000
44	Farm Processed Tea	0.000	0.000	0.000	0.000	0.000	0.000	0.000	0.000
45	Processed Tea	0.000	0.000	0.000	0.000	0.000	0.000	0.000	0.000
46	Dried and Salted Fish	0.000	0.000	0.000	0.000	0.000	0.000	0.000	0.000
47	Canned Fish	0.000	0.000	0.000	0.000	0.000	0.000	0.000	0.000
48	Brown Sugar	0.000	0.000	0.000	0.000	0.000	0.006	0.000	0.000
49	Refined Sugar	0.001	0.051	0.036	0.000	0.000	0.024	0.000	0.000
50	Canning (s+c)	0.000	0.000	0.000	0.000	0.000	0.000	0.000	0.000
51	Canning (m+l)	0.000	0.000	0.000	0.000	0.000	0.000	0.000	0.000
52	Kretek Cigs	0.000	0.000	0.000	0.000	0.000	0.000	0.000	0.000
53	White Cigs	0.000	0.000	0.000	0.000	0.000	0.000	0.000	0.000
54	Other Fbt	0.000	0.000	0.018	0.196	0.064	0.107	0.000	0.000
55	Wood and Construction	0.008	0.000	0.000	0.002	0.001	0.005	0.032	0.005
56	Textiles, etc	0.009	0.051	0.018	0.000	0.000	0.002	0.001	0.293
57	Paper, Transport, Metal, etc.	0.031	0.051	0.071	0.029	0.010	0.002	0.040	0.011
58	Chemical, Cement, etc	0.009	0.040	0.038	0.005	0.002	0.000	0.077	0.006
59	Coal Mining	0.001	0.000	0.000	0.000	0.000	0.000	0.000	0.000
60	Petroleum Mining, etc	0.000	0.000	0.000	0.000	0.000	0.000	0.000	0.000
61	Gasoline	0.003	0.005	0.007	0.005	0.003	0.001	0.002	0.002
62	Fuel Oil	0.003	0.005	0.009	0.000	0.000	0.001	0.001	0.001
63	Electricity	0.052	0.000	0.000	0.004	0.011	0.009	0.001	0.019
64	City Gas	0.000	0.000	0.000	0.000	0.000	0.000	0.000	0.000
65	Water	0.001	0.000	0.018	0.000	0.002	0.000	0.000	0.004
66	Trade	0.036	0.051	0.125	0.087	0.154	0.188	0.130	0.074
67	Restaurants	0.002	0.000	0.000	0.002	0.001	0.002	0.010	0.002
68	Hotel, etc	0.001	0.000	0.000	0.001	0.001	0.001	0.000	0.000
69	Road Transport, etc	0.009	0.000	0.018	0.010	0.007	0.022	0.036	0.010
70	Air Transport, etc	0.003	0.000	0.018	0.005	0.003	0.016	0.021	0.006
71	Banking and Insurance	0.005	0.000	0.000	0.014	0.013	0.009	0.008	0.007
72	Real Estate	0.000	0.000	0.000	0.000	0.000	0.001	0.006	0.002
73	Public Services, etc	0.001	0.000	0.000	0.000	0.000	0.000	0.001	0.000
74	Personal Services, etc	0.004	0.000	0.018	0.000	0.000	0.003	0.001	0.002
	Sum of Endogenous Accounts	0.922	0.949	0.964	0.824	0.739	0.976	0.801	0.786
75	Government	0.000	0.000	0.000	0.000	0.000	0.000	0.000	0.000
76	Capital Accounts	0.000	0.000	0.000	0.000	0.000	0.000	0.000	0.000
77	Net Indirect Taxes	0.033	0.051	0.036	0.164	0.229	0.012	0.011	0.006
78	Rest of World	0.046	0.000	0.000	0.011	0.032	0.012	0.188	0.208
	Sum of Exogenous Accounts	0.078	0.051	0.036	0.175	0.261	0.024	0.199	0.214
	Total	1.000	1.000	1.000	1.000	1.000	1.000	1.000	1.000

Factors of production — Institutions — Production activities — M Exo ac M

Table II.5: Cont

	Name	Procuction Activities							
		Paper Transport Metal, Etc	Chemical Cement, Etc	Coal Mining	Petroleum Mining, Etc	Gasoline	Fuel Oil	Electricity	City Gas
		57	58	59	60	61	62	63	64
1	Ag Paid Rural	0.000	0.000	0.000	0.000	0.000	0.000	0.000	0.000
2	Ag Paid Urban	0.000	0.000	0.000	0.000	0.000	0.000	0.000	0.000
3	Ag Unpaid Rural	0.000	0.000	0.000	0.000	0.000	0.000	0.000	0.000
4	Ag Unpaid Urban	0.000	0.000	0.000	0.000	0.000	0.000	0.000	0.000
5	Prod Paid Rural	0.026	0.036	0.212	0.001	0.008	0.008	0.001	0.000
6	Prod Paid Urban	0.035	0.020	0.021	0.001	0.007	0.007	0.063	0.113
7	Prod Unpaid Rural	0.018	0.021	0.000	0.000	0.000	0.000	0.001	0.000
8	Prod Unpaid Urban	0.005	0.001	0.000	0.000	0.000	0.000	0.006	0.000
9	Cler Paid Rural	0.006	0.011	0.046	0.000	0.004	0.004	0.022	0.000
10	Cler Paid Urban	0.019	0.014	0.017	0.002	0.006	0.006	0.021	0.045
11	Cler Unpaid Rural	0.001	0.000	0.000	0.000	0.000	0.000	0.000	0.000
12	Cler Unpaid Urban	0.001	0.000	0.000	0.000	0.000	0.000	0.000	0.000
13	Prof Paid Rural	0.001	0.003	0.005	0.000	0.002	0.002	0.011	0.000
14	Prof Paid Urban	0.009	0.008	0.000	0.005	0.004	0.003	0.046	0.067
15	Prof Unpaid Rural	0.001	0.002	0.000	0.000	0.000	0.000	0.000	0.000
16	Prof Unpaid Urban	0.003	0.001	0.000	0.000	0.000	0.000	0.000	0.000
17	Uninc Capital Land	0.000	0.000	0.000	0.000	0.000	0.000	0.000	0.000
18	Uninc Capital Housing	0.000	0.000	0.000	0.000	0.000	0.000	0.000	0.000
19	Uninc Capital Rural	0.013	0.016	0.000	0.000	0.000	0.000	0.001	0.000
20	Uninc Capital Urban	0.025	0.023	0.000	0.000	0.000	0.000	0.009	0.000
21	Inc Capital Domestic	0.111	0.049	0.000	0.000	0.000	0.000	0.047	0.324
22	Inc Capital Government	0.035	0.124	0.347	0.203	0.236	0.232	0.297	0.000
23	Inc Capital Foreign	0.050	0.029	0.000	0.720	0.000	0.000	0.038	0.000
24	Ag Employees								
25	Farm Size 1								
26	Farm Size 2								
27	Farm Size 3								
28	Rural Lower								
29	Rural Middle								
30	Rural Higher								
31	Urban Lower								
32	Urban Middle								
33	Urban Higher								
34	Companies								
35	Food Crop	0.001	0.004	0.000	0.000	0.000	0.000	0.000	0.000
36	Nonfood Crop	0.000	0.011	0.000	0.000	0.000	0.000	0.000	0.000
37	Livestock and Products	0.001	0.000	0.000	0.000	0.000	0.000	0.000	0.000
38	Forestry and Hunting	0.007	0.005	0.001	0.000	0.000	0.000	0.000	0.000
39	Fishery	0.000	0.000	0.000	0.000	0.000	0.000	0.000	0.000
40	Metal Ore Mining	0.000	0.000	0.000	0.000	0.000	0.000	0.000	0.000
41	Other Mining	0.000	0.014	0.000	0.000	0.000	0.000	0.000	0.000
42	Handpounded Rice	0.000	0.000	0.000	0.000	0.000	0.000	0.000	0.000
43	Milled Rice	0.000	0.000	0.000	0.000	0.000	0.000	0.000	0.000
44	Farm Processed Tea	0.000	0.000	0.000	0.000	0.000	0.000	0.000	0.000
45	Processed Tea	0.000	0.000	0.000	0.000	0.000	0.000	0.000	0.000
46	Dried and Salted Fish	0.000	0.000	0.000	0.000	0.000	0.000	0.000	0.000
47	Canned Fish	0.000	0.000	0.000	0.000	0.000	0.000	0.000	0.000
48	Brown Sugar	0.000	0.000	0.000	0.000	0.000	0.000	0.000	0.000
49	Refined Sugar	0.000	0.002	0.000	0.000	0.000	0.000	0.000	0.000
50	Canning (s+c)	0.000	0.000	0.000	0.000	0.000	0.000	0.000	0.000
51	Canning (m+l)	0.000	0.000	0.000	0.000	0.000	0.000	0.000	0.000
52	Kretek Cigs	0.000	0.000	0.000	0.000	0.000	0.000	0.000	0.000
53	White Cigs	0.000	0.000	0.000	0.000	0.000	0.000	0.000	0.000
54	Other Fbt	0.000	0.024	0.000	0.000	0.000	0.000	0.000	0.000
55	Wood and Construction	0.023	0.012	0.003	0.001	0.005	0.005	0.025	0.002
56	Textiles, etc	0.002	0.004	0.003	0.000	0.000	0.000	0.000	0.001
57	Paper, Transport, Metal, etc.	0.039	0.018	0.086	0.005	0.015	0.020	0.017	0.017
58	Chemical, Cement, etc	0.031	0.025	0.007	0.000	0.022	0.021	0.004	0.020
59	Coal Mining	0.000	0.000	0.016	0.000	0.000	0.000	0.005	0.000
60	Petroleum Mining, etc	0.000	0.225	0.000	0.002	0.479	0.471	0.000	0.000
61	Gasoline	0.002	0.003	0.007	0.000	0.000	0.000	0.017	0.004
62	Fuel Oil	0.001	0.008	0.007	0.001	0.002	0.002	0.090	0.087
63	Electricity	0.007	0.016	0.083	0.004	0.010	0.009	0.020	0.018
64	City Gas	0.000	0.000	0.000	0.000	0.000	0.000	0.000	0.001
65	Water	0.007	0.000	0.000	0.000	0.000	0.000	0.000	0.000
66	Trade	0.099	0.074	0.015	0.000	0.006	0.006	0.027	0.031
67	Restaurants	0.003	0.002	0.001	0.000	0.002	0.002	0.002	0.001
68	Hotel, etc	0.000	0.000	0.001	0.000	0.000	0.000	0.001	0.000
69	Road Transport, etc	0.013	0.021	0.002	0.000	0.001	0.002	0.005	0.015
70	Air Transport, etc	0.009	0.013	0.005	0.001	0.002	0.003	0.013	0.012
71	Banking and Insurance	0.016	0.017	0.003	0.002	0.021	0.021	0.007	0.003
72	Real Estate	0.006	0.004	0.002	0.003	0.003	0.003	0.003	0.002
73	Public Services, etc	0.001	0.001	0.001	0.000	0.001	0.001	0.000	0.000
74	Personal Services, etc	0.003	0.004	0.000	0.001	0.002	0.000	0.001	0.003
	Sum of Endogenous Accounts	0.633	0.870	0.890	0.954	0.839	0.828	0.803	0.766
75	Government	0.000	0.000	0.000	0.000	0.000	0.000	0.000	0.000
76	Capital Accounts	0.000	0.000	0.000	0.000	0.000	0.000	0.000	0.000
77	Net Indirect Taxes	0.011	0.014	0.007	0.037	0.001	0.001	0.010	0.005
78	Rest of World	0.357	0.117	0.103	0.009	0.160	0.171	0.187	0.228
	Sum of Exogenous Accounts	0.367	0.130	0.110	0.046	0.161	0.172	0.197	0.234
	Total	1.000	1.000	1.000	1.000	1.000	1.000	1.000	1.000

Factors of production — Institutions — Production activities — Exo ac M — M

31

		Production Activities							
	Name	Water	Wholesale and Retail Trade	Resturants	Hotel Etc	Road Transport Etc	Air Transport Etc	Banking Insurance	Real Estate
		65	66	67	68	69	70	71	72
Factors of production									
1	Ag Paid Rural	0.000	0.000	0.000	0.000	0.000	0.000	0.000	0.000
2	Ag Paid Urban	0.000	0.000	0.000	0.000	0.000	0.000	0.000	0.000
3	Ag Unpaid Rural	0.000	0.000	0.000	0.000	0.000	0.000	0.000	0.000
4	Ag Unpaid Urban	0.000	0.000	0.000	0.000	0.000	0.000	0.000	0.000
5	Prod Paid Rural	0.000	0.002	0.000	0.002	0.077	0.015	0.001	0.003
6	Prod Paid Urban	0.041	0.003	0.000	0.003	0.086	0.038	0.006	0.003
7	Prod Unpaid Rural	0.000	0.000	0.000	0.000	0.072	0.009	0.000	0.000
8	Prod Unpaid Urban	0.000	0.000	0.000	0.000	0.049	0.003	0.000	0.000
9	Cler Paid Rural	0.000	0.018	0.006	0.044	0.011	0.006	0.013	0.008
10	Cler Paid Urban	0.016	0.032	0.005	0.139	0.015	0.049	0.137	0.011
11	Cler Unpaid Rural	0.000	0.158	0.054	0.002	0.001	0.000	0.000	0.000
12	Cler Unpaid Urban	0.000	0.085	0.029	0.002	0.002	0.001	0.000	0.000
13	Prof Paid Rural	0.000	0.001	0.000	0.005	0.001	0.003	0.005	0.001
14	Prof Paid Urban	0.024	0.007	0.000	0.018	0.005	0.043	0.095	0.009
15	Prof Unpaid Rural	0.000	0.009	0.005	0.001	0.000	0.001	0.000	0.000
16	Prof Unpaid Urban	0.000	0.034	0.009	0.015	0.004	0.002	0.001	0.002
17	Uninc Capital Land	0.000	0.000	0.000	0.000	0.000	0.000	0.000	0.000
18	Uninc Capital Housing	0.000	0.000	0.000	0.000	0.000	0.000	0.000	0.642
19	Uninc Capital Rural	0.000	0.077	0.086	0.025	0.080	0.017	0.003	0.002
20	Uninc Capital Urban	0.000	0.118	0.113	0.114	0.137	0.021	0.005	0.055
21	Inc Capital Domestic	0.000	0.203	0.010	0.015	0.094	0.018	0.048	0.112
22	Inc Capital Government	0.130	0.059	0.000	0.084	0.010	0.312	0.452	0.010
23	Inc Capital Foreign	0.000	0.037	0.001	0.019	0.000	0.000	0.032	0.000
Institutions									
24	Ag Employees								
25	Farm Size 1								
26	Farm Size 2								
27	Farm Size 3								
28	Rural Lower								
29	Rural Middle								
30	Rural Higher								
31	Urban Lower								
32	Urban Middle								
33	Urban Higher								
34	Companies								
Production activities									
35	Food Crop	0.000	0.001	0.077	0.007	0.000	0.001	0.000	0.000
36	Nonfood Crop	0.000	0.000	0.011	0.004	0.000	0.000	0.000	0.000
37	Livestock and Products	0.000	0.000	0.068	0.019	0.000	0.003	0.000	0.000
38	Forestry and Hunting	0.000	0.000	0.002	0.000	0.000	0.000	0.000	0.000
39	Fishery	0.000	0.000	0.034	0.002	0.000	0.000	0.000	0.000
40	Metal Ore Mining	0.000	0.000	0.000	0.000	0.000	0.000	0.000	0.000
41	Other Mining	0.000	0.000	0.000	0.000	0.000	0.000	0.000	0.000
42	Handpounded Rice	0.000	0.000	0.021	0.000	0.000	0.000	0.000	0.000
43	Milled Rice	0.000	0.000	0.044	0.023	0.004	0.003	0.000	0.000
44	Farm Processed Tea	0.000	0.000	0.002	0.000	0.000	0.000	0.000	0.000
45	Processed Tea	0.000	0.000	0.001	0.003	0.000	0.000	0.000	0.000
46	Dried and Salted Fish	0.000	0.000	0.008	0.000	0.000	0.000	0.000	0.000
47	Canned Fish	0.000	0.000	0.002	0.000	0.000	0.000	0.000	0.000
48	Brown Sugar	0.000	0.000	0.002	0.000	0.000	0.000	0.000	0.000
49	Refined Sugar	0.000	0.000	0.030	0.012	0.000	0.001	0.000	0.000
50	Canning (s+c)	0.000	0.000	0.000	0.000	0.000	0.000	0.000	0.000
51	Canning (m+l)	0.000	0.000	0.000	0.001	0.000	0.000	0.000	0.000
52	Kretek Cigs	0.000	0.000	0.000	0.001	0.000	0.000	0.000	0.000
53	White Cigs	0.000	0.000	0.000	0.001	0.000	0.000	0.000	0.000
54	Other Fbt	0.000	0.000	0.151	0.061	0.000	0.003	0.000	0.000
55	Wood and Construction	0.087	0.006	0.007	0.040	0.005	0.023	0.016	0.097
56	Textiles, etc	0.002	0.001	0.004	0.011	0.001	0.007	0.000	0.000
57	Paper, Transport, Metal, etc.	0.000	0.005	0.008	0.024	0.010	0.046	0.018	0.003
58	Chemical, Cement, etc	0.016	0.000	0.000	0.008	0.000	0.000	0.000	0.000
59	Coal Mining	0.000	0.000	0.000	0.000	0.000	0.000	0.000	0.000
60	Petroleum Mining, etc	0.000	0.000	0.000	0.000	0.000	0.000	0.000	0.000
61	Gasoline	0.000	0.006	0.001	0.001	0.022	0.024	0.002	0.001
62	Fuel Oil	0.000	0.001	0.012	0.009	0.012	0.013	0.000	0.001
63	Electricity	0.068	0.002	0.003	0.021	0.001	0.004	0.004	0.001
64	City Gas	0.000	0.000	0.001	0.002	0.000	0.000	0.000	0.000
65	Water	0.000	0.000	0.001	0.010	0.001	0.001	0.000	0.000
66	Trade	0.300	0.007	0.088	0.056	0.032	0.051	0.032	0.003
67	Restaurants	0.007	0.009	0.003	0.009	0.004	0.015	0.004	0.004
68	Hotel, etc	0.003	0.003	0.000	0.001	0.000	0.001	0.013	0.000
69	Road Transport, etc	0.061	0.012	0.015	0.015	0.017	0.007	0.006	0.004
70	Air Transport, etc	0.000	0.006	0.009	0.023	0.004	0.063	0.021	0.002
71	Banking and Insurance	0.022	0.045	0.009	0.057	0.008	0.033	0.008	0.011
72	Real Estate	0.005	0.014	0.008	0.011	0.002	0.011	0.017	0.004
73	Public Services, etc	0.000	0.002	0.002	0.001	0.003	0.009	0.017	0.001
74	Personal Services, etc	0.048	0.009	0.004	0.004	0.168	0.009	0.008	0.003
	Sum of Endogenous Accounts	0.831	0.973	0.946	0.927	0.938	0.867	0.962	0.994
75	Government	0.000	0.000	0.000	0.000	0.000	0.000	0.000	0.000
76	Capital Accounts	0.000	0.000	0.000	0.000	0.000	0.000	0.000	0.000
77	Net Indirect Taxes	0.000	0.010	0.011	0.015	0.014	0.004	0.001	0.002
78	Rest of World	0.168	0.017	0.043	0.058	0.048	0.129	0.037	0.004
	Sum of Exogenous Accounts	0.169	0.027	0.054	0.073	0.062	0.133	0.038	0.006
	Total	1.000	1.000	1.000	1.000	1.000	1.000	1.000	1.000

Table II.5: Cont

		Name	Production Activities	
			Public Services Etc	Personal Services
			73	74
Factors of production	1	Ag Paid Rural	0.000	0.000
	2	Ag Paid Urban	0.000	0.000
	3	Ag Unpaid Rural	0.000	0.000
	4	Ag Unpaid Urban	0.000	0.000
	5	Prod Paid Rural	0.006	0.077
	6	Prod Paid Urban	0.016	0.073
	7	Prod Unpaid Rural	0.000	0.052
	8	Prod Unpaid Urban	0.001	0.053
	9	Cler Paid Rural	0.049	0.102
	10	Cler Paid Urban	0.098	0.098
	11	Cler Unpaid Rural	0.001	0.031
	12	Cler Unpaid Urban	0.002	0.023
	13	Prof Paid Rural	0.286	0.009
	14	Prof Paid Urban	0.308	0.008
	15	Prof Unpaid Rural	0.004	0.005
	16	Prof Unpaid Urban	0.008	0.008
	17	Uninc Capital Land	0.000	0.000
	18	Uninc Capital Housing	0.000	0.000
	19	Uninc Capital Rural	0.008	0.005
	20	Uninc Capital Urban	0.036	0.011
	21	Inc Capital Domestic	0.022	0.016
	22	Inc Capital Government	0.034	0.002
	23	Inc Capital Foreign	0.000	0.000
Institutions	24	Ag Employees		
	25	Farm Size 1		
	26	Farm Size 2		
	27	Farm Size 3		
	28	Rural Lower		
	29	Rural Middle		
	30	Rural Higher		
	31	Urban Lower		
	32	Urban Middle		
	33	Urban Higher		
	34	Companies		
Production activities	35	Food Crop	0.003	0.000
	36	Nonfood Crop	0.000	0.000
	37	Livestock and Products	0.004	0.000
	38	Forestry and Hunting	0.000	0.000
	39	Fishery	0.001	0.000
	40	Metal Ore Mining	0.000	0.000
	41	Other Mining	0.000	0.000
	42	Handpounded Rice	0.002	0.000
	43	Milled Rice	0.002	0.000
	44	Farm Processed Tea	0.000	0.000
	45	Processed Tea	0.000	0.000
	46	Dried and Salted Fish	0.000	0.000
	47	Canned Fish	0.000	0.000
	48	Brown Sugar	0.000	0.000
	49	Refined Sugar	0.000	0.000
	50	Canning (s+c)	0.000	0.000
	51	Canning (m+l)	0.000	0.000
	52	Kretek Cigs	0.000	0.000
	53	White Cigs	0.000	0.000
	54	Other Fbt	0.002	0.000
	55	Wood and Construction	0.009	0.004
	56	Textiles, etc	0.002	0.023
	57	Paper, Transport, Metal, etc.	0.010	0.057
	58	Chemical, Cement, etc	0.005	0.074
	59	Coal Mining	0.000	0.000
	60	Petroleum Mining, etc	0.000	0.000
	61	Gasoline	0.001	0.004
	62	Fuel Oil	0.001	0.002
	63	Electricity	0.004	0.002
	64	City Gas	0.000	0.000
	65	Water	0.001	0.001
	66	Trade	0.013	0.067
	67	Restaurants	0.001	0.003
	68	Hotel, etc	0.000	0.000
	69	Road Transport, etc	0.002	0.014
	70	Air Transport, etc	0.002	0.005
	71	Banking and Insurance	0.003	0.008
	72	Real Estate	0.004	0.011
	73	Public Services, etc	0.006	0.001
	74	Personal Services, etc	0.003	0.012
M		Sum of Endogenous Accounts	0.962	0.861
Exoac	75	Government	0.000	0.000
	76	Capital Accounts	0.000	0.000
	77	Net Indirect Taxes	0.005	0.005
	78	Rest of World	0.033	0.134
M		Sum of Exogenous Accounts	0.038	0.139
		Total	1.000	1.000

agricultural employees (row 24), 19.1% to the household group
headed by small farmers owning or operating less than half a
hectare (row 25) etc.; 2) Reading down column 24 one can, likewise, capture the consumption expenditure pattern of the household
group headed by agricultural employees and it shows, among others,
that 18.2% of their expenditures went for food crops (row 35),
2.3% for livestock products (row 37) and 24.8% for milled rice
(row 43). Interestingly enough, this particular group did dissave
to the tune of 6.4% of total expenditures as can be seen by
looking at the intersection of column 24 and row 76 (capital
account); 3) The last example reflects the relative allocation of
food production into value added going to the different factors of
production and intermediate input requirements. Thus, reading
down column 35 one can see that 12.5% of the gross output of farm
food crops went to compensate agricultural paid rural workers (row
1), 35.1% went to agricultural unpaid rural workers (row 3) and
40% to land rent (17) etc. With regard to intermediate input
requirements, 2.2% came from within the same sector (row 35), 2.9%
went for wholesale and retail trade margins (row 66) and, finally,
it can be seen that 1.4% was imported from the rest of the world.
In a general sense, matrices A_n and A_1 capture the structure of
the Indonesian economy as of 1975.

From the definition of A_n, it follows that in the transaction
matrix, each endogenous total income (y_n) is given as follows

$$y_n = A_n y_n + x \qquad (2.1)$$

which states that row sums of the endogenous accounts (1-74 in
SAM-Tech) can be obtained by multiplying the average expenditure
propensities for each row of the endogenous accounts by the level
of income recorded in each column and adding exogenous income x.

Equation (2.1) can be rewritten as

$$y_n = (I - A_n)^{-1} x \qquad (2.2)$$
$$= M_a x$$

Thus, from (2.2), endogenous incomes y_n (i.e. factor incomes,
y_1; institutions incomes, y_2; and production activities incomes,
y_3 as shown in Table II.4) can be derived by multiplying injection
x by a multiplier matrix M_a. This matrix has been referred to as
the accounting multiplier matrix because it explains the results
obtained in a SAM and not the process by which they are generated.[7] The latter would require the specification of a dynamic
model including the different SAM accounts and variables. The
construction of such a model to explore the macroeconomic effects
of the choice of technologies is clearly beyond the scope of the
present study but might be considered as a natural extension of
it.[8]

Returning to accounting multipliers, it is important to analyse further the endogenous transactions matrix T_n and its corresponding coefficient matrix A_n. Table II.4 shows that T_{nn} is, in fact, partitioned as follows:

$$T_{nn} = \begin{bmatrix} 0 & 0 & T_{13} \\ T_{21} & T_{22} & 0 \\ 0 & T_{32} & T_{33} \end{bmatrix} \qquad (2.3)$$

The exogenous accounts are collapsed into one column sum (x_i) representing injections and one row sum representing leakages (l_i). Corresponding to the partitioning of T_{nn} in (2.3), we have

$$A_n = \begin{bmatrix} 0 & 0 & A_{13} \\ A_{21} & A_{22} & 0 \\ 0 & A_{32} & A_{33} \end{bmatrix} \qquad (2.4)$$

The five submatrices which together constitute A_n appear in Table II.5. Thus A_{13} allocates the value added generated by the various production activities to the various factors as a proportion of the value of gross output of each activity and appears in columns 35-74 and rows 1-23 of Table II.5. Likewise, A_{33} represents the intermediate (input-output) demand and is shown in the square matrix embracing, respectively, columns and rows 34-74. Each column of the production activities account in A_{13} and A_{33} represents, in fact, a linear Leontief-type sectoral production function. In turn, A_{21} (embracing columns 1-23 and rows 24-34 in Table II.5) yields the incomes accruing to the different household groups by factorial source, and A_{22} represents transfers among households and between companies and households. Finally, A_{32} (columns 24-34 and rows 35-74) reflects the consumption behavior of the different socioeconomic household groups. More specifically, it shows the proportion of incomes (equal expenditures) of each household class which is spent on each production activity (i.e. commodity).

One limitation of the accounting multiplier matrix M_a as derived in equation (2.2) is that it implies unitary expenditure elasticities (the prevailing average expenditure propensities in A_n are assumed to apply to any incremental injection). A more realistic alternative is to specify a matrix of marginal expenditure propensities (C_n below) corresponding to the observed income and expenditure elasticities of the different agents, under the assumption that prices remain fixed. Expressing the changes in incomes (d_{y_n}) resulting from changes in injections (dx) (see Pyatt and Round op.cit.), one obtains,

$$d_{y_n} = C_n d_{y_n} + dx$$

$$= (I-C_n)^{-1} dx = M_c dx \qquad (2.5)$$

M_c has been coined a fixed price multiplier matrix and its advantage is that it allows any nonnegative income and expenditure elasticities to be reflected in M_c. In particular, in exploring the macroeconomic effects of exogenous changes in the output of different product-cum-technologies on other macroeconomic variables, it would be very unrealistic to assume that consumers reacted to any given proportional change in their income by increasing expenditures on the different commodities by exactly that same proportion (i.e. assuming that the income elasticities of demand of the various socioeconomic household groups for the various commodities were all unitary). Consequently, an attempt was made to estimate the likely magnitudes of these elasticities (see Appendix Table C). Given the lack of information on the magnitude of these elasticities for the socioeconomic groups, many of the specific elasticities had to be guessed at. Whenever possible, (e.g. in the case of rice) whatever available empirical evidence was used.[9] In any case, the estimates appearing in Appendix Table C should be taken as illustrative of the likely magnitudes of expenditure elasticities of the various socio-economic groups rather than on empirically derived parameters. Since the expenditure (income) elasticity (ε_{y_i}) is equal to the ratio of the marginal expenditure propensity (MEP_i) to the average expenditure propensity (AEP_i) for any given good i, it follows that the marginal expenditure propensity can be readily obtained once the expenditure elasticity and the average expenditure propensities are known, i.e.

$$\varepsilon_{y_i} = \frac{MEP_i}{AEP_i}$$

$$MEP_i = \varepsilon_{y_i} \cdot AEP_i \qquad (2.6)$$

$$\text{and} \quad \sum_i MEP_i = 1^{10}$$

Thus, given the matrix A_{32} of average expenditure propensities, (columns 24-34 and rows 35-74 of Table II.5) and the corresponding expenditure elasticities of demand as given in Appendix Table C the corresponding marginal expenditure propensities matrix C_{32} could easily be derived. This matrix is given in Appendix Table D. One example will suffice to illustrate the above relationship (2.6), i.e. the marginal expenditure propensity of agricultural employees for milled rice was taken as .175 in Appendix Table D (see element corresponding to column 24 and row 43). This ratio is obtained as the product of the corresponding expenditure elasticity equal to .71 (see Appendix Table C) and the average expenditure propensity .248.

In principle, a similar procedure could be used to obtain the marginal expenditure propensities corresponding to the other four submatrices (in addition to C_{32}) of C_n. The mapping of factorial income into household income (T_{21}) reflects the asset and wealth distribution, i.e. the ownership pattern of factors of production by household groups. As long as this pattern remains constant, the corresponding average propensities (A_{21} appearing in Table II.5) remain in effect (i.e. $A_{21}=C_{21}$). Conversely, should a change in the underlying pattern of ownership of factors occur--such as a land reform--this would have to be reflected by a new matrix of marginal propensities incorporating the structural changes. We assume that the ownership pattern of factors of production remains constant throughout our simulation exercises and therefore retain the existing average propensities, i.e. A_{21} in Table II.5. Likewise, we shall assume that the pattern of interinstitutional transfers, i.e. A_{22} remains as given.

Finally, in a somewhat similar vein, certain types of technological changes--to the extent that they may be foreseen--could be incorporated into a matrix of marginal expenditures coefficients with regard to both the allocation of value added generated by production activities accruing to factors and the matrix of intermediate inputs. In the absence of such information on technological change, it is also assumed that any incremental output of any of the production activities within the system will be produced using the same prevailing technology, i.e. the incremental technological coefficients are assumed to be the same as the existing average technological coefficients.

In summary, for simulation purposes, we are using the following matrix of marginal expenditure propensities C_n,

$$
C_n = \begin{bmatrix} 0 & 0 & C_{13}=A_{13} \\ C_{21}=A_{21} & C_{22}=A_{22} & 0 \\ 0 & C_{32} & C_{33}=A_{33} \end{bmatrix} \quad (2.7)
$$

which assumes that the ownership pattern of factors remains constant, as well as the pattern of interinstitutional transfers and the technological coefficients for any given activity. In contrast, realistic income elasticities of demand are postulated for the different socioeconomic groups yielding matrix C_{32}. Incidentally, another advantage of using a marginal expenditure propensity matrix with regard to the expenditure behavior of the different household groups is that it allows taking into account, as well, the marginal leakages of the households such as their marginal expenditure to save, to pay taxes and to import which may be quite different from their corresponding average expenditure propensities.[11]   (The coefficients which appear in Appendix Table D, columns 24-34 and rows 75-78 provide these marginal leakages.)

Thus returning to the fixed price multiplier matrix derived in equation (2.5), where M_c equals $(I-C_n)^{-1}$, it follows that given the average expenditure propensities for A_{21}, A_{22}, A_{13} and A_{33} from Table II.5 and the marginal expenditure propensities for C_{32} given in Appendix Table D, C_n in equation (2.5) is fully known and the corresponding fixed price multiplier matrix M_c can likewise be derived. This matrix is reproduced on Table II.6. The multipliers in this table should be interpreted as follows: an incremental injection of 100 units (i.e. Indonesian Rupiahs) into any particular column will typically be responsible for some part of every incremental endogenous income. More specifically, we are interested in the effects on the major policy objectives of the increased output of production activities incorporating given technologies. Thus, for example, it can be asked what the macroeconomic consequences would be of an injection of 100 additional units of exogenous demand for a product using a traditional technology as opposed to the same product using a modern technology. Suppose, for example, that one wanted to estimate the macroeconomic effects of an increase of 100 units of exogenous demand for handpounded rice, (activity 42) as compared to milled rice (activity 43). This exogenous demand might be through exports or government expenditures, or even through the natural diffusion process of a modern technology becoming relatively more important over time.[12]

Both direct and indirect effects are generated by this injection circulating around the economy. The fixed price multiplier column for handpounded rice (42) in Table II.6 as well as for milled rice (43) estimates these effects. Thus, reading down the multipliers numbers down column 42 it can be seen that an increase of 100 rupiahs of handpounded rice output would lead ultimately to an increase of 25.2 units of income accruing to agricultural paid rural workers (row 1), 0.7 rupiah to agricultural paid urban workers, 62.4 rupiahs to agricultural unpaid rural workers (row 3) and so on and so forth. Similarly, reading down the milled rice column (43) it can be seen that an increase of 100 rupiah of milled rice output would yield ultimately increases in income going to the above three labour groups of, respectively, 16.9 rupiahs, 0.6 and 43.7 rupiahs. Some of the more aggregate effects of this injection can be seen by looking at total factor income, total income of institutions and total output effects, respectively. Thus, these aggregate multipliers are 2.73 for handpounded rice as opposed to 2.52 for milled rice for factorial income (implying that an addition of output of 100 rupiahs would ultimately yield 273 rupiahs of increased income going to all factors as compared to 252 for milled rice, as can be seen in row 23b and column 42 and 43, respectively of Table II.6).

Likewise, the corresponding household and companies' income aggregate multipliers are 2.81 for handpounded rice and 2.59 for milled rice (see row 34b and columns 42 and 43) and, finally, the aggregate output multipliers turn out to be 4.81 and 4.58, respectively (see row 74b and columns 42 and 43).

In the next chapter, these fixed price multipliers are used more systematically to estimate the likely effects of different product-cum- technology activities on the whole macroeconomic system, particularly with regard to our twelve dualistic production activities. The purpose of the above example was simply to illustrate the significance of fixed price multipliers and how they might be interpreted.

It will be seen subsequently in Chapter III that the observed greater aggregate effects on factor incomes, household incomes and gross output of handpounded rice as compared to milled rice in the preceding example can, in fact, be generalised within our set of dualistic sectors. In each instance, the traditional technology generated greater feedbacks--as measured by effects on total factor incomes, household incomes and gross output than its modern counterpart.[13]

Table II.6: Fixed Price Multiplier Matrix, Indonesian SAM-Tech, 1975*

			Factors of Production							
		Name	Ag Paid Rural	Ag Paid Urban	Ag Unpaid Rural	Ag Unpaid Urban	Prod Paid Rural	Prod Paid Urban	Prod Unpaid Rural	Prod Unpaid Urban
			1	2	3	4	5	6	7	8
Factors of Production	1	Ag Paid Rural	1.103	0.090	0.092	0.090	0.094	0.068	0.091	0.064
	2	Ag Paid Urban	0.005	1.004	0.004	0.004	0.004	0.003	0.004	0.003
	3	Ag Unpaid Rural	0.244	0.212	1.217	0.212	0.221	0.156	0.215	0.148
	4	Ag Unpaid Urban	0.010	0.009	0.008	1.008	0.009	0.007	0.009	0.006
	5	Prod Paid Rural	0.055	0.053	0.048	0.049	1.054	0.050	0.052	0.049
	6	Prod Paid Urban	0.053	0.052	0.048	0.048	0.053	1.051	0.051	0.050
	7	Prod Unpaid Rural	0.043	0.041	0.038	0.038	0.042	0.039	1.041	0.037
	8	Prod Unpaid Urban	0.018	0.018	0.017	0.017	0.018	0.018	0.018	1.018
	9	Cler Paid Rural	0.039	0.038	0.035	0.035	0.038	0.036	0.037	0.035
	10	Cler Paid Urban	0.066	0.063	0.059	0.059	0.064	0.061	0.063	0.059
	11	Cler Unpaid Rural	0.090	0.084	0.080	0.080	0.085	0.077	0.083	0.074
	12	Cler Unpaid Urban	0.050	0.047	0.044	0.044	0.047	0.042	0.046	0.041
	13	Prof Paid Rural	0.048	0.047	0.043	0.043	0.047	0.048	0.046	0.047
	14	Prof Paid Urban	0.066	0.065	0.058	0.060	0.064	0.065	0.063	0.063
	15	Prof Unpaid Rural	0.008	0.007	0.007	0.007	0.007	0.007	0.007	0.007
	16	Prof Unpaid Urban	0.023	0.022	0.021	0.021	0.022	0.020	0.021	0.019
	17	Uninc Capital Land	0.389	0.346	0.345	0.340	0.357	0.273	0.348	0.261
	18	Uninc Capital Housing	0.096	0.097	0.084	0.087	0.090	0.097	0.089	0.096
	19	Uninc Capital Rural	0.110	0.102	0.092	0.093	0.104	0.093	0.100	0.089
	20	Uninc Capital Urban	0.159	0.152	0.144	0.145	0.154	0.151	0.150	0.145
	21	Inc Capital Domestic	0.197	0.187	0.177	0.178	0.189	0.175	0.185	0.169
	22	Inc Capital Government	0.146	0.139	0.132	0.132	0.141	0.133	0.138	0.129
	23	Inc Capital Foreign	0.071	0.068	0.063	0.064	0.069	0.064	0.068	0.062
Σ		Sub-Total	3.090	2.942	2.856	2.856	2.973	2.735	2.926	2.670
Institutions	24	Ag Employees	0.752	0.649	0.122	0.117	0.161	0.097	0.177	0.094
	25	Farm Size 1	0.443	0.323	0.615	0.639	0.341	0.198	0.401	0.195
	26	Farm Size 2	0.236	0.198	0.412	0.363	0.216	0.139	0.254	0.136
	27	Farm Size 3	0.353	0.315	0.586	0.527	0.322	0.234	0.348	0.227
	28	Rural Lower	0.273	0.193	0.202	0.180	0.876	0.177	0.586	0.170
	29	Rural Middle	0.060	0.044	0.057	0.047	0.085	0.037	0.074	0.036
	30	Rural Higher	0.111	0.093	0.094	0.086	0.144	0.088	0.277	0.085
	31	Urban Lower	0.264	0.388	0.236	0.308	0.255	1.125	0.249	0.934
	32	Urban Middle	0.042	0.069	0.038	0.049	0.041	0.093	0.040	0.087
	33	Urban Higher	0.249	0.388	0.222	0.268	0.240	0.296	0.235	0.466
	34	Companies	0.385	0.366	0.347	0.349	0.372	0.346	0.364	0.335
Σ		Sub-Total	3.167	3.025	2.932	2.934	3.052	2.830	3.005	2.765
Production activities	35	Food Crop	0.576	0.498	0.491	0.481	0.517	0.357	0.499	0.336
	36	Nonfood Crop	0.108	0.098	0.099	0.098	0.098	0.083	0.097	0.079
	37	Livestock and Products	0.132	0.125	0.129	0.128	0.125	0.113	0.126	0.111
	38	Forestry and Hunting	0.015	0.013	0.012	0.012	0.013	0.009	0.013	0.009
	39	Fishery	0.068	0.063	0.061	0.061	0.067	0.058	0.065	0.056
	40	Metal Ore Mining	0.000	0.000	0.000	0.000	0.000	0.000	0.000	0.000
	41	Other Mining	0.007	0.006	0.006	0.006	0.006	0.005	0.006	0.005
	42	Handpounded Rice	0.101	0.083	0.128	0.121	0.095	0.059	0.099	0.056
	43	Milled Rice	0.281	0.245	0.185	0.185	0.252	0.173	0.231	0.160
	44	Farm Processed Tea	0.007	0.006	0.007	0.006	0.006	0.004	0.006	0.004
	45	Processed Tea	0.003	0.002	0.002	0.002	0.002	0.002	0.002	0.002
	46	Dried and Salted Fish	0.044	0.040	0.040	0.040	0.043	0.035	0.042	0.034
	47	Canned Fish	0.008	0.007	0.006	0.006	0.007	0.006	0.007	0.006
	48	Brown Sugar	0.015	0.013	0.014	0.014	0.013	0.010	0.013	0.009
	49	Refined Sugar	0.042	0.038	0.038	0.037	0.039	0.034	0.038	0.033
	50	Canning (s+c)	0.000	0.000	0.000	0.000	0.000	0.000	0.000	0.000
	51	Canning (m+l)	0.000	0.000	0.000	0.000	0.000	0.000	0.000	0.000
	52	Kretek Cigs	0.099	0.085	0.081	0.080	0.079	0.059	0.080	0.055
	53	White Cigs	0.016	0.017	0.017	0.017	0.024	0.024	0.021	0.023
	54	Other Fbt	0.189	0.186	0.198	0.198	0.194	0.212	0.190	0.200
	55	Wood and Construction	0.048	0.046	0.043	0.043	0.046	0.043	0.045	0.042
	56	Textiles, etc	0.169	0.165	0.156	0.160	0.174	0.175	0.168	0.168
	57	Paper, Transport, Metal, etc.	0.119	0.121	0.105	0.108	0.126	0.121	0.124	0.123
	58	Chemical, Cement, etc	0.069	0.066	0.060	0.061	0.066	0.061	0.064	0.059
	59	Coal Mining	0.000	0.000	0.000	0.000	0.000	0.000	0.000	0.000
	60	Petroleum Mining, etc	0.031	0.030	0.027	0.028	0.030	0.029	0.030	0.028
	61	Gasoline	0.015	0.015	0.013	0.013	0.015	0.014	0.014	0.014
	62	Fuel Oil	0.018	0.018	0.015	0.016	0.018	0.017	0.017	0.016
	63	Electricity	0.028	0.029	0.024	0.025	0.027	0.032	0.027	0.031
	64	Gas	0.000	0.000	0.000	0.000	0.000	0.000	0.000	0.000
	65	Water	0.007	0.006	0.006	0.006	0.006	0.007	0.006	0.006
	66	Trade	0.489	0.452	0.440	0.438	0.457	0.399	0.450	0.383
	67	Restaurants	0.136	0.138	0.108	0.114	0.128	0.156	0.122	0.147
	68	Hotel, etc	0.005	0.005	0.004	0.004	0.005	0.005	0.005	0.005
	69	Road Transport, etc	0.128	0.125	0.116	0.119	0.130	0.133	0.124	0.127
	70	Air Transport, etc	0.051	0.049	0.046	0.046	0.051	0.048	0.050	0.046
	71	Banking and Insurance	0.050	0.048	0.045	0.045	0.049	0.045	0.048	0.043
	72	Real Estate	0.150	0.150	0.131	0.136	0.140	0.151	0.138	0.149
	73	Public Services, etc	0.151	0.150	0.134	0.137	0.148	0.153	0.145	0.150
	74	Personal Services, etc	0.124	0.120	0.110	0.112	0.121	0.115	0.118	0.113
Σ		Sub-Total	3.498	3.259	3.099	3.102	3.320	2.947	3.233	2.830
Exog Accts.	75	Government	0.181	0.177	0.169	0.171	0.175	0.177	0.173	0.174
	76	Capital Accounts	0.420	0.433	0.485	0.477	0.434	0.443	0.446	0.455
	77	Net Indirect Taxes	0.041	0.038	0.037	0.037	0.039	0.035	0.038	0.033
	78	Rest of World	0.358	0.351	0.309	0.316	0.352	0.345	0.343	0.338
Σ		Sub-Total	1.000	1.000	1.000	1.000	1.000	1.000	1.000	1.000

* For explanation, see text in particular eqs. 2.5 and 2.7.

Table II.6: Cont

		Name	Factors of Production							
			Cler Paid Rural	Cler Paid Urban	Cler Unpaid Rural	Cler Unpaid Urban	Prof Paid Rural	Prof Paid Urban	Prof Unpaid Rural	Prof Unpaid Uban
			9	10	11	12	13	14	15	16
Factors of Production	1	Ag Paid Rural	0.090	0.057	0.091	0.063	0.080	0.048	0.087	0.058
	2	Ag Paid Urban	0.004	0.003	0.004	0.003	0.004	0.003	0.004	0.003
	3	Ag Unpaid Rural	0.213	0.131	0.215	0.144	0.187	0.110	0.205	0.132
	4	Ag Unpaid Urban	0.009	0.006	0.009	0.006	0.008	0.005	0.008	0.006
	5	Prod Paid Rural	0.053	0.046	0.053	0.048	0.049	0.042	0.051	0.046
	6	Prod Paid Urban	0.052	0.047	0.052	0.049	0.049	0.043	0.051	0.047
	7	Prod Unpaid Rural	0.041	0.035	0.041	0.037	0.038	0.031	0.040	0.035
	8	Prod Unpaid Urban	0.018	0.017	0.018	0.017	0.017	0.015	0.018	0.017
	9	Cler Paid Rural	1.037	0.034	0.037	0.035	0.036	0.032	0.037	0.034
	10	Cler Paid Urban	0.063	1.057	0.063	0.059	0.060	0.053	0.062	0.057
	11	Cler Unpaid Rural	0.083	0.069	1.083	0.073	0.078	0.061	0.081	0.069
	12	Cler Unpaid Urban	0.046	0.038	0.046	1.040	0.043	0.034	0.045	0.038
	13	Prof Paid Rural	0.046	0.046	0.046	0.047	1.046	0.043	0.046	0.046
	14	Prof Paid Urban	0.064	0.062	0.063	0.063	0.062	1.058	0.063	0.062
	15	Prof Unpaid Rural	0.007	0.006	0.007	0.007	0.007	0.006	1.007	0.006
	16	Prof Unpaid Urban	0.021	0.018	0.022	0.019	0.020	0.016	0.021	1.018
	17	Uninc Capital Land	0.346	0.238	0.348	0.255	0.314	0.205	0.335	0.238
	18	Uninc Capital Housing	0.089	0.095	0.089	0.096	0.086	0.093	0.087	0.095
	19	Uninc Capital Rural	0.101	0.082	0.101	0.087	0.093	0.072	0.098	0.082
	20	Uninc Capital Urban	0.150	0.135	0.150	0.143	0.141	0.121	0.147	0.136
	21	Inc Capital Domestic	0.186	0.161	0.186	0.167	0.177	0.147	0.182	0.161
	22	Inc Capital Government	0.139	0.122	0.138	0.127	0.132	0.111	0.136	0.122
	23	Inc Capital Foreign	0.068	0.059	0.068	0.061	0.065	0.054	0.067	0.059
M		Sub-Total	2.926	2.563	2.929	2.647	2.791	2.403	2.875	2.565
Institutions	24	Ag Employees	0.167	0.081	0.169	0.089	0.170	0.069	0.159	0.079
	25	Farm Size 1	0.332	0.164	0.371	0.184	0.249	0.143	0.319	0.163
	26	Farm Size 2	0.206	0.117	0.229	0.127	0.177	0.101	0.197	0.117
	27	Farm Size 3	0.324	0.199	0.339	0.216	0.308	0.173	0.350	0.201
	28	Rural Lower	0.719	0.160	0.666	0.168	0.289	0.144	0.594	0.160
	29	Rural Middle	0.083	0.034	0.079	0.035	0.127	0.031	0.084	0.034
	30	Rural Higher	0.283	0.081	0.266	0.084	0.704	0.074	0.380	0.081
	31	Urban Lower	0.250	0.678	0.250	0.897	0.236	0.244	0.244	0.712
	32	Urban Middle	0.040	0.097	0.040	0.090	0.039	0.089	0.039	0.082
	33	Urban Higher	0.236	0.731	0.236	0.520	0.226	1.143	0.231	0.715
	34	Companies	0.365	0.317	0.365	0.331	0.347	0.290	0.357	0.318
M		Sub-Total	3.007	2.659	3.009	2.742	2.873	2.499	2.956	2.661
Production activities	35	Food Crop	0.496	0.296	0.499	0.326	0.430	0.243	0.475	0.297
	36	Nonfood Crop	0.096	0.071	0.097	0.077	0.089	0.060	0.093	0.071
	37	Livestock and Products	0.124	0.108	0.125	0.110	0.122	0.103	0.123	0.108
	38	Forestry and Hunting	0.013	0.008	0.013	0.009	0.012	0.007	0.012	0.008
	39	Fishery	0.066	0.052	0.066	0.055	0.064	0.047	0.065	0.052
	40	Metal Ore Mining	0.000	0.000	0.000	0.000	0.000	0.000	0.000	0.000
	41	Other Mining	0.006	0.005	0.006	0.005	0.006	0.004	0.006	0.005
	42	Handpounded Rice	0.092	0.049	0.096	0.054	0.080	0.042	0.089	0.049
	43	Milled Rice	0.240	0.139	0.236	0.156	0.205	0.107	0.227	0.140
	44	Farm Processed Tea	0.006	0.004	0.006	0.004	0.006	0.003	0.006	0.004
	45	Processed Tea	0.002	0.002	0.002	0.002	0.002	0.002	0.002	0.002
	46	Dried and Salted Fish	0.042	0.031	0.042	0.033	0.040	0.027	0.042	0.031
	47	Canned Fish	0.007	0.005	0.007	0.006	0.006	0.005	0.007	0.005
	48	Brown Sugar	0.013	0.008	0.013	0.009	0.012	0.007	0.013	0.008
	49	Refined Sugar	0.038	0.030	0.038	0.032	0.036	0.025	0.037	0.030
	50	Canning (s+c)	0.000	0.000	0.000	0.000	0.000	0.000	0.000	0.000
	51	Canning (m+l)	0.000	0.000	0.000	0.000	0.000	0.000	0.000	0.000
	52	Kretek Cigs	0.078	0.047	0.079	0.053	0.072	0.036	0.076	0.047
	53	White Cigs	0.023	0.022	0.022	0.023	0.021	0.020	0.022	0.022
	54	Other Fbt	0.188	0.183	0.190	0.197	0.175	0.155	0.183	0.184
	55	Wood and Construction	0.045	0.041	0.045	0.042	0.043	0.038	0.044	0.040
	56	Textiles, etc	0.170	0.158	0.170	0.166	0.159	0.142	0.166	0.159
	57	Paper, Transport, Metal, etc.	0.127	0.127	0.125	0.124	0.133	0.132	0.127	0.126
	58	Chemical, Cement, etc	0.065	0.057	0.065	0.059	0.061	0.052	0.063	0.057
	59	Coal Mining	0.000	0.000	0.000	0.000	0.000	0.000	0.000	0.000
	60	Petroleum Mining, etc	0.030	0.027	0.030	0.028	0.028	0.025	0.029	0.027
	61	Gasoline	0.015	0.014	0.015	0.014	0.014	0.014	0.014	0.014
	62	Fuel Oil	0.017	0.015	0.017	0.016	0.016	0.014	0.017	0.015
	63	Electricity	0.027	0.031	0.027	0.031	0.026	0.029	0.026	0.031
	64	Gas	0.000	0.000	0.000	0.000	0.000	0.000	0.000	0.000
	65	Water	0.006	0.006	0.006	0.006	0.005	0.005	0.006	0.006
	66	Trade	0.449	0.358	0.450	0.378	0.424	0.320	0.439	0.358
	67	Restaurants	0.124	0.136	0.123	0.145	0.113	0.116	0.120	0.136
	68	Hotel, etc	0.005	0.004	0.005	0.005	0.005	0.004	0.005	0.004
	69	Road Transport, etc	0.126	0.119	0.125	0.125	0.114	0.105	0.121	0.119
	70	Air Transport, etc	0.050	0.044	0.050	0.046	0.049	0.040	0.049	0.044
	71	Banking and Insurance	0.048	0.041	0.048	0.043	0.046	0.037	0.047	0.041
	72	Real Estate	0.138	0.148	0.138	0.149	0.134	0.145	0.136	0.148
	73	Public Services, etc	0.147	0.146	0.146	0.149	0.145	0.139	0.145	0.146
	74	Personal Services, etc	0.119	0.110	0.119	0.113	0.115	0.105	0.117	0.110
M		Sub-Total	3.239	2.642	3.241	2.790	3.007	2.356	3.151	2.645
Exog Accts.	75	Government	0.173	0.169	0.173	0.173	0.167	0.161	0.170	0.169
	76	Capital Accounts	0.441	0.470	0.443	0.457	0.458	0.497	0.450	0.470
	77	Net Indirect Taxes	0.038	0.031	0.038	0.033	0.036	0.027	0.037	0.031
	78	Rest of World	0.348	0.330	0.346	0.337	0.339	0.316	0.342	0.330
M		Sub-Total	1.000	1.000	1.000	1.000	1.000	1.000	1.000	1.000

Table II.6: Cont.

		Name	Factors of Production							
			Unic Capital Land	Unic Capital Housing	Unic Capital Rural	Unic Capital Urban	Inc Capital Domestic	Inc Capital Government	Inc Capital Foreign	Ag Employees
			17	18	19	20	21	22	23	24
Factors of Production	1	Ag Paid Rural	0.081	0.075	0.095	0.062	0.009	0.009	0.006	0.106
	2	Ag Paid Urban	0.004	0.004	0.004	0.003	0.000	0.000	0.000	0.005
	3	Ag Unpaid Rural	0.189	0.175	0.223	0.142	0.021	0.020	0.013	0.251
	4	Ag Unpaid Urban	0.007	0.007	0.009	0.006	0.001	0.001	0.001	0.010
	5	Prod Paid Rural	0.044	0.049	0.053	0.048	0.007	0.007	0.005	0.057
	6	Prod Paid Urban	0.043	0.049	0.052	0.049	0.007	0.007	0.005	0.054
	7	Prod Unpaid Rural	0.034	0.038	0.042	0.037	0.005	0.005	0.004	0.044
	8	Prod Unpaid Urban	0.015	0.017	0.018	0.017	0.003	0.002	0.002	0.019
	9	Cler Paid Rural	0.032	0.035	0.038	0.035	0.005	0.005	0.003	0.040
	10	Cler Paid Urban	0.054	0.059	0.063	0.059	0.009	0.009	0.006	0.067
	11	Cler Unpaid Rural	0.073	0.076	0.085	0.072	0.011	0.010	0.007	0.092
	12	Cler Unpaid Urban	0.040	0.042	0.047	0.040	0.006	0.006	0.004	0.051
	13	Prof Paid Rural	0.039	0.046	0.046	0.047	0.007	0.007	0.005	0.049
	14	Prof Paid Urban	0.054	0.062	0.064	0.063	0.010	0.009	0.006	0.067
	15	Prof Unpaid Rural	0.006	0.007	0.007	0.007	0.001	0.001	0.001	0.008
	16	Prof Unpaid Urban	0.019	0.020	0.022	0.019	0.003	0.003	0.002	0.024
	17	Uninc Capital Land	1.307	0.294	0.359	0.253	0.037	0.036	0.024	0.399
	18	Uninc Capital Housing	0.076	1.093	0.090	0.096	0.016	0.015	0.010	0.099
	19	Uninc Capital Rural	0.083	0.090	1.102	0.087	0.013	0.012	0.008	0.115
	20	Uninc Capital Urban	0.130	0.142	0.153	1.143	0.021	0.020	0.013	0.161
	21	Inc Capital Domestic	0.161	0.173	0.188	0.167	1.026	0.024	0.016	0.201
	22	Inc Capital Government	0.120	0.129	0.140	0.127	0.019	1.018	0.012	0.148
	23	Inc Capital Foreign	0.058	0.063	0.068	0.061	0.009	0.009	1.006	0.073
		Sub-Total	2.671	2.744	2.967	2.644	1.246	1.236	1.159	2.138
Institutions	24	Ag Employees	0.113	0.153	0.250	0.083	0.012	0.012	0.008	1.122
	25	Farm Size 1	0.360	0.312	0.427	0.171	0.025	0.024	0.016	0.259
	26	Farm Size 2	0.361	0.213	0.256	0.123	0.018	0.017	0.012	0.190
	27	Farm Size 3	0.791	0.334	0.368	0.211	0.031	0.030	0.020	0.329
	28	Rural Lower	0.196	0.273	0.583	0.168	0.025	0.024	0.016	0.211
	29	Rural Middle	0.060	0.071	0.087	0.035	0.014	0.014	0.009	0.048
	30	Rural Higher	0.090	0.135	0.174	0.084	0.036	0.034	0.023	0.099
	31	Urban Lower	0.218	0.409	0.253	0.921	0.035	0.034	0.023	0.268
	32	Urban Middle	0.035	0.109	0.040	0.098	0.022	0.021	0.014	0.042
	33	Urban Higher	0.205	0.481	0.238	0.515	0.157	0.150	0.101	0.254
	34	Companies	0.316	0.339	0.369	0.331	1.058	1.013	0.683	0.392
		Sub-Total	2.745	2.829	3.045	2.740	1.434	1.372	0.925	3.215
Production activities	35	Food Crop	0.427	0.400	0.519	0.322	0.046	0.044	0.030	0.599
	36	Nonfood Crop	0.088	0.085	0.100	0.076	0.011	0.010	0.007	0.110
	37	Livestock and Products	0.119	0.118	0.127	0.110	0.018	0.017	0.011	0.131
	38	Forestry and Hunting	0.011	0.011	0.013	0.009	0.001	0.001	0.001	0.015
	39	Fishery	0.057	0.058	0.066	0.055	0.008	0.008	0.005	0.069
	40	Metal Ore Mining	0.000	0.000	0.000	0.000	0.000	0.000	0.000	0.000
	41	Other Mining	0.005	0.005	0.006	0.005	0.001	0.001	0.000	0.007
	42	Handpounded Rice	0.112	0.080	0.102	0.052	0.008	0.008	0.005	0.087
	43	Milled Rice	0.160	0.179	0.241	0.155	0.021	0.020	0.013	0.316
	44	Farm Processed Tea	0.006	0.005	0.007	0.004	0.001	0.001	0.000	0.007
	45	Processed Tea	0.002	0.002	0.002	0.002	0.000	0.000	0.000	0.003
	46	Dried and Salted Fish	0.037	0.036	0.043	0.033	0.005	0.005	0.003	0.044
	47	Canned Fish	0.006	0.006	0.007	0.006	0.001	0.001	0.001	0.008
	48	Brown Sugar	0.013	0.011	0.014	0.009	0.001	0.001	0.001	0.015
	49	Refined Sugar	0.035	0.034	0.039	0.032	0.005	0.004	0.003	0.043
	50	Canning (s+c)	0.000	0.000	0.000	0.000	0.000	0.000	0.000	0.000
	51	Canning (m+l)	0.000	0.000	0.000	0.000	0.000	0.000	0.000	0.000
	52	Kretek Cigs	0.069	0.064	0.083	0.052	0.007	0.007	0.004	0.106
	53	White Cigs	0.018	0.021	0.021	0.023	0.003	0.003	0.002	0.014
	54	Other Fbt	0.181	0.189	0.194	0.198	0.027	0.026	0.017	0.180
	55	Wood and Construction	0.039	0.043	0.046	0.042	0.007	0.006	0.004	0.050
	56	Textiles, etc	0.143	0.161	0.169	0.167	0.024	0.023	0.016	0.167
	57	Paper, Transport, Metal, etc.	0.098	0.123	0.122	0.124	0.022	0.021	0.014	0.121
	58	Chemical, Cement, etc	0.055	0.060	0.065	0.059	0.009	0.009	0.006	0.071
	59	Coal Mining	0.000	0.000	0.000	0.000	0.000	0.000	0.000	0.000
	60	Petroleum Mining, etc	0.025	0.028	0.030	0.028	0.004	0.004	0.003	0.032
	61	Gasoline	0.012	0.014	0.014	0.014	0.014	0.002	0.002	0.015
	62	Fuel Oil	0.014	0.016	0.017	0.016	0.002	0.002	0.002	0.019
	63	Electricity	0.022	0.028	0.027	0.031	0.005	0.005	0.003	0.029
	64	Gas	0.000	0.000	0.000	0.000	0.000	0.000	0.000	0.000
	65	Water	0.005	0.006	0.006	0.006	0.001	0.001	0.001	0.007
	66	Trade	0.399	0.405	0.459	0.377	0.057	0.054	0.037	0.500
	67	Restaurants	0.076	0.127	0.125	0.147	0.019	0.018	0.012	0.145
	68	Hotel, etc	0.004	0.004	0.005	0.005	0.001	0.001	0.000	0.005
	69	Road Transport, etc	0.104	0.120	0.126	0.126	0.018	0.017	0.011	0.128
	70	Air Transport, etc	0.042	0.046	0.050	0.046	0.007	0.007	0.004	0.051
	71	Banking and Insurance	0.041	0.044	0.049	0.043	0.007	0.006	0.004	0.051
	72	Real Estate	0.117	0.144	0.140	0.150	0.024	0.023	0.016	0.154
	73	Public Services, etc	0.123	0.145	0.146	0.150	0.024	0.023	0.015	0.154
	74	Personal Services, etc	0.101	0.113	0.119	0.113	0.018	0.017	0.011	0.127
		Sub-Total	2.790	2.931	3.301	2.786	0.414	0.396	0.267	3.581
Exog. Accts.	75	Government	0.159	0.170	0.175	0.173	0.405	0.431	0.261	0.182
	76	Capital Accounts	0.524	0.463	0.441	0.456	0.516	0.493	0.333	0.407
	77	Net Indirect Taxes	0.033	0.034	0.039	0.033	0.005	0.005	0.003	0.042
	78	Rest of World	0.283	0.332	0.345	0.338	0.074	0.071	0.403	0.368
		Sub-Total	1.000	1.000	1.000	1.000	1.000	1.000	1.000	1.000

Table II.6: Cont

		Name	Institutions							
			Farm Size 1	Farm Size 2	Farm Size 3	Rural Lower	Rural Middle	Rural Higher	Urban Lower	Urban Middle
			25	26	27	28	29	30	31	32
Factors of Production	1	Ag Paid Rural	0.110	0.099	0.064	0.093	0.094	0.071	0.068	0.073
	2	Ag Paid Urban	0.005	0.004	0.003	0.004	0.004	0.004	0.003	0.004
	3	Ag Unpaid Rural	0.260	0.230	0.148	0.219	0.219	0.165	0.156	0.169
	4	Ag Unpaid Urban	0.010	0.009	0.006	0.009	0.009	0.007	0.007	0.007
	5	Prod Paid Rural	0.057	0.048	0.037	0.055	0.056	0.047	0.051	0.057
	6	Prod Paid Urban	0.055	0.048	0.037	0.054	0.055	0.048	0.052	0.058
	7	Prod Unpaid Rural	0.044	0.038	0.028	0.043	0.045	0.036	0.039	0.043
	8	Prod Unpaid Urban	0.019	0.017	0.013	0.019	0.019	0.016	0.018	0.020
	9	Cler Paid Rural	0.040	0.035	0.027	0.038	0.040	0.035	0.037	0.041
	10	Cler Paid Urban	0.067	0.059	0.045	0.064	0.068	0.059	0.061	0.070
	11	Cler Unpaid Rural	0.093	0.082	0.061	0.084	0.089	0.074	0.077	0.085
	12	Cler Unpaid Urban	0.051	0.045	0.034	0.047	0.049	0.041	0.043	0.047
	13	Prof Paid Rural	0.048	0.043	0.034	0.047	0.051	0.045	0.048	0.056
	14	Prof Paid Urban	0.067	0.059	0.046	0.065	0.070	0.061	0.065	0.076
	15	Prof Unpaid Rural	0.008	0.007	0.005	0.007	0.008	0.006	0.007	0.008
	16	Prof Unpaid Urban	0.024	0.021	0.016	0.022	0.023	0.019	0.020	0.022
	17	Uninc Capital Land	0.408	0.357	0.249	0.355	0.363	0.287	0.274	0.294
	18	Uninc Capital Housing	0.098	0.086	0.064	0.089	0.103	0.083	0.097	0.128
	19	Uninc Capital Rural	0.110	0.090	0.069	0.106	0.107	0.087	0.094	0.103
	20	Uninc Capital Urban	0.165	0.150	0.109	0.155	0.170	0.133	0.153	0.169
	21	Inc Capital Domestic	0.204	0.181	0.137	0.189	0.203	0.169	0.176	0.198
	22	Inc Capital Government	0.150	0.137	0.101	0.142	0.155	0.126	0.134	0.149
	23	Inc Capital Foreign	0.073	0.064	0.049	0.070	0.073	0.063	0.064	0.070
M		Sub-Total	2.168	1.909	1.382	1.975	2.073	1.684	1.745	1.947
Institutions	24	Ag Employees	0.125	0.110	0.076	0.110	0.113	0.089	0.089	0.098
	25	Farm Size 1	1.264	0.231	0.159	0.231	0.236	0.186	0.184	0.202
	26	Farm Size 2	0.194	1.170	0.117	0.169	0.173	0.136	0.133	0.145
	27	Farm Size 3	0.337	0.295	1.203	0.292	0.299	0.235	0.228	0.248
	28	Rural Lower	0.210	0.181	0.135	1.196	0.203	0.168	0.178	0.199
	29	Rural Middle	0.049	0.045	0.051	0.052	1.043	0.057	0.037	0.040
	30	Rural Higher	0.099	0.087	0.065	0.093	0.099	1.083	0.088	0.100
	31	Urban Lower	0.273	0.243	0.181	0.256	0.275	0.226	1.249	0.281
	32	Urban Middle	0.043	0.039	0.029	0.041	0.042	0.038	0.071	1.044
	33	Urban Higher	0.256	0.227	0.171	0.241	0.261	0.218	0.236	0.271
	34	Companies	0.398	0.356	0.267	0.373	0.402	0.333	0.349	0.389
M		Sub-Total	3.247	2.983	2.454	3.055	3.146	2.768	2.841	3.018
Production activities	35	Food Crop	0.602	0.505	0.332	0.517	0.503	0.377	0.357	0.386
	36	Nonfood Crop	0.115	0.104	0.072	0.096	0.103	0.081	0.084	0.086
	37	Livestock and Products	0.142	0.137	0.105	0.122	0.137	0.118	0.113	0.124
	38	Forestry and Hunting	0.015	0.013	0.009	0.013	0.013	0.011	0.009	0.010
	39	Fishery	0.069	0.062	0.050	0.068	0.072	0.062	0.059	0.062
	40	Metal Ore Mining	0.000	0.000	0.000	0.000	0.000	0.000	0.000	0.000
	41	Other Mining	0.007	0.006	0.005	0.006	0.006	0.005	0.005	0.006
	42	Handpounded Rice	0.136	0.182	0.081	0.085	0.102	0.067	0.057	0.063
	43	Milled Rice	0.243	0.151	0.124	0.266	0.250	0.182	0.176	0.185
	44	Farm Processed Tea	0.008	0.007	0.005	0.006	0.008	0.005	0.004	0.005
	45	Processed Tea	0.003	0.002	0.002	0.003	0.002	0.002	0.002	0.002
	46	Dried and Salted Fish	0.045	0.041	0.032	0.044	0.046	0.039	0.036	0.037
	47	Canned Fish	0.007	0.006	0.005	0.007	0.007	0.006	0.006	0.006
	48	Brown Sugar	0.017	0.015	0.010	0.013	0.015	0.011	0.010	0.010
	49	Refined Sugar	0.042	0.039	0.031	0.039	0.042	0.033	0.035	0.036
	50	Canning (s+c)	0.000	0.000	0.000	0.000	0.000	0.000	0.000	0.000
	51	Canning (m+l)	0.000	0.000	0.000	0.000	0.000	0.000	0.000	0.000
	52	Kretek Cigs	0.102	0.080	0.054	0.076	0.056	0.068	0.059	0.056
	53	White Cigs	0.015	0.018	0.019	0.027	0.033	0.020	0.024	0.022
	54	Other Fbt	0.208	0.247	0.143	0.190	0.287	0.155	0.216	0.229
	55	Wood and Construction	0.050	0.044	0.033	0.046	0.051	0.042	0.044	0.052
	56	Textiles, etc	0.183	0.149	0.125	0.179	0.171	0.155	0.177	0.197
	57	Paper, Transport, Metal, etc.	0.117	0.104	0.085	0.129	0.140	0.140	0.120	0.153
	58	Chemical, Cement, etc	0.070	0.060	0.046	0.067	0.070	0.059	0.061	0.067
	59	Coal Mining	0.000	0.000	0.000	0.000	0.000	0.000	0.000	0.000
	60	Petroleum Mining, etc	0.032	0.027	0.021	0.031	0.032	0.028	0.029	0.032
	61	Gasoline	0.015	0.013	0.010	0.015	0.015	0.015	0.014	0.017
	62	Fuel Oil	0.018	0.015	0.012	0.018	0.018	0.015	0.017	0.019
	63	Electricity	0.028	0.024	0.018	0.028	0.029	0.026	0.032	0.038
	64	Gas	0.000	0.000	0.000	0.000	0.000	0.000	0.000	0.001
	65	Water	0.007	0.006	0.004	0.006	0.006	0.005	0.007	0.006
	66	Trade	0.509	0.449	0.338	0.454	0.484	0.402	0.401	0.437
	67	Restaurants	0.131	0.104	0.077	0.133	0.124	0.106	0.159	0.182
	68	Hotel, etc	0.005	0.004	0.004	0.005	0.005	0.005	0.005	0.005
	69	Road Transport, etc	0.136	0.117	0.086	0.134	0.128	0.107	0.135	0.145
	70	Air Transport, etc	0.052	0.047	0.036	0.052	0.054	0.048	0.048	0.054
	71	Banking and Insurance	0.052	0.046	0.035	0.049	0.052	0.045	0.045	0.050
	72	Real Estate	0.153	0.133	0.099	0.139	0.160	0.129	0.151	0.200
	73	Public Services, etc	0.152	0.135	0.106	0.149	0.163	0.144	0.154	0.179
	74	Personal Services, etc	0.127	0.111	0.085	0.122	0.122	0.113	0.116	0.132
M		Sub-Total	3.614	3.203	2.299	3.331	3.505	2.825	2.968	3.291
Exog Accts.	75	Government	0.186	0.173	0.143	0.174	0.188	0.161	0.178	0.184
	76	Capital Accounts	0.413	0.486	0.588	0.428	0.403	0.468	0.440	0.381
	77	Net Indirect Taxes	0.042	0.037	0.028	0.039	0.040	0.034	0.036	0.037
	78	Rest of World	0.358	0.304	0.241	0.358	0.369	0.336	0.346	0.398
M		Sub-Total	1.000	1.000	1.000	1.000	1.000	1.000	1.000	1.000

	Name	Urban Higher 33	Companies 34	Food Crop 35	Nonfood Crop 36	Livestock and Products 37	Forestry and Hunting 38	Fishery 39	Metal Ore Mining 40
1	Ag Paid Rural	0.047	0.009	0.212	0.205	0.117	0.092	0.165	0.037
2	Ag Paid Urban	0.003	0.000	0.008	0.007	0.011	0.006	0.021	0.002
3	Ag Unpaid Rural	0.106	0.021	0.556	0.242	0.307	0.196	0.248	0.086
4	Ag Unpaid Urban	0.005	0.001	0.021	0.011	0.016	0.008	0.020	0.003
5	Prod Paid Rural	0.041	0.007	0.047	0.045	0.045	0.042	0.044	0.158
6	Prod Paid Urban	0.043	0.007	0.046	0.042	0.044	0.037	0.043	0.050
7	Prod Unpaid Rural	0.031	0.005	0.037	0.033	0.035	0.036	0.033	0.024
8	Prod Unpaid Urban	0.015	0.003	0.016	0.015	0.016	0.014	0.015	0.012
9	Cler Paid Rural	0.031	0.005	0.034	0.034	0.035	0.031	0.031	0.055
10	Cler Paid Urban	0.052	0.009	0.058	0.053	0.056	0.048	0.053	0.062
11	Cler Unpaid Rural	0.060	0.011	0.080	0.072	0.083	0.061	0.072	0.066
12	Cler Unpaid Urban	0.033	0.006	0.044	0.040	0.044	0.033	0.039	0.036
13	Prof Paid Rural	0.043	0.007	0.040	0.041	0.039	0.029	0.035	0.030
14	Prof Paid Urban	0.058	0.010	0.056	0.051	0.054	0.041	0.050	0.046
15	Prof Unpaid Rural	0.005	0.001	0.008	0.006	0.007	0.005	0.006	0.005
16	Prof Unpaid Urban	0.016	0.003	0.020	0.018	0.021	0.015	0.018	0.016
17	Uninc Capital Land	0.200	0.037	0.725	0.713	0.971	0.509	0.813	0.145
18	Uninc Capital Housing	0.093	0.016	0.080	0.068	0.076	0.056	0.070	0.065
19	Uninc Capital Rural	0.070	0.013	0.090	0.079	0.087	0.064	0.080	0.063
20	Uninc Capital Urban	0.118	0.021	0.139	0.123	0.135	0.101	0.126	0.101
21	Inc Capital Domestic	0.145	0.026	0.175	0.176	0.194	0.359	0.216	0.138
22	Inc Capital Government	0.109	0.019	0.139	0.204	0.129	0.128	0.125	0.322
23	Inc Capital Foreign	0.053	0.009	0.063	0.080	0.061	0.119	0.086	0.202
	Sub-Total	1.377	0.246	2.694	2.357	2.582	2.031	2.410	1.724
24	Ag Employees	0.066	0.012	0.195	0.182	0.137	0.101	0.166	0.062
25	Farm Size 1	0.136	0.025	0.445	0.308	0.366	0.227	0.324	0.126
26	Farm Size 2	0.098	0.018	0.338	0.252	0.323	0.187	0.275	0.083
27	Farm Size 3	0.167	0.031	0.598	0.491	0.650	0.359	0.548	0.131
28	Rural Lower	0.141	0.025	0.205	0.184	0.199	0.152	0.183	0.223
29	Rural Middle	0.030	0.014	0.056	0.048	0.055	0.039	0.050	0.033
30	Rural Higher	0.073	0.036	0.093	0.087	0.091	0.075	0.084	0.079
31	Urban Lower	0.202	0.035	0.232	0.208	0.227	0.176	0.213	0.195
32	Urban Middle	0.076	0.022	0.037	0.034	0.036	0.032	0.035	0.034
33	Urban Higher	1.199	0.157	0.219	0.210	0.216	0.200	0.209	0.217
34	Companies	0.286	1.058	0.351	0.427	0.360	0.562	0.395	0.580
	Sub-Total	2.474	1.434	2.769	2.430	2.659	2.110	2.481	1.764
35	Food Crop	0.234	0.046	1.470	0.362	0.430	0.269	0.378	0.197
36	Nonfood Crop	0.058	0.011	0.091	1.253	0.088	0.056	0.078	0.041
37	Livestock and Products	0.102	0.018	0.120	0.099	1.421	0.075	0.102	0.057
38	Forestry and Hunting	0.007	0.001	0.012	0.011	0.011	1.065	0.014	0.007
39	Fishery	0.046	0.008	0.057	0.048	0.054	0.037	1.049	0.029
40	Metal Ore Mining	0.000	0.000	0.000	0.000	0.000	0.000	0.000	1.000
41	Other Mining	0.004	0.001	0.006	0.003	0.006	0.004	0.005	0.004
42	Handpounded Rice	0.040	0.008	0.109	0.084	0.105	0.062	0.090	0.036
43	Milled Rice	0.102	0.021	0.178	0.149	0.170	0.110	0.152	0.093
44	Farm Processed Tea	0.003	0.001	0.006	0.003	0.006	0.004	0.005	0.003
45	Processed Tea	0.002	0.000	0.002	0.002	0.002	0.001	0.002	0.001
46	Dried and Salted Fish	0.027	0.005	0.037	0.031	0.035	0.023	0.032	0.018
47	Canned Fish	0.005	0.001	0.006	0.005	0.005	0.004	0.005	0.003
48	Brown Sugar	0.007	0.001	0.013	0.010	0.012	0.008	0.011	0.005
49	Refined Sugar	0.024	0.005	0.035	0.029	0.033	0.022	0.030	0.017
50	Canning (s+c)	0.000	0.000	0.000	0.000	0.000	0.000	0.000	0.000
51	Canning (m+l)	0.000	0.000	0.000	0.000	0.000	0.000	0.000	0.000
52	Kretek Cigs	0.034	0.007	0.074	0.059	0.067	0.043	0.061	0.030
53	White Cigs	0.020	0.003	0.017	0.015	0.017	0.012	0.015	0.011
54	Other Fbt	0.151	0.027	0.180	0.148	0.174	0.116	0.165	0.091
55	Wood and Construction	0.037	0.007	0.046	0.051	0.045	0.048	0.049	0.053
56	Textiles, etc	0.140	0.024	0.148	0.125	0.140	0.099	0.133	0.083
57	Paper, Transport, Metal, etc.	0.132	0.022	0.104	0.097	0.099	0.085	0.116	0.071
58	Chemical, Cement, etc	0.051	0.009	0.067	0.060	0.055	0.041	0.051	0.035
59	Coal Mining	0.000	0.000	0.000	0.000	0.000	0.000	0.000	0.007
60	Petroleum Mining, etc	0.025	0.004	0.028	0.029	0.026	0.022	0.029	0.030
61	Gasoline	0.014	0.002	0.013	0.013	0.013	0.012	0.013	0.011
62	Fuel Oil	0.013	0.002	0.015	0.015	0.015	0.014	0.024	0.016
63	Electricity	0.029	0.005	0.023	0.021	0.023	0.020	0.021	0.089
64	Gas	0.000	0.000	0.000	0.000	0.000	0.000	0.000	0.000
65	Water	0.005	0.001	0.005	0.005	0.005	0.004	0.005	0.003
66	Trade	0.314	0.057	0.439	0.395	0.441	0.328	0.394	0.368
67	Restaurants	0.113	0.019	0.103	0.090	0.098	0.071	0.091	0.073
68	Hotel, etc	0.004	0.001	0.004	0.004	0.004	0.005	0.005	0.010
69	Road Transport, etc	0.104	0.018	0.111	0.107	0.109	0.097	0.107	0.082
70	Air Transport, etc	0.039	0.007	0.045	0.045	0.046	0.041	0.042	0.057
71	Banking and Insurance	0.037	0.007	0.052	0.048	0.045	0.050	0.048	0.076
72	Real Estate	0.144	0.024	0.124	0.105	0.119	0.088	0.108	0.101
73	Public Services, etc	0.138	0.024	0.126	0.107	0.120	0.084	0.110	0.081
74	Personal Services, etc	0.104	0.018	0.105	0.101	0.101	0.096	0.092	0.089
	Sub-Total	2.311	0.414	3.973	3.732	4.139	3.115	3.634	2.978
75	Government	0.159	0.405	0.170	0.197	0.173	0.239	0.183	0.249
76	Capital Accounts	0.501	0.516	0.481	0.462	0.497	0.462	0.469	0.394
77	Net Indirect Taxes	0.026	0.005	0.036	0.034	0.039	0.031	0.037	0.081
78	Rest of World	0.313	0.074	0.313	0.307	0.290	0.268	0.311	0.276
	Sub-Total	1.000	1.000	1.000	1.000	1.000	1.000	1.000	1.000

Factors of Production (rows 1–23)
Institutions (rows 24–34)
Production activities (rows 35–74)
Exog Accts. (rows 75–78)

Table II.6: Cont

		Name	Production Activities							
			Other Mining	Handpounded Rice	Milled Rice	Farm. Proc Tea	Processed Tea	Dried and Salted Fish	Canned Fish	Brown Sugar
			41	42	43	44	45	46	47	48
Factors of Production	1	Ag Paid Rural	0.067	0.252	0.169	0.254	0.120	0.109	0.099	0.133
	2	Ag Paid Urban	0.003	0.007	0.006	0.004	0.004	0.011	0.009	0.005
	3	Ag Unpaid Rural	0.155	0.624	0.437	0.401	0.168	0.194	0.179	0.218
	4	Ag Unpaid Urban	0.006	0.018	0.017	0.008	0.007	0.012	0.011	0.009
	5	Prod Paid Rural	0.079	0.048	0.070	0.044	0.090	0.062	0.048	0.118
	6	Prod Paid Urban	0.102	0.047	0.055	0.041	0.066	0.093	0.046	0.049
	7	Prod Unpaid Rural	0.091	0.038	0.062	0.032	0.031	0.083	0.033	0.110
	8	Prod Unpaid Urban	0.066	0.016	0.016	0.015	0.015	0.032	0.015	0.017
	9	Cler Paid Rural	0.052	0.034	0.035	0.036	0.039	0.035	0.033	0.045
	10	Cler Paid Urban	0.069	0.059	0.060	0.054	0.066	0.059	0.057	0.061
	11	Cler Unpaid Rural	0.089	0.081	0.078	0.084	0.089	0.092	0.087	0.085
	12	Cler Unpaid Urban	0.046	0.045	0.043	0.046	0.049	0.050	0.048	0.046
	13	Prof Paid Rural	0.043	0.041	0.039	0.042	0.038	0.037	0.034	0.045
	14	Prof Paid Urban	0.066	0.057	0.056	0.049	0.054	0.054	0.051	0.057
	15	Prof Unpaid Rural	0.010	0.008	0.007	0.007	0.007	0.007	0.007	0.007
	16	Prof Unpaid Urban	0.020	0.021	0.020	0.021	0.022	0.023	0.022	0.021
	17	Uninc Capital Land	0.264	0.644	0.581	0.392	0.429	0.688	0.447	0.481
	18	Uninc Capital Housing	0.087	0.081	0.076	0.068	0.064	0.072	0.068	0.080
	19	Uninc Capital Rural	0.285	0.092	0.169	0.085	0.085	0.092	0.257	0.439
	20	Uninc Capital Urban	0.533	0.141	0.146	0.130	0.134	0.145	0.208	0.142
	21	Inc Capital Domestic	0.179	0.177	0.173	0.195	0.198	0.235	0.232	0.191
	22	Inc Capital Government	0.159	0.139	0.140	0.275	0.247	0.136	0.150	0.168
	23	Inc Capital Foreign	0.063	0.064	0.064	0.072	0.083	0.075	0.093	0.076
M		Sub-Total	2.534	2.734	2.519	2.354	2.106	2.395	2.235	2.603
Institutions	24	Ag Employees	0.121	0.220	0.176	0.209	0.124	0.130	0.135	0.192
	25	Farm Size 1	0.235	0.466	0.386	0.329	0.223	0.285	0.257	0.342
	26	Farm Size 2	0.154	0.340	0.284	0.225	0.171	0.239	0.190	0.235
	27	Farm Size 3	0.241	0.575	0.489	0.367	0.314	0.467	0.339	0.391
	28	Rural Lower	0.306	0.209	0.250	0.188	0.210	0.222	0.245	0.405
	29	Rural Middle	0.049	0.056	0.054	0.046	0.042	0.049	0.047	0.065
	30	Rural Higher	0.118	0.094	0.101	0.092	0.089	0.098	0.096	0.138
	31	Urban Lower	0.591	0.235	0.243	0.216	0.248	0.293	0.278	0.239
	32	Urban Middle	0.068	0.037	0.037	0.036	0.038	0.041	0.041	0.038
	33	Urban Higher	0.366	0.222	0.220	0.222	0.235	0.235	0.242	0.229
	34	Companies	0.374	0.354	0.351	0.509	0.492	0.417	0.438	0.404
M		Sub-Total	2.621	2.809	2.591	2.439	2.185	2.475	2.309	2.679
Production activities	35	Food Crop	0.355	1.261	1.136	0.357	0.292	0.361	0.342	0.426
	36	Nonfood Crop	0.077	0.092	0.083	0.419	0.621	0.075	0.076	0.553
	37	Livestock and Products	0.105	0.121	0.110	0.094	0.082	0.100	0.090	0.110
	38	Forestry and Hunting	0.013	0.012	0.011	0.013	0.014	0.017	0.013	0.015
	39	Fishery	0.053	0.058	0.053	0.046	0.040	0.484	0.416	0.055
	40	Metal Ore Mining	0.000	0.000	0.000	0.000	0.000	0.000	0.000	0.000
	41	Other Mining	1.007	0.006	0.005	0.005	0.005	0.011	0.005	0.006
	42	Handpounded Rice	0.064	1.111	0.115	0.078	0.062	0.081	0.069	0.088
	43	Milled Rice	0.168	0.185	1.180	0.152	0.127	0.149	0.144	0.190
	44	Farm Processed Tea	0.005	0.006	0.005	1.005	0.004	0.005	0.004	0.005
	45	Processed Tea	0.002	0.002	0.002	0.002	1.001	0.002	0.002	0.002
	46	Dried and Salted Fish	0.033	0.038	0.034	0.030	0.026	1.031	0.028	0.036
	47	Canned Fish	0.006	0.006	0.005	0.005	0.004	0.005	1.005	0.006
	48	Brown Sugar	0.010	0.013	0.012	0.010	0.008	0.010	0.010	1.012
	49	Refined Sugar	0.031	0.036	0.032	0.028	0.024	0.030	0.029	0.033
	50	Canning (s+c)	0.000	0.000	0.000	0.000	0.000	0.000	0.000	0.000
	51	Canning (m+l)	0.000	0.000	0.000	0.000	0.000	0.000	0.000	0.000
	52	Kretek Cigs	0.057	0.076	0.067	0.059	0.047	0.058	0.052	0.068
	53	White Cigs	0.020	0.017	0.016	0.014	0.014	0.016	0.015	0.018
	54	Other Fbt	0.176	0.182	0.167	0.143	0.128	0.161	0.212	0.168
	55	Wood and Construction	0.089	0.048	0.044	0.045	0.045	0.059	0.046	0.052
	56	Textiles, etc	0.154	0.153	0.140	0.121	0.123	0.134	0.123	0.145
	57	Paper, Transport, Metal, etc.	0.128	0.105	0.106	0.094	0.110	0.108	0.108	0.118
	58	Chemical, Cement, etc	0.060	0.066	0.062	0.052	0.058	0.053	0.064	0.063
	59	Coal Mining	0.000	0.000	0.000	0.000	0.000	0.000	0.000	0.000
	60	Petroleum Mining, etc	0.030	0.028	0.031	0.025	0.037	0.028	0.031	0.031
	61	Gasoline	0.017	0.013	0.015	0.013	0.020	0.014	0.015	0.014
	62	Fuel Oil	0.017	0.015	0.021	0.015	0.028	0.019	0.020	0.020
	63	Electricity	0.028	0.024	0.038	0.020	0.043	0.023	0.040	0.025
	64	Gas	0.000	0.000	0.000	0.000	0.000	0.000	0.000	0.000
	65	Water	0.006	0.006	0.007	0.005	0.004	0.005	0.005	0.005
	66	Trade	0.387	0.446	0.431	0.469	0.508	0.517	0.493	0.458
	67	Restaurants	0.126	0.105	0.101	0.092	0.088	0.098	0.093	0.108
	68	Hotel, etc	0.004	0.004	0.004	0.004	0.006	0.005	0.005	0.005
	69	Road Transport, etc	0.125	0.114	0.111	0.108	0.113	0.116	0.108	0.124
	70	Air Transport, etc	0.045	0.046	0.044	0.041	0.053	0.046	0.045	0.049
	71	Banking and Insurance	0.044	0.051	0.051	0.047	0.058	0.055	0.051	0.050
	72	Real Estate	0.135	0.126	0.118	0.105	0.099	0.112	0.105	0.125
	73	Public Services, etc	0.134	0.128	0.120	0.105	0.100	0.114	0.104	0.124
	74	Personal Services, etc	0.110	0.107	0.101	0.100	0.094	0.096	0.090	0.121
M		Sub-Total	3.819	4.809	4.580	3.919	4.091	4.198	4.061	4.429
Exog Accts.	75	Government	0.181	0.171	0.168	0.228	0.219	0.192	0.197	0.187
	76	Capital Accounts	0.432	0.476	0.444	0.459	0.435	0.466	0.430	0.444
	77	Net Indirect Taxes	0.046	0.036	0.034	0.032	0.047	0.041	0.033	0.041
	78	Rest of World	0.341	0.316	0.354	0.280	0.299	0.301	0.340	0.328
M		Sub-Total	1.000	1.000	1.000	1.000	1.000	1.000	1.000	1.000

Table II.6: Cont

		Name	Production Activities							
			Refined Sugar 49	Canning (s+c) 50	Canning (m+l) 51	Kretex Cigs 52	White Cigs 53	Other Fbt 54	Wood and Construction 55	Textiles etc 56
Factors of Production	1	Ag Paid Rural	0.079	0.099	0.113	0.093	0.045	0.096	0.042	0.041
	2	Ag Paid Urban	0.003	0.004	0.004	0.003	0.002	0.004	0.002	0.002
	3	Ag Unpaid Rural	0.142	0.244	0.281	0.142	0.080	0.206	0.097	0.094
	4	Ag Unpaid Urban	0.006	0.010	0.011	0.006	0.003	0.008	0.004	0.004
	5	Prod Paid Rural	0.097	0.187	0.107	0.051	0.040	0.054	0.116	0.093
	6	Prod Paid Urban	0.069	0.115	0.066	0.042	0.031	0.053	0.086	0.097
	7	Prod Unpaid Rural	0.066	0.078	0.037	0.036	0.018	0.057	0.068	0.053
	8	Prod Unpaid Urban	0.018	0.020	0.017	0.014	0.008	0.024	0.020	0.021
	9	Cler Paid Rural	0.035	0.047	0.038	0.028	0.021	0.036	0.033	0.027
	10	Cler Paid Urban	0.059	0.081	0.065	0.049	0.037	0.063	0.051	0.054
	11	Cler Unpaid Rural	0.062	0.075	0.085	0.068	0.058	0.094	0.067	0.060
	12	Cler Unpaid Urban	0.035	0.041	0.047	0.037	0.031	0.052	0.037	0.034
	13	Prof Paid Rural	0.035	0.042	0.036	0.028	0.020	0.036	0.028	0.027
	14	Prof Paid Urban	0.051	0.063	0.055	0.041	0.030	0.053	0.046	0.044
	15	Prof Unpaid Rural	0.006	0.007	0.007	0.006	0.004	0.009	0.007	0.007
	16	Prof Unpaid Urban	0.018	0.025	0.022	0.018	0.014	0.027	0.019	0.019
	17	Uninc Capital Land	0.294	0.360	0.401	0.333	0.166	0.351	0.172	0.170
	18	Uninc Capital Housing	0.061	0.072	0.067	0.050	0.036	0.068	0.054	0.051
	19	Uninc Capital Rural	0.193	0.148	0.120	0.072	0.079	0.095	0.092	0.115
	20	Uninc Capital Urban	0.228	0.195	0.171	0.134	0.111	0.276	0.140	0.181
	21	Inc Capital Domestic	0.201	0.198	0.198	0.205	0.253	0.220	0.254	0.178
	22	Inc Capital Government	0.201	0.138	0.167	0.151	0.097	0.227	0.145	0.118
	23	Inc Capital Foreign	0.094	0.074	0.084	0.113	0.180	0.072	0.067	0.079
M		Sub-Total	2.052	2.321	2.199	1.719	1.365	2.183	1.646	1.569
Institutions	24	Ag Employees	0.110	0.128	0.127	0.097	0.058	0.109	0.069	0.069
	25	Farm Size 1	0.205	0.270	0.273	0.178	0.109	0.225	0.142	0.138
	26	Farm Size 2	0.143	0.189	0.197	0.136	0.077	0.164	0.095	0.093
	27	Farm Size 3	0.239	0.311	0.337	0.248	0.133	0.285	0.151	0.149
	28	Rural Lower	0.246	0.315	0.236	0.155	0.121	0.198	0.214	0.193
	29	Rural Middle	0.042	0.049	0.045	0.033	0.024	0.040	0.032	0.030
	30	Rural Higher	0.094	0.106	0.090	0.070	0.055	0.091	0.080	0.072
	31	Urban Lower	0.301	0.341	0.273	0.206	0.162	0.344	0.253	0.291
	32	Urban Middle	0.042	0.045	0.040	0.032	0.027	0.047	0.035	0.037
	33	Urban Higher	0.244	0.259	0.236	0.194	0.166	0.278	0.208	0.208
	34	Companies	0.457	0.381	0.416	0.426	0.465	0.488	0.439	0.345
M		Sub-Total	2.123	2.395	2.270	1.773	1.397	2.270	1.720	1.624
Production activities	35	Food Crop	0.291	0.609	0.713	0.268	0.165	0.481	0.216	0.209
	36	Nonfood Crop	0.278	0.084	0.099	0.436	0.159	0.204	0.047	0.058
	37	Livestock and Products	0.079	0.097	0.090	0.067	0.045	0.096	0.061	0.082
	38	Forestry and Hunting	0.011	0.010	0.010	0.008	0.005	0.010	0.054	0.007
	39	Fishery	0.040	0.048	0.044	0.032	0.022	0.043	0.031	0.031
	40	Metal Ore Mining	0.000	0.000	0.000	0.000	0.000	0.000	0.000	0.000
	41	Other Mining	0.004	0.005	0.005	0.004	0.002	0.004	0.041	0.003
	42	Handpounded Rice	0.055	0.071	0.070	0.049	0.030	0.063	0.039	0.038
	43	Milled Rice	0.129	0.157	0.141	0.103	0.070	0.146	0.100	0.097
	44	Farm Processed Tea	0.004	0.005	0.004	0.003	0.002	0.004	0.003	0.003
	45	Processed Tea	0.001	0.002	0.002	0.001	0.001	0.002	0.001	0.001
	46	Dried and Salted Fish	0.025	0.031	0.028	0.020	0.014	0.026	0.019	0.019
	47	Canned Fish	0.004	0.005	0.005	0.003	0.002	0.004	0.003	0.003
	48	Brown Sugar	0.008	0.010	0.009	0.008	0.005	0.015	0.006	0.006
	49	Refined Sugar	1.024	0.079	0.063	0.025	0.015	0.052	0.018	0.018
	50	Canning (s+c)	0.000	1.000	0.000	0.000	0.000	0.000	0.000	0.000
	51	Canning (m+l)	0.000	0.000	1.000	0.000	0.000	0.000	0.000	0.000
	52	Kretek Cigs	0.045	0.056	0.052	1.037	0.024	0.047	0.033	0.033
	53	White Cigs	0.014	0.017	0.015	0.011	1.008	0.015	0.011	0.011
	54	Other Fbt	0.127	0.153	0.161	0.322	0.143	1.257	0.102	0.100
	55	Wood and Construction	0.044	0.040	0.041	0.035	0.022	0.043	1.064	0.033
	56	Textiles, etc	0.122	0.203	0.146	0.088	0.061	0.120	0.089	1.500
	57	Paper, Transport, Metal, etc.	0.118	0.152	0.167	0.100	0.060	0.094	0.113	0.083
	58	Chemical, Cement, etc	0.055	0.096	0.093	0.044	0.027	0.049	0.117	0.043
	59	Coal Mining	0.001	0.000	0.000	0.000	0.000	0.000	0.000	0.000
	60	Petroleum Mining, etc	0.029	0.039	0.042	0.023	0.015	0.025	0.038	0.022
	61	Gasoline	0.014	0.017	0.020	0.015	0.010	0.014	0.013	0.012
	62	Fuel Oil	0.019	0.019	0.023	0.011	0.008	0.016	0.012	0.013
	63	Electricity	0.073	0.027	0.026	0.022	0.023	0.032	0.018	0.043
	64	Gas	0.000	0.000	0.000	0.000	0.000	0.000	0.000	0.000
	65	Water	0.005	0.005	0.023	0.004	0.004	0.005	0.004	0.009
	66	Trade	0.334	0.412	0.478	0.381	0.333	0.526	0.368	0.326
	67	Restaurants	0.088	0.101	0.091	0.070	0.051	0.095	0.080	0.073
	68	Hotel, etc	0.005	0.004	0.004	0.005	0.004	0.005	0.003	0.004
	69	Road Transport, etc	0.095	0.102	0.114	0.087	0.058	0.117	0.108	0.081
	70	Air Transport, etc	0.039	0.041	0.058	0.039	0.025	0.057	0.052	0.036
	71	Banking and Insurance	0.042	0.045	0.049	0.052	0.041	0.057	0.043	0.040
	72	Real Estate	0.095	0.112	0.104	0.078	0.057	0.105	0.084	0.079
	73	Public Services, etc	0.096	0.114	0.103	0.077	0.055	0.103	0.077	0.076
	74	Personal Services, etc	0.084	0.093	0.109	0.070	0.048	0.094	0.071	0.066
M		Sub-Total	3.501	4.062	4.205	3.599	2.615	4.030	3.140	3.260
Exog Accts.	75	Government	0.204	0.177	0.189	0.186	0.193	0.220	0.189	0.154
	76	Capital Accounts	0.403	0.411	0.417	0.362	0.321	0.443	0.345	0.304
	77	Net Indirect Taxes	0.060	0.084	0.069	0.190	0.246	0.044	0.036	0.029
	78	Rest of World	0.334	0.328	0.325	0.262	0.240	0.294	0.430	0.513
M		Sub-Total	1.000	1.000	1.000	1.000	1.000	1.000	1.000	1.000

Table II.6: Cont

		Production Activities							
	Name	Paper T'sport Metal, etc	Chemical Cement, Etc	Coal Mining	Petroleum Mining, etc	Gasoline	Fuel Oil	Electricity	City Gas
		57	58	59	60	61	62	63	64
Factors of Production									
1	Ag Paid Rural	0.026	0.032	0.036	0.007	0.011	0.011	0.021	0.022
2	Ag Paid Urban	0.001	0.001	0.002	0.000	0.001	0.001	0.001	0.001
3	Ag Unpaid Rural	0.059	0.071	0.085	0.016	0.025	0.025	0.049	0.051
4	Ag Unpaid Urban	0.002	0.003	0.003	0.001	0.001	0.001	0.002	0.002
5	Prod Paid Rural	0.051	0.063	0.244	0.007	0.019	0.019	0.023	0.022
6	Prod Paid Urban	0.060	0.049	0.055	0.008	0.019	0.019	0.086	0.137
7	Prod Unpaid Rural	0.036	0.042	0.021	0.005	0.008	0.008	0.016	0.016
8	Prod Unpaid Urban	0.013	0.011	0.009	0.002	0.004	0.003	0.012	0.008
9	Cler Paid Rural	0.023	0.030	0.066	0.005	0.012	0.011	0.036	0.015
10	Cler Paid Urban	0.051	0.048	0.052	0.010	0.023	0.023	0.047	0.072
11	Cler Unpaid Rural	0.047	0.045	0.041	0.009	0.015	0.014	0.030	0.032
12	Cler Unpaid Urban	0.026	0.025	0.022	0.005	0.008	0.008	0.016	0.018
13	Prof Paid Rural	0.018	0.022	0.028	0.006	0.010	0.010	0.027	0.017
14	Prof Paid Urban	0.037	0.039	0.035	0.013	0.021	0.020	0.071	0.094
15	Prof Unpaid Rural	0.004	0.006	0.004	0.001	0.001	0.001	0.003	0.003
16	Prof Unpaid Urban	0.014	0.013	0.011	0.002	0.004	0.004	0.008	0.008
17	Uninc Capital Land	0.103	0.125	0.142	0.030	0.044	0.044	0.086	0.091
18	Uninc Capital Housing	0.038	0.040	0.043	0.014	0.019	0.019	0.034	0.036
19	Uninc Capital Rural	0.058	0.066	0.048	0.010	0.017	0.017	0.034	0.036
20	Uninc Capital Urban	0.096	0.106	0.075	0.017	0.028	0.028	0.063	0.059
21	Inc Capital Domestic	0.211	0.150	0.105	0.022	0.038	0.038	0.119	0.400
22	Inc Capital Government	0.117	0.264	0.461	0.222	0.378	0.372	0.400	0.098
23	Inc Capital Foreign	0.080	0.234	0.050	0.730	0.365	0.359	0.102	0.062
	Sub-Total	1.181	1.485	1.638	1.143	1.071	1.056	1.287	1.301
Institutions									
24	Ag Employees	0.042	0.050	0.061	0.010	0.016	0.016	0.033	0.033
25	Farm Size 1	0.086	0.100	0.126	0.021	0.033	0.033	0.066	0.067
26	Farm Size 2	0.057	0.068	0.082	0.015	0.023	0.023	0.045	0.047
27	Farm Size 3	0.092	0.109	0.127	0.025	0.038	0.038	0.075	0.078
28	Rural Lower	0.120	0.139	0.265	0.022	0.042	0.042	0.082	0.071
29	Rural Middle	0.020	0.025	0.034	0.010	0.013	0.012	0.019	0.017
30	Rural Higher	0.052	0.063	0.077	0.026	0.032	0.031	0.053	0.043
31	Urban Lower	0.183	0.177	0.159	0.032	0.061	0.060	0.172	0.225
32	Urban Middle	0.027	0.030	0.029	0.016	0.018	0.018	0.030	0.035
33	Urban Higher	0.167	0.190	0.181	0.116	0.128	0.127	0.205	0.237
34	Companies	0.383	0.558	0.582	0.711	0.640	0.631	0.572	0.538
	Sub-Total	1.229	1.509	1.724	1.004	1.046	1.031	1.352	1.390
Production activities									
35	Food Crop	0.134	0.160	0.197	0.037	0.056	0.056	0.111	0.115
36	Nonfood Crop	0.029	0.050	0.040	0.009	0.013	0.013	0.025	0.027
37	Livestock and Products	0.041	0.045	0.054	0.014	0.019	0.019	0.037	0.040
38	Forestry and Hunting	0.013	0.011	0.007	0.001	0.002	0.002	0.005	0.004
39	Fishery	0.020	0.023	0.028	0.007	0.009	0.009	0.018	0.019
40	Metal Ore Mining	0.000	0.000	0.000	0.000	0.000	0.000	0.000	0.000
41	Other Mining	0.004	0.017	0.003	0.001	0.001	0.001	0.003	0.002
42	Handpounded Rice	0.024	0.028	0.036	0.006	0.010	0.010	0.019	0.020
43	Milled Rice	0.062	0.071	0.094	0.017	0.026	0.026	0.052	0.054
44	Farm Processed Tea	0.002	0.002	0.002	0.001	0.001	0.001	0.001	0.002
45	Processed Tea	0.001	0.001	0.001	0.000	0.000	0.000	0.001	0.001
46	Dried and Salted Fish	0.012	0.014	0.017	0.004	0.006	0.006	0.011	0.012
47	Canned Fish	0.002	0.002	0.003	0.001	0.001	0.001	0.002	0.002
48	Brown Sugar	0.004	0.004	0.005	0.001	0.002	0.002	0.003	0.003
49	Refined Sugar	0.012	0.016	0.016	0.004	0.005	0.005	0.010	0.011
50	Canning (s+c)	0.000	0.000	0.000	0.000	0.000	0.000	0.000	0.000
51	Canning (m+l)	0.000	0.000	0.000	0.000	0.000	0.000	0.000	0.000
52	Kretek Cigs	0.021	0.024	0.030	0.006	0.009	0.008	0.017	0.018
53	White Cigs	0.008	0.008	0.010	0.003	0.004	0.004	0.007	0.008
54	Other Fbt	0.066	0.100	0.085	0.021	0.031	0.031	0.060	0.067
55	Wood and Construction	0.044	0.035	0.029	0.007	0.015	0.015	0.043	0.020
56	Textiles, etc	0.061	0.070	0.080	0.019	0.027	0.027	0.053	0.060
57	Paper, Transport, Metal, etc.	1.089	0.074	0.151	0.023	0.043	0.047	0.065	0.069
58	Chemical, Cement, etc	0.058	1.052	0.040	0.008	0.034	0.034	0.029	0.045
59	Coal Mining	0.000	0.000	1.017	0.000	0.000	0.000	0.005	0.000
60	Petroleum Mining, etc	0.021	0.250	0.028	1.006	0.492	0.484	0.064	0.060
61	Gasoline	0.008	0.011	0.016	0.002	1.004	0.004	0.024	0.010
62	Fuel Oil	0.008	0.017	0.023	0.003	0.006	1.006	0.098	0.095
63	Electricity	0.019	0.030	0.100	0.008	0.018	0.017	1.032	0.031
64	Gas	0.000	0.001	0.000	0.000	0.000	0.000	0.000	1.001
65	Water	0.009	0.003	0.003	0.001	0.001	0.001	0.002	0.003
66	Trade	0.254	0.248	0.220	0.046	0.077	0.076	0.161	0.173
67	Restaurants	0.050	0.054	0.060	0.016	0.024	0.024	0.046	0.050
68	Hotel, etc	0.003	0.003	0.003	0.001	0.001	0.001	0.003	0.002
69	Road Transport, etc	0.061	0.073	0.061	0.015	0.023	0.023	0.047	0.060
70	Air Transport, etc	0.029	0.035	0.030	0.007	0.012	0.013	0.031	0.030
71	Banking and Insurance	0.040	0.042	0.028	0.008	0.032	0.031	0.027	0.024
72	Real Estate	0.059	0.062	0.067	0.021	0.030	0.030	0.053	0.057
73	Public Services, etc	0.052	0.058	0.067	0.019	0.026	0.026	0.048	0.053
74	Personal Services, etc	0.048	0.054	0.054	0.015	0.023	0.021	0.040	0.046
	Sub-Total	2.366	2.748	2.706	1.355	2.085	2.073	2.255	2.294
Exog. Accts.									
75	Government	0.162	0.235	0.254	0.282	0.264	0.260	0.245	0.221
76	Capital Accounts	0.272	0.361	0.384	0.352	0.334	0.329	0.352	0.350
77	Net Indirect Taxes	0.026	0.039	0.027	0.041	0.026	0.025	0.024	0.020
78	Rest of World	0.540	0.364	0.336	0.325	0.377	0.386	0.378	0.409
	Sub-Total	1.000	1.000	1.000	1.000	1.000	1.000	1.000	1.000

		Production Activities							
	Name	Water	Wholesale and Retail Trade	Resturants	Hotel etc	Road Transport etc	Air Transport etc	Banking Insurance	Real Estate
		65	66	67	68	69	70	71	72
1	Ag Paid Rural	0.034	0.050	0.095	0.053	0.057	0.030	0.027	0.061
2	Ag Paid Urban	0.002	0.002	0.005	0.003	0.003	0.001	0.001	0.003
3	Ag Unpaid Rural	0.080	0.116	0.219	0.122	0.132	0.070	0.062	0.142
4	Ag Unpaid Urban	0.003	0.005	0.009	0.005	0.005	0.003	0.003	0.006
5	Prod Paid Rural	0.044	0.039	0.050	0.045	0.132	0.044	0.026	0.053
6	Prod Paid Urban	0.087	0.040	0.049	0.048	0.141	0.069	0.032	0.051
7	Prod Unpaid Rural	0.032	0.028	0.041	0.033	0.113	0.029	0.018	0.037
8	Prod Unpaid Urban	0.017	0.013	0.017	0.015	0.073	0.013	0.009	0.016
9	Cler Paid Rural	0.034	0.045	0.040	0.074	0.058	0.026	0.032	0.039
10	Cler Paid Urban	0.073	0.082	0.064	0.196	0.083	0.091	0.172	0.065
11	Cler Unpaid Rural	0.091	0.212	0.140	0.067	0.073	0.045	0.038	0.066
12	Cler Unpaid Urban	0.050	0.115	0.076	0.038	0.042	0.026	0.021	0.037
13	Prof Paid Rural	0.025	0.033	0.037	0.037	0.038	0.027	0.031	0.040
14	Prof Paid Urban	0.067	0.056	0.055	0.071	0.057	0.082	0.132	0.064
15	Prof Unpaid Rural	0.007	0.013	0.012	0.006	0.007	0.005	0.003	0.006
16	Prof Unpaid Urban	0.022	0.048	0.031	0.032	0.022	0.014	0.011	0.020
17	Uninc Capital Land	0.138	0.197	0.392	0.219	0.223	0.123	0.111	0.242
18	Uninc Capital Housing	0.053	0.072	0.077	0.070	0.072	0.049	0.054	0.723
19	Uninc Capital Rural	0.079	0.142	0.183	0.100	0.158	0.066	0.046	0.082
20	Uninc Capital Urban	0.126	0.221	0.276	0.239	0.259	0.100	0.077	0.182
21	Inc Capital Domestic	0.178	0.329	0.199	0.170	0.246	0.122	0.139	0.273
22	Inc Capital Government	0.269	0.177	0.157	0.241	0.138	0.433	0.529	0.132
23	Inc Capital Foreign	0.058	0.085	0.070	0.079	0.067	0.049	0.065	0.057
	Sub-Total	1.570	2.120	2.296	1.963	2.200	1.517	1.639	2.397
24	Ag Employees	0.057	0.087	0.126	0.077	0.098	0.048	0.041	0.118
25	Farm Size 1	0.115	0.176	0.260	0.157	0.198	0.096	0.083	0.241
26	Farm Size 2	0.077	0.114	0.187	0.110	0.130	0.066	0.058	0.165
27	Farm Size 3	0.123	0.180	0.320	0.185	0.203	0.107	0.096	0.260
28	Rural Lower	0.155	0.247	0.251	0.181	0.290	0.120	0.095	0.229
29	Rural Middle	0.027	0.040	0.047	0.034	0.043	0.024	0.023	0.056
30	Rural Higher	0.071	0.109	0.105	0.086	0.108	0.062	0.062	0.112
31	Urban Lower	0.264	0.348	0.355	0.361	0.444	.0.215	0.199	0.372
32	Urban Middle	0.038	0.049	0.047	0.052	0.053	0.037	0.043	0.086
33	Urban Higher	0.244	0.309	0.279	0.344	0.292	0.257	0.348	0.41
34	Companies	0.477	0.558	0.397	0.455	0.425	0.573	0.692	0.440
	Sub-Total	1.648	2.216	2.374	2.041	2.285	1.605	1.741	2.493
35	Food Crop	0.181	0.266	0.492	0.277	0.304	0.158	0.140	0.325
36	Nonfood Crop	0.040	0.057	0.114	0.071	0.064	0.035	0.033	0.070
37	Livestock and Products	0.056	0.079	0.186	0.102	0.087	0.055	0.050	0.097
38	Forestry and Hunting	0.010	0.007	0.012	0.009	0.009	0.006	0.005	0.013
39	Fishery	0.028	0.040	0.085	0.040	0.044	0.025	0.024	0.048
40	Metal Ore Mining	0.000	0.000	0.000	0.000	0.000	0.000	0.000	0.000
41	Other Mining	0.006	0.004	0.005	0.005	0.005	0.003	0.003	0.008
42	Handpounded Rice	0.032	0.048	0.091	0.045	0.054	0.028	0.024	0.063
43	Milled Rice	0.085	0.124	0.196	0.135	0.147	0.074	0.065	0.146
44	Farm Processed Tea	0.002	0.003	0.006	0.003	0.004	0.002	0.002	0.004
45	Processed Tea	0.001	0.001	0.003	0.005	0.002	0.001	0.001	0.002
46	Dried and Salted Fish	0.017	0.024	0.037	0.023	0.028	0.015	0.014	0.030
47	Canned Fish	0.003	0.004	0.007	0.004	0.005	0.002	0.002	0.005
48	Brown Sugar	0.005	0.007	0.013	0.007	0.008	0.004	0.004	0.009
49	Refined Sugar	0.016	0.023	0.062	0.035	0.026	0.015	0.014	0.028
50	Canning (s+c)	0.000	0.000	0.000	0.000	0.000	0.000	0.000	0.000
51	Canning (m+l)	0.000	0.000	0.000	0.001	0.000	0.000	0.000	0.000
52	Kretek Cigs	0.028	0.042	0.054	0.039	0.048	0.024	0.022	0.051
53	White Cigs	0.011	0.015	0.016	0.015	0.017	0.009	0.010	0.017
54	Other Fbt	0.093	0.128	0.320	0.193	0.145	0.085	0.080	0.158
55	Wood and Construction	0.118	0.038	0.049	0.077	0.041	0.049	0.039	0.138
56	Textiles, etc	0.083	0.112	0.135	0.122	0.132	0.079	0.070	0.134
57	Paper, Transport, Metal, etc.	0.074	0.091	0.109	0.114	0.115	0.110	0.081	0.111
58	Chemical, Cement, etc	0.058	0.043	0.053	0.054	0.061	0.031	0.029	0.059
59	Coal Mining	0.000	0.000	0.000	0.000	0.000	0.000	0.000	0.000
60	Petroleum Mining, etc	0.027	0.024	0.032	0.030	0.043	0.033	0.015	0.026
61	Gasoline	0.013	0.016	0.015	0.014	0.035	0.033	0.010	0.013
62	Fuel Oil	0.016	0.013	0.028	0.023	0.026	0.022	0.008	0.014
63	Electricity	0.086	0.022	0.030	0.045	0.025	0.019	0.018	0.025
64	Gas	0.001	0.000	0.001	0.003	0.000	0.000	0.000	0.000
65	Water	1.004	0.004	0.006	0.014	0.006	0.005	0.003	0.005
66	Trade	0.521	1.284	0.472	0.352	0.356	0.237	0.204	0.353
67	Restaurants	0.075	0.098	1.103	0.097	0.106	0.073	0.062	0.112
68	Hotel, etc	0.007	0.007	0.005	1.006	0.004	0.004	0.015	0.004
69	Road Transport, etc	0.131	0.095	0.120	0.102	1.115	0.062	0.060	0.109
70	Air Transport, etc	0.030	0.040	0.052	0.061	0.042	1.090	0.044	0.043
71	Banking and Insurance	0.063	0.077	0.057	0.095	0.047	0.061	1.031	0.050
72	Real Estate	0.082	0.111	0.121	0.109	0.112	0.076	0.084	1.125
73	Public Services, etc	0.072	0.101	0.115	0.097	0.112	0.073	0.082	0.122
74	Personal Services, etc	0.119	0.088	0.100	0.085	0.260	0.061	0.059	0.100
	Sub-Total	3.195	3.137	4.301	3.509	3.634	2.660	2.407	3.620
75	Government	0.209	0.242	0.184	0.207	0.193	0.251	0.302	0.202
76	Capital Accounts	0.355	0.446	0.424	0.405	0.405	0.385	0.450	0.453
77	Net Indirect Taxes	0.024	0.034	0.046	0.042	0.043	0.022	0.017	0.032
78	Rest of World	0.412	0.278	0.346	0.345	0.359	0.342	0.231	0.313
	Sub-Total	1.000	1.000	1.000	1.000	1.000	1.000	1.000	1.000

Table II.6: Cont

		Name	Production Activities: Public Services etc 73	Personal Services 74
Factors of Production	1	Ag Paid Rural	0.059	0.054
	2	Ag Paid Urban	0.003	0.003
	3	Ag Unpaid Rural	0.138	0.125
	4	Ag Unpaid Urban	0.006	0.005
	5	Prod Paid Rural	0.049	0.123
	6	Prod Paid Urban	0.060	0.118
	7	Prod Unpaid Rural	0.033	0.086
	8	Prod Unpaid Urban	0.016	0.068
	9	Cler Paid Rural	0.081	0.133
	10	Cler Paid Urban	0.152	0.152
	11	Cler Unpaid Rural	0.067	0.100
	12	Cler Unpaid Urban	0.038	0.062
	13	Prof Paid Rural	0.328	0.043
	14	Prof Paid Urban	0.365	0.058
	15	Prof Unpaid Rural	0.010	0.011
	16	Prof Unpaid Urban	0.025	0.026
	17	Uninc Capital Land	0.240	0.213
	18	Uninc Capital Housing	0.083	0.074
	19	Uninc Capital Rural	0.085	0.083
	20	Uninc Capital Urban	0.160	0.135
	21	Inc Capital Domestic	0.176	0.176
	22	Inc Capital Government	0.152	0.133
	23	Inc Capital Foreign	0.057	0.072
M		Sub-Total	2.386	2.053
Institutions	24	Ag Employees	0.103	0.091
	25	Farm Size 1	0.182	0.186
	26	Farm Size 2	0.128	0.122
	27	Farm Size 3	0.217	0.193
	28	Rural Lower	0.219	0.299
	29	Rural Middle	0.061	0.042
	30	Rural Higher	0.266	0.118
	31	Urban Lower	0.310	0.382
	32	Urban Middle	0.061	0.048
	33	Urban Higher	0.566	0.289
	34	Companies	0.361	0.353
M		Sub-Total	2.474	2.122
Production activities	35	Food Crop	0.312	0.288
	36	Nonfood Crop	0.068	0.062
	37	Livestock and Products	0.106	0.083
	38	Forestry and Hunting	0.009	0.009
	39	Fishery	0.050	0.042
	40	Metal Ore Mining	0.000	0.000
	41	Other Mining	0.005	0.005
	42	Handpounded Rice	0.057	0.052
	43	Milled Rice	0.144	0.137
	44	Farm Processed Tea	0.004	0.004
	45	Processed Tea	0.002	0.002
	46	Dried and Salted Fish	0.030	0.026
	47	Canned Fish	0.005	0.004
	48	Brown Sugar	0.009	0.008
	49	Refined Sugar	0.028	0.025
	50	Canning (s+c)	0.000	0.000
	51	Canning (m+l)	0.000	0.000
	52	Kretek Cigs	0.049	0.045
	53	White Cigs	0.019	0.016
	54	Other Fbt	0.155	0.138
	55	Wood and Construction	0.047	0.041
	56	Textiles, etc	0.140	0.152
	57	Paper, Transport, Metal, etc.	0.126	0.153
	58	Chemical, Cement, etc	0.057	0.124
	59	Coal Mining	0.000	0.000
	60	Petroleum Mining, etc	0.027	0.043
	61	Gasoline	0.015	0.016
	62	Fuel Oil	0.015	0.016
	63	Electricity	0.029	0.026
	64	Gas	0.000	0.000
	65	Water	0.006	0.006
	66	Trade	0.352	0.378
	67	Restaurants	0.108	0.099
	68	Hotel, etc	0.004	0.004
	69	Road Transport, etc	0.104	0.107
	70	Air Transport, etc	0.042	0.043
	71	Banking and Insurance	0.042	0.048
	72	Real Estate	0.130	0.115
	73	Public Services, etc	1.133	0.105
	74	Personal Services, etc	0.102	1.099
M		Sub-Total	3.532	3.520
Exog Accts.	75	Government	0.177	0.164
	76	Capital Accounts	0.450	0.365
	77	Net Indirect Taxes	0.034	0.034
	78	Rest of World	0.339	0.437
M		Sub-Total	1.000	1.000

Notes

1 Central Bureau of Statistics, <u>Social Accounting Matrix Indonesia, 1975</u>, Vols. 1 and 2, August 1982. Volumes 1 and 2 of this publication describe in great detail how the original SAM was constructed. It describes the procedures which were used to estimate entries in the SAM and the classification schemes underlying the three levels of aggregation i.e. 27 X 27, 62 X 62 and 116 X 116. Other sources which describe the CBS and SAM are Roger A. Downey "Indonesian Inequality: Integrated National Accounting of Who Gets What, Ph.D. Thesis, Cornell University, 1984; Roger A. Downey and Steven J. Keuning, "Introduction to the Indonesian Social Accounting Matrix, Institute of Social Studies Working Paper Series No. 25, 1985; and Steven J. Keuning, "Modelling the Indonesian Social Accounting Matrix", Institute of Social Studies Working Paper Series No. 1, 1984. The CBS-SAM evolved from a joint project between CBS in Jakarta, Professor Erik Thorbecke of Cornell University and the Institute of Social Studies in the Hague. The CBS provided invaluable help for which we are very grateful.

2 A.S. Bhalla, <u>Technology and Employment in Industry</u>, ILO, Geneva, 1975; J. Svejnar and E. Thorbecke, "Determinants and Effects of Technological Choice," Paper presented at the annual meeting of the American Association for the Advancement of Science, 1980; J. Svejnar and E. Thorbecke, "The Determinants and Effects of Technological Choices," in Barbara Lucas, (Ed.) <u>Internal and External Constraints on Technological Choice in Developing Countries</u>, Tooley-Bowker Publishing Company, London, 1982 and H. Khan, "Technology, Energy, Employment and Basic Needs: A Study of the Korean Manufacturing Sector," Report submitted to the Technology and Employment Branch, World Employment Programme, International Labour Office, Geneva, 1982.

3 It is important to note that this information does not exist either for 1975 (the base year for the SAM) nor for subsequent years. The survey done by the World Bank with the Central Bureau of Statistics in 1980-81 failed to bear fruit. A new special investment survey undertaken by the Industrial Statistics Division of the CBS, is in the process of yielding a time series which is still inadequate for our purposes for two reasons. First, it does not go back to 1975; and, secondly, even if it did, there is still no way to distinguish technology within sectors.

4 It should be kept in mind that some differences in output and employment between the different size firms are results of characteristics other than technologies such as the economy of scale. Strictly speaking, one should separate of economies scale and other non-technological effects so that only <u>pure</u> technological differences stand out. This, however, is impossible to do without a large scale survey. However, it is important to remember that scale and technology may <u>not</u> be entirely independent of each other, <u>i.e.</u> in some cases economies of scale exist only with a certain (perhaps modern) technique. To the extent that this is true, firm size can be

a good indicator of differences in both technology and economies of scale. If the two are inseparable, in the sense
described above the technological differences can be explored
reasonably without reference to the economies of scale.
Ideally one could distinguish between both firm sizes and
different technologies. Our data base here, however, did not
permit the latter.

5 Thorbecke designed and initiated this methodology and applied
it to the case of Korea in connection with a National Science
Foundation project. (See Svejnar-Thorbecke, op.cit.) Subsequently Khan applied this methodology in exploring more systematically the energy requirements of different production
activities in Korea as well as some of the implications of
more recent development trends in Korea on energy use. The
section which follows which describes how the SAM methodology
can be applied to the exploration of the macroeconomic effects
of technology is largely based on Svejnar-Thorbecke 1980 and
on G. Pyatt and E. Thorbecke, Planning Techniques for a
Better Future, International Labour Office, Geneva, 1976.

6 Companies receive only nonlabour income and some groups of
households receive both labour and nonlabour (capital and
land) income.

7 See G. Pyatt and J.I. Round, "Accounting and fixed-price
multipliers in a social accounting matrix framework,"
Economic Journal, 1979, Vol. 89, pp. 850-73for the distinction
between accounting multiplier matrix and fixed price multiplier matrix which is discussed subsequently.

8 There exists a number of computable general equilibrium models
which are either implicitly or explicitly based on a SAM-
framework. For a recent review of these models see S.
Robinson, "Multisectoral Models of Developing Countries: A
Survey", California Agricultural Experiment Station, Giannini
Foundation of Agricultural Economics, University of California, Working Paper No. 401, April 1986.

9 Thus, for example, C.P. Timmer and H. Alderman, "Estimating
Consumption Parameters for Food Policy Analysis," American
Journal of Agricultural Economics, Vol. 61, No. 5, pp. 982-87,
1979 have estimated on the basis of the Susenas survey data
the expenditure elasticity of demand for rice for four income
levels in both urban and rural areas. These estimates ranged
from 1.0-1.17 (urban-rural) for the poorest income group to
.07-.36 (urban-rural) for the highest income group. These
estimates provided the basis for our own estimates of demand
elasticities for both handpounded and milled rice by the
various socioeconomic groups contained in Appendix Table C.

10 This condition allowed not only different MEP's than AEP's to
be chosen to reflect the consumption patterns of the different
socio-economic groups but, in addition, marginal (saving,
import, and taxation) propensities could be postulated for
each socio-economic group which differed from their respective
average propensities.

11 This means that the matrix C_1 is likely to be different from
A_1.

12 Note that the initial impulse or injection could be an exogenous increase (or decrease) in output directly as the examples in section III.H show.

13 In Chapter VI, some of the limitations of this demand-oriented approach and, particularly, the assumption of excess capacity and no supply constraints are discussed. The existence of supply constraints complicates the picture in real life and can alter some of the findings of the present analysis--as is shown in Chapter VI (section C).

III Analysis of macroeconomic effects of alternative product-cum-technologies based on SAM-Tech and other sources

This chapter includes a number of sections. It starts in section A with a synopsis of other studies which explored the macro-economic effects of technology choices in Indonesia. Next, in section B the increasing relative importance of the modern techno-logical alternative in selected dualistic sectors over time is described focusing on the extent to which the modern technology displaced the corresponding traditional one in these same sectors. This is followed by four short sections which use the fixed price multipliers derived from SAM-Tech to explore the implications of the above trend on, respectively, national and sectoral output and energy requirements (in section C); factor income and employment (in section E); and on household income distribution (in section F). In addition, the linkages between and among traditional activities, modern activities and other sectors are examined in section D.

The final part of Chapter III is devoted to a review of the methodology underlying structural path analysis and the trans-mission of economic influence within the SAM framework (in section G). This methodology is next applied to the Indonesian SAM-Tech to illustrate on the basis of thirteen selected examples, the whole network of paths through which the impact of a change in output originating in the dualistic product-cum-technologies sec-tion gets transmitted within the Indonesian SAM structure.

A. Synopsis of other studies

This section is devoted to a brief review of the methodologies and findings of existing studies on the macroeconomic effects of industrial policies including technology choices in Indonesia.[1] Very little scholarly research on this topic was done before the mid-sixties.[2] In no small measure, this was due to the relative insignificance of the manufacturing sector until the late sixties.[3] In the seventies more attention was devoted to the industrial sector than before and a number of good studies appeared. Broadly speaking, they can be divided into descriptive and sectoral studies, on the one hand, and analytical studies using input-output and econometric techniques, on the other. The surveys in the Bulletin for Indonesian Economic Studies (BIES), the work by Peter McCawley on "The Growth of the Industrial Sector", and the excellent chapter by Poot on the development of labour-intensive industries in Indonesia are examples of the first approach.[4] The Input-Output approach is of even more relatively recent origin. This work received its impetus from the publication of 1971 and 1975 input-output tables by the CBS. There are two ongoing projects; one undertaken by the ILO in cooperation with the Department of Manpower in Indonesia, and the other by the Netherlands Economic Institute (NEI). The ILO/Department of Manpower studies by Douglas S. Paauw and Stan Stavenuiter use the 1975 input-output table, whereas the NEI studies rely on an updated version of it for 1980. We discuss the sectoral and the I/O approaches in sequence.

The major contribution of the sectoral studies has been to identify the industrial structure of Indonesia from the existing data base. Using national income statistics, surveys and censuses of manufacturing industries as well as information on institutional arrangements, McCawley presents the reader with a thorough description of the industrial sector in the 70's and its overall role in the Indonesian economy.

Poot's chapter in the ARTEP volume relates more closely to our concern with labour intensive industries. There is some overlap in the area of description between his study and that of McCawley, but the focus is on the structure of labour-intensive industries. Using all available survey information during the 70's, he discusses cottage and household industries and small scale enterprises as well as large and medium scale enterprises. The analysis relies largely on limited technical information regarding such variables as productivity and growth of value added and identification of the influence of government policies on the growth of small scale enterprises.

In contrast with the above approach, the input-output approach tends to be much broader in scope. Simple macroeconomic modelling based on multipliers is relied upon for the projection of employment and output in the future. The papers by Douglas Paauw and Stan Stavenuiter look at the employment implications of export promotion and government expenditures.[5] The methodology uses the standard Leontief inverse to compute the change in output from a change in the vector of final demand, i.e.

$$x = (I - A)^{-1} \ f$$

where f = change in final demand vector

      x = change in output vector

      A = the intermediate input-coefficients matrix
         or the 'technology' matrix.

The resulting change in employment is computed by using the direct and indirect employment coefficients for the 1975 Indonesian input-output table.[6] This approach can be contrasted with the SAM multipliers using the "generalised inverse" rather than simply the "Leontief inverse" based only on the I-O submatrix. As explained in the previous section, the SAM average propensities' matrix A contains the Input/Output coefficients as a sub-matrix (A_{33} in eq. 2.4) in addition to four other submatrices. As such, the SAM approach captures a number of interdependencies which are excluded in the straightforward Leontief approach. This issue is discussed further at the end of this section.

Paauw starts out by allocating export demands for the base year 1982 for 50 of the 66-sector input-output table for 1975. Then, two cases with different export targets are considered. Case I looks at the effect of policies for promotion of labour-intensive exports in selected sectors. Case II considers the impact of REPELITA IV provisional export targets on output and employment. Under case I employment is projected to increase by 1.36 million during REPELITA IV. The contribution of manufacturing exports is deemed to be the largest (644,600) followed by agriculture (461,860) and service (204,600). Under case II, only two sectors, manufacturing and services contribute to export-generated employment. Agricultural employment is actually projected to fall by 59 thousand between 1983/84 and 1988/89, at a rate of -1.1% per year. Total employment will grow by 253 thousand at an annual growth rate of 2.4 percent. The difference between the two cases is largely explained by a lower target growth of exports in the second case. However, it is the switch from more capital-intensive to the relatively labour-intensive sectors in manufacturing and services that leads to the overall increase in employment in both instances.

Similar experiments are conducted with respect to an increase in government expenditures in the development budget. In order to use the I/O methodology the spending on budget programs (by function and ministry) had to be transformed into final demands for each I/O sector. With considerable ingenuity, this was accomplished by an interagency group. The final demands were then deflated to 1975 prices using the price indices for the year 1982. The rate of inflation between 1982 and 1984/85 (the year for which projections were made) was assumed to be 11% for all sectors. It was estimated the government expenditures alone would create over 4.7 million jobs in 1984/85. Compared with the corresponding figures in 1982/83, this would be an increment of more than 607 thousand jobs. These new jobs result from a) an absolute increase in the size of 1984/85 budget when compared with the development budget in 1982/83, and b) a shift in final demand from products of the capital-intensive sectors such as fertilizers to the products of relatively labour-intensive manufacturing sectors.[7]

To this date the most extensive use of input/output technique for the study of the Indonesian manufacturing sector has been made by the Netherlands Economic Institute in collaboration with the Indonesian Ministry of Industry.[8] In addition to extending the I/O method to a consideration of skills and factor intensities, a survey of selected establishments in the manufacturing sector was conducted in order to estimate the capital utilisation in the manufacturing sector.[9]

The capital utilisation survey covered ten of the 27 provinces. The most industrialised provinces were included, but a few provinces with some industry were still excluded. In terms of 3-digit IIC/ISIC classification, the sectors surveyed were:

331	Wood and Wood Products
341	Paper and Paper Products
351	Industrial Chemicals
352	Other Chemical Products
361	Pottery, China, Earthenware
362	Glass and Glass Products
363	Cement, Lime and Cement Products
371	Iron and Steel Industries
372	Basic Non-ferrous Metals
381	Cuttlery, Hardware
382	Machinery
383	Electrical Machinery
394	Transport Equipment

Using two different measures of capital utilisation, it was found that both scale of production and the capital-labour ratio are positively related to capacity utilisation. As our study acknowledges, there is a crying need for such measurements of capital use for the identification of technologies in use. The previous work, though an important beginning, does not allow one to classify and distinguish among technologies at the sectoral level.

The input-output studies of NEI attempt to identify the most promising export possibilities for Indonesia in the 80's and on that basis project capital and employment requirements for the period 1980-1990. Two strategies for industrialisation for Indonesia are discussed. Strategy (a) stresses self-reliance through the reduction of dependence on the world market for manufactured capital, and intermediate and consumer goods. This strategy stresses the development of basic industries. Strategy (b) calls for the development of industries in which Indonesia has a comparative advantage. This leads to the development of labour-intensive industries. However, both strategies emphasise the priority of natural resource based industries as well, because of the abundance of Indonesia's natural resource endowment.

Two scenarios, based on strategies (a) and (b), respectively, for change in the manufacturing sector between the years 1980-1990 are developed. A comparison of these two scenarios shows the following:

1) For the same production volume (GDP) strategy (b) leads to 50% more employment creation than does strategy (a).

2) Strategy (a) requires 46% more investment funds than strategy (b).

3) Total value added is slightly higher for the scenario based on strategy (a) than the scenario arising from strategy (b).

4) Imports of inputs, the capital-labour ratio and value added per worker are higher for scenario following strategy (a) than for scenario resulting from strategy (b).

The above discussed existing studies are no doubt useful. However, they capture only partially the interdependencies in the economy. In particular the impact of changes in the structure of production on the household income distribution and the effects of the latter on final demand are left out. A general equilibrium approach will have to take into account not only the effects of an exogenous change in final demand on output and employment, but also close the loop by including the allocation of the value added to the households and so on and so forth. The input-output approach is not designed for this. In contrast, the Social Accounting Matrix approach is a logical extension of, and an improvement over, the input-output approach. As mentioned at the beginning of this section, SAM includes the household income distribution and consumption pattern along with the intermediate inputs used. Thus, the use of fixed price multipliers goes considerably farther than the Leontief inverse in capturing the general equilibrium effects of changes in technologies or of any macro economic policy instruments, as is demonstrated in the following sections.

B. **Increasing relative importance of modern technological alternative in selected dualistic sectors**

The manufacturing sector in Indonesia is still relatively small in comparison with other sectors accounting for only 8.9% of GDP at current prices in 1975. It has, however, continued to grow at a high rate reaching a share of 11.6% of total GDP in 1980. (The corresponding relative shares at constant 1973 prices were 11.1 and 15.3 percent, respectively.) It is interesting to note, as Table III.1 reveals, that in 1975 small scale establishments (SE's) and household and cottage establishments (HCE's) together contributed only about 19% of total output and value added of the manufacturing sector while accounting for approximately 75% of total employment in this sector. This means, of course, that

TABLE III.1

Output Value Added and Employment by Size Class of Manufacturing Industries in 1974/75

Size Class	Output			Value Added			Employment	
	Amount (million Rs.)	per man-day	%	Amount (million Rs.)	per man-day	%	Number (Thousand persons)	%
Large and medium	1295.3	8029	78.3	478.4	2965	77.9	665.8	22.8
Small	157.3	2745	9.5	52.8	922	8.6	269.0	9.4
Household and cottage	200.8	468	12.2	82.6	192	13.5	1934.1[1]	67.8
Total	1653.4	-	100.0	613.8[2]	-	100.0	2858.9	100

[1] To improve comparability with small and large industries, employment in household and cottage industries has been expressed in man years rather than total persons employed, since a high proportion of participants in these industries work only part time.

[2] It should be noted that there is a considerable gap between value added data for manufacturing from these sources and from national accounts data. According to the latter, GDP in manufacturing amounted to 890 billion in 1974 and 1124 billions in 1975.

Source: BPS, *Sensus Industri 1974/75.*

major differences in productivity exist between the different
firm sizes. In general, the technology in use within a sector
tends to be correlated with firm size. Small establishments and
household and cottage establishments are very likely to use traditional technology and vice versa for medium and large establishments (MLE's). As Poot 1981, p.89 [10] has indicated the main
difference is that MLE's use some kind of power equipment whereas
only a small minority of the SE's (341 out of 47,845 establishments) do so.

One tendency which appears to be taking place in Indonesia, and
in many other developing countries, is the displacement of small
industries. MLE's producing products similar to those in SE's and
HCE's have increasingly taken over a larger share of the market
and affected employment quite negatively in the latter.

This tendency is highlighted next with regard to our dualistic
activities in Table III.2,--all of which, incidentally, are classified as manufacturing according to the International Standard
Industrial Code. (The corresponding 5-digit ISIC numbers are
given in Table III.2.) Together, these dualistic activities con-
stituted 4.26% of total national output (col. 1) in 1975. Perhaps, a better way of gauging the relative importance of these
activities in the economy is to realise that their combined output
represented roughly half of the manufacturing sector output in
that year--largely due to the importance of rice milling.

In general, Table III.2 suggests that the modern technology
displaced the traditional technology as judged by its increasing
share, respectively, of total output (cols. 2 and 3) and of value
added (cols. 5 and 6) between 1975 and 1980 for each product with
the exception of clove cigarettes (presumably but not clearly the
traditional technology) which captured a larger share of the
cigarette market over the same timespan.[11]

Next, let us examine the trend towards displacement of the
traditional technology by the modern one at the product level on
the basis of the data in Table III.2. Between 1975 and 1980 the
share of milled rice rose from 65 to 71% of total rice output and
the corresponding value added share rose from 59 to 76%. It
should be noted, however, that L. Mears,[12] gives a different
picture of the diffusion of milled rice technology. By his account, the arrival of small mills near the villages led to a much
more rapid shift from handpounded to milled rice production than
the CBS input-output statistics (upon which Table III.2 was based)
indicate. According to Mears, by 1979, the share of handpounded
rice had fallen to only 6% of total rice output.[13] Hence, the
displacement might, in fact, have been even faster and more pronounced than indicated in Table III.2.

In fish processing, the modern technology increased its share of
total output and value added only quite moderately (from, respectively, 15 to 17% and from 7 to 13%). Even though canning of
fruits and vegetables is an almost insignificantly small sector in
terms of total output as shown in column 1 of Table III.2, by

Table III.2.: Indonesia: Dualistic Sectors: 1975 Output, Rate of Growth of Real Output, 1975-80 and Percentage Shares of Output and Value Added for Each contributed by Traditional and Modern Technology.

Sector	SAM Code	ISIC Code	1975 Output[a] in billion Rupiahs (1)	Percentage Share of Total Output Produced with Traditional and Modern Technology 1975 (2)	1980[b] (3)	Percentage Change in 1980 Compared to 1975 Output[c] (4)	Percentage Share of Total Value Added Produced with Traditional and Modern Technology[d] 1975 (5)	1980 (6)
Rice								
Handpounded (T)	(42)	31161	617	35	29	- 8	41	33
Milled (M)	(43)	31161	1145	65	71	17	59	76
Tea								
Farm Processed (T)	(44)	31211	41	84	na	na	na	na
Off-farm Processing (M)	(45)	31211	8	16	na	na	na	na
Fish								
Drying and Salting (T)	(46)	31141	139	85	83	-29	93	87
Canned (M)	(47)	31141	24	15	17	-14	7	13
Cigarettes		31420						
Clove (T)	(52)	31490	232	73	84	99	60	79
White (M)	(53)	31430	84	27	16	27	40	21
Canning of Fruits and Vegetables								
Small (T)	(50)	31130	.2	32	(7)	na	49	5
Medium and Large (M)	(51)	31130	.6	68	(93)	na	51	95

Sugar							
Brown (T)	(48)	31181	47	26	na	na	na
Refined (M)	(49)	31181	137	74	na	na	na

A. Total Output of Dualistic
   Sectors Above   2469

B. Total National (SAM) Output   57978

Share of A to B (%)   4.26

Sources and Methodology:

[a]From Appendix Table B.

[b]From i) CBS Table Input-Output 1980, and ii) Census of Manufactures 1975 and 1979. Notice that in some instances the 1979 or 1980 output figures came from source ii) above so that the comparison between relative shares in 1975 and 1980 is based on two different sources.

[c]For the sake of comparability, the same data source either (i) or (ii) under b above was used in both years to compute the percentage change. The following sectoral deflators were used with SAM-Tech sector numbers and price deflators (1975=100) given next: 42, 224.2; 43, 241.0; 44 and 45, 208.0; 46 and 47, 286.6; 52, 194.3; 53, 221.4. Sectoral price deflators are from CBS.

[d]

[e]Mears (1981) gives a different picture of the diffusion of milled rice technology. According to him, by 1979, the share of handpounded rice had fallen to only 6 percent (see text for more detail).

1980, the medium and large firms seem to have taken over the quasi totality of that sector's production.

Even though we could not estimate the prevailing share of refined sugar as compared to brown sugar output in 1980, there is evidence quoted by other sources that the modern technology continued to make major inroads on the traditional one. Indeed as Poot (1981, p.124) remarked in connection with the threat to the continued existence of small firms in a number of areas,

> "For example, considerable resources have been allocated to the development of large scale sugar refineries. Once they start production, they are likely to force many of the cottage sugar mills out of production (which in 1975 employed over 780,000 workers in HCE's alone). A similar threat is faced by small scale rice mills as mechanised rice mills are expanding rapidly. Increased competition from large scale enterprises constitutes therefore a formidable threat to small scale firms in many sectors."

The cigarette sector is peculiar in the sense that clove cigarettes (Kretek i.e. the traditional product using a traditional technology) are often produced in large firms. Hence, in this case, it would be a mistake to associate the traditional technology with the size of the establishment.[14] In any case, the data in Table III.2 suggest that in contrast with the other dualistic products, the share of clove cigarettes in total cigarette output increased markedly between 1975 to 1980 from 73 to 84% (the corresponding share of value added grew from 60 to 79%). In fact, in this case we are not only comparing two technologies but also two reasonably distinct products, and it is more than likely that the increasing relative importance of clove cigarettes reflects a change in the consumers' taste pattern towards the latter rather than a technological change. Whereas, in general, consumers' preferences shift towards the modern product throughout the process of economic development, this is not always the case as this last example suggests.[15]

C. Effects on national and sectoral output and energy requirements

The above analysis has shown that during the only period (i.e. 1975-1980) for which information was available, the modern alternative technology has increasingly replaced the traditional one for five of the six types of products (rice, tea, processed fish, sugar and canned fruits and vegetables) which were broken down by technology along dualistic lines in SAM-Tech. It appears interesting, next, to explore the implications of this trend on a variety of macroeconomic variables. First, the effects of this trend on, respectively, overall output in the economy, the output of various aggregated sectors and energy requirements are estimated.

Table III.3 was prepared for this purpose. It estimates on the basis of the previously derived fixed price multipliers the effects of given (exogenous) unit changes in the demand for selected dualistic production activities on aggregate national output and different sectoral components of national output. Again, one example will suffice to illustrate the way in which this table can be interpreted. Reading along the first row, it can be seen that an exogenous increase of 100 rupiahs of handpounded rice production would result through its circular effects working themselves out within the whole economy to increments of, respectively, 155 rupiahs of agricultural and mining output, 124.4 rupiahs of aggregate output of the six traditional activities (within our set of twelve dualistic sectors), 24.6 rupiahs of aggregate output in the corresponding six modern activities, 8 rupiahs of combined energy output, 168.9 rupiahs of other sectors' output for a combined aggregate effects of 480.9 rupiahs (see column 6 of Table III.3).

The major inferences which can be drawn from Table III.3 are the following. In general, it appears that the traditional technology generates greater aggregate output effects on the whole economic system than the corresponding modern technology. This is particularly noticeable with regard to comparing clove cigarettes and white cigarettes (with fixed price multipliers of 3.599 and 2.615, respectively) and brown vs. refined sugar (4.429 as opposed to 3.501). As can be seen from column 6 of Table III.3, the total output multiplier was higher for the traditional than the modern technology in the case of four of the six products, and in the other remaining two cases, the difference was marginal. Furthermore, the direct and indirect energy requirements were in every instance greater for the modern technological alternative than for the traditional one with the exception of clove cigarettes vs. white cigarettes.[16]

D. Linkages between and among traditional activities, modern activities and other sectors

A key question in a developing country relates to the nature and magnitude of the linkages between the informal sector and the formal sector. We can examine this issue with reference to our six products. Table III.3 demonstrates that the combined output effects of a given increase in a traditional product-cum-technology (e.g. handpounded rice) on both the set of other traditional activities (thus excluding the activity's own multiplier) and the set of modern activities were in every instance greater than for a similar increase in the corresponding modern alternative (e.g. milled rice). This can be seen by looking at columns 2 and 3, respectively, of Table III.3. What this suggests is that, at least within the twelve dualistic sectors included in this study, the direct and indirect linkages generated by any one traditional (informal) activity vis-a-vis all other traditional activities as well as vis-a-vis modern activities were greater than those generated by the corresponding (product-wise) modern alternative. In addition, in four of the six products shown in Table III.3, the aggregate output effects on agriculture and

Table III 3: Estimated Effects of Changes in Output of Selected
Dualistic Production Activities (Traditional and Modern) on
Aggregate Output of Agriculture and Mining, Dualistic Sectors,
Energy, Others and the Whole Economy Using Fixed Price
Multipliers[a]

Dualistic Sectors[2]		Aggregate Effects on Agriculture and Mining (1)	Aggregate Effects on Six Traditional Dualistic Activities Listed in First Column (2)	
Rice				
T. Handpounded	(42)	1.550	1.244	(0.133)[c]
M. Milled	(43)	1.387	0.233	(0.118)[d]
Tea				
T. Farm Processed	(44)	0.934	1.182	(0.177)
M. Off-farm Processed	(45)	1.054	0.147	(0.143)
Fish				
T. Dried and Salted	(46)	1.048	1.185	(0.154)
M. Canned	(47)	0.942	0.163	(0.135)
Sugar				
T. Brown	(48)	1.165	1.209	(0.197)
M. Refined	(49)	0.703	0.137	(0.129)
Canning of Fruits and Vegetables				
T. Small Firms	(50)	0.853	1.173	(0.173)
M. Medium & Large Firms	(51)	0.961	0.163	(0.163)
Cigarettes				
T. Clove	(52)	0.815	1.117	(0.080)
M. White	(53)	0.398	0.075	(0.051)

Sources and Methodology:
[a]The figures in this table are the fixed price multipliers obtained
from Table II.6. For methodology, see text.
[b]In each instance the traditional technological alternative is
listed first.

Aggregate Effects on Six Modern Dualistic Activities Listed in First Column (3)		Aggregate Effects on Energy Sectors (4)	Aggregate Effects on Other Sectors (5)	Aggregate National Effects (6)
0.246	(0.061)d	0.080	1.689	4.809
1.235	(0.055)c	0.105	1.620	4.580
0.201	(0.199)	0.073	1.529	3.919
1.170	(0.169)	0.128	1.592	4.091
0.202	(0197)	0.084	1.679	4.198
1.195	(0.190)	0.106	1.655	4.061
0.249	(0.216)	0.090	1.716	4.429
1.172	(0.148)	0.136	1.353	3.501
0.260	(0.260)	0.102	1.674	4.062
1.226	(0.226)	0.111	1.744	4.205
0.143	(0.132)	0.071	1.453	3.599
1.096	(0.088)	0.056	0.990	2.615

cNumber in parentheses is obtained by excluding own multiplier.
dNumber in parentheses is obtained by excluding effects on, respectively, traditional (handpounded) rice and modern (milled) rice for the sake of comparability and similarly for each pair of dualistic activities.

mining (i.e. primary sectors) were greater for the traditional than for the corresponding modern technology (within each pair of each pair of product-cum-technologies), while in the other two instances, the difference was fairly marginal. (See column 1 of Table III.3.) Given the very high labour intensity of these primary activities, it will be seen subsequently that this observation has important implications for income distribution and employment as well.[17]

Another element which is likely to further reinforce the magnitude of the direct and indirect output effects generated by the traditional technique as compared to the modern one within the same sector is that there is likely to be more excess capacity available within the former than the latter.

E. Effects on factor income and employment

The effects of changes in the output of any one of our twelve dualistic activities on the factorial income distribution (and indirectly on employment as will be seen subsequently) can be gathered by examining the fixed price multipliers in Table II.6. More specifically, the relevant submatrix of M_c, i.e. M_{31} is that embraced by columns 42 to 53 and rows 1 to 23. Scrutinising the above submatrix suggests the following inferences. First, somewhat surprisingly, comparing the traditional and modern activity within each pair of product-cum-technology, it does not appear that the modern technology generates more total capital (e.g. land) income than the corresponding traditional technology. This is largely caused by the fact that the traditional alternative tends to generate more rent going to land and other agricultural capital than the modern alternative and vice versa for incorporated capital. Secondly, with regard to labour income, it can be seen that the traditional technology consistently yields significantly greater labour income effects than the corresponding modern technology. Thus, for example, adding the fixed price multipliers for all the labour factors, one obtains the following results: a 100 unit (rupiah) increase in the output of handpounded rice would yield 139.6 units increase in labour incomes (SAM codes 1-16) as compared to 117 rupiahs in the case of milled rice. The corresponding figures for farm processed tea are 113.7 as compared to 86.6 for processed tea; 102.6 for brown sugar as compared to 78 for refined sugar; and, 66.1 for clove cigarettes as compared to 44.3 for white cigarettes.

Moreover, from an income distribution standpoint, it is clear that the effects of increased production by the traditional technology has a considerably greater impact on the incomes of lower skilled workers than the corresponding modern alternative. Again, this can be verified by looking at Table II.6, e.g. it can be seen that the fixed price multiplier of handpounded rice on agricultural paid rural workers is .252 as opposed to .169 for milled rice and, likewise, with regard to agricultural unpaid rural workers, the corresponding multiplier values are .624 and .437, respectively. This finding is generalisable to other products as well, as the reader can verify.[18]

The information in our multiplier table can yield interesting and much more specific information relating, for instance, to the impact of each technological alternative on not only the rural-urban income distribution but also the distribution between the incomes of paid vs. unpaid workers (self-employed and family workers) and higher vs. lower skilled workers, as the classification breakdown into 16 different labour groups shows.

The employment effects, per se, can be readily derived from the effects on each labour factor given the average wage per full time equivalent prevailing for the corresponding labour skill group. The CBS in its Social Accounting Matrix Indonesia, 1975, Volume 1 provides the average wages and salaries per worker equivalent by labour factor and production sectors in 1975 (see Table 3.1.4 of above volume). Thus, Table III.4 illustrates how the actual employment effects can be derived from a knowledge of the fixed price multipliers. The specific example presented in that table compares the employment effects of an exogenous increase of 1 million rupiahs in the output of handpounded vs. milled rice. The employment effects computed in terms of number of worker equivalents are derived for the 16 labour groups in SAM-Tech. In columns 4 and 5, respectively, of Table III.4 it can be seen that a million rupiahs of additional handpounded rice would yield 3.32 additional agricultural paid rural workers as opposed to 2.23 for milled rice, 8.76 additional agricultural unpaid rural workers as opposed to 6.14, and so on and so forth for the 16 labour groups. By analogy, the same methodology can be used to derive the employment effects generated by an increase in output of any of the 40 production activities in our SAM-Tech, not just the dualistic activities.

F. Effects on household income distribution

The household income distribution for the ten household groups in SAM-Tech is endogenously determined mainly through the mapping of the factorial income distribution into the household income distribution. In addition, the household income distribution is also marginally affected by interhousehold transfers and transfers between companies and households. An examination of the submatrix of the fixed price multiplier matrix M_c (i.e. M_{32}) which yields the household income distribution resulting from changes in the output of any production activity is given by columns 35-74 and rows 24-33 in Table II.6. Table III.5 reproduces these multipliers for three pairs of dualistic activities i.e. handpounded vs. milled rice, brown sugar vs. refined sugar and clove cigarettes vs. white cigarettes. A quick perusal of Table III.5 reveals that for each pair of dual product-cum-technology, the traditional alternative yielded greater total (combined) household income than the corresponding modern activity. In turn, making pair-wise comparisons between the traditional and modern technological alternatives for the three pairs of production activities shown in Table III.5, the following observations suggest them-

Table III.4.: Derivation of Employment Effects from Fixed Price Multipliers, Handpounded Rice vs. Milled Rice.

SAM Code	Labor Factor	Effects on Labor Income of Increase of 1 Million Rupiahs in Output of	
		Handpounded Rice (in thousand Rupiahs) (1)	Milled Rice (2)
1	Ag Paid Rural	252	169
2	Ag Paid Urban	7	6
3	Ag Unpaid Rural	624	437
4	Ag Unpaid Urban	18	17
5	Prod Paid Rural	48	70
6	Prod Paid Urban	47	55
7	Prod Unpaid Rural	38	62
8	Prod Unpaid Urban	16	16
9	Cler Paid Rural	34	35
10	Cler Paid Urban	59	60
11	Cler Unpaid Rural	81	78
12	Cler Unpaid Urban	45	43
13	Prof Paid Rural	41	39
14	Prof Paid Urban	57	56
15	Prof Unpaid Rural	8	7
16	Prof Unpaid Urban	21	20

Sources and Methodology:
Columns (1) and (2) are obtained by multiplying the postulated injection (1 million Rupiahs of output) by the corresponding fixed price multipliers in Table II.6); column (3) comes from CBS, Social Accounting Matrix of Indonesia, 1975, vol. 1, Table 3.1.3; columns (4) and (5), respectively, are obtained by dividing col. (1) by col. (3) and col. (2) by col. (3), respectively.

Average Wages and Salaries per Worker Equivalent (in Thousand Rupiahs) (3)	Effects on Employment of	
	Handpounded Rice (Number of worker equivalent) (4)	Milled Rice (Number of worker equivalent) (5)
75.9	3.32	2.23
98.5	.07	.06
71.2	8.76	6.14
89.4	.20	.19
126.3	.38	.55
189.7	.25	.29
102.1	.37	.61
160.0	.10	.10
111.6	.30	.31
198.9	.30	.30
80.3	1.01	.97
117.7	.38	.37
349.2	.12	.11
556.3	.10	.10
101.0	.08	.07
419.1	.05	.05

Table III.5: Fixed Price Multipliers Giving Effects of Selected Dualistic Production Activities on Household Income Distribution.

SAM Code	Production Activities Households & Companies	Handpounded Rice (42)	Milled Rice (43)	Brown Sugar (48)	Refined Sugar (49)	Clove Cigarettes (52)	White Cigarettes (53)
24	Ag Employees	.220	.176	.192	.110	.097	.058
25	Farm Size 1	.466	.386	.342	.205	.178	.109
26	Farm Size 2	.340	.284	.235	.148	.136	.077
27	Farm Size 3	.575	.489	.391	.239	.248	.133
28	Rural Lower	.209	.250	.405	.246	.155	.121
29	Rural Middle	.056	.054	.065	.042	.033	.024
30	Rural Higher	.094	.101	.138	.094	.070	.055
31	Urban Lower	.235	.243	.239	.301	.206	.162
32	Urban Middle	.037	.037	.038	.042	.032	.027
33	Urban Higher	.222	.220	.229	.244	.194	.166
	Total Household Income	2.455	2.240	2.275	1.666	1.347	.932
34	Companies	.354	.351	.404	.457	.426	.465
	Total Income of Institutions	2.809	2.591	2.679	2.123	1.773	1.397

Source: Taken directly from Table II.6.

selves. In each case, the traditional activity showed higher multiplier values for the following household groups: agricultural employees and the three different groups of farmers defined according to amount of land owned or operated. On the other hand, milled rice yielded more income to the lower income level rural households group than handpounded rice with the opposite being the case for brown sugar vs. refined sugar and clove cigarettes vs. white cigarettes.

In contrast to labour income, most of the modern technologies display higher income multipliers with respect to income of companies than do the corresponding traditional alternative.

Generally speaking, the above findings hold true for the whole set of dualistic sectors in our sample.

G. Structural path analysis methodology: transmission of economic influence within the SAM framework

Recently, Defourny and Thorbecke (1984)[19] have applied structural path analysis to a SAM framework. Because the SAM is a comprehensive--essentially general equilibrium--data system, the whole network through which influence is transmitted can be identified and specified through structural path analysis. Since the application of the latter to the SAM framework is quite new, the principal elements and components of the structural path methodology are presented very briefly in this section before applying them to SAM-Tech in the next section.

The starting point is to equate the notion of expenditure to that of "influence". Graphically this means that each average expenditure propensity a_{ji} (or, alternatively, marginal expenditure propensity c_{ji}) of an "arc" (i,j) linking two poles of the structure and oriented in the direction of the expenditure is to be interpreted as the magnitude of the influence transmitted from pole i to pole j.

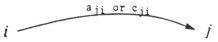

$$i \xrightarrow{\quad a_{ji} \text{ or } c_{ji} \quad} j$$

The average expenditure propensity a_{ji} (or alternatively) the marginal expenditure propensity c_{ji}) reflects the "intensity of arc (i,j). Hence, as will become clearer subsequently, an analysis based on accounting multipliers derived from the matrix of average expenditure propensities, A_n, of which a_{ji} is an element presumes that influence is reflected by the latter. On the other hand, fixed price multipliers derived from the matrix of marginal expenditure propensities, C_n, assumes that the intensity of the influence between any two poles is captured by the corresponding value of the marginal expenditure propensities. Since the empirical analysis which follows is based on fixed price multipliers, the analysis proceeds by equating influence with marginal expenditure propensity.

A path which does not pass more than one time through the same pole is called an "elementary path". Finally, a "circuit" is a path for which the first pole (pole of origin) coincides with the last one (pole of destination). In Figure III.2 below the path (i,x,y,j) is an elementary path while path (x,y,z,x) is a circuit.

The concept of influence can be given three different quantitative interpretations, namely, (1) direct influence, (2) total influence, and (3) global influence which are discussed below.

1. Direct influence

The direct influence of i on j transmitted through an elementary path is the change in income (or production) of j induced by a unitary change in i, the income (or the production) of all other poles except those along the selected elementary path remaining constant. The direct influence can be measured, respectively, along an arc or an elementary path as follows,

(a) Case of direct influence of i on j along arc (i,j)

$$I^D_{(i \to j)} = c_{ji}, \qquad (3.1)$$

where c_{ji} is the (j,i)th element of the matrix of marginal expenditure propensities C_n. Matrix C_n can therefore be called the matrix of direct influences--it being understood that the direct influence is measured along arc (i,j).

(b) Case of direct influence along an elementary path (i,...,j). The direct influence transmitted from a pole i to a pole j along a given elementary path is equal to the product of the intensities of the arcs constituting the path. Thus,

$$I^D_{(i...j)} = c_{jn} \cdots c_{mi}. \qquad (3.2)$$

For example, Figure III.1 below represents a given elementary path, $p = (1,x,y,j)$[20]

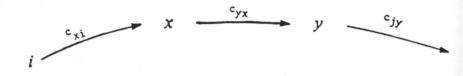

Figure III.1. Elementary path

and

72

$$I^D_{(i \to j)_p} = I^D_{(i,x,y,j)} = c_{xi}c_{yx}c_{jy}. \qquad (3.3)$$

2. Total influence

In most structures, there exists a multitude of interactions among poles. In particular, poles along any elementary path are likely to be linked to other poles and other paths forming circuits which amplify in a complex way, the direct influence of that same elementary path. To capture these indirect effects, the concept of total influence was introduced.

Given an elementary path $p = (i,...,j)$ with origin i and destination j, the total influence is the influence transmitted from i to j along the elementary path p including all indirect effects within the structure imputable to that path. Thus, total influence cumulates, for a given elementary path p, the direct influence transmitted along the latter and the indirect effects induced by the circuits adjacent to that same path (i.e. these circuits which have one or more poles in common with path p). Figure III.2 reproduces the same elementary path $p = (i,x,y,j)$ appearing in Figure III.1 and in addition incorporated explicitly all circuits adjacent to it.

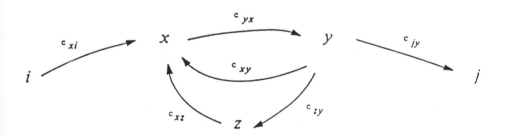

Figure III.2. Elementary path including adjacent circuits

It can readily be seen that between poles i and y the direct influence is $c_{xi}c_{yx}$ which is then transmitted back from y to x via the two loops yielding an effect $(c_{xi}c_{xy})(c_{xy}+c_{zy}c_{xz})$ which in turn has to be transmitted back from x to y. This process yields a series of dampened impulses between x and y

$$c_{xi}c_{yx}\left\{ 1 + c_{yx}(c_{xy} + c_{zy}c_{xz}) + [c_{yx}(c_{xy} + c_{zy}c_{xz})]^2 + ... \right\}$$

$$= c_{xi}c_{yx} [I-c_{yx}(c_{xy}+c_{zy}c_{xz})]^{-1} \qquad (3.4)$$

To complete the transmission of influence along the above elementary path p the above effects have to travel along the last arc (y,j) so that the above effects have to be multiplied by c_{jy} to obtain the total influence along this path,

$$I^T_{(i \to j)_p} = c_{xi}c_{yx}c_{jy}[1-c_{yx}(c_{xy}+c_{zy}c_{xz})]^{-1} \qquad (3.5)$$

It can readily be seen that the first term on the right-hand side represents the previously defined direct influence, $I^D_{(i \to j_p)}$ and the second term is the path multiplier M_p, i.e.

$$I^T_{(i \to j)_p} = I^D_{(i \to j)_p}M_p. \qquad (3.6)$$

M_p captures the extent to which the direct influence along path p is amplified through the effects of adjacent feedback circuits.[21]

3. Global influence

Global influence, in contrast with direct and total influences, does not refer to topology, namely, the specific paths followed in the transmission of influence. Global influence from pole i to pole j simply measures the total effects on income or output of pole j consequent to an injection of one unit of output or income in pole i.

The global influence is captured by the reduced form of the SAM model derived previously

$$dy_n = (I-C_n)^{-1} \ dx = M_c dx \qquad (3.7) = (2.5)$$

Let $m_{c\ ji}$ be the (j,i)th element of the matrix of fixed price multipliers M_c then, as was seen previously, it captures the full effects of an exogenous injection dx_i on the endogenous variable dy_j. Hence

$$I^G_{(i \to j)} = m_{cji},$$

and matrix $M_c = (I-C_n)^{-1}$ can be called the matrix of global influences.

It is important to understand clearly the distinction between global influence and direct influence. The latter is linked to a particular elementary path which is entirely isolated from the rest of the structure (i.e. assuming ceteris paribus). It captures what could be called the immediate effect of an impulse following this particular path. Global influence, in contrast, differs from direct influence for two fundamental reasons:

74

(a) It captures the direct influence transmitted by all elementary paths linking (spanning) the two poles under consideration. Indeed, given two poles i and j, the effects of an injection affecting the output or income of i on the output or income of j manifest themselves through the intermediary of all paths with origin i and destination j. The direct influence, transmitted by pole i to pole j along different elementary paths with the same origin and destination, is equal to the sum of the direct influences transmitted along each elementary path.

(b) In addition, these paths are not considered in isolation but as an integral part of the structure from which they were separated to calculate the direct influence. Hence, global influence cumulates all induced and feedback effects resulting from the existence of circuits in the graph and is equal to the sum of the total influences of all elementary paths spanning pole i and pole j (see. eq. 3.10).

An example should clarify this point. Figure III.3 reproduces the elementary path and adjacent circuits explored in Figure III.2 and adds two other elementary paths with the same origin i and destination j, i.e. (i,s,j) and (i,v,j).

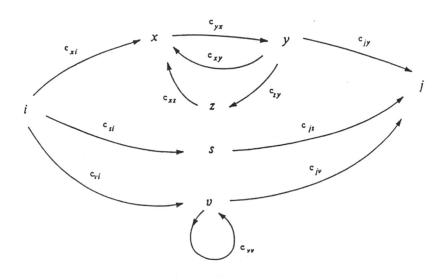

Figure III.3. Network of elementary paths and adjacent circuits linking poles i and j.

In the above example, it is clear that path (i,s,j) is an elementary path without any adjacent circuit while path (i,v,j) contains one loop centered on v. For simplicity, we can refer to these last two paths as 2 and 3, respectively--the initial path being referred to as 1.

$$\overset{G}{I}(i{\to}j) = m_{cji} = \overset{T}{I}(i,x,y,j) + \overset{T}{I}(i,s,j) + \overset{T}{I}(i,v,j)$$

$$= \overset{T}{I}(i{\to}j)_1 + \overset{T}{I}(i{\to}j)_2 + \overset{T}{I}(i{\to}j)_3 \qquad (3.9)$$

$$= \overset{D}{I}(i{\to}j)_1 \, M_1 + c_{si}c_{js} + (c_{vi}c_{jv}) \, (I-c_{vv})^{-1}$$

$$= \overset{D}{I}(i{\to}j)_1 \, M_1 + \overset{D}{I}(i{\to}j)_2 + \overset{D}{I}(i{\to}j)_3 \, M_3$$

Note that in the case of the second path, the multiplier is one since the path has no adjacent circuits. Thus, in general, the global influence linking any two poles of a structure can be decomposed into a series of total influences transmitted along each and all elementary paths spanning i and j, i.e.

$$\overset{G}{I}(i{\to}j) = m_{cji} = \sum_{p=1}^{n} \overset{T}{I}(i{\to}j)_p = \sum_{p=1}^{n} \overset{D}{I}(i{\to}j)_p \, M_p, \qquad (3.10)$$

where p stands for elementary paths $1,2,k,\ldots,n$.

H. Structural path analysis applied to Indonesian SAM-Tech

In this section structural path analysis is used to analyse the effects of changes in output of the selected twelve dualistic product-cum-technologies on the whole economic system (structure) as represented by the Indonesian SAM-Tech. Because of some of the guesstimates which had to be made in building SAM-Tech and deriving the fixed price multipliers (in particular, the marginal expenditure propensities to consume production activities by the different household groups) this application should be considered more as a demonstration exercise yielding not only the approximate order of magnitude of quantitative effects but also, just as importantly, the whole network of paths through which the impact of a change in output in any of our twelve activities is propagated to the whole Indonesian SAM structure.

In Table III.6, thirteen selected examples are presented. They have in common that in each instance the pole of origin (i.e. the pole through which the exogenous injection enters the structure)

Table III.6: Structural Path Analysis: Global Influence, Direct Influence and total Influence for Selected Paths Involving Dualistic Activities, Indonesian SAM-TECH.

	(1) Path Origin (i)	(2) Path Destination (j)	(3) Global Influence $I^G_{(i \to j)} = m_{ji}$	(4) Elementary Paths $(i \to j)_p$	(5) Direct Influence $I^D_{(i \to *)p}$	(6) Path Multiplier M_p	(7) Total Influence $I^T_{(i \to j)p}$	(8) $\dfrac{I^T_{(i \to j)p}}{I^G_{(i \to j)}}$ (in %)
						= M_p x		
			A. Effects of Production Activities on Factors					
Ia	Hand Pounded Rice (HPR)	Agricultural Unpaid Rural Labor (AUR)	0.624	HPR-Farm Food Crops-AUR HPR-AUR	0.275 0.141	1.522 1.271	0.418 0.180	67.0 28.8
Ib	Rice Milling (RM)	Agricultural Unpaid Rural Labor (AUR)	0.437	RM-Farm Food Crops-AUR	0.241	1.579	0.381	87.2
IIa	Farm Processed Tea (FPT)	Agricultural Unpaid Rural Labor (AUR)	0.401	FPT-AUR FPT-Farm Non-Food Crops-AUR	0.221 0.021	1.220 1.502	0.270 0.031	67.3 7.7
IIb	Processed Tea (PT)	Agricultural Unpaid Rural Labor (AUR)	0.168	PT-Farm Non-Food Crops-AUR	0.033	1.501	0.050	29.8
			B. Effects of Production Activities on Household Groups					
IIIa	Hand Pounded Rice (HPR)	Agricultural Employees (AE)	0.220	HPR-Farm Food Crops-Agr Paid Rural-AE HPR-Agr Paid Rural-AE HPR-Farm Food Crops-Land-AE HPR-Farm Food Crops-Agr Unpaid Rural-AE	0.062 0.041 0.006 0.004	1.565 1.256 1.695 1.582	0.097 0.052 0.010 0.007	44.1 23.6 4.5 3.2
IIIb	Rice Milling (RM)	Agricultural Employees (AE)	0.176	RM-Farm Food Crops-Agr Paid Rural-AE RM-Uninc Rural Cap-AE RM-Farm Food Crops-Land-AE RM-Farm Food Crops-Agr Unpaid Rural-AE	0.054 0.011 0.005 0.004	1.601 1.338 1.731 1.635	0.087 0.015 0.009 0.006	49.4 8.5 5.1 3.4
IVa	Canning & Preserving of Fruits & Vegetables (T) (CPFV)	Rural Lower (RL)	0.315	CPFV(T)-Prod Paid Rural-RL CPFV(T)-Uninc Rural Cap-RL CPFV(T)-Prod Urban Rural-RL CPFV(T)-Clerical Unpaid Rural-RL	0.093 0.022 0.016 0.008	1.213 1.257 1.220 1.214	0.113 0.027 0.020 0.010	35.9 8.6 6.3 3.2
IVb	Canning & Preserving of Fruits & Vegetables (M) (CPFV)	Rural Lower (RL)	0.236	CPFV(M)-Prod Paid Rural-RL CPFV(M)-Uninc Rural Cap-RL CPFV(M)-Trade-Clerical Unpaid Rural-RL CPFV(M)-Farm Food Crops-Land-RL	0.039 0.011 0.009 0.005	1.213 1.257 1.249 1.792	0.047 0.014 0.012 0.009	19.9 5.9 5.1 5.8

Table III.6 (cont.)

	(1) Path Origin (i)	(2) Path Destination (j)	(3) Global Influence $I_{(i\to j)}^G = m_{ji}$	(4) Elementary Paths $(i\to j)_p$	(5) Direct Influence $I_{(i\to j)_p}^D$	(6) Path Multiplier M_p	(7) Total Influence $I_{(i\to j)_p}^T$	(8) $\dfrac{I_{(i\to j)_p}^T}{I_{(i\to j)}^G}$ (in %)
Va	Brown Sugar (BS)	Farm Size 1 (F1)	0.342	BS-Uninc Rural Cap-F1	0.067	1.352	0.091	26.6
				BS-Farm Non-Food Crops-Land-F1	0.025	1.807	0.045	13.2
				BS-Farm Non-Food Crops-Agr Unpaid Rural-F1	0.011	1.685	0.018	5.3
				BS-Prod Unpaid Rural-F1	0.012	1.306	0.016	4.7
				BS-Farm Non-Food Crops-Agr Paid Rural-F1	0.009	1.640	0.014	4.1
				BS-Prod Paid Rural-F1	0.007	1.321	0.010	2.9
Vb	Refined Sugar (RS)	Farm Size 1 (F1)	0.205	RS-Uninc Rural Cap-F1	0.024	1.364	0.033	16.1
				RS-Farm Non-Food Crops-Land-F1	0.012	1.821	0.021	10.2
				RS-Farm Non-Food Crops-Agr Unpaid Rural-F1	0.005	1.699	0.009	4.4
				RS-Prod Paid Rural-F1	0.006	1.333	0.008	3.9
				RS-Prod Unpaid Rural-F1	0.006	1.319	0.008	3.9
				RS-Farm Non-Food Crops-Agr Paid Rural-F1	0.004	1.654	0.007	3.4
VIa	Brown Sugar (BS)	Farm Size 3 (F3)	0.391	BS-Farm Non-Food Crops-Land-F3	0.083	1.661	0.137	35.0
				BS-Uninc Rural Cap-F3	0.025	1.306	0.033	8.4
				BS-Farm Non-Food Crops-Agr Unpaid Rural-F3	0.008	1.679	0.014	3.6
VIb	Refined Sugar (RS)	Farm Size 3 (F3)	0.239	RS-Farm Non-Food Crops-Land-F3	0.039	1.674	0.065	27.2
				RS-Uninc Rural Cap-F3	0.009	1.318	0.012	5.0
				RS-Farm Non-Food Crops-Agr Unpaid Rural-F3	0.004	1.693	0.007	2.9
VIIa	Hand Pounded Rice (HPR)	Farm Size 3 (F3)	0.575	HPR-Farm Food Crops-Land-F3	0.169	1.666	0.281	48.9
				HPR-Farm Food Crops-Agr Unpaid Rural-F3	0.083	1.613	0.134	23.3
				HPR-Agr Unpaid Rural-F3	0.043	1.418	0.061	10.6
VIIb	Rice Milling (RM)	Farm Size 3 (F3)	0.489	RM-Farm Food Crops-Land-F3	0.148	1.709	0.253	51.7
				RM-Farm Food Crops-Agr Unpaid Rural-F3	0.073	1.671	0.122	24.9

Table III.6 (cont.)

(1)	(2)	(3)	(4)	(5)	(6)	(7)	(8)
Path Origin	Path Destination	Global Influence	Elementary Paths	Direct Influence	Path Multiplier	Total Influence	$\frac{I^T_{(i \to j)_p}}{I^G_{(i \to j)}}$
(i)	(j)	$I^G_{(i \to j)} = m_{ji}$	$(i \to j)_p$	$I^D_{(i \to j)_p}$	M_p	$= I^T_{(i \to j)_p}$	(in %)
					$\times$	$=$	
		C. Effects of Production Activities on Other Production Activities					
VIIIa Hand Pounded Rice (HPR)	Farm Food Crops (FFC)	1.261	HPR-FFC	0.783	1.495	1.171	92.7
VIIIb Rice Milling (RM)	Farm Food Crops (FFC)	1.136	RM-FFC	0.686	1.533	1.052	92.6
IXa Farm Processed Tea (FPT)	Farm Food Crops (FFC)	0.357	FPT-Agr Unpaid Rural-Farm Size 1-FFC	0.012	1.621	0.019	5.3
			FPT-Agr Paid Rural-Agr Employees-FFC	0.012	1.549	0.018	5.0
IXb Processed Tea (PT)	Farm Food Crops (FFC)	0.292	PT-Farm Non-Food Crops-Land-Farm Size 3-FFC	0.006	1.972	0.012	4.1
			PT-Farm Non-Food Crops-Land-Farm Size 1-FFC	0.004	2.039	0.008	2.7
			PT-Farm Non-Food Crops-Land-Farm Size 2-FFC	0.004	1.882	0.008	2.7
Xa Farm Processed Tea (FPT)	Farm Non-Food Crops (FNFC)	0.419	FPT-FNFC	0.294	1.257	0.370	88.3
Xb Processed Tea (PT)	Farm Non-Food Crops (FNFC)	0.621	PT-FNFC	0.475	1.254	0.595	95.8
XIa Brown Sugar (BS)	Farm Food Crops (FFC)	0.426	BS-Uninc Rural Cap-Rural Lower-FFC	0.013	1.720	0.022	5.2
			BS-Uninc Rural Cap-Farm Size 1-FFC	0.009	1.680	0.016	3.8
XIb Refined Sugar (RS)	Farm Food Crops (FFC)	0.291	BS-FFC	0.009	1.496	0.013	4.5
			BS-Uninc Rural Cap-Rural Lower-FFC	0.005	1.731	0.008	2.7
XIIa Brown Sugar (BS)	Farm Non-Food Crops (FNFC)	0.553	BS-FNFC	0.398	1.262	0.502	90.8
XIIb Refined Sugar (RS)	Farm Non-Food Crops (FNFC)	0.278	BS-FNFC	0.186	1.275	0.237	85.3
XIIIa Clove Cigarette (CC)	Farm Non-Food Crops (FNFC)	0.436	CC-FNFC	0.305	1.273	0.389	89.2
			CC-Other Food, Beverage & Tobacco-FNFC	0.020	1.557	0.031	7.1
XIIIb White Cigarette (WC)	Farm Non-Food Crops (FNFC)	0.159	WC-FNFC	0.100	1.260	0.126	79.2
			WC-Other Food, Beverage & Tobacco-FNFC	0.006	1.545	0.010	6.3

is one of the twelve dualistic product-cum-technology activities.

Before exploring these paths, it should be noted that the triangular interrelationship of the endogenous structure of the SAM means that an elementary path must always travel in the triangular direction as shown on Figure II.1. Since in all of the examples selected here the injection occurs in a production activity, all elementary paths originating with that activity would affect, first, other production activities (through the induced demand for intermediate inputs represented by the I-O matrix A_{33}) and factor demand (through the distribution of the value added among factors, i.e. matrix A_{13}) before the influence is transmitted to institutions (in particular, the different household groups) through matrix A_{21}. Next in this sequence, transfers among institutions would be captured through A_{22} before the final link back to production activities (reflecting the consumption pattern of institutions, i.e. C_{32}) can take place.

All the thirteen cases which are analysed in Table III.6 follow the same methodology. Each case, 1) takes a given pole of origin (i) and destination (j) and measures the corresponding global influence; 2) identifies the more important elementary paths spanning these two poles and measures the direct and total influences, respectively; and 3) gives the proportion of global influence between i and j transmitted through each specific path p.

Since the main purpose of the exercise is to examine the differential macroeconomic effects of a change in the output of a modern as opposed to the corresponding traditional technological alternative, each case entails a pairwise comparison for a given product of the two technologies. Thus, in each of the thirteen cases which are explored, the pole of origin consists of a given pair of product-cum-technologies while the poles of destination consist of selected other production activities, factors, and socioeconomic household groups. Thereby, the differential effects of e.g. handpounded rice as compared to rice milling on selected factors of production, different household groups, and other production activities can be ascertained quantitatively and, more importantly, the various paths through which influence is transmitted can be identified explicitly.

Before exploring a few specific cases in more detail, one interesting generalisation revealed by Table III.6 (col. 3) is that the global influence (i.e. the fixed price multiplier) in each of the thirteen pairwise comparisons is higher when the injection occurs in the traditional technology.

Since it would be rather tedious and somewhat repetitive to go through each one of the thirteen cases in detail, two of them are selected as typical examples and scrutinised next. The reader, of course, is encouraged to go through the other cases to see the common pattern which appears to prevail.

The two prototype cases analyse in detail below the effects of a change in the output of a) handpounded vs. milled rice, respectively, on the income of household group consisting of agricultural employees (case IIIa and IIIb) and b) brown sugar vs. refined sugar, respectively, on the income of the household group headed by small farmers (case Va and Vb). The most important paths through which influence is transmitted (i.e. those paths carrying at least 2.5% of the global influence) are shown explicitly in Table III.6. Furthermore, the corresponding networks of paths are presented graphically for the two selected cases in Figures III.4 and III.5. These diagrams illustrate clearly the nature of path analysis and should be consulted in the analysis which follows.

Case IIIa in Table III.6 explores the structural path analysis from an injection into the handpounded rice activity (as pole of origin) to its ultimate effects on the household group of agricultural employees (the pole of destination). From the matrix of fixed price multipliers, the global influence can be obtained-- i.e. an increment of 100 Rupiahs into that activity yields an increase of 22 Rupiah in the income of agricultural employees (see col. 3 of Table III.6). The path analysis in col. 8 reveals that 44.1% of the additional income accruing to agricultural employees follows a path consisting of three consecutive arcs from handpounded rice to farm food crops (reflecting mainly the intermediate demand for paddy), to income accruing to the labour group "agricultural paid rural workers" involved in paddy production to its ultimate destination, i.e. income of household group headed by agricultural employees.

The second path (consisting of two consecutive arcs) through which 23.6% of the global influence is transmitted goes from handpounded rice to payments to agricultural paid rural workers to agricultural employees. The other two elementary paths shown in Case III.a reveal that a small part of the global influence goes from handpounded rice to farm food crops (paddy) to land rent to agricultural employees. This last arc represents the imputed land rent value of the paddy produced on marginal plots of land belonging to agricultural employees, implying that the latter are not necessarily totally landless. The final elementary path links handpounded rice to farm food crops (paddy) to Agricultural Unpaid Rural workers to Agricultural Employees. This path represents the imputed income--presumably in the form of rice--received by agricultural employees' households as a compensation for their (unpaid) labour in the production of paddy which, in turn, went into the initial increase in the output of handpounded rice.

The above four paths appear in Figure III.4, where they are numbered, from one to four, respectively. It can be noticed by looking at that diagram that path 1, 3 and 4 all use the same first arc from handpounded rice to farm food crops. It should also be noted in interpreting the diagram that next to the origin of each arc the corresponding marginal expenditure propensity (c_{ji}) is specifically indicated. Likewise, the product of two or more consecutive arcs along any elementary path (i.e. the direct

Figure III.4: Structural Network Illustrating Effects of Handpounded Rice and Milled Rice, Respectively, on Income of Agricultural Employees.

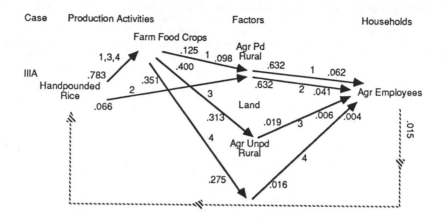

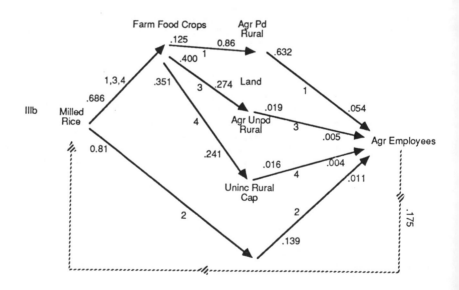

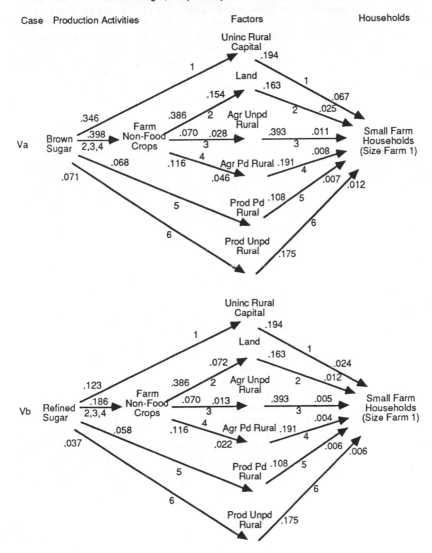

Figure III.5: Structural Network Illustrating Effects of Brown Sugar and Refined Sugar, Respectively, on Small Farmers' Income

influence) is also given at the end of each relevant arc. Thus for example, path 1 in Figure III.4.a shows that the marginal expenditure propensity from handpounded rice to farm food crops amounts to .783. In turn, the MEP from farm food crops to agricultural paid rural labour amounts to .125 with the product of these last two MEPs equalling .098. Finally, the MEP from agricultural paid rural labour which goes to agricultural employees as income is .632 yielding a direct influence along path 1 of .062.[22] Perhaps a simpler way of expressing the above relationship is to ask the following question -- What is the magnitude of the direct influence from handpounded rice to agricultural employees travelling along path 1? This direct influence as has been shown previously would be equal to the product of the relevant MEPs i.e. an increase of 100 Rupiahs in the production of handpounded rice would yield 78.3 additional Rupiahs of farm food crops output (mainly paddy production), 9.8 additional Rupiahs earned by agricultural paid rural labour (78.3 Rupiahs X .125 = 9.8 Rupiahs). Finally, the household group of agricultural employees would receive 6.2 Rupiahs of the initial injection of 100 Rupiahs into handpounded rice (in other words, 9.8 Rupiahs X .632 = 6.2 Rupiahs).

A few additional observations should be made about the diagram in Figure III.4.a. First, it shows clearly the other three paths described previously. Secondly, the direct influence transmitted through path 1, or any of the other three paths shown in the figure, is amplified through the effects of adjacent feedback circuits. The magnitude of these feedback circuits is given by the path multiplier M_p. As was seen in equation 3.6 the product of the direct influence and the corresponding path multiplier yields the total influence which is transmitted along that particular path. It would have been practically impossible to draw all of the adjacent circuits and feedbacks systems in this or for that matter, the other diagrams appearing in Figures III.4 and III.5. Just one feedback is shown explicitly (in broken line), i.e. the induced consumption of handpounded rice by agricultural employees' households. (The corresponding MEP amounts to .015.) If this were the only feedback then the corresponding path multiplier (which would apply to all four paths) would be equal to 1/(1-.015)=1.015. Thirdly, the four paths appearing on Figure III.4.a account together for 75.4% of the global influence (see Col. 8 of Table III.6). This means that a multitude of paths not explicitly shown, because each transmits only a small part of the global influence between the poles of origin and destination, account together for almost one-fourth of the global influence.

Case III.b takes milled rice as the pole of origin and agricultural employees as the pole of destination. It can be seen from both Table III.6 and Figure III.4.b that the transmission of influence follows many of the same paths as in the case of the traditional technology (handpounded rice). More specifically, paths 1, 3 and 4 are similar in the two instances (i.e. they go through the same poles)--the only difference consisting of the higher intensity of the first common arc of these paths linking handpounded rice and farm food crops (the MPE amounting to .783) compared to the corresponding link between milled rice and farm food crops (MPE = .686). This indicates, of course, that the traditional technology requires relatively more paddy inputs per unit of output than the corresponding modern technology. In other words, the linkage of the former product-cum-activity to paddy production is greater than the latter which, in contrast, requires more nonagricultural intermediate inputs per unit of output. The only two paths which differ in Case III.b as compared to III.a are i) the path going from handpounded rice to agricultural paid rural labour to agricultural employees (denoted as path 2 in Figure III.4.a). and ii) the path linking milled rice to unincorporated rural capital to agricultural employees (i.e. path 2 in Figure III.4.b).

A final point worth noting with regard to the structural network of influence spanning milled rice and agricultural employees relates to the much larger intensity of the feedback from agricultural employees to milled rice, i.e. the marginal propensity to consume of the latter for milled rice amounting to .175. If this were the only feedback in the above structure (which it isn't) the corresponding path multiplier for all four paths appearing in III.b would be equal to 1/(1-.175)=1.212.

In summary, the higher global influence (fixed price multiplier) of handpounded rice vis-a-vis, agricultural employees compared to rice milling vis-a-vis agricultural employees, i.e. .22 as opposed to .176, is to a large extent attributable to the greater backward linkages between handpounded rice and farm food crops as compared to milled rice and farm food crops.

The last prototype example entails a comparison between the effects of a change in the production of brown sugar and refined sugar, respectively, on the incomes of the household group consisting of small farmers (farmers owning or operating less than half a hectare). Here again, the network through which influence is transmitted can be seen clearly by looking at Figure III.5 and Table III.6. Thus, in contrast with the preceding case, the traditional and modern technologies affect the economic system through the same set of six paths.

Comparing the global influence of traditional vs. modern sugar production, it can be seen that the former is substantially higher than the latter (.342 vs. .205, see col. 3, Table III.6). Describing, first, the transmissions of influence by the traditional technology, the most important path (denoted as path 1 in Figure III.5.a) is that linking brown sugar to unincorporated rural capital which represents that part of value added from brown sugar production which accrues as profits to the small farmers engaged in this activity. As can be seen from col. 8 of Table III.6, 26.6% of the global influence of traditional sugar on small farmers income travels along this first path. Paths 2, 3 and 4 have the first arc in common which constitutes the backward linkages to farm nonfood crops (i.e. to purchase respectively, palm sugar and sugar cane) before splitting up via, respectively, land, agricultural paid and unpaid rural labour before converging on small farm households. The other two paths (5 and 6) represent payments to, respectively, paid and unpaid production workers in the rural areas involved directly in the actual processing and preparation of brown sugar--a part of which labour income accrues ultimately to small farm households.

The major difference between the two influence graphs (see Figure III.5) consists of the considerably smaller backward linkages to sugar cane (which in our SAM classification comes under farm nonfood crops) of the modern technological alternative (refined sugar) compared to the traditional one (brown sugar) which is made out of palm sugar. More specifically, this link (which paths 2-4 have in common) displays marginal expenditure propensity of .398 in the traditional brown sugar case and only .186 in the case of refined sugar. Likewise the linkages to the factors of production i.e. unincorporated rural capital, and the two labour groups of paid and unpaid production workers in the rural areas were significantly higher for brown than for refined sugar.

Notes

1 See C.P. Timmer's study of "Choice of Techniques in Rice Milling on Java", Bulletin of Indonesian Economic Studies, July 1973, where isoquants are derived for five different techniques ranging from handpounding to large capital intensive mills, is an important contribution to the microeconomic literature on choice of techniques. However, in this section we concentrate exclusively on macroeconomic or sectoral studies.

2 One important exception is the work by Douglas S. Paauw, "From Colonial to Guided Economy," in Ruth T. McVey (Ed.) Indonesia, New Haven: Human Relations Area File Press, 1963.

3 See Anne Booth and Peter McCawley, "The Indonesian Economy in the Mid-Sixties," in Anne Booth and Peter McCawley, (eds.), The Indonesian Economy During the Soeharto Era, Kuala Lampur, Oxford University Press, 1981, p. 1.

4 See for example various issues of BIES including other references in this study; Peter McCawley, "The Growth of the Industrial Sector", in Anne Booth and Peter McCawley, Eds., The Indonesian Economy During the Soeharto Era, Oxford University Press, Oxford, 1981; H. Poot, "The Development of Labour Intensive Industries in Indonesia", in Rashid Amjad, (Ed.), The Development of Labour Intensive Industry in ASEAN Countries, ARTEP, Bangkok, 1978.

5 Douglas S. Paauw, Export Promotion and Employment Creation During REPELITA IV, Working Paper, Employment and Income Distribution Strategy Project, ILO/ Dept. of Manpower, Government of Indonesia, Jakarta, 1984; Stan Stavenuiter, The Employment Effects of Indonesia's 1982/83 Development Budget Working Paper, Employment and Income Distribution Strategy Project, Jakarta, 1984.

6 Actually total amount of employment is calculated according to the following formula:

$$L = \ell[I -(I-M)A]^{-1}f$$

where
L = total employment (direct and indirect)
ℓ = A diagonal matrix of each sector's labour input per unit of output
f = final demand vector
$[I - (I-M)A]^{-1}$ = The Leontief inverse matrix adjusted for import effects (M). It is not clear from the ILO study (Appendix A) whether M consists only of imported intermediate inputs or includes final demand for imports as well.

7 Stavenuiter, op.cit., p. 5.

8 Netherlands Economic Institute, "Industrial Development in Indonesia, Selected Prospects and Options,", Rotterdam, 1983; Netherlands Economic Institute, Structural Analysis of the Indonesian Manufacturing Sector, 1983.

9 Netherlands Economic Institute, MANKAP Project: Final Report, 1983, 1984. Arie Kuyvenhoven and Huib Pot, Industrial Development in Indonesia--Analysis and Options.

10 H. Poot, "The Development of Labour Intensive Industries in Indonesia," in Rashid Amjad (Ed.) The Development of Labour Intensive Industry in ASEAN Countries, Asian Employment Programme, International Labour Organisation, 1981.

11 Even though it was not possible to obtain an accurate estimate of the share of total sugar output and value added in 1980 accounted for by brown sugar (the traditional technology) as opposed to refined sugar, there is strong evidence that the latter had become relatively much more important by 1980 as is indicated subsequently in the text.

12 L. Mears, The New Rice Economy of Indonesia, Gadjah Madah University Press, 1981.

13 Mears also refers to a study by a team from the Agricultural University at Bogor which reports that even as early as 1974, the share of handpounded rice amounted to only 17% of the total.

14 In conversations with experts, however, it was pointed out that large numbers of people are often employed in making Kreteks by traditional technology. The authors would like to acknowledge their debt to Mr. Vikram Nehru of the World Bank on this point.

15 It is interesting to note that clove cigarettes are not only increasingly popular in Indonesia but also in the industrialised Western world particularly among the young.

16 Even though clove cigarettes required slightly less energy per unit of output than white cigarettes (the average expenditure propensity on energy being .009 and .011, respectively, as shown on Table II.2), the greater linkages of clove cigarettes production to primary inputs (reflected by higher multiplier values) account for higher direct and indirect energy requirements of the latter compared to white cigarettes output. For more detail, see Chapter IV.

17 This needs to be qualified since agriculture and quarrying are labour-intensive but most mining is not.

18 The corresponding multiplier values for farm processed tea and processed tea vis-a-vis the above two labour skill groups were .254 vs. .120 and .401 vs. .168, respectively.

19 The brief review of structural path analysis which follows draws heavily on J. Defourny and E. Thorbecke, "Structural Path Analysis and Multiplier Decomposition within a Social Accounting Matrix Framework," The Economic Journal, 94, March 1984, pp. 111-136 which should be consulted for more detail.

20 As will be seen subsequently, a multitude of different elementary paths may go from i to j. In any case, a number of examples of elementary paths and, more generally, of the whole network of paths applied to the Indonesian SAM are presented in the next section. Hopefully these concrete examples will bring some added realism to these concepts.

21 For a formal derivation of M_p, see Appendix in Defourny-Thorbecke, op.cit.

22 I.e. the product of the three consecutive arcs of this path equals (.783 X .125 X .632 = .062).

IV Macroeconomic and SAM analysis of the energy sector in Indonesia

Introduction

The Republic of Indonesia is fortunate to have abundant energy
sources. Apart from the most well-known and exploited source,
i.e. petroleum, the country is richly endowed with natural gas,
coal, and biomass. It also has hydroelectric and geothermal
potential. We hasten to add that only oil and gas have been
extensively explored and exploited. The other energy sources are
either in early stages of exploitation, as in the case of coal or
biomass, or are being explored slowly (e.g. geothermal resources).
Nevertheless, the Indonesian economy in the 1980s faces challenges
in energy planning from at least two directions. Both the fluctuations in oil prices and the growth in domestic demand for
energy tend to make any strategy for development based on oil an
increasingly precarious proposition. The growth in domestic
demand may actually turn Indonesia into an energy-importing country by the year 2000 (World Bank/UNDP, 1981). There are, however,
good prospects for diversification and increase of energy supply.
Furthermore, domestic pricing policy of energy could be altered to
ration the existing supply.[1]

Given the manifest importance of the energy sector in the Indonesian economy, a detailed analysis of this sector from a technological perspective is critical. This chapter attempts such an
analysis mainly within the previous SAM framework, but it also
utilises much additional and detailed information from other
sources as well. Using the information in the 1975 SAM, the
energy sector is disaggregated along the lines described later in
the chapter.

In addition to the SAM, time-series information on the oil
sector, balance of payments data and government budgetary statistics are used to address the following macroeconomic issues:

1) The role of the petroleum and natural gas sector in the Indonesian economy. More specifically, the balance of payments effects of a change in demand for or in the price of petroleum in the world market are investigated for the decade of the 70's and beyond.

2) The consequences of the above for the government budget are analysed.

3) The relationship between labour-intensity and energy-intensity of the technologies for the dualistic sectors is explored. According to the labour-energy intensity hypothesis, some labour-intensive techniques also turn out to be energy-intensive (Keddie and Cleghorn, 1980; Khan, 1985). Here this hypothesis is examined for the dualistic sectors.

4) The overall income distributional impact of the energy sector and, in particular, the impact of a decline in petroleum exports and revenues on incomes received by households is investigated.

5) In a similar fashion, the impact of a change in incomes of the various household groups on their energy consumption is also investigated.

The large and complex role of the energy sector in Indonesia has been studied by several international and national bodies.[2] Still the link between technology, on the one hand, and energy and income distribution on the other, remains largely unexplored. While we do not claim, of course, to have the final word on the subject, the present approach tries to look at the above link in a systematic fashion.

This chapter is subdivided into two sections. Section A is a macroeconomic analysis of the role of the energy sector with respect to the balance of payments and the government budget (issues 1 and 2 above). Section B deals with the remaining macroeconomic issues including the question of the energy-content of technologies within a SAM framework. The appendix at the end of the chapter will provide the interested reader with a discussion of production, consumption and reserves of energy in Indonesia.

A. Macroeconomic analysis: energy, balance of payments and government revenue

In Indonesia oil, natural gas and coal are the most exploited energy sources, with oil playing the leading role. (For a detailed discussion, see appendix.) Accordingly, most of the emphasis in this section is on oil, even though it has to be recognised that natural gas production is increasing very rapidly.

Export of crude oil by Indonesia rose from 56% of total production in 1961 to 82% in 1976.[3] Since that time the ratio of exports to total output has fallen so that in 1982 exports were only 66 percent of total production. Increase in export price index of crude in the 1970s is shown in Table IV.1 Further in- creases took place in the world oil price in the late seventies and early 80s. Starting in 1982/83, however, the trend seems to be reversing. Of course, exports by themselves have little meaning. We need to know the amount of foreign exchange that the petroleum industry actually brings into the economy. This can be done by borrowing the concept of "retained values" for an industry from the literature on the primary export sectors.[4]

Table IV.1

Export Price Index of Crude Export, 1967-1983[*]
(in U.S. $)

Year	Average Price (f.o.b.) per barrel	Index
1967	1.62	100
1968	1.62	100
1969	1.62	100
1970	1.62	100
1971	2.38	144
1972	2.73	169
1973	4.41	272
1974	12.08	746
1975	12.38	771
1976	12.49	775
1977	12.40	932
1978	12.70	955
1979	17.26	1298
1980	28.67	2155
1981	32.50	2444
1982	33.47	2517
1983	29.31	2204

[*]Prices for 1977-83 are for Saudi Arabian Crude. The high grade Indonesian crude oil has a premium, but can be expected to move in tandem with the Saudi Arabian crude.
Sources: 1967-1976, Sritua Arief, "The Indonesian Petroleum Industry: A Study of Its Impact on the Indonesian Economy, Ph.D. Dissertation, 1979, University of Hull, United Kingdom, p. 104. Base year, 1967 = 100; 1977-1983, International Monetary Fund, International Financial Statistics, 1984, pp. 504-5. Base year, 1967 = 100 (for Saudia Arabian crude).

Subtracting all foreign payments incurred to support the extrac- tion of oil and its shipment from the receipts gives us the "re- tained value of petroleum exports". More explicitly, Retained Value of Petroleum Exports = Value of Gross Output - Production Costs in Foreign Exchange (incurred by foreign companies +

Pertamina) - Factor Payments Abroad - Foreign Exchange Costs related to the domestic consumption of oil products - Foreign Exchange Expenditures by Pertamina for other than its direct Petroleum Production, Refining and Marketing operations.

Table IV.2 gives the retained values for petroleum exports (including petroleum products) for 1970 to 1980. Over the decade the retained value has more than tripled, though there are some year-to-year fluctuations. It should also be noted that the increase slowed down after an actual decline in 1977. With oil price decreases in the 1980s the retained value is likely to stabilise or even decline.

Oil's special position in the Indonesian economy is quite clear. It was the first oil boom in 1973-74 that permitted the unforeseen increase in government expenditure. Then, in 1976 and 1977, the Pertamina crisis forced the government to curtail the ambitious public expenditure program. By 1978 experts were predicting an end to the oil boom episode in the Indonesian economy (Arndt, 1978). However, the second oil boom in 1979 gave bona fide justification for government spending backed up by a healthy current account surplus. Subsequently the slackening of the oil market and a price cut in March 1983 put the projected government expenditures and revenues in question.

Table IV.2
Retained Values of Petroleum Earnings
(millions of U.S. dollars--constant 1970 prices)

1970	160
1971	141
1972	225
1973	308
1974	361
1975	382
1976	429
1977	544
1978	413
1979	499
1980	501

Source: 1970-76 Sritua Arief, op.cit, p. 145; 1977-80 Authors' calculations from International Monetary Fund, International Financial Statistics and Balance of Payments Yearbook, various years.

To further emphasise the nexus between oil, the balance of payments and government revenue, it is sufficient to mention that even in 1982 the oil sector contributed 80% of the export receipts and over 65% of non-aid central government revenues. The figures during preceding years are of the same order of magnitude.

It is clear from the current account figures in Table IV.3 that oil exports as a percentage of total exports have increased during the 1970s. Total volume of imports has also increased in recent years, resulting in a deterioration of the trade balance. If

TABLE IV.3
Current Account: Indonesian Balance-of-Payments
(Except and excluding financing) (in millions of SDR's)

	1974	1975	1976	1977	1978	1979	1980	1981
Current Account Balance	497	- 913	- 788	- 40	-1136	755	2197	- 625
Merchandise: exports f.o.b.	6041	5673	7462	9216	8802	11717	16720	19760
Oil Sector	4212	4174	5267	6210	5879	7404	12007	16084
Other Sectors	1829	1499	2195	3006	2922	4313	4713	3676
Merchandise: imports f.o.b.	-3853	-4504	-5906	-6401	-6695	-7152	- 9680	-14038
Trade balance	2188	1169	1556	2815	2106	4565	7040	5723
Other goods, services, and income: credit	165	113	139	142	232	308	343	539
Other goods, services, and income: debit	-1897	-2217	-2496	-3018	-3485	-4141	- 5228	- 6984
Shipment and other transportation	- 546	- 667	- 871	- 957	- 933	- 989	- 1318	- 1861
Investment Income	-1105	-1141	-1050	-1443	-1612	- 1908	- 2556	- 2653
Other	- 246	- 409	- 575	- 618	- 940	- 1244	- 1354	- 2470
Total: goods, services and income	456	- 935	- 801	- 61	-1147	732	2155	- 721
Private unrequited transfers	--	--	--	--	--	--	--	--
Total, excl. official unrequited transfers	456	- 935	- 801	- 61	-1147	732	2155	- 721
Official unrequited transfers	41	22	13	21	11	23	42	96

Source: International Monetary Fund Balance of Payments Yearbook, Vol. 34, Part 1, 1983, p. 266.

these trends continue, then overall current account deficits may grow. In fact, it is reported that by the end of March 1982 the current account deficit was $2.3 billion which was small compared to the 1983 deficit of close to $5.5 billion.[5] One bright spot might be the recent increase in the shipment of Liquified Natural Gas (LNG) as foreign demand rose. It is unlikely, however, that this will be sufficient to reverse the effects of a fall in oil revenue. Between 1982 and 1983, oil revenue fell from $19.4 billion to $16.1 billion--a drop of almost 17%.

The effect of this loss of oil revenue on the government budget cannot but be pronounced. In fact on January 6, 1983, President Soeharto introduced an austerity budget in the Parliament as a response to this decline in revenue. As Figures IV.1 and IV.2 show, over the past decade the Public sector spending grew with oil revenues pari passu. The two oil booms actually transformed the financing of Indonesian budget from non-oil sources (mostly indirect taxes) to mostly oil revenues. By the end of 1970s government non-aid revenues grew from 10% of the GDP to 23%, as a result of the oil bonanza.

As oil receipts show signs of decline (Figure IV.1), there is concern about tightening the belt. It will be an important question of public policy as to which items in the budget should be cut and by how much. As yet, no clear trend has emerged and especially for socioeconomic expenditures no cuts have been discussed or announced. Yet, some decline is expected as shown by Figure IV.2.

In the next section, we analyse inter alia, the income distributional effects of a fall in oil exports in the 1980s.

B. An analysis of the energy sector within a Social Accounting Matrix framework

The Social Accounting Matrix constructed earlier can be very useful in the macroeconomic modelling of the energy sector. The approach here follows Khan (1982, 1985) in breaking down the energy sector in the SAM for Indonesia. The CBS SAM had only one bona fide energy sector--petroleum and natural gas. In constructing the new SAM, several sectors needed to be disaggregated. Thus, coal was separated from metal ore and other mining, fuel oil, avigas, gasoline etc. were extracted from chemical and clay products, and electricity and gas taken out of the electricity, gas and water sector. In the disaggregated SAM five new energy sectors are added bringing the total to six. This classification includes both energy sources (coal, petroleum and natural gas, fuel oil and gasoline) and final energy outputs (electricity and gas).[6]

One traditional source of energy namely, the biomass is missing from among the six energy subsectors above. As mentioned before, this is a very important energy source in Indonesia. Unfortunately, not enough is known about the macroeconomics of biomass

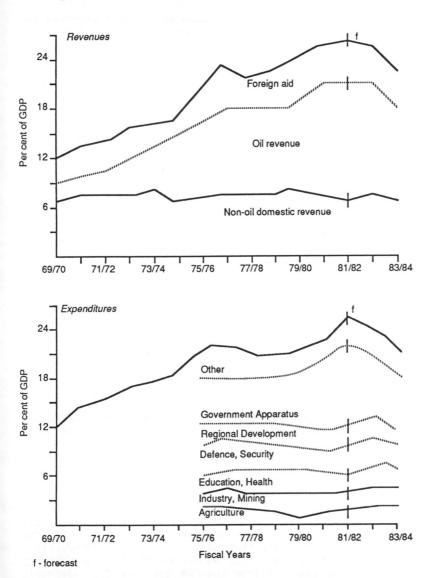

FIGURES IV.1 AND IV.2
Budget Revenues and Expenditures as a Proportion of GDP, 1969/70 - 1983/84

Revenues

Per cent of GDP

24 —

18 —

12 —

6 —

Foreign aid

Oil revenue

Non-oil domestic revenue

69/70   71/72   73/74   75/76   77/78   79/80   81/82   83/84

Expenditures

Per cent of GDP

24 —

18 —

12 —

6 —

Other

Government Apparatus

Regional Development

Defence, Security

Education, Health

Industry, Mining

Agriculture

69/70   71/72   73/74   75/76   77/78   79/80   81/82   83/84

Fiscal Years

f - forecast

Source: Peter McCawley, Survey of Recent Developments, BIES, April, 1983, p. 14.

which is of precise, quantitative nature. For this reason, it was not possible to separate out it in the SAM. However, biomass is included under other (non-energy) productive activities.

The starting point for the construction of the disaggregated SAM is the input-output table. The problem of reconciling the input-output table and the SAM were considerable. Both new columns and new rows needed to be introduced. Since the imported inputs are distinguished from domestic inputs, the first step in both rows and columns was to calculate an import coefficient. These were computed for the new SAM sectors from the I/O table according to the following formula:

$$\text{import coefficient} = \frac{\text{imported intermediate inputs}}{\text{total intermediate inputs}}$$

In general, these coefficients are different for each new activity. Using these coefficients, total intermediate inputs were separated into imported and domestic intermediate inputs. Subsequently the CBS SAM along with the input-output table for 1975 were used to create the submatrix of intermediate inputs for the energy sectors as well as to calculate the energy inputs required by the other productive activities in the new SAM.

The computation of value added and consumption was fraught with difficulties as well. The SAM coefficients for value added could be used only for petroleum and natural gas. Here, too, inconsistencies existed between the SAM and the I/O estimates. Information from Keuning's estimate of distribution of the operating surplus in the Indonesian economy,[7] along with broad aggregated sectoral coefficients were used to derive these figures. In a number of places informal judgements and educated guesses were necessary.

For consumption several sources other than the aggregate SAM were available. The most useful was Downey 1984 giving consumption of electricity, kerosene, fuel oil and gasoline by households. Since households did not consume any petroleum or coal in 1975, the only remaining item to be allocated was gas consumption. It was assumed that only the urban households consumed gas in proportion to their consumption of electricity.

The final SAM transaction matrix has 78 rows (and columns), and incorporates the transactions between the energy sector and the rest of the economy in a consistent manner. Thus, production, consumption, and distribution of value added of the six energy sectors all can be read off from the SAM quite readily (Appendix Table B). As an illustration, we reproduce here the household consumption of energy in 1975. These are only estimates, but so far the only consistent estimate of household consumption of energy for the year 1975.

The breakdown into rural/urban household categories in Table IV.4 allows us to look at their consumption patterns separately.[8]

Table IV.4

Consumption of Energy by Households
(in billions of Rupiahs)

		Agricultural Employees 24	Farm Size 1 25	Farm Size 2 26	Farm Size 3 27	Rural Lower 28	Rural Middle 29	Rural Higher 30	Urban Lower 31	Urban Middle 32	Urban Higher 33	Totals
Coal	59	0.00	0.00	0.00	0.00	0.00	0.00	0.00	0.00	0.00	0.00	0.00
Petroleum & Gas	60	0.00	0.00	0.00	0.00	0.00	0.00	0.00	0.00	0.00	0.00	0.00
Gasoline	61	0.42	0.53	0.38	0.90	1.63	0.43	1.61	2.07	0.65	6.14	14.76
Fuel Oil	62	1.68	2.63	1.50	2.03	2.81	0.58	1.32	3.67	0.57	2.38	19.17
Electricity	63	1.36	2.16	1.30	2.10	2.67	0.61	2.49	11.67	3.07	17.89	45.32
City Gas	64	0.00	0.00	0.00	0.00	0.00	0.00	0.00	0.14	0.05	0.27	.334
Population (millions)		14.74	31.33	15.60	15.89	20.80	3.06	7.00	12.42	3.02	6.72	130.58

Source: Social Accounting Matrix for Indonesia, 1975, Appendix Table B. For household populations, Downey (1984) and Keuning (1984).

For example, gas is consumed only by the city dwellers. Electricity consumption increases with income both in the rural and urban areas showing that it is a normal good for all households. The total consumption of electricity for any rural household group is lower than the lowest urban consuming group. This puts the urban/rural disparity in electricity and gas consumption in bold relief. The pattern for fuel oil (which includes kerosene) and gasoline is less clear cut. On the whole, the urban sector (especially the upper income group) is the larger consumer. However, rural consumption of kerosene and gasoline is not negligible. Furthermore, biomass consumption in rural areas is ignored here.

According to Hadi Soesastro biomass and kerosene are the two most important sources of energy in the rural areas.[9] According to the energy consumption survey in 1980 73.9% of the rural households used biomass and 24.6% of the households used kerosene for cooking. An overwhelming 85% used kerosene for lighting.[10]

Keuning (1984) gives the per capita expenditure of both the urban and the rural households on firewood. In rural areas, per capita expenditures on firewood range from a low of Rp 372/year for farmers with more than 1 hectare of land to a high of Rp 510/year for rural inactive households. The corresponding figures for the urban area are Rp 163/year for urban upper income level households and Rp 250/year for urban inactive households.[11] Thus, it would seem that biomass is a much more important energy source for the rural areas than for the urban areas. Moreover, time-series data indicate a rise in consumption from .50 cubic metre/capita year in 1956 to .84 cubic metre/ capita year in 1976.[12] It was claimed that in the absence of subsidies for kerosene, biomass consumption would increase even more, perhaps leading to serious deforestation. However, recent studies by Mark Pitt and Howard Dick question this claim.[13]

In any case, kerosene consumption is rising in both the urban and rural areas. However, Pitt shows that the urban households receive a disproportionate share of kerosene subsidy. Thus, it will not be surprising to discover that the consumption was increasing faster in the urban areas than in the rural areas during the 1970s.[14]

We now turn to the more substantive issue of testing the energy-labour intensity hypothesis. According to this hypothesis, confirmed by some earlier findings (see Keddie & Cleghorn 1980 , Khan 1985) in some sectors the labour-intensive technique also turns out to be the more energy-intensive one (e.g. for the sugar processing sector in India and for textiles in Korea). At this point, however, it is relevant to mention the exact scope and limitations of this hypothesis before proceeding further. The hypothesis is about the physical energy-content of technologies and has no bearing on the economics of this energy content ipso facto. From the economic point of view what is important is the social cost of technology, including the cost of energy used up. Thus a labour-intensive technology may still be socially optimal even if the energy-labour intensity hypothesis is true.

Unlike the Korean SAM, the Indonesian SAM does not have a break-down of the textiles sector according to technologies.[15] Further-more, biomass as an energy input is not listed as a separate row. This means that the hypothesis canot be tested in its strictest formulation which includes all energy inputs. In what follows we examie the available data for sugar production and for the other dualistic sectors in order to examine the hypothesis in the Indo-nesian context. The data in terms of use of energy by various technologies are presented in Table IV.5. Table IV.5 is a sub-matrix of A_{33} in Table II.5 and, thus gives the amount of energy used as a fraction of total output for any dualistic sector. This enables us to compare the energy-content of technologies in a straightforward manner by comparing the columns.

Columns 48 and 49 are brown sugar and sugar, respectively. The coefficients in the A-matrix do not confirm the Keddie-Cleghorn finding or the labour-energy intensity hypothesis. On the whole the sugar produced by modern technology uses 12 times more energy per rupiah of output than the brown sugar. It is interesting to note, however, that brown sugar does use at least one energy input more intensively than does refined sugar. This energy input is fuel oil. The actual ratio is about 1.33:1. However, the elec-tricity consumption (per unit of output) of refined sugar is so much larger than that of brown sugar that the latter energy input dominates. These observations point to the necessity to disaggre-gate the energy inputs carefully, as we have tried to do.

Further work using even more disaggregated energy inputs will be useful. It is worth re-emphasising that biomass as an energy source is omitted in the SAM. It is certainly true that the labour-intensive OPS (open pan sulphitation) method of making brown sugar does use considerable amount of biomass energy mainly in the form of firewood and charcoal.[16] Therefore, the hypothesis that is falsified needs to be couched in the following modified from: In sugar production the traditional technique is more intensive in commercial, non-traditional forms of energy use. Our work thus points to the necessity for collecting more information on the traditional sources of energy used in the traditional techniques of production.

In going through the rest of the columns, we find that this modified labour-energy intensity hypothesis MLE-hypothesis is not confirmed in most sectors. As expected, handpounded rice uses no commercial energy whatsoever. Farm processed tea uses some kerosene, gasoline and other fuel oils. Drying and salting of fish does not require much commercial energy either. In fruits and vegetables, the same pattern holds, except that the differ-ences here are much less than the previous ones. Finally, the technologies for cigarette manufacturing also show the same pat-tern. However, the actual use of energy is quite miniscule. Also, clove cigarettes are a different product than the white cigarettes.

Table IV.5

Submatrix of Average Propensities for Consuming Energy by Dual Techniques

		Hand-Pounded Rice 42	Rice Milling 43	Farm Processed Tea 44	Processed Tea 45	Dried & Salted Fish 46	Canned Fish 47	Brown Sugar 48	Refined Sugar 49	Canning (S+C) 50	Canning (M+L) 51	Clove Cigarettes 52	White Cigarettes 53
Coal	59	0.00	0.00	0.00	0.00	0.00	0.00	0.00	0.00	0.00	0.00	0.00	0.00
Petroleum & Gas	60	0.00	0.00	0.00	0.00	0.00	0.00	0.00	0.00	0.00	0.00	0.00	0.00
Gasoline	61	0.00	0.002	0.001	0.007	0.00	0.002	0.00	0.003	0.005	0.007	0.005	0.003
Fuel Oil	62	0.00	0.005	0.002	0.013	0.001	0.002	0.004	0.003	0.005	0.009	0.000	0.000
Electricity	63	0.00	0.015	0.000	0.022	0.001	0.018	0.001	0.052	0.000	0.000	0.004	0.011
City Gas	64	0.00	0.00	0.00	0.00	0.00	0.00	0.00	0.00	0.00	0.00	0.00	0.00

Source: Table II.5.

An important fact which emerges from Table IV.5 is also that on the whole, the energy intensities in this table are unusually low. The exclusion of the traditional sources of energy partially explains this. However, compared to some more capital-intensive sector (cement etc., for example), these sectors have all fairly low energy-intensity.

It may also be useful in this context to compare a relatively labour-intensive sector with a capital-intensive one. Since the textiles sector is viewed as a labour-intensive candidate for the export market it is useful to compare the energy-intensity of this sector with a more capital-intensive sector. It is clear that the capital-intensive goods sector is the more energy intensive, especially in the use of petroleum and natural gas. It is noteworthy, though, that the textiles sector uses more electricity per unit of output than the other capital intensive industries. This may occur because of inefficient use of technologies in textiles sector.[17]

Table IV.6

Average Propensities to Spend on Energy

Energy Sectors	Textiles	Cement etc.
Coal	0.000	0.000
Petroleum & Natural Gas	0.000	0.225
Gasolene	0.002	0.003
Fuel Oil	0.001	0.008
Electricity	0.019	0.016
Gas	0.000	0.000

Source: Table II.5.

It is possible to determine the direct and indirect energy use by the two techniques via both backward and forward linkages when demand for the product of either technique changes. This can be done by using the fixed price multipliers introduced before (Tables IV.7 & IV.8 below). For instance, in the case of brown sugar vs. refined sugar, for every one thousand rupiah increase in expenditure on each, the energy component receives 90 and 136 rupiahs respectively (see Table IV.7). So, the refined sugar sector leads to more energy consumption for the conventional energy sources indirectly as well. The total fixed price multipliers for these dualistic sectors for the energy rows are given in Table IV.7. They are broken down by the six energy sectors in Table IV.8.

A closer look at Table IV.8 reveals that petroleum and natural gas, and electricity receive most of the indirect expenditures on energy from the six dualistic sectors. In two of these six sectors, namely brown sugar vs. refined sugar and clove cigarettes vs. white cigarettes, the traditional technology actually leads to more indirect expenditure on petroleum and natural gas than the modern technique. This holds true for clove and white cigarettes for fuel oil as well.

Table IV.7

Energy Fixed Price Multipliers for the Dualistic Sectors

Sector	(SAM Column)	Fixed Price Multiplier
Handpounded Rice	42	0.080
Milled Rice	43	0.105
Farm Processed Tea	44	0.073
Tea Processing	45	0.128
Dried and Salted Fish	46	0.084
Canned Fish	47	0.106
Brown Sugar	48	0.090
Refined Sugar	49	0.136
Canning & Preserving of Fruits & Vegetables (Trad)	50	0.102
Canning & Preserving of Fruits & Vegetables (Modern)	51	0.111
Clove Cigarettes	52	0.071
White Cigarettes	53	0.056

Source: Table II.6.

However, it should be noted that in Table IV.7, for all sectors except clove cigarettes and white cigarettes the amount going to the energy sectors for an equal increase in demand for each product-cum-technology within a dualistic sector is higher for the modern technique. For clove cigarettes and white cigarettes, an increase in expenditure of 1000 rupiahs will lead to 71 and 56 rupiahs of expenditure on energy, respectively. However, it appears that both these figures are low compared even with the other subsectors. Secondly, there is more uncertainty about the energy inputs in these two subsectors than the others since the reliability of components other than electricity and fuel oils are not known exactly.

A question which can be addressed next, is the effects on households' incomes of changes in the pattern of energy production. The fixed price multipliers for the household incomes with respect to exogenous increases in demand for the energy sectors are given in Table IV.9 below.

102

Table IV.8

Submatrix of Fixed-Price Multipliers

		Hand-Pounded Rice 42	Rice Milling 43	Farm Processed Tea 44	Processed Tea 45	Dried & Salted Fish 46	Canned Fish 47	Brown Sugar 48	Refined Sugar 49	Canning (S+C) 50	Canning (M+L) 51	Clove Cigarettes 52	White Cigarettes 53
Coal	59	0.00	0.00	0.00	0.00	0.00	0.00	0.00	0.00	0.00	0.00	0.00	0.00
Petroleum & Gas	60	0.028	0.031	0.025	0.037	0.028	0.031	0.031	0.029	0.039	0..042	0.023	0.015
Gasoline	61	0.013	0.015	0.013	0.020	0.014	0.015	0.014	0.014	0.017	0.020	0.015	0.010
Fuel Oil	62	0.015	0.021	0.015	0.028	0.019	0.02	0.02	0.019	0.019	0.023	0.011	0.008
Electricity	63	0.024	0.038	0.020	0.043	0.023	0.04	0.025	0.073	0.027	0.026	0.022	0.023
City Gas	64	0.00	0.000	0.000	0.000	0.00	0.00	0.00	0.00	0.00	0.00	0.00	0.00

Source: Table II.6.

Table IV.9

Energy and Household Income Distribution
(Fixed Price Multipliers)

Energy Sectors Households	Coal	Petroleum & Natural Gas	Gaso- line	Fuel	Elec- tricity	Gas
Ag.Employees	0.061	0.010	0.016	0.016	0.033	0.033
Ag. Operator 0-0.5	0.126	0.021	0.033	0.033	0.066	0.067
Ag. Operator 0.501-1.0	0.082	0.015	0.023	0.023	0.045	0.047
Ag. Operator >1.0	0.127	0.025	0.038	0.038	0.075	0.078
Rural Lower	0.265	0.022	0.042	0.042	0.082	0.071
Rural Inactive	0.034	0.010	0.013	0.012	0.019	0.017
Rural Upper	0.077	0.026	0.032	0.031	0.053	0.043
Urban Lower	0.159	0.032	0.061	0.060	0.172	0.225
Urban Inactive	0.029	0.016	0.018	0.018	0.030	0.035
Urban Upper	0.181	0.116	0.128	0.127	0.205	0.237

Source: Table II.6.

It appears that the overall impact of a change in demand for the
energy sector is more pronounced on the resulting incomes of the
urban than on the rural households. Within the urban areas the
upper income households stand to gain or lose the most from an
increase or a decrease in demand for energy, respectively. The
effect, however, is relatively less significant for petroleum and
natural gas as opposed to the other subsectors within energy.
This is because much of the earnings accrue to foreign nationals
as factor payments abroad as well as to the government.

A seeming anomaly in the above table is that rural lower income
households marginally gain more from an increase in expenditures
on the energy sector than do the rural upper income households
(though this does not hold for the petroleum and natural gas
subsector).

It is very hazardous to try to use the 1975 SAM to make any
predictions on the effects of a change in oil demand on household
income distribution in 1985. Not only have relative prices
changed but some structural changes have taken place (manufacturing and service sectors have grown relative to agriculture and
mining). The latter change, though not dramatic, must have affected the SAM coefficients and hence the fixed price multipliers.
Changes in relative prices will mean that the pure quantity adjustment assumption is untenable. Here we offer some results of
the declne of demand for petroleum in the world market and a fall
in revenue subject to the above qualifications.

It is assumed that internationally the recent price decline and OPEC quota for Indonesia will lead to a fall of about 15 percent from the total value of output of 1983. Assuming an export/output ratio of two-thirds, in constant 1975 prices this corresponds to a fall of 585 million dollars of petroleum export based on the fixed price multipliers from the 1975 SAM. The consequent loss of income will be the highest for urban income groups--more than $60 million. Agricultural employees lose the least--$5.85 million.[18] In terms of real income loss, it is probably slightly more, since the deflator used was the international oil price index which increased faster than many domestic prices during this period. Furthermore, even though the precise quantitative estimate is questionable, the qualitative judgement that the fall in oil price, ceteris paribus will lower the standard of living of just about everybody in Indonesia seems valid. Even though the greater relative loss by the upper income households than by the lower income ones may indicate a lessening of income inequality marginally this is very little consolation to about half of the Indonesians who either already live in poverty or are at the margin of it. Various social and economic policies will be needed urgently to cope with the problem of increasing poverty as a result of the oil price decline.

If the effects of energy price decontrol, especially withdrawal of subsidies on kerosene and other petroleum products are considered, then the fall in real income will be even higher than before. It may hit hard specifically those urban groups currently enjoying the benefits of these subsidies.

It is also of some interest to consider the opposite question, namely that of the effects of an increase in the incomes of various socioeconomic groups on energy consumption. This is what in fact happened during the seventies in Indonesia. Table IV.10 reproduces the submatrix of fixed price multipliers for energy consumption by household groups from the 1975 SAM. Looking at the column sums, it can be readily seen that for an equal increase in income the urban inactive households will spend the most and the Agricultural Operators with more than 1.0 hectares will spend the least amount on energy. For every 1000 rupiahs increase in income the former group will spend 107 rupiahs on energy while the latter group will spend only 61 rupiahs.[19]

The highest and lowest expenditures on energy (not including firewood) coming from an increase in income of the urban and rural household groups, respectively, are consistent with earlier observations on urban/rural disparities in energy consumption.[20] This means that the pattern of rural/ urban disparities in expenditures on energy holds for indirect expenditures on energy as well. Finally, it can also be noted from Table IV.10 that on the whole the increased receipts going to the energy sector as a consequence of assumed income growth of the households are relatively low.

Table IV.10

Fixed Price Multipliers for the Energy Subsectors by Household Groups

Households / Energy	Ag. Employees 24	Agricultural Operators 0 - 15 25	.501-1.000 26	> 1.000 27	Rural Lower 28	Rural Inactive 29	Rural Upper 30	Urban Lower 31	Urban Inactive 32	Urban Upper 33
Coal 61	0.000	0.000	0.000	0.000	0.000	0.000	0.000	0.000	0.000	0.000
Petroleum 62	0.032	0.032	0.027	0.021	0.031	0.032	0.028	0.029	0.032	0.025
Gasoline 63	0.015	0.015	0.013	0.010	0.015	0.015	0.015	0.014	0.017	0.014
Fuel Oil 64	0.019	0.018	0.015	0.012	0.018	0.018	0.015	0.017	0.019	0.013
Electricity 65	0.029	0.028	0.024	0.018	0.028	0.029	0.026	0.032	0.038	0.029
City Gas 66	0.000	0.000	0.000	0.000	0.000	0.000	0.000	0.000	0.001	0.000
Total	0.095	0.093	0.079	0.061	0.092	0.094	0.084	0.092	0.107	0.081

Source: Table II.6.

Two factors may have contributed to these low observed values of receipts by the energy sector. The first is, as mentioned earlier, the omission of biomass from the energy sources.[21] Not only has this biased the total energy consumption of rural households downwards, but it has also resulted in a lower overall energy coefficient for certain production activities (e.g. brown sugar). Insofar as the households consume some of these commodities, the indirect receipts of the energy sector from the consumption of these commodities are not captured here. The second factor has to do with the date of these observations. Since the mid-seventies both the income elasticity of demand for energy by the households and the energy-content of productive activities in industry have been increasing (see appendix). Consequently, it would be logical to expect the corresponding multipliers in a more recent SAM, (were one to be constructed for the eighties) to be higher than those shown in Table IV.15.

Most of the receipts of the energy sector from a rise in household incomes accrue to four energy subsectors--petroleum and natural gas, gasoline, fuel oil and electricity. According to Table IV.10, for an increase in income of 1000 rupiahs for each household group the consequent receipts range from 21 rupiahs to 32 rupiahs for petroleum and natural gas, from 10 rupiahs to 17 rupiahs for gasoline, from 12 rupiahs to 19 rupiahs for fuel oil and from 18 to 38 rupiahs for electricity. Again, the magnitude of any of these components is not very high.

Within the four groups of energy sources, the increase in the receipts by petroleum and natural gas seem to be relatively high. This is particularly true if one compares multipliers for petroleum and natural gas with those for gasoline and fuel oil. From Table IV.4 in this section, it is clear that the households do not consume any petroleum or natural gas directly. Therefore, the magnitude of the multiplier is to be explained entirely by an indirect expenditure on energy via other commodities consumed by the households. Some of these commodities, consumed by both rural and urban households, are rice, farm food crops, textile products, cigarettes and other food, beverage and tobacco. The direct consumption of energy by these commodities can be found in the A-matrix (i.e. Table II.5). The direct energy input into these commodities is also not very high. As Table IV.5 shows, hand-pounded rice uses no conventional energy input at all and the energy input in milled rice is low, with no petroleum and natural gas used. The situation is similar for the other commodities consumed by the households as well.

In the final analysis, then, it is the indirect demand for energy generated by the production of commodities such as rice and farm food crops, that explains the 'relatively high' multipliers for petroleum and natural gas. In other words, the inputs which enter into the production of commodities such as farm food crops, textiles and cigarettes use petroleum and natural gas as one of their intermediate inputs. For example, even though the textiles sector does not use petroleum and natural gas directly, it uses some of the products from "other chemicals, clay products, cement

107

and basic metals". The latter sector is, in turn, a heavy user of petroleum and natural gas. In addition to this, gasoline and fuel oil are also used as inputs into textiles production. The A-matrix indicates that the gasoline and fuel oil accounts spend 48% and 47% of their column totals respectively on petroleum and natural gas. It may be noted that households also consume petroleum and natural gas indirectly through their regular consumption of gasoline and fuel oil.

The above analysis is yet another illustration of the usefulness of the SAM in elucidating both the direct and indirect linkages between consumption and production activities for the economy as a whole. As we have emphasised, the analysis would have been more realistic if a SAM were available for a more recent year.[22] But even with this limitation, it can be readily seen how even the simple fixed price modelling based on SAM goes considerably further than the input/output or any other partial equilibrium approach in exploiting the intersectoral linkages and demand-supply interactions for the entire economy.

This completes our discussion of the energy-content of technologies as well as the macroeconomic analysis of the energy sector. The major contribution of this chapter has been to demonstrate the usefulness of the SAM framework for analysing these issues. In the next chapter, we leave the static framework used so far and turn to some of the dynamic aspects of technology choice by considering the effects of research and development on generation and adoption of technology along with an analysis of diffusion of technology in Indonesia during the last decade.

Notes

1 For implications of the energy price decontrol policies, see William H. Branson: <u>Macroeconomic Analysis of the Effects of Energy Price Decontrol in Indonesia</u>, World Bank Report, 1982. For an analysis of income distributional implications of price decontrol, see Mark M. Pitt and Lung-Fei Lee, "The Income Distributional Implications of Increasing Energy Prices in Indonesia", mimeo, Dept. of Economics, University of Minnesota, 1983.

2 Some of the more important of the studies are: World Bank/UNDP: Indonesia, Issues and Options for the Energy Sector, 1981; World Bank/UNDP: Report No. 2026-IND. Recent Developments, Short-Term Prospects and Development Issues, 1978; World Bank/UNDP: Report No. 2788-IND, Indonesia: Long-Run Development and Short-Run Adjustment, 1980; Asian Development Bank: <u>Energy Sector Indonesia</u>, 1980; Asian Development Bank: <u>Survey of Energy Utilisation</u>, Vols. 1 & 2, 1980; BPPT/Bechtel National Inc.: <u>Energy Planning Study for Indonesia</u>, 1981; Directorate General for Power and Energy/Development International, <u>Energy Planning for Development in Indonesia</u>, Jakarta, October, 1981.

3 Sritua Arief, "The Indonesian Petroleum Industry: A Study of Its Impact on the Indonesian Economy, Ph.D. Dissertation, 1979, University of Hull, United Kingdom.

4 See Zuhayr Mikdashi, The Community of Oil Exporting Countries: A Study in Governmental Co-operations: London: George Allen & Unwin Ltd., 1972. see also Raymond F. Miksell et al., Foreign Investment in the Petroleum and Mineral Industries: Case Studies of Investor-Host Country Relations, Baltimore and London: The Johns Hopkins Press, 1971.

5 Peter McCawley Survey of Recent Developments, BIES, April 1983, pp. 3-7 and International Monetary Fund, International Financial Statistics, 1984, pp. 331-333.

6 Due to unavailability of data on value added going to the 23 disaggregated factors and the consumption by the 10 different household groups, it was not possible to disaggregate the energy sector further. It would of course have been useful to separate coal from natural gas and kerosene from fuel oil etc. Such refinements will require collection of data in the SAM format in the future.

7 Steven J. Keuning: "The Distribution of Profits in Indonesia", Institute of Social Studies Working Paper Series No. 3, 1984.

8 The figures in Table IV.4 have to be interpreted carefully. They are <u>aggregate</u> consumption figures for the household categories listed. The <u>per capita</u> consumption figures (i.e. total aggregate consumption of a given socio-economic household group divided by the total number of people in the same group) are quite different. Thus even though the rural lower group consumes more total gasoline than either rural middle or upper groups, in per capita terms the ratio between the three groups is roughly 1:2:4. The same general relative order of magnitude obtains also among the urban socio-economic groups when energy consumption is expressed on per capita terms.

9 Hadi Soesastro, Rural Household Energy Survey in West Jawa in Energi dan Pemerataan. Hadi Soesastro et al., ed. Centre for International Studies, Jakarta, 1983, p. 240.

10 Ibid, p. 240, Table 10.1.

11 Steven Keuning, Modelling the Indonesian Social Accounting Matrix, BPS/Institute for Social Studies Project Working Paper No. 1, 1984, p. 16.

12 Soesastro, op.cit., p. 242.

13 Howard Dick, The Oil Price Subsidy, Deforestation and Equity, Bulletin of Indonesian Economic Studies 16(3), November, 1980, pp. 32-60; Mark Pitt, Equity, Externalities and Energy Subsidies: The Case for Kerosene in Indonesia, Center for Economic Research, Department of Economics, the University of Minnesota, Discussion Paper No. 181, August 1983.

14 Mark Pitt, op.cit., p. 14. Pitt claims that in 1978 "urban households received more than two and one-half times the subsidy of the rural households.

15 Though several good studies exist at the industry level, using sample surveys none investigates this particularl issue of labour-energy substitutability. See for example, Hal Hill, Choice of Technique in the Indonesian Weaving Industry, Economic Development and Cultural Change, Jan. 1983, Vol. 31, No. 2, pp. 337-353; Mark M. Pitt and Lung-Fei Lee, The Measurement and Sources of Technical Inefficiency in the Indonesian Weaving Industry, Journal of Development Economics, Vol. 9, No. 1, August 1981, pp. 43-64.

16 In fact, both the technologies use a considerable amount of biomass, mainly bagasse, but the modern technologies may burn this more efficiently. We are indebted to Dr. Armand Pereira for pointing this out.

17 Mark Pitt and Lung-Fei Lee, "The Measurement and Sources of Technical Inefficiency in the Indonesian Weaving Industry", Journal of Development Economics, Vol. 9, No. 1, August 1981, pp. 43-64.

18 Expressed in per capita terms urban households lose $13.03 as opposed to only 43 U.S. cents for agricultural employees.

19 These figures do not include the expenditure on firewood by the household groups. For some rural households firewood is the main source of energy.

20 See for example the World Bank Survey discussed in the appendix. The result here assumes that the income elasticities of energy for each group remains constant during the period of analysis.

21 As stated before, the SAM does include biomass, but lack of data did not permit the inclusion as a separate energy sector.

22 As pointed out previously a SAM for 1980 is just about to be completed by a joint team from the Central Statistical Bureau and the Institute of Social Studies.

Appendix to Chapter IV --
Consumption, production and reserves of energy in Indonesia

The general trends in consumption of energy are discussed, first, followed by a more detailed examination of a) some of its components, viz. petroleum and petroleum products, coal, natural gas and electricity, and, finally, b) production performance and reserves of energy in Indonesia.

Commercial energy consumption in Indonesia for several recent years are given below: (in million barrels of oil equivalent)[1]

	1983/84	1979/80	1978/79	1977/78
Total	210.2	162.0	160.1	143.0

There is an unmistakable rising trend in consumption of energy shared by all components (i.e. oil, natural gas, coal, hydropower and geothermal). Non-commercial fuels (agricultural residues and fuel wood) comprised 48% of the total energy consumption in 1978 as compared to 62% in 1960 and 57% in 1970. These energy sources are also used primarily in the rural areas whereas the commercial fuels are used mainly in the urban areas.

Energy consumption grew at an annual rate of 12.6%, far greater than the 7.9% annual growth of G.D.P. during 1970-78. From these figures the average elasticity of energy consumption with respect to GDP can be computed as 1.59 for this period. According to the World Bank sources, the recent elasticity is even higher--2.1.[2] In 1975, the industrial sector became the largest consumer of commercial energy. The higher elasticity in recent years shows the impact of this change. The electric power sector and the transport sector also account partially for this trend with average annual growth rates of demand for energy of 18% and 14%, respectively.[3]

An important feature of energy consumption is the heavy dependence on petroleum. The industrial sector's reliance on oil increased from 59% of its total energy requirements in 1969 to 70% in 1977. In the electricity sector, the corresponding figures are from 68% to 86% over the same period. During this time, there was actually a decline in coal consumption and very small increases in the use of natural gas and hydropower capacity. Most of the natural gas was used as feedstock for the fertilizer industry.

These trends were further accentuated by an increase in the consumption of petroleum products during this decade at an average annual rate of 15.2%. Automotive diesel, gasoline, fuel oil, industrial diesel oil and aviation fuel all contributed to this. Though the consumption of kerosene decreased from 42% to 33% of the total in 1979, in absolute terms the amount of kerosene consumed was still greater than the consumption of any other petroleum products.

The allocation of kerosene between the household and the

industrial sector is controversial. According to BPPT and BPS sources shown in Table IV.A, there is a growing level of kerosene consumption in the industrial sector, in addition to the large volume consumed by the household sector. Other sources show consumption by the household sector only.[4] Where the breakdown between the two sectors is given as in Table IV.A, the growth rate for the industrial sector (20%) outstrips that for the households (13%).

As for the other sources and types of energy, the consumption of coal actually declined until the end of the 70's. Current estimated domestic consumption is about 1.1 million barrels oil equivalent annually, almost a three-fold increase since 1979. However, it is only one-half of one percent of the total energy consumption. The use of natural gas by industry has grown at an average annual rate of 22% since 1975. The fertilizer and steel industries are the major consumers of natural gas.

Electricity is used by both households and industries. Even though estimates of households using electricity vary (6% of the total number of households according to the World Bank, 8% according to the Ministry of Mining and Energy) they use as much electricity as the industrial sector (36% of the total electricity used). The bulk of the latter industrial use is by the large industries (33%). Small industries use a miniscule 3%. These figures do not include production and consumption from own-generated electricity used almost exclusively in the industrial sector.

Turning now to the production and reserves of energy, we note that oil and biomass account for 45% and 48%, respectively, of the current total energy supply.[5] Fortunately, there are substantial reserves of natural gas and coal. Likewise, geothermal energy and hydroelectric power potentials should not be overlooked. Next, we discuss both the existing and potential supply of the major energy sources. Because of the obvious importance of petroleum, this

source is discussed first and more extensively than the others.

In 1980, Indonesia was fourteenth among the world's crude producers with a production rate of 1.58 million barrels per day (MBD). The production more than doubled between 1969 and 1976. After reaching a peak of 615.1 MB in 1977, it declined to 488 MB in 1982. Since then, it is showing signs of increase again. According to experts, the maximum feasible annual production level for this decade is about 700 MB.

Table IV.A

Kerosene Consumption and Prices 1969-78

Year	Consumption (litres x 10^9)			Annual Growth Rates (%)			Price (Rp/l)
	Households	Industry	Total	Households	Industry	Total	(I April)
(1)	(2)	(3)	(4)	(5)	(6)	(7)	(8)
1969	2.158	0.539	2.697				
1970	2.184	0.538	2.722	1.2	0.0	0.9	
1971	2.252	0.748	3.000	3.1	39.0	10.2	
1972	2.643	0.644	3.287	17.4	-13.9	9.6	
1973	2.943	0.733	3.676	11.4	13.8	11.8	
1974	3.404	0.848	4.252	15.7	15.7	15.7	13
1975	3.903	0.961	4.864	14.7	13.3	14.4	16
1976	4.239	0.844	5.083	8.6	-12.2	4.5	18
1977	4.713	1.122	5.835	11.2	32.9	14.8	18
1978	5.137	1.489	6.626	9.0	32.7	13.6	18
FY 78/79			6.917			4.4	18
79/80			7.335			6.2	25
80/81			7.883				37.5

Sources: 1969–1978 Draft I, BPPT Report, Appendix A, Tables A-5 and A-6.
FY 1978/79 and 1979/80: Ministry of Mines and Energy.
International Financial Statistics, 1984, pp. 504-5

113

Table IV.B
Total Indonesian Crude Oil Production, 1969-83
(million barrels per year)

Year	Production
1969	270.9
1974	501.8
1975	476.9
1976	550.3
1977	615.1
1978	597.0
1979	580.0
1980	577.0
1981	585.0
1982	488.0
1983	518.0

Source: 1969-77 World Bank, op.cit., p. 22.
1978-83 Hal Hill, Survey of Current Development, Bulletin
for Indonesian Economic Studies, August 1984, p. 29.

Previously, a substantial part of the crude oil used to be
refined abroad. The government initiatives to make refining an
indigenous production activity have been successful. By 1984 the
government plans for expanding domestic refining capacity with the
new plants at Cilicap and Balikpapan were complete. A long
chapter in the economic relations of Singapore and Indonesia ended
in August 1984 with the cessation of the refining of the
Indonesian crude in Singapore.

Foreign investment in the oil sector in recent years has been
growing. Table IV.C shows the investment in both oil and non-oil
sectors. The U.S. is the most important investor. The overall
importance of U.S. investment in this sector is indicated by the
fact that excluding oil, Japan appears to be the leading investor
in Indonesia until 1983. In reality, when the oil sector is
added, it is seen that the U.S. had been the leading investor
since 1980. The importance of foreign investment is also
underlined in the SAM by the fact that more than two-thirds of the
value added going to capital in the petroleum and natural gas
sector accrues to foreign capital.

Finally it can be noted that a firm estimate of
petroleum reserves in Indonesia is still not available. The
existing geological surveys of both East and West Indonesia put
undiscovered reserves from 10 to 40 billion barrels. In 1980 the
figure for the proven remaining reserves was 9.5 billion barrels.
At the then rate of production (575 million barrels/year) this
meant 16 years of production. With the higher figure for
undiscovered reserves, the date when Indonesia will no longer be
an oil-producing country can be postponed for another 65 years.
However, it is clear that unless these are confirmed or further

massive deposits are discovered, Indonesian planners must decide
on a reasonable production schedule and on possible substitutes
for oil.

Table IV.C

Total Foreign Investment (including
investment in the oil sector), 1980-83
(millions of $)

Year	Total Investment		Country Shares			
	BKPM[a]	Oil	Oil Excluded		Oil Included	
			U.S.	Japan	U.S.	Japan
1980	752	1318	15	15	66	7
1981	859	2245	2	25	62	8
1982	1648	2656	6	42	55	16
1983[b]	1439	1501	22	17	54	9

[a]The Investment Coordinating Board.
[b]January-June

Source: Hal Hill, Survey of Recent Developments, BIES, August
         1984, p. 32.

The next step is to consider the production and reserves of
substitute energy sources, viz. natural gas, coal,
hydroelectricity, geothermal energy and biomass. The production
of natural gas increased four-fold from 1974 to 1979. 1979
production was 958,000 MCF (2,700 MCFD).[6] This was one third of
oil production in terms of BTU's. Nearly one-half was exported in
LNG (Liquefied Natural Gas) form to Japan from liquefaction
centers at Arun and Badak. Others uses include NGL (Natural Gas
Liquids), (1979: 19 MB) and LPG (Liquefied Petroleum Gas). As
for reserves, the 69 trillion cubic feet (TCF) of proven reserves
of natural gas are equivalent to 8.22 billion barrels of oil.
Most of the sites, however, are far from major industrial and
population centers. Main fields are: Arun in North Sumatra (17
TCF), Badak in Kalimantan (7 TCF) and Natuna in the South China
Sea (35 TCF).

Both anthracite and lignite varieties of coal together with
various intermediate varieties are found in Indonesia. Known
reserves are located in Sumatra and East Kalimantan, West
Kalimantan, Java, Sulawesi, Timor and Irian Java. The estimates
range from 2.6 billion tons of "mineable" coal (Department of
Mines and Energy) to 10 and 15 billion tonnes (World Bank, 1981).
Present production is undertaken mainly by the state and mining
company, PN Batubara (PNB). Current production level is about
300,000 tons annually. The two fields at Bukit Asam and Ombelin

in Sumatra produce almost all the current output. During the last few years, the government has taken steps to encourage the production and consumption of coal especially for domestic purposes.

Even though no comprehensive river reconnaissance has been ever taken, at least 127,000 gwh/year of hydroelectric potential has been identified. The government estimates indicate 31,000 MW of capacity. The full exploitation of this source is further hampered by the fact that the geographical distribution lies mostly outside Java. Nearly half is located in Irian Jaya with less than 1% of the total population. However, the possible use of this source for rural electrification outside of Java should not be overlooked.

Estimates of geothermal energy are not reliable. Table IV.D shows that identified reserves amount to some 1500 MW. Most of this is located in Java. Geothermal development is now one of the priorities in government energy policy.

Table IV.D

Estimated Geothermal Resources
(in mega watts)

Region	Potential Reserves	Identified Reserves
Java	5500	890
Sumatra	1100	270
Sulawesi	1400	180
Other areas	2000	120
Total	10000	1460

Source: Asian Development Bank - Energy Sector in Indonesia (Issues and Strategies). T.L. Sankar, Manila, September, 1980, World Bank, p. 29.

The World Bank estimate for the biomass potential from the vast forests (see Table IV.E) is about 650 million tons per year.[7] A second source of biomass are the agricultural residues. In Java some households obtain about 70% of their fuelwood requirement from home gardens. After harvesting and milling straws and rice husks are used as energy sources for cooking etc. The bulk of this biomass potential (estimated at 91.1 million tons) remains untapped so far.[8] However, the benefits of further use of firewood must be weighted against potential ecological disaster from forest depletion.

This completes the background discussion of the energy sector. In the next section the macroeconomic implications of changes in the energy sector on balance of payments and the government budget are investigated.

Table IV.E

Distribution of Forest Land by Island
(million ha.)

Island Groups	Land Area	Forested Area	% Forest Area[b]
Sumatra	47.36	28.45	60
Java (incl. Madura)	13.22	2.88	22
Bali	0.56	0.13	23
East Nusa Tenggara[a]	4.79	0.68	14
West Nusa Tenggara	2.02	0.85	42
Kalimantan	53.95	41.48	77
Maluku	7.45	6.00	81
Sulawesi	18.92	14.09	77
East Timor	1.49	n.a.	--
Irian Jaya	42.20	31.50	75

[a]0.53 million ha. of the forested lands on East Nusa Tenggara is designated as protected areas.
[b](Area forest land/area total land) X 100.
Source: UNDP/World Bank, op.cit, p. 33

Notes to Appendix to Chapter IV

1 These figures are from Hal Hill, Survey of Recent Developments, BIES, Vol. XX, No. 2, August 1984. The total for
1977/78 is from World Bank 1981 .

2 Indonesia: "Issues and Options in the Energy Sector," Report
of the joint UNDP/World Bank Energy Sector Assessment Program,
November 1981, p. ix. Unless otherwise stated, all the
figures in this section are from this study.

3 Ibid, p. 10.

4 World Bank/UNDP op.cit., p. 4, footnote 1.

5 Biomass consists of mainly firewood and agricultural residues.

6 MCF = Million Cubic Feet
MCFD = Million Cubic Feet per Day

7 UNDP/World Bank, op.cit., p. 33.

8 Ibid, p. 34.

V Research and development and diffusion of technology: new theoretical approaches and some examples from Indonesia

This chapter consists of two parts dealing, respectively, with A) the relation between research and development and technology and B) the diffusion of technology.

A. Research and development (R & D) and technology

The systematic study of the economic impact of R & D is quite a recent development even for the economies of developed countries.[1] It is, therefore, not surprising that no such macroeconomic study exists for Indonesia. Even at the sectoral level, very little competent work has been done so far.[2] The lack of data on R & D has been a major stumbling block. The present study, while unable to overcome the problem of data availability, focuses on a number of conceptual issues in order to highlight both the modelling problems and data requirements in linking R & D with technology generation and adoption in an economy-wide framework. More specifically, using the available qualitative and quantitative information on R & D in Indonesia, this chapter addresses the following three sets of issues:

(1) The conceptual issue of including R & D in an economy-wide model is addressed by attempting to identify R & D as a separate productive activity within a SAM. Although quite promising, this approach turns out to be problematic at the same time. The major problem is the seeming contradiction between the static nature of the SAM framework and the dynamic effects of R & D on the economy. In the first part of this section we discuss the possible resolution of this difficulty within the SAM framework.

(2) Empirically, the existing studies and information on several sectors, e.g. agricultural mechanisation, rice and textiles production, are reviewed in order to explore the possibilities of utilising these examples for the construction of a SAM along the lines discussed in the first part of this section.

At the same time, the need for further information emerges as a severe constraint on such an undertaking at present.

(3) Nevertheless, the SAM approach to R & D, appears to be conceptually appealing if one contrasts the possible policy experiments which can be undertaken within a SAM framework with the apparently ad hoc science and technology policy in existence. In particular, the priority areas for technology development are reviewed in what follows along with the high technology focus within these areas. The conceptual discussion, together with admittedly very limited empirical information, raises some doubts about the wisdom of an exclusively high technology emphasis, given the employment and income distributional objectives of the Indonesian government.

The message of the first part of this chapter is simply that incorporation of R & D in SAM is conceptually possible and desirable from the policymaker's standpoint. However, in order to fully assess the impact of R & D on the related macroeconomic variables such as output, employment, income distribution etc. one needs a series of SAMs for successive time periods. For the purpose of forecasting as a guide to policy this calls for a dynamic approach. The second part of this chapter attempts to address this issue by including diffusion of technology in the SAM. Here it becomes clear that for the time being we lack an acceptable (or even available) theory of "dynamising" SAM, and hence some partial approaches are discussed instead.

1. R & D policy in an economy-wide setting: the SAM approach

Choice of new technology in a developing country is affected by research and development in two ways. A developing country can attempt to develop new, "appropriate" technology through R & D, or it can adapt the existing technology to its needs. In the latter case, research in modification of existing technology may be necessary. This includes the adaptation of imported technology to suit local conditions as well as the updating of traditional technology to increase its productivity. In what follows R & D expenditures are assumed to be used for both generation of new technologies and the re-shaping of existing technologies.

In the literature on R & D in developed countries a distinction is made between research (sometimes between 'basic' and 'applied' research) and 'development'. Whereas the end result of research is 'pure' or applicable knowledge, development "attempts to reduce research findings to practice".[3] Thus, for new technologies, products or processes to be realised, research is a necessary but not sufficient condition. For the modification of existing technology 'development' may be presumed to be the major requirement. In practice, however, it is often very difficult to identify research and development as two separate categories because the same branch and in some cases the same personnel may be involved in both activities. Furthermore the linkages between research and development are difficult to quantify. How much research is necessary before development can begin? Once development begins, is there no need for further research? There are no unambiguous answers to these questions. Therefore, in this study, we treat R & D as a symbiotic whole when looking at their impact on technology and the economy at large.

Here the Social Accounting Matrix is proposed as a framework for linking R & D with the generation and adoption of technologies. A rather straight-forward approach is to include R & D as a separate productive activity, i.e. augment T_{33} (in Table II.4) by a column and a row. This will naturally mean that the whole SAM transactions matrix will now have one more row and column than before. In an accounting sense, this poses no problems whatsoever. The current flows from and to the R & D account are captured by the entries in R & D column and row respectively. Incidentally, this could also capture the financing of R & D by domestic or foreign and by public or private sources.[4]

The public financing of R & D is captured by the flow of funds from the government account to the R & D and to a lesser extent by the R & D entries of public owned corporations (e.g. Pertamina, in the oil industry in Indonesia). For this latter information to be shown, however, the productive activities need to be identified according to the types of ownership. This will also capture the foreign financing of R & D as the flows from foreign owned firms. The residual will be domestic private financing of R & D (see section V.A.3. for a description of the public financing of R & D in Indonesia.) A more comprehensive and direct way to capture R & D according to the mode of financing is to break down the R & D column according to how it is financed. Thus, there should be one column for foreign private R & D, one for domestic private R & D and so on. However, this requires an even more detailed break down of R & D data than before.

The above proposal, though useful as an accounting device runs into serious difficulties as a basis for the macroeconomic modelling of technology. The major problem, as alluded to before, is that the effects of R & D on technology are essentially dynamic whereas the above framework is completely static. In other words, R & D on a particular sector is very unlikely to generate or modify a technology within the accounting period (usually a year). Typically, several years of lead time will be necessary for a new technology to be developed; or even for an existing technology to be modified adequately. Thus, the accounting or fixed price multipliers cannot reveal the dynamic effects of R & D on technology. This, of course, does not imply that econometric models incorporating R & D cannot be based on such SAMs, or that the SAM entries cannot be used as a base year solution for such models.

However, the SAM framework as such, holds further possibilities for R & D modelling. One way to capture the dynamic effects discussed previously is through introduction of lags in the R & D accounts, treating R & D as an intermediate input of production. It is assumed that the expenditure on R & D in a sector in the past caused the present increase in its productivity. By analogy, current R & D expenditures on a sector will lead to increases of productivity in the future. Thus, if R_{j,t_0} is the expenditure of the jth sector on R & D at period t_0, the output effect on this sector may be observed for a period t $(>t_0)$ in the future. The value of t will depend on the industry characteristics and the type of R & D undertaken. Thus it may be a long period for the aircraft industry where a large amount of R & D, perhaps financed by foreign sources will be necessary. It may be relatively short for the modification of small tractors for use on a particular type of soil. In any case then, theoretically, the impact of R & D on the productivity of existing technologies and productive activities may be captured to some extent once lags are taken into account. The impact of R & D on the productivity of technologies and processes can be reflected more accurately if the marginal effect on input-output coefficients can be computed for an increase in R & D.

Symbolically,

$a_{ij(t)}$ = input of activity i into activity j in period t

$R_{j(t)}$ = research and development input into the activity j in time t

Then

$$a_{ij(t_1)} = f(R_{j(t_0)}, A_k), \quad t_1 > t_0 \qquad (5.1)$$

$$i,j = 1,2,\ldots n \qquad k = 1,2,\ldots m$$

where A_k are other factors which also shift productivity.

It may seem that with technological progress one should observe $a_{ij(t_1)} \leq a_{ij(t_0)}$ in sector j. However, this is too restrictive, since technological progress may very well call for less use of one type of intermediate input and more of another. Thus one may observe a decrease in the use of cotton fibers along with an increase in the use of synthetic fibers in modern technology in the textiles sector. However, output per unit of labour or capital must increase.

In terms of the matrix of average propensities, the above can be rewritten in the following manner:

As in (2.4), let

$$A_n = \begin{bmatrix} 0 & 0 & A_{13} \\ A_{21} & A_{22} & 0 \\ 0 & A_{32} & A_{33} \end{bmatrix}$$

A_n, of course, now includes R & D as another productive activity.

After an increase in R & D expenditures, R_j, a new average propensities matrix, A_n', can be otained for the future period.

$$A_n' = \begin{bmatrix} 0 & 0 & A_{13}' \\ A_{21} & A_{22} & 0 \\ 0 & A_{32} & A_{33}' \end{bmatrix}$$

where a_{ij} and a_{ij}' are the intermediate input requirements in A_n and A_n' respectively. Usually technological change will mean that the entries in the value-added matrix (A_{13}) might change also. This is likely, as technological progress typically enhances the productivity of labour and/or capital. Unless technical change is neutral in a very specific manner, the shares of value added going to various factors will be different after technical progress has occurred.[5]

The above approach still involves considerable simplification of reality. In particular, it abstracts to some extent from the external effects of expenditure of R & D. In the real world frequently R & D in one activity will also lead to productivity gains in other, perhaps related activities. Thus, expenditure for research on rice may lead to productivity gains for other food crops as well. As the next part illustrates, econometric estimation of such external effects is not so easily obtained. Another neglected feature in the proposed framework is the cumulative effect of R & D. R & D expenditure in one period may lead to not a one shot increase in productivity, but rather to a cumulative effect for several periods like a decaying process till the effects become negligible. Econometric work involving distributed lags may be necessary to estimate these effects over the relevant time periods. Thus, the SAM framework is not a mechanical device to be used without discretion. It still remains a _framework_ within which econometric results of the impact of R & D on productivity can be integrated.

Assuming that the average propensities matrix, A_n', and the marginal expenditure propensities matrix can be constructed, then accounting multipliers and fixed price multipliers matrices can be computed. The procedure for arriving at the impact of a change in R & D expenditures on production, consumption, employment and income distribution is the same as those described earlier in Chapters II and III.

So far the issue of the generation of completely new productive activities or technologies through research and development has not been discussed. For technologies within SAM-Tech this means the introduction of a dualistic technology-cum-product sector where previously there was only one sector (i.e. the addition of a new column vector representing the linear production function of the new technology). In the same way, for the introduction of an entirely new product a new column and a corresponding row are to be added to the SAM. In section V.B, we discuss the problem further in the context of an evolutionary model of technological change for the generation of new technology.

It should not be surprising that the amount of detailed information necessary to operationalise the proposed SAM framework for R & D is not available for Indonesia. In the next subsection we review briefly the available data in order to identify further information requirements for constructing such a SAM.

2. Studies of agricultural mechanisation research on rice and textiles

Agricultural mechanisation, rice and textiles production are the few areas of the Indonesian economy where some work has been done on the impact of R & D on the generation and adoption of technologies. Here the methodologies and results of these studies are reviewed briefly in order to evaluate their usefulness for building a SAM incorporating R & D activity.

The mechanised technology in paddy production was introduced in the form of small tractors in Indonesia in the seventies. The demand for mechanisation of land preparation was a result of the alleged labour shortage during the peak period, caused by the introduction of high-yielding varieties of rice. Aided by the government BIMAS (rice intensification) program certain areas in Sumatra and Java have introduced small tractors for land preparation.[6]

These tractors were developed originally not in Indonesia, but rather in developed countries and especially at international organisations such as the International Rice Research Institute. As an engineering study by Reddy points out,

> "...small farm equipment technology developed at IRRI, is the appropriate one in the sense that it is simple enough to be handled by small farmers and then fabricatable in small workshops with initial guidance."[7]

West Sumatra was chosen as a pilot project area and field extension work was carried out (funded by the USAID). After initial demonstrations, two small local workshops were motivated to start manufacturing the equipment. This 'joint venture' between IRRI and the local firms resulted in the production and sale of several hundreds of hand weeders and more than 200 paddy threshers within three years by March 1982. In the judgement of the project engineers,

> West Sumatra has attained the take off stage with regard to the local production of some of the above farm equipment in the sense that the spread of manufacturers and their production has been rapidly increasing without requiring any further outside assistance.[8] (Emphasis in the original text.)

Further field extension work was undertaken in South Sulawesi,

South Kalimantan and West Java. In South Sulawesi, actually ten locally produced hand made tractors met the technical and economic test admirably.[9] However, further R & D expenditures will still be necessary to make these tractors, developed originally for 10 to 15 ha. farm sizes, totally appropriate for the much smaller size farms in Indonesia.

Table V.1 compares the costs of traditional, locally improved modern and imported modern technology. Except for harvesting and winnowing, the improved modern technology seems to enjoy a comparative cost advantage. However, the initial investments are often large. This is another area where appropriate government credit and investment policies are necessary.

Let us briefly indicate the way agricultural mechanisation could be incorporated in a SAM. Assuming for simplicity, mechanisation for paddy production only, this would mean first of all further dissaggregating the SAM so that paddy production is shown as a distinct production activity. With some effort, this can be done. In addition, the paddy production activity itself will have to be broken down into paddy produced by modern (mechanised) and traditional (non-mechanised) technologies.[10] At present sufficient information for this breakdown does not exist. It is also clear that more detailed information on the intermediate inputs, value added going to the factors and consumption will be necessary in addition to the data on R & D expenditures.

A second example of the relationship between R & D and productivity is the previously cited study of rice research in Indonesia by David Salmon. This study treats R & D as an input in the production function which is to some extent analogous to our treatment of R & D. Salmon's work distinguishes between centralised and decentralised research (both public) on bunded and non-bunded rice and takes into account other productivity shifters (A_k in eq. 5.1) such as BIMAS and literacy program, and land quality. Using a translog production function with the aforementioned R & D and other variables, he finds that the R & D variables have a positive effect on productivity showing increasing marginal returns. The overall returns are very high--151 percent a year. This was partly a reflection of low budget base in 1965, the initial year for which data existed. It also contained effects of 'the residual of investments in rice research made in Indonesia before 1965'.[11] Even discounting for these factors, the return to R & D in rice would still be quite high.

Including R & D for paddy production in SAM would be very attractive not only because the return to R & D is high, but also because the financing is known with certainty to be public and good time series data exist for R & D. Table V.2 shows the research expenditure on rice during the 70's. Salmon's work also takes into account the lags in the relationship between R & D expenditures and productivity shift. However, the external effects of research in other activities on rice productivity are neglected although the (external) effect of rice research in one region to the region adjacent to it is taken into account. It

Table V.1

COMPARATIVE COST OF MAJOR OPERATIONS FOR RICE CULTIVATION IN INDONESIA

May 1982

No	Operation	Traditional — Man days Required per Ha	Traditional — Cost/Ha-in Fp. inner Islands* (outer Islands)	Traditional — Initial Investment in Rp.	IRRI-TYPE ** Locally made improved Equipment — Man Days Required per Ha	IRRI-TYPE ** — Cost/Ha-in Rp. inner islands* (outer islands)	IRRI-TYPE ** — Initial Investment in Rp.	Imported Equipment — Man Days Required per Ha	Imported Equipment — Cost/Ha-in Rp. inner islands* (outer islands)	Imported Equipment — Initial Investment in Rp.
1.	Land Ploughing	40 (manual) / 16 (animal)	40,000 (80,000) / 40,000 (56,000)	2,000 / 300,000	3 days x 2 opr (6HP HT) / 4 days x 2 opr (4HP HT)	35,000 (41,000) / 28,000 (36,000)	$1\frac{1}{2} \times 10^6$ / 800,000	2 day x 1 opr (13HP MT) / $2\frac{1}{2}$ daysx2 opr (6HP RT)	45,000 (47,000) / 50,000 (55,000)	$4\frac{1}{2} \times 10^6$ / 2.8×10^6
2.	Transplanting	22 (manual) "Women	17,600 (35,200)	-	8 (5 row hand operated)	(10,000) (18,000)	180,000	-	-	-
3.	Weeding (2 times)	40 (manual) " Women	32,000 (64,000)	1,000	14 (Weeder)	14,000 (28,000)	8,000	-	-	-
4.	Harvesting	12 (sickle)	12,000 (24,000)	1,000	$\frac{1}{2}$ x 2 opr (6HP HT Reap) / $\frac{1}{2}$ x 2 opr (4HP HT Reap)	13,000 (14,000) / 10,000 (11,000)	2.0×10^6 / 1.2×10^6	$\frac{1}{2}$ x 2 (5HP reaper)	12,500 (13,500)	1.8×10^6
5.	Threshing	22 (using legs) / 18 (using wood platform)	22,000 (44,000) / 18,000 (36,000)	- / 2,000	1.5 (5HP TH) / 9 (pedal TH)	11,000*** (12,500) / 10,000 (19,000)	500,000 / 35,000	2 (small combine)	90,000 (92,000)	500,000
6.	Winnowing	6 (manual)	6,000 (12,000)	-	2.5 (m. Winnower)	3,000 (5,500)	25,000			
7.	Drying	6	6,200 (12,000)	1,000 (plastic mat)	2.5	16,000 (18,500)		1.5	20,000 (21,500)	

T. = Hand Tractor M.T. = mini tractor R.T. = rotary tiller m = manual opr = operator $1 = Rp. 650,-
*1. assuming rice yields are 4 tons/Ha & thresher cap. 350 Kg/hr
2. assumption: daily agric. women labor wahe Rp. 800/day in inner Islands & Rp. 1,600/ in outer Islands
3. assumption: daily agric. men labour wage Rp. 1,000/day in inner Islanmds & Rp. 2,000/day in outer Islands
** Estimates from pilot projects
Source: Reddy, op.rlt, p.9

Table V.2

Expenditure on Rice Research
(millions of rupiahs)

Year	Research Expenditure
1970/71	167
1971/72	240
1972/73	541
1973/74	738
1974/75	936
1975/76	1576
1976/77	1707
1977/78	1749
1978/79	1612

Source: Mears, The New Rice Economy in Indonesia pp. 423 and 580.

would also be possible to estimate the consumption of rice from available information. The major problems are the intermediate input and the value added matrices. So far, information on these categories have been gathered for a few villages in Java only (see subsection V.B.2). Hence, it is not possible to include R & D in rice research for Indonesia as a whole in a SAM framework at present without a detailed survey covering the entire country.

The final example of a sectoral study is the case study of R & D for the textiles sector by LIPI (Indonesian Institute of Sciences).[12] According to this study, the domestic development of textiles is receiving an increased impetus for two reasons. First of all, the goal of increasing Indonesia's non-oil, labour-intensive exports can be served by increased production in this sector. Secondly, the fulfillment of clothing needs for the population requires an increase in production.

Although to an outsider the textile technology may appear to be simple, there are actually a bewildering array of products, processes and techniques. For the sake of simplicity, we discuss only spinning and weaving for natural fibers. Table V.3 shows the main stages in cotton spinning.

Most of the technical improvements have occurred in roving, spinning and winding. As discussed later, the spinning technology had been modernised by 1975. The future problem is to maintain an indigenous supply of machines and skilled personnel.

In weaving technology, the types of looms are the main consideration. Here, as the section on diffusion discusses extensively the number of semi-automatic and automatic looms is on the increase. The growth of equipment and production of textiles during REPELITA II are given in Tables V.4 and V.5, respectively.

Table V.3

The Cotton Spinning Process

Production Stage	Name of Machine	Input	Output	Standard Workers /Machine
Blowing	Blowing Machine	Cotton Fibre	Lap	2
Carding	Carding Machine	Lap	Card Sliver	20
Combing & Drawing	Sliver/ribbon Lap Machine	Card Sliver		2
	Combing Machine		Combed Sliver	10
Roving	Roving Machine	Drawing Sliver	Roving	2
Ring Spinning	Spinning Machine	Roving	Yarn (cop)	3-8
Winding	Winding Machine	Cop	Cheese	1

Source: Khan 1982 , p. 35.

Based on the distinctions between technologies in spinning and weaving, it is possible to break these two important subsectors of textiles into traditional and modern technology-cum-products (Khan 1982). The LIPI study indicates that within each of these activities, some R & D expenditures will occur in order to create more domestic capabilities in terms of both improved domestic equipment and workers. However, the seventy page document which is very rich in the description of processes and institutional detail gives no figures for actual or planned expenditures on R & D in textiles. Therefore, none of the components of the SAM can be computed. Given the importance of textiles and the obvious emphasis on it during REPELITA IV, this is very disappointing. It is of utmost importance for the appropriate government or international agency to collect the required information on R & D.

3. Current priority areas in R & D and the SAM approach

The government of Indonesia seems to be committed to a policy of science and technology to meet the needs of the country. This was stated recently in general terms by the Minister of Research and Technology, Prof. B.J. Habibie:

"...a clear, realistic and consistently applied concept of the nature of the society to be developed and the technologies needed for the realization of this future society must also be evolved. These technologies need not be the most primitive. They may indeed in many cases be the most advanced in the world. The only criterion for the appropriateness of technologies for any particular country including technologically less developed countries, is their utility in solving actual problems in that particular country."[13]

Table V.4 The growth of equipment and production of textile industry in PELITA I

No.	Items	Unit	1967/70	70/71	71/72	72/73	73/74
A.	Equipment						
1.	False Twisting	Set	-	2	18	35	44
2.	Spinning	1000 mp	481.8	481.8	552.5	631.3	729.6
3.	Weaving	1000 ATBM	50	50	50	50	50
		1000 ATM	35.3	35.6	43.4	48.3	53.7
4.	Knitting	1000 ARBM	2.5	2.5	2.5	2.6	2.7
		1000 ARM	5.4	5.9	6.2	6.4	6.7
5.	Garments	1000 units	3.5	3.8	4.2	4.9	6.2
B.	Production						
6.	Fiber Making	1000 tons	-	-	-	-	6.5
7.	Yarn	1000 balls	182.1	217.5	238.0	262.1	316.1
8.	Weaving Fabric	million meters	322.3	400.8	574.7	667.7	733.3
9.	Knitting Fabrics	million meters	127.5	147.5	155.3	185.1	193.3
10.	Batik	million meters	60.7	66.7	73.2	80.4	88.2
11.	Garments	million meters	6.8	7.3	8.3	9.6	12.3

Source: LIPI - Case Study - Textiles, p.25

Table V.5 The growth of equipment and production of textile industry in PELITA II (1974 - 1979)

No.	Items	Unit	1974/75	75/76	76/77	77/78	78/79
A.	Equipment						
1.	False Twisting	Set	142	147	164	164	100
2.	Spinning	million mp	0.9	1.2	1.4	1.5	1.5
3.	Weaving	1000 ATBM	55	60	66.3	66.3	60
		1000 ATM	57.8	60.4	61.5	66.9	65
4.	Knitting	1000 ARBM	2.9	3.0	3.1	3.2	-
		1000 ARM	6.8	7.2	7.5	8.0	8.2
5.	Garments	1000 units	6.4	6.5	6.8	7.2	12.8
B.	Production						
6.	Fiber Making	1000 tons	12.1	47.7	59.1	59.1	95.0
7.	Yarn	1000 balls	364.0	445.4	622.9	678.0	900.0
8.	Weaving Fabric	million meters	777.1	809.1	993.9	1073.4	1400.0
9.	Knitting Fabrics	million meters	196.3	208	293.1	316.8	-
10.	Batik	million meters	95.3	115	148.1	149.2	125
11.	Garments	million meters	12.5	12.8	13.4	14.7	15

Source: LIPI - Case Study - Textiles, p.28.

In the same speech, the minister emphasised the need for experimentation and actual application of technologies, imported or produced indigenously, in order to develop them further.

Another general and influential idea in the policy formulations on science and technology in Indonesia is the dynamic needs of the economy at different phases of development. Both Prof. Habibie and the LIPI study on "Science and Technology Policy Research" stress this aspect. The latter document mentions that

> "the utilization of science and technology should coincide with the phases of development which starts with the agricultural sector development to create self-sufficiency in food and gradually comes to the industrial sector development to process raw materials into industrial products."[14]

In practice, however, the pattern of R & D is not always as consistent.

The existing S & T in Indonesia is the product of mostly factors other than the economic development needs of the country. However, a coherent S & T policy must be cognisant of national development objectives and goals. Clear policy criteria derived from both development needs as well as other factors such as national security must be used to formulate such a S & T policy.

It is generally agreed among Indonesia's policymakers that high growth with equity in income distribution and the fulfillment of basic needs are the primary development goals. Accordingly, the basic needs (food, housing, health care, clothing, education) areas should also be a focus of intense research and development activities. The present study emphasises the usefulness of a SAM framework for policy analysis precisely to meet these development goals. If a SAM incorporating both R & D and technologies can be constructed, then the effect of change of any expenditure on R & D will be shown by the fixed price multipliers. In particular, the effects of such policies on household income distribution and consumption will indicate to what extent the goals of equity in income distribution and of basic needs fulfillment are being met.

In the absence of such a framework, very careful cost-benefit studies of specific R & D projects may serve as a substitute. The existing evidence does not suggest that such studies have been or are being made. The specific commitments of the government in terms of priority areas (which will be discussed presently) therefore appear to be somewhat ad hoc. The existing information on the allocation of R & D expenditures by institutions and broad categories does not clarify the situation very much.

The Ministry of State for Research and Technology directs all research activities financed with public funds. This constitutes the bulk of R & D activities in Indonesia. Together with the research institutions of the specific industries, there are four categories of research institutions in Indonesia:

1) Research institutions under the Ministries;

2) Research institutions under the non-ministerial government
    agencies;

3) Research institutions within the universities;

4) Research institutions of the industries.

The government has taken a major policy decision to create a
National Center for Research, Science and Technology in Serpong,
Jakarta. In 1982/83 there were 240 R & D institutions of which
141 were ministerial, 30 non-ministerial, 58 university and 11
industrial. Of the 2238 R & D activities financed by the
government, 28% were undertaken by ministerial institutions, 6% by
non-ministerial institutions and 66% by the universities. According to Prof. Mohamadi of LIPI, 47% of them were in human basic
needs, 19% in natural resources and energy, 13% on industrialisation and 21% in social sciences and humanities. It would be
extremely interesting to explore further the nature of these R & D
projects, but lack of information prevents us from this endeavor.
There is also no rupiah figure so that budgetary allocation among
the categories cannot be determined. The only available figures
relate to the four-fold functional classification. According to
this, of the total 296 trillion rupiahs (approximately $296
million) in R & D, 127 trillion rupiahs or 43% went to the ministerial institutions, 59 trillion rupiahs or 20% went to the non-
ministerial institutions and 110 trillion rupiahs or 37% went to
the universities. This total was .5% of the GDP in 1982/83 and
grew at an annual rate of 41%.[15]

Mainly due to the paucity of data from the foregoing discussion
it is not clear how R & D is allocated to basic needs category
especially. Other available information on sectors receiving
priority regarding R & D shows concern with both basic needs
industries as well as other industries. However, the emphasis
seems to lie with the latter.

On the one hand, there are the agricultural R & D and R & D in
textiles. These seem to reflect a commitment to the fulfillment
of basic needs. On the other hand, the transportation (including
aircrafts, shipbuilding and land-transportation) and telecommunications sectors seem to have top priorities with several high
visibility capital-intensive projects.[16] For example, the an-
nouncement of the first Indonesian made aircraft recently drama-
tised the emphasis given to the aircraft industry. In the context
of Indonesia, a country with 13000 islands stretching over a vast
distance, transportation, naturally, has to be a high priority
area. However, inland water transportation probably deserves more
attention than the production of expensive aircrafts with little
domestic content.[17]

In shipbuilding, the manufacturing of 400-dwt, 30-knot FPB-57
and 60 dwt,30-knot FPB patrol boats under license from Friedrich
Luerssen Werf in Bremen GDR has been planned. Improvement of dry

docking, maintenance and overhauling capabilities is also underway.

In land transportation, both the automotive industry and the rolling stock industries are in the first phase of their development. The former is largely privately owned with firms from Europe, Japan and U.S. Therefore, R & D, if it takes place in Indonesia at all, is foreign financed. The rolling-stock manufacturing is controlled by a single government-owned corporation, P.T. Industri Kereta Api (PT INKA). Here the R & D expenditure is presumably for improvement of quality especially for exports. Recently PT INKA submitted a joint bid (together with Nippon Sharyo) for delivery of freight cars to Thailand.

In telecommunications most of R & D is concentrated in the development of digital telephone switching systems, automobile telephones and various short-wave radio transmitters for defense purposes. Along with defense industries, energy and engineering industries are also mentioned prominently as candidates for R & D expenditures.

The high technology focus of the existing policy is very clear from the foregoing discussion. What is not clear are the impacts of these policies on output, employment and income distribution. Some of these sectors may indeed generate high growth, but perhaps at the expense of employment in more labour-intensive industries, where the same investment may lead to a higher employment. The initial balance-of-payment effects are almost certainly going to be deficit producing, since most of the technology will be imported, at least initially. Thus, given the long-run goals of both growth and equity in terms of adequate income and basic needs fulfillment for the people, the impact of these policies seems unclear. It is especially in such a context that policy experiments with both efficient labour-intensive technologies and a blending of labour and capital-intensive technologies, as R & D expenditures change, can be extremely useful. Thus, devoting some resources for a long-term project to construct a SAM embodying R & D and technologies, or at least generating enough information so that alternative R & D and technology policies can be evaluated by comparing their effects on output, employment, income distribution and balance of payments would seem to have a high pay off.

In the next section, the relationship between R & D and the diffusion of technology is pursued further by synthesising the results of an evolutionary model of technical change in the SAM framework.

B. Diffusion of technology

Whether a technology is generated domestically or transferred from abroad, its use has to become widespread in the economy before any significant impact is felt. In this section an attempt will be made to understand the dynamics of technology diffusion.

In one important respect, the discussion on R & D logically precedes that on diffusion. R & D expenditures can often lead to a more rapid diffusion of technology than would be the case otherwise. However, even without significant R & D expenditures, a new technology may still be used extensively. The two cases are distinguished here by identifying the diffusion caused or preceded by significant R & D expenditures as R-diffusion. The second type of diffusion which occurs even without much R & D expenditures may be called market-forces led or M-diffusion. The distinction is one of degree only, for even in the first case the market forces have to be present. But the presence or absence of R & D in a sector can be operationally relevant for an explanation of diffusion. The necessity of R & D in some sector (e.g. aircraft industry or new varieties of rice) for the introduction of novel technologies, gives the concept of R-diffusion further meaning.

In the empirical literature on diffusion both types can be identified. The work done on the U.S. by A. Wade Blackman et al.,[18] uses factor analysis to isolate the effect of R & D as a major contributor to the diffusion of technologies in certain sectors. On the other hand, the pioneering work of Zvi Griliches, the work by Mansfield as well as the model described later on in this study are examples of M-diffusion approaches.[19] The recently published study by James Keddie on choice of technology in Indonesian firms also follows this line of argument when it claims that the search for premium through product heterogeneity leads to the choice of relatively capital-intensive technology in many cases.[20]

In discussing diffusion of technology in Indonesia, the major problem is the availability of information. The existing information, even at the micro level is very scanty and its reliability often questionable. At the macro level there is no systematic time series which corresponds precisely to the distinctions between techniques made in this study. In this part we focus on the linkages between the micro and macroeconomic aspects of technological diffusion at a conceptual level. The main result is the demonstration of such linkages between micro-models of evolutionary change and macro-models based on SAM.

Before moving on to a theoretical discussion of the nexus between diffusion of technology within a sector and other macroeconomic variables such as output, employment and income distribution, it will be instructive to review some studies of these linkages at the micro level for Indonesia. Appendix A to this chapter contains a further description and explanation of the trends of output, employment and value added in some of the dualistic and other selected industries for both the traditional and modern techniques in the Indonesian case.

1. Some microeconomic studies of technology, employment and income distribution

Hayami and Kikuchi (1981) and Kasryno (1981) discuss the impact of technology in rice paddy production on the income distribution for two and three villages in Java respectively. In this section these two studies are reviewed.

Of the two villages selected for their study by Hayami and Kikuchi, one is technologically stagnant and the other is technologically progressive. In the first village no technological change except for some increase in the fertilizer use had taken place. The gains in rice yields have not been significant as a result. The increase in the labor force through population growth led to a decline in the marginal product of labor. Finally, an institutional change in harvesting from <u>bawon</u> to <u>ceblokan</u> system led to an increase in inequality of labor income. Under the <u>bawon</u> system, harvesting was open to any villager and the output would be shared. The <u>ceblokan</u> system restricted entry and introduced a wage system corresponding to the market mechanism.

Between 1968-71 and 1978 the total farmer's (owner) income increased by 25% in this village whereas the average income of hired laborer rose by only 4%. Consequently the conclusion can be drawn that "the size distribution of income between farmers and laborers became more skewed." It is also supported by the fact that over the same period the number of landless and near-landless households increased more rapidly than that of farmers.[21]

In contrast to the dismal, almost Ricardian stationary state of the previous village, the technologically progressive village is a picture of rapid growth without adverse distributional consequences. Here is a village which is not unlike the other one in terms of physical and social characteristics with only one exception. Use of irrigation, fertilizer and high yield variety seeds led to a 40% increase in yield/acre. Even though the <u>bawon</u> system was retained, the share of the workers was one-tenth instead of one-fifth. But with the increased yield, the post-harvest real wages did not fall in most cases.[22] Tables V.6 and V.7 show the changes in shares of income from rice production per ha. of crop area in the two villages. In the technologically progressive village (North Subang) shown in Table V.7, the share of income received by hired laborers falls by only one percent between 1968-71 and 1978. As stated earlier, the absolute incomes of these hired laborers did not fall. In contrast to this village, in South Subang, their income share fell relatively (from 36.8 to 32.6 percent during the same period) despite a very small increase in real wages.

Two aspects of this very interesting study should be noted. First, one can hardly generalize from a study of only two villages. Second and more important is the fact that the stability of income distribution in the second village depended at least partly in its nonadoption of the <u>ceblokan</u> system. The reason for this, it is admitted by the authors, is sociological rather than economic. It is explained by the "loose community structure of the village." As the villagers were recent settlers from various ethnic groups, the kind of restrictions required by the ceblokan system could not be introduced smoothly under patron-client relationships already in existence in the other village.[23] Furthermore, it is not clear that in the future the marginal product of labor will not fall with population growth or in-migration. It is also possible that restricted entry systems

134

Table V. 6,

Changes in shares of income from rice production
per ha. of crop area in the South Subang Village,
1968-71 to 1978.

	Income in paddy (kg/ha)		Income share (%)	
	1968–71	1978	1968–71	1978
Value added[a]	2,255	2,649	100.0	100.0
Farmer:				
Family labor	427	438	19.0	16.5
Capital	136	125	6.0	4.7
Operator's surplus	862	1,223	38.2	46.2
Total	1,425	1,786	63.2	67.4
Hired laborer:				
Preharvest work	397	443	17.6	16.7
Harvest & postharvest work	433	420	19.2	15.9
Total	830	863	36.8	32.6

Source: Y. Hayami and M. Kikuchi, Asian Village at the Crossroads, p. 192.

Table V. 7

Changes in shares of income from rice production
per ha. of crop area in the North Subang Village,
from 1968-71 to 1978/79.

	Income in paddy (kg/ha)		Income share (%)	
	1968–71	1978/79	1968–71	1978/79
Value added[a]	2,191	2,903	100.0	100.0
Farmer:				
Family labor	117	252	5.3	8.7
Capital	47	154	2.2	5.2
Operator's surplus	1,197	1,427	54.6	49.2
Total	1,361	1,833	62.1	63.1
Hired laborer:				
Preharvest work	467	686	21.3	23.7
Harvest & postharvest work	363	384	16.6	13.2
Total	730	1,070	37.9	36.9

Source: Hayami and Kikuchi, p. 207.

analogous to the ceblokan system may be introduced in the future by the owner-farmers.

The other study of three villages by Kasryno was a part of the agroeconomic survey.[24] Modern technology reached these villages as part of the BIMAS (rice intensification through mass guidance) package of high-yielding seed varieties, chemical fertilizers, pesticides, extension services and a favorable procurement policy. The following tables show the change in the technology in the three villages (Tables V.8, V.9, V.10). In one of the villages (Mariuk), there has been also a change in the land preparation technology. In 1971, 75% of the farmers used animals and only 3% power tillers for land preparation. In 1981 most of the farmers (83%) used power tillers. It needs to be emphasized that this technological change was a direct result of the government rice intensification program. From Tables V.8, V.9 and V.10 it is clear that the increase in fertilizer (ranging from 36% to 91% of the 1969/71 figures) is positively correlated with the increase in yield (ranging from 24.4% to 51%) per ha. of paddy.

Although the productivity of land increased in each village, in two of them, the number of landless households increased significantly. In the most technologically advanced village (Mariuk) one-third of the households were landless in 1971. Ten years later 70% were landless. The percentage of sharecropping families among the landless also dropped from 22% in 1971 to only 10% in 1981. Thus, the number of purely landless households increased by more than five times. New market types of wage contracts began to be used along with the bawon system in the wake of the technological change. In Kasryno's words:

"During the wet season crop landless laborers worked as permanent agricultural laborers with daily wage payments. The laborers in the wet season were employed in every phase of rice production from seedbed preparation, land preparation, transplanting, weeding, harvesting and post-harvest tasks, even the wife of a laborer took part in this work especially in transplanting, weeding and harvesting. In the dry season, the laborers became tenants through a sharecropping contract. In addition, landowners extended credits for the dry season production expenses as well as living expenses for the tenants...(Thus) a market interlinkage emerged. From the land owner's view, he gets assurance of a supply of labor for the wet season, assurance of qualified tenants for the dry season, and reliable borrowers for the surplus capital he has accumulated.[25]

In terms of the Gini coefficient, the size distribution of income in all three villages became more unequal in 1981 than in 1971. In Sentul, Jatisari and Mariuk villages, the Gini coefficients of income distribution were .56, .56 and .53, respectively in 1971. The corresponding figures for 1981 were .59, .71 and .87, respectively. Therefore, clearly inequality of income distribution as measured by the Gini coefficient increased for all three villages.

Table V.8

Changes in Inputs Per Hectare of Rice Area and Input Price for Rice Production in Mariuk Village, West Java, 1969/71 to 1980/81.

Items	Wet Season 1969/71 [a]	Wet Season 1980/81 [a]	% changes from 1969/71 to 1980/81
Yield (kgs paddy/Ha)	2884	4365	51.0
Paddy Price (Rp/kg)	19.30	96	397
Inputs:			
Fertilizer (kgs/Ha) [b]	131 (59)	250 (105)	91
Labour (hours/Ha):			
Land preparation (male)	265	227	-14.3
Total preharvest	692	686	-1.0
Animal	59	1	-98
Tractor	0.5	16	2400
Real Input Prices (in kg paddy): [c]			
Fertilizer (kg/Ha)	1.4	0.67	-52.0
Male labour (kg/day)	8.3(100)[d]	10.4(500)[d]	25.0
Animal rental (kg/day) [e]	13.0	27.5	115.0
Tractor rental (kg/ha) [f]	278	315	13.3

a. Average for wet seasons 1969/70 and 1970/71 and wet season 1980/81
b. Urea and TSP; figures in parentheses are in kgs of plant nutrients (N and P)
c. Nominal price divided by paddy price.
d. Figures in parentheses are daily money wage alone where wage rates in kg/day are total wage which include money wage and value of 3 meals and cigarettes given to labourers.
e. Both for animal and tractor rental fees, they included wages for operators.
f. Tractor rental based on piece of work contract such as for a piece of land (Ha) which was most common.

Source: Faisal Kasryno: Technological Progress and Its Effects on Income Distribution, p. 11.

Table V.9

Changes in Inputs per Hectare of Rice Crop Area and Input Price for Rice Production in Sentul Village, West Java, 1969/71 to 1980/81.

Items	Wet Season 1969/71 [a]	Wet Season 1980/81 [a]	% changes from 1969/71 to 1980/81
Yield (kgs paddy/Ha)	1534	2129	38.8
Paddy Price (Rp/kg)	16.25	85.0	425
Inputs:			
Fertilizer (kgs/Ha) [b]	67 (28)	100 (43)	49
Labour (hours/Ha):			
Land preparation (male)	228	194	-15
Total preharvest	458	439	-5
Animal for land preparation	49	52	6
Real Input Prices: [c]			
Fertilizer (kg/Ha)	2.1	0.67	-69
Labour wage (kg/day)	7.35	7.6	4
Animal rental (kg/day) [d]	15.0	16.7	11

a. Average for wet seasons 1969/70 and 1970/71.
b. Urea and TSP; figures in parentheses are in kgs of plant nutrients (N and P)
c. Nominal price divided by paddy price.
d. Rental on per day basis which was more common in this village.

Source: Faisal Kasryno: Technological Progress and Its Effects on Income Distribution, p. 9.

Table V.10

Changes in Inputs per Hectare of Rice Crop Area and Input Price for Rice Production in Jatisari Village, West Java, 1969/71 to 1980/81.

Items	Wet Season 1969/71 [a]	Wet Season 1980/81 [a]	% changes from from 1969/71 to 1980/81
Yield (kgs paddy/Ha)	3420	4253	24.4
Paddy Price (Rp/kg)	22.0	115.0	423
Inputs:			
Fertilizer (kgs/Ha) [b]	257 (108)	350 (147)	36
Labour (hours/Ha):			
Land preparation (male)	955	593	-38
Total preharvest	1702	1263	-26
Animal for land preparation	9.2	12.9	40
Real Input Prices (kg paddy): [c]			
Fertilizer (kg/Ha)	1.36	0.61	-55
Male labour (kg/day) [d]	6.1(80)	5.2(500)	-19
Male labour (kg/hour)	0.87	1.04	19
Animal rental (kg/day) [e]	19.2	21.7	13

a. Average for wet seasons 1969/70 and 1970/71.
b. Urea and TSP; figures in parentheses are in kgs of plant nutrients (N and P)
c. Nominal price divided by paddy price.
d. Figures in parentheses are daily money wages, where figures in kgs paddy/day are included values of meals and cigarettes which are given to labourers. In 1969/71 average working hours was 7 hours a day where for 1981 it was 5 hours a day.
e. Rental on per day basis which was more common in this village. Wage for operator included in the rental fee.

Source: Faisal Kasryno: Technological Progress and Its Effects on Income Distribution, p. 10.

According to Kasryno, this increase in inequality is directly attributable to an increase in landholding inequality. With the caveat of the paucity of information in mind, it seems fair to conclude on the basis of the two foregoing studies that ceteris paribus at present technological change in rice paddy cultivation is equally likely to increase or decrease income inequality among the farmers and agricultural labourers. What needs to be understood are institutional arrangements which may ameliorate or exacerbate the existing inequality of income distribution. More research on diffusion of technology and institutional change in the organization of labor process is an urgent necessity before the distributional effects of diffusion can be predicted with any reliability.

2. Incorporation of microeconomic technology diffusion models into a SAM framework at conceptual level

At the macro level, assuming that institutional arrangements do not change along with the introduction of technology (an unrealistic but simplifying assumption) it is possible to model the linkage between diffusion of technology within a sector and the macroeconomic effects on production, employment and income distribution within a SAM framework. The strategy here is to link microeconomic models of evolutionary technical change with the macroeconomic framework. We use here a model of technology diffusion developed by Nelson et al. for Colombia to illustrate this novel approach.[26]

The purpose of this particular model for Colombia was to explain the existence of different technologies in the same productive activity and the diffusion path of modern technology over time. The theory of product life cycle in international trade suggests a diffusion of technology from the advanced to the less developed countries over time. Similarly, the diffusion of this modern technology within the LDC requires time as well. Therefore, at any point in time the observation on value added/worker for an industry in an LDC actually represents a weighted average distributed over firms using quite different technologies, i.e.

$$Q/L = \sum_{(Q/L)\ min}^{(Q/L)\ max} (Q_i/L_i)\ L_i/L$$

where Q = total value added in a particular sector

L = total employment in a particular sector

Q_i = value added of firms using technology i

L_i = employment in firms using technology i.

Since value added/worker is a measure of labor-intensity, the above expression is consistent with the coexistence of techniques with varying degrees of labor intensities. In the model itself, the techniques are reduced to two in number (for simplicity) which corresponds exactly to the dualistic classification of technologies in Chapter II.

The starting point for the model is a sector of the less developed economy using only traditional technology. Then, a new technology which is more productive than the existing one is introduced from abroad, or generated domestically through R & D efforts. The new technology is required to pay higher rewards to the factors, perhaps because of the existence of labor unions and other factor market imperfections. As a result, the transition to the long-run competitive equilibrium involves a period when both the techniques can be sustained. It is the diffusion pattern of the new technology during this period that is of utmost importance. Our strategy is to use the results regarding the pattern of diffusion in order to adjust the SAM coefficients during the transition period, if necessary. This approach will lead to a partial relaxation of the static features of the SAM. We now summarize the relevant aspects of the Nelson model and show how the results of this model can be integrated with the SAM framework.

For simplicity, assume that capital and labor are the only factors. Suppose at time t_o, Q/L, the per capita output in dollar terms to be the following:

$$Q/L = f(K/L) = g(w,r)$$

where $g(\cdot)$ is homogeneous of degree zero and w and r are the costs of labor and capital respectively. Let us also assume that at the same time a new technology is invented that is α times more productive than the old one for every factor mix. At time $t_{o+\theta}$ the new technology is first brought to use at a small level. After $t_o + \theta$ productivity will be

$$Q/L = g(w_1, r_1) L_1/L + g(w_2, r_2) L_2/L$$

$$L_1 + L_2 = L$$

where L_1 = labor in the old technology

L_2 = labor in the new technology

w_1, w_2 = wages under the old and new techniques respectively

r_1, r_2 = prices of capital under the old and new techniques respectively.

It can be shown that the relative importance of the two technologies can be traced through time in the following manner: (for the derivation of this, see the appendix)

$$d/dt[\log (Q_2/Q_1)] = (\dot{Q}_2/Q_2) - (\dot{Q}_1/Q_1) =$$

$$\lambda[(1-b) (1 - 1/\alpha) h_1 (\bar{r},\bar{w})]$$

where $\lambda > 0$ is a diffusion index, $0 \leq b \leq 1$ is an adjustment coefficient and $\bar{w}$ and $\bar{r}$ are competitive (normal profit) wages and rentals. $h_1 (\cdot)$ is the unit cost function of the traditional technology. Given a certain value for α (a technical parameter) the diffusion process varies directly with λ and inversely with b.

This is a simple, and in some respects a misspecified model.[27] However, as a first approximation, even under the assumptions of constant returns to scale and a value of λ which is the same for the expanding and the declining firms, we can obtain an estimate of the increase in total sectoral output through the introduction of new technology as an outcome of R & D expenditures or adoption of foreign technology. This will allow us to adjust our SAM entries for the next period. Here there are two cases to consider:

Case 1: In case of any one of our dualistic sectors such as handpounded rice vs. milled rice, or farm processed tea vs. modern tea processing, the diffusion index λ and the adjustment coefficient b can be estimated from time-series data to reallocate output between the techniques for the next period. This will not alter the SAM multipliers but only the composition of output between the traditional and modern subsectors.

Case 2: However, we also have sectors where the dualistic breakdown has not been made explicitly. Here (e.g. textiles, paddy production) a separate technology-cum-productive activity can be introduced in the next period. As a result, the matrix for average expenditure propensities will change. Consequently, we will arrive at a new matrix of accounting multipliers.

It may be possible to obtain different estimates for α, λ and b for each sector and also devise an iterative procedure to project their values into the future for dynamic simulation exercises. More research with similar models is also likely to pay off.

It was not possible to estimate the parameters λ or b for Indonesia as the data for small enterprises exist for only two points in time (1975 and 1979) and information on returns to capital is virtually non-existent at the sectoral level. Conceptually, the approach still has a great deal of appeal and perhaps can be applied to other developing countries with better time-series data (e.g. Korea).

Given that data are available on R & D, the previous section extended the SAM framework by incorporating the relationship between R & D and the development and use of new technology. In this section the link is further extended to some of the technical and market characteristics captured by λ, α and b. Thus, conceptually both R-diffusion and M-diffusion can be handled by the proposed integration of R & D, evolutionary models and SAM.

C. Summary

This chapter dealt with a number of issues related to R & D and diffusion of technology. It may be useful to summarize the main issues discussed and results obtained here.

The first section (V.A) of this chapter proposes a method for treating R & D in a macroeconomic setting by identifying it as a separate productive activity within the SAM. As a device for integrating R & D data with other macroeconomic variables and analyzing the impacts of R & D on technology, employment and income distribution, the proposal seems to have considerable merit. However, a look at the existing data and econometric work on R & D in Indonesia reveals the impossibility of operationalising the suggested approach without extensive collection of information on R & D expenditures in specific sectors of the economy. Further econometric work dealing with sectoral productivity changes as a result of R & D will also be necessary. Nevertheless, a critical review of the current government R & D policies giving priority to high technology, clearly confirms the appropriateness of a SAM approach for R & D policy analysis. Given multiple objectives of R & D policy such as growth of output, employment and 'equitable' income distribution, no ad hoc or partial equilibrium approach can be a good substitute for the SAM approach.

The second section begins with a review of microeconomic linkages between technology diffusion in rice paddy production and income distribution which shows the link between them to be complex, involving significant institutional changes. These linkages at the macroeconomic level are explored further conceptually in the final subsection. There a synthesis of the results of an evolutionary model of technical change with the SAM framework shows the potential for micro-macro linkages in the area of technology diffusion. In this way, this chapter highlights the crucial connection between R & D and technological change over time and their implications at both micro and macro levels.

Notes

1 See for example, Edwin Mansfield, Industrial Research and Technological Innovation: An Econometric Analysis, W.W. Norton, New York, 1968, Preface and Introduction for a discussion of the relative neglect of R & D by economists prior to the 1960's.

2 In fact, other than the work done on the impact of rice research on productivity by David Salmon, economists have not looked at the impact of R & D on the Indonesian economy at all. See David Salmon, An Evaluation of Investment in Agricultural Research in Indonesia, unpublished Ph.D. dissertation, The University of Minnesota, 1984.

3 Edwin Mansfield, et al, The Production and Application of New Industrial Technology, W.W. Norton, New York, 1977, p. 2.

4 Note that payment for patents, copyrights and royalties has been included in an aggregate way in the 1975-SAM. The total amount shows up under transfers of companies to rest of world (column 34 and row 78 of Appendix Table B.

5 The exceptions are generalised Harrod and Solow-neutral technical progress as characterised for an n-factor multi-ware production function. Parvin and Khan have called this case the generalised input augmenting technical progress for such a production function. See M. Parvin and H. Khan, "Technological Progress and Productivity Change with Environmental Regulations and Labor-Management Conflict," unpublished manuscript, The University of Akron, 1984.

6 Soedjatmiko, Merle Esmay and Robert Stevens, Appropriate Primary Tillage Mechanisation for Rice in Indonesia, Paper presented at ASAE meeting at Madison, Wisconsin, June 1982, p.5.

7 V.R. Reddy, Small Farm Equipment Technology Transfer to Developing countries, (Experiences Gained in Indonesia), paper presented at the meeting of the American Society of Agricultural Engineers, Madison, Wisconsin, 1982, p. 1.

8 Reddy, op.cit., p. 3.

9 Reddy, p. 4.

10 This issue and related issues of identifying different production processes in the SAM are discussed in Chapter VI (section B).

11 Salmon. op.cit., p. 93.

12 LIPI, Science and Technology Policy Research, Case Study - Textiles, Jakarta, 1983.

13 Prof. Dr. Ing. B.J. Habibie, "Some Thoughts Concerning a Strategy for the Industrial Transformation of a Developing Country," address delivered to the Deustsche Gesellshaft fur Luft-und Raumfabt Bonn, GDR, June 1983, p. 23.

14 LIPI, Science and Technology Policy Research: A View from the Demand Side, Supply Side and the Linkage Area, 1983, p. 3.

15 Prof. Dr. Muhammadi and Dr. Lebdo Suwarto, Science and Technology for Development in Indonesia, Paper presented at the ASEAN-EEC Seminar on Science and Technology Indicators and Science Policy, Royal Society, London, 1983, pp. 41-43. It is not clear from this source whether the growth rate refers to that from the previous year, or over a longer time horizon.

However, given the very recent emphasis on R & D by the government, it is likely that this high growth rate reflects a jump from a not-too-distant base year with a low R & D budget.

16 Habibie, op.cit..

17 Even though the figure of 90% has been mentioned as the local content of the aircraft manufactured, this is for the frame only. The engine and other components are imported. Hal Hill, Survey of Recent Development, BIES, August 1984, p. 19-20.

18 A. Wade Blackman Jr., et al., "An Innovation Index Based on Factor Analysis" in Harold A. Linstone and Devendra Sahal (Eds.), Technological Substitution: Forecasting Techniques and Applications, Elsevier, New York, 1976.

19 Zvi Griliches, Hybrid Corn: An Exploration in the Economics of Technological Change, Econometrica, October, 1957, pp. 501-522; Edwin Mansfield, Industrial Research and Techological Innovation, W.W. Norton, New York, 1968.

20 James Keddie, "More on Production Techniques in Indonesia", in Robert Stobaugh and Louis T. Wells, Jr., (Ed.) Technology Crossing Borders, Harvard Business School Press, Boston, Mass., 1984.

21 Y. Hayami and M. Kikuchi: Asian Village Economy at the Crossroads, University of Tokyo Press, 1981, p. 192.

22 Ibid, pp. 195-208.

23 Ibid, p. 204.

24 Faisal Kasryno: Technological Progress and Its Effects on Income Distribution and Employment in Rural Areas: A Case Study of Three Villages in West Java, Indonesia, Agro-Economic Survey--Rural Dynamics Study, Bogor, Indonesia, 1981.

25 Ibid, p. 22.

26 R.R. Nelson, T.P. Schultz and R.L. Sllighton, Structural Change in a Developing Economy, Princeton University Press, Princeton, 1971.

27 See Nelson et al., op.cit., p. 112-113 for a discussion of some of these specification problems. Strictly speaking, this does not neatly capture the real effect of productivity change. In order to capture this, the underlying production function needs to be specified explicitly. Once this is done, further problems emerge. We discuss here the following two cases:

1) Leontief production functions: Here the change in intermediate coefficients can be captured by considering:

$$z = x - f = [(I-A)^{-1} - I]f = Cf$$

where z = intermediate input
x = output
f = final demand

$$z_t - z_{t-1} = C_t f_t - C_{t-1} f_{t-1}$$
$$= C_t(f_t - f_{t-1}) + (C_t - C_{t-1})f_{t-1}$$
$$= C_{t-1}(f_t - f_{t-1}) + (C_t - C_{t-1})f_t$$

Define $C^* = (C_t + C_{t-1})/2$
$\qquad f^* = (f_t + f_{t-1})/2$
$\qquad \Delta C = C_t - C_{t-1}$
$\qquad \Delta f = f_t - f_{t-1}$

Then,

$$\Delta Z = C^* \, \Delta f + \Delta C f^*$$

The first term is the effect of change in final demand holding C constant on the change in intermediate demand. The second term is the effect of coefficient change holding final demand constant. H. Simon interpreted this last effect as technological change. But the I/O coefficients are the result of both ex-ante technology and relative input and factor prices. The effects of the latter must be discounted before Simon's claim can be accepted.

2) Cobb-Douglas: $\qquad Q = f(R, \lambda L) = AR^\alpha (\lambda L)^\beta$

where R = intermediate input
$\qquad$ L = efficiency units of labor

With production change, the profit-maximisation condition gives

$$d(R/Q)/dQ > 0 \quad \text{if} \quad \alpha + \beta < 1$$

Here the estimation process is simple for the factor-shares. Then intermediate inputs can be calculated as residuals. As long as $\alpha + \beta < 1$ we are assured of results that are not absurd.

Studies using this type of approach will require long time-series data in many sectors and substantial research effort.

Appendix A to Chapter V --
  Description and explanation of trends in output, employment and
  value added in selected dualistic and other sectors

In Chapter II of this study, six sectors were broken down dualistically according to technologies used. These were 1) handpounded
rice vs. milled rice; 2) farm processed tea vs. tea processing; 3)
brown sugar vs. refined sugar; 4) drying and salting of fish vs.
canning of fish; 5) clove cigarettes vs. white cigarettes and 6)
preservation of fruits and vegetables (traditional vs. modern
techniques). In tracing the diffusion of these technologies over
time, we use the information from the I/O tables for handpounded
rice vs. rice milling, tea processing and fish preservation. Two
of our six dualistic sectors are lost because the current 1980
input-output table does not provide information on clove cigarettes or brown sugar separately. Using the census and surveys of
manufactures we recover clove and white cigarettes. By comparing
the 1975 and 1979 surveys of small firms and large and medium
firms the changes in canning and preserving of fruits and vegetables can be captured. The quality of the existing data especially on the small scale and the household and cottage production
activities suffers from lack of consistency in some cases. In
what follows the survey data are used in conjunction with other
information whenever such information is available.

In addition to the sectors mentioned in Chapter II, here several
additional industries with dualistic technological characteristics
are discussed. These are: 1) a further breakdown by firm size of
rice milling and polishing; 2) weaving (except jute mills); and 3)
saw mills and other wood mills. The first breakdown augments the
discussion of handpounded and milled rice by breaking the latter
activity further dualistically into small rice mills and the large
and medium rice mills. Weaving has traditionally been one of the
few important manufacturing sectors in Indonesia. It figures
prominently in most discussions of export promotion of labour-
intensive industries in Indonesia. Wood cutting and finishing
(including plywood manufacturing) has become a significant sector
in manufacturing in recent years.

Some aspects of the changes in output, employment and value
added for the dualistic sectors have already been discussed in
Chapter II. It is interesting to compare the technological indicators between the various years. Data limitations permit us to
compare systematically only the value added per worker. If value
added per worker decreases (increases) over time, then this is an
indication of increasing labour-intensity (capital-intensity).[1]
Thus, using value added per worker as a measure of labour-
intensity, it can be seen from Table V.A that the labour-
intensity decreased further (i.e. value added per worker rose) for
most modern techniques. Rice milling is an important exception.
The next subsection takes up the developments in rice milling
where the diffusion of small rice milling units explains the rise
in labour intensity for this technique.

1.a) Handpounded rice vs. milled rice

The output comparison from the 1975 and 1980 I/O tables shows that the share of the milled rice increased from 65 to 71 percent of the total with a corresponding decline in the output share of the handpounded variety. As mentioned previously, Mears 1981 quotes a figure as low as 6% for the share of handpounded rice by 1979. Timmer's study on choice of techniques in rice milling in Java speculates that the share of handpounded rice on that island may have fallen to 10% already by 1973.[2] In any case, even by the optimistic CBS I/O estimate the handpounding activity has been steadily declining in importance for the last 15 years. Over a five-year period since 1978, the CBS estimated a 7.5% decline, in absolute terms, of rice produced by handpounding. There was a corresponding decline in the total value added as well as share of value added going to the handpounding activity.

Table V.A

Real Value Added Per Worker
(in 000's of rupiahs, 1975 constant rupiahs)

Sector	1975	1980
Handpounded Rice	183.23	--
Rice Milling	1494.72	725.00
Farm Processed Tea	114.6	--
Tea Processing	136.46	174.14
Dried and Salted Fish	96.67	--
Canned Fish	97.31	269.66
Brown Sugar	54.40	--
Refined Sugar	1127.18	829.36
Clove Cigarettes	967.15	2181.9
White Cigarettes	7440.81	9919.95
Weaving (Small & Household)	74.26	276*
Weaving (Large & Medium)	292.89	387*
Saw Mills and Other Wood Mills (Small & Household)	197	178.9*
Saw Mills and Other wood Mills (Large & Medium)	551.73	733*

*1979
-- = indicates data not available.

Source: Sensus Industrii 1975 and 1979, 1980. The deflators used are based on the CPI for the various years given for Indonesia in the International Financial Statistics by the International Monetary Fund. For rice, the wholesale price index of the CBS is used. The data for large and medium firms are published in volumes entitled Statistik Industrii.

Even though the total employment figures are not available for both these years (or the intervening years for that matter) the loss of jobs from this conversion seems to have been considerable. Collier et al. claim that more than 1 million jobs (held mostly by women) may have been lost in the process.[3] This is associated with an income loss of $50 million annually.[4] Much of this was the result of the proliferation of small rice milling units.

In the 1960s and 1970s both the handpounding and large rice mills in existence since the early 19th century, faced the challenge from Japanese rubber roller hullers as well as from Indonesian-made small rice milling units (RMU's). The small mill had the productivity advantage over the handpounding technique. At the same time it was possible to operate these units more profitably than their larger counterparts during the harvest season near the village. Thus the small RMU's had a cost advantage over the large ones.[5]

In 1969 as part of REPELITA I along with reduction of control on rice milling, investment in this branch was encouraged in line with the general policy of supporting agriculture-related industries. Forty new large rice mills were established between 1969 and 1973 and more than two-thirds of the older large rice mills were rehabilitated. Total investment in these projects amounted to over Rp. 3 billion.

During the same period, the number of small rice mills rose from less than 5000 to nearly 35000. After 1974, when the Central Bank stopped capital investment credit for all rice millers (except cooperatives[6]), large mills were faced with the rigors of competition. As a result, within a few years many of them were forced to close. The small RMU's continued operation, partly because of their lower capital intensity and partly because of their flexibility. As Mears points out, "With little overhead, the owner could profitably continue to operate to meet the day to day milling needs of the farm families after the crop season."[7] In Table V.B a sampling of rice mill break-even prices for 1978/79 compiled by BULOG (the national food stock authority) shows a uniformly higher break-even price for the large mills than for the small RMU's.

A comparison of the variable costs from BULOG sources in Tables V.C and V.D shows that the variable cost is uniformly higher for the large mills than for the small RMU's. However at full capacity the large mills are capable of producing at a competitive milling cost/ton--between 5000-6000 Rp/ton as opposed to Rp 5000-7000 for the small RMU's.

The market advantages of the small rice mills are also pointed out by Timmer in his 1973 article. According to this study,

"Where market forces--low wages, high interest rates, and cheap rice prices--have been allowed to work, the overwhelming superiority of small rice mills as a generic class has been apparent to investors and these facilities have indeed mushroomed throughout Java."[8]

Table V.B

**Sampling of Rice Mill Break-even Prices and Quantities
In Selected Provinces, October 1978 - October 1979[1]
(Prices in Rp/ton and Quantities in tons/year of Milled Rice)**

	Break-even Price at 1978/79 1978/79 Operating Level		Level of Operation of Sample Mill	Break-even Quantities at Charge for Milling in Rp/kg of:					
	With Bran Sales	Without Bran Sales		With Bran Sales			Without Bran Sales		
				5	6	7	5	6	7
Large Mills									
North Sumatra	4,204	6,604	3,200	2,600	2,103	1,766	5,990	3,881	2,870
South Sumatra	4,134	6,534	1,900	1,459	1,150	949	4,093	2,336	1,634
West Java	4,645	7,045	2,400	2,222	1,838	1,567	4,455	3,140	2,424
Central Java	3,774	6,174	4,290	3,200	2,650	2,262	6,366	4,508	3,489
East Java	3,987	6,387	6,000	4,640	3,792	3,206	10,017	6,755	5,096
South Sulawesi	4,360	6,760	1,600	1,346	1,084	907	3,210	2,036	1,491
Small Mills									
North Sumatra	5,590	7,090	540	612	499	421	926	690	550
South Sumatra	5,444	6,944	500	563	438	359	980	656	493
West Java	5,454	6,954	700	766	621	522	1,181	868	686
Central Java	5,463	6,963	410	451	371	315	668	506	407
East Java	5,440	5,940	265	235	- 195	167	337	261	213
South Sulawesi	5,394	6,894	340	373	299	249	594	426	332

Source: Leon Mears, The New Rice Economy of Indonesia, p. 182.

Table V.C.

Cost Study of Milling, Small Rice Mills (1978/1979)

	N. Sumatra	S. Sumatra	W. Java	C. Java	E. Java	S. Sulawes
Capacity (ton of milled rice/hour)	1.5	2.25	1.5	2.5	4.5	1.5
Investment Cost [1] (Rp.)						
1. Rice Mill	5,020,000	2,775,000	4,613,000	7,951,000	10,510,000	3,800,000
2. Engine	2,400,000	2,250,000	2,492,000	6,980,000	7,177,000	2,500,000
3. Installation	-	-	-	900,000	413,000	200,000
4. Land	8,640,000	5,000,000	10,364,000	9,130,000	14,375,000	8,500,000
5. Building	12,320,000	4,250,000	10,680,000	12,610,000	10,290,000	5,000,000
6. Others	2,000,000	635,000	600,000	1,984,000	3,902,000	275,000
Total Investment Cost	30,380,000	14,910,000	28,749,000	39,555,000	46,667.000	20,275,000
Operating Cost (Rp./Year)						
A. Fixed Costs						
1. Depreciation of [2]						
a. Rice Mill	837,000	462,000	769,000	1,325,000	1,752,000	633,000
b. Engine	343,000	321,000	356,000	997,000	1,025,000	357,000
c. Building & Installation	821,000	283,000	712,000	901,000	714,000	347,000
d. Others	348,000	63,000	150,000	90,000	390,000	28,000
2. Maintenance						
a. Rice Mill	374,000	225,000	730,000	1,070,000	1,224,000	275,000
b. Engine	250,000	125,000	400,000	920,000	2,899,000	150,000
c. Building	200,000	175,000	200,000	300,000	250,000	50,000
3. Taxes	483,000	347,000	185,000	511,000	600,000	77,000
4. Insurance [3]	-	-	-	49,000	200,000	-
5. Interest @ 12% /Year	3,646,000	1,789,000	3,450,000	4,745,000	5,600,000	2,433,000
6. Salaries						
a. Mill Operation Mechanic	1,584,000	1,080,000	600.000	614,000	1,380,000	596,000
b. Mill Operation Helper	1,116,000	360,000	2,952.000	2,149,000	540,000	395,000
c. Others	720,000	210,000	-	1,368,000	3,972,000	100,000
7. Others	300,000	-	135.000	400,000	200,000	125,000
Total Fixed Costs	11,022,000	5,440,000	10,639.000	15,439,000	20,746,000	5,566,000
B. Variable Costs (Rp./Year)						
1. Engine and Mill						
a. Fuel	976,000	1,520,000	694,000	1,237,500	3,244,000	1.450,000
b. Lubricating Oil	468,000	158,000	360,000	530,000	150,000	350,000
c. Rubber Roll	3,675,000	2,560,000	1,968,000	4,096,000	8,100,000	2,250,000
2. Handling Expenses (Incl. Wages)						
a. Scale to Mill	1,830,009	1,537,000	1,107,000	1,538,000	2,160,000	600,000
b. Stacking and Weighing	915,000	200,000	600,000	1,000,000	702,000	150,000
c. Scale to Pile	915,000	1,000,000	600,000	1,000,000	1,404,000	400,000
3. Others	1,332,000	-	940,000	1,648,000	165,000	25,000
Total Variable Costs	10,111,000	6,975,000	6,269,000	11,049,500	17,575,000	5,225,000
Tons of Paddy/Year	4,920	2,923	3,700	6,600	9,231	2,461
Total Number of Tons of Milled Rice/Year	3,200	1,900	2,400	4,290	6,000	1,600
Number of Operation Days 1977/78	250	175	240	280	250	225
1978/79	300	200	200	200	225	200
Milling Cost of Paddy (Rp./ton)	3,900	3,250	3,900	3,250	3,250	3,250
Milling Cost of Milled Rice (Rp/Ton)	6,000	6,250	6,000	5,000	5,000	5,750
Variable Cost ton of Milled Rice (Rp.)	3,160	3,671	2,612	2,575	2,929	3,266
Revenue from Rice Bran & Husk (Rp/ton Rice) [4]	2,400	2,400	2,400	2,400	2,400	2,400

1) Investment cost valued at 1975 prices
2) Depreciation periods assumed: Mills - 6 years
   Engine - 7 years
   Building and Installation - 15 years
   Others vary with type of goods.
3) Formal insurance purchased by only part of millers interviewed.
4) Assumes bran as % of rice output   Large Mills 12 % @ Rp. 20/Kg
   Small Mills 10% @ Rp. 15/Kg

Source: Mears, p. 526.

Table V.D.

Cost Study of Milling, Small Rice Mills (1978/1979)

	N. Sumatra	S. Sumatra	W. Java	C. Java	E. Java	S. Sulawes
Capacity (ton of milled rice/hour)	0.5	0.6	0.6	0.4	0.6	0.5
Investment Cost [1] (Rp.)						
1. Rice Mill	2,107,000	1,050,000	1,688,000	1,726,000	794,000	950,000
2. Engine	903,000	1,240,000	951,000	929,000	640,000	1,250,000
3. Installation	-	-	-	-	-	-
4. Land	1,505,000	2,500,000	870,000	1,400,000	750,000	750,000
5. Building	1,704,000	1,500,000	2,560,000	1,200,000	1,000,000	1,000,000
6. Others	100,000	85,000	320,000	200,000	110,000	55,000
Total Investment Cost	6,319,000	6,375,000	6,389,000	5,455,000	3,294,000	4,005,000
Operating Cost (Rp./Year)						
A. Fixed Costs						
1. Depreciation of [2]						
a. Rice Mill	351,000	175,000	281,000	288,000	132,000	158,000
b. Engine	129,000	177,000	136,000	133,000	91,000	178,000
c. Building & Installation	100,000	100,000	170,000	80,000	67,000	67,000
d. Others	30,000	8,000	35,000	28,000	11,000	6,000
2. Maintenance						
a. Rice Mill	50,000	49,000	270,000	125,000	21,000	120,000
b. Engine	71,000	38,000	300,000	75,000	19,000	20,000
c. Building	100,000	75,000	50,000	25,000	15,000	45,000
3. Taxes	32,000	72,000	40,000	20,000	4,000	21,000
4. Insurance [3]	-	-	-	-	-	-
5. Interest @ 12% /Year	758,000	765,000	767,000	655,000	395,000	481,000
6. Salaries						
a. Mill Operation Mechanic	240,000	525,000	360,000	90,000	216,000	385,000
b. Mill Operation Helper	830,000	-	600,000	541,500	180,000	-
c. Others	-	-	240,000	-	-	-
7. Others	17,000	-	25,000	25,000	9,000	25,000
Total Fixed Costs	2,708,000	1,984,000	3,274,000	2,085,500	1,160,000	1,506,000
B. Variable Costs (Rp./Year)						
1. Engine and Mill						
a. Fuel	161,500	128,000	380,000	150,000	50,000	95,000
b. Lubricating Oil	91,000	60,000	140,000	80,000	17,000	16,000
c. Rubber Roll	575,000	795,000	834,000	340,000	65,000	276,000
2. Handling Expenses (Incl. Wages)					282,000	411,000
a. Scale to Mill	-	505,000	-	-	-	-
b. Stacking and Weighing	-	-	-	-	-	-
c. Scale to Pile	-	-	-	-	-	-
3. Others	293,000	-	240.000	200,000	-	40,000
Total Variable Costs	1,120,500	1,488,000	1.594.000	770,000	414,000	838,000
Tons of Paddy/Year	830	769	1.080	630	408	523
Total Number of Tons of Milled Rice/Year	540	500	700	410	265	340
Number of Operation Days 1977/78	150	175	200	220	200	200
1978/79	200	185	200	180	175	175
Milling Cost of Paddy (Rp./ton)	4,550	4,225	3,900	3,575	3,400	3,737
Milling Cost of Milled Rice (Rp/Ton)	7,000	6,500	6,000	5,500	5,230	5,750
Variable Cost ton of Milled Rice (Rp.)	2,075	2,976	2,229	1,878	1.562	2,465
Revenue from Rice Bran & Husks (Rp/ton Rice) [4]	1,500	1,500	1,500	1,500	1,500	1,500

1) Investment cost valued at 1975 prices
2) Depreciation periods assumed: Mills - 6 years
　　　　　　　　　　　　　　　　　Engine - 7 years
　　　　　　　　　　　　　　　　　Building and Installation - 15 years
　　　　　　　　　　　　　　　　　Others vary with type of goods.
3) Formal insurance purchased by only part of millers interviewed.
4) Assumes bran as % of rice output   Large Mills 12 % @ Rp. 20/Kg
　　　　　　　　　　　　　　　　　　Small Mills 10% @ Rp. 15/Kg

Source: Mears, p. 527.

It is thus clear that the diffusion of small rice milling units reflect technological flexibility and advantageous market forces. On the whole then this is an example of M-diffusion as very little R & D was necessary.

1.b) Textiles: spinning and weaving

Historically the textiles sector has been one of the strongest manufacturing sectors in Indonesia. By the early seventies in both spinning and weaving subsectors in this industry, major technological transformations had taken place. This transformation was complete for spinning at a much earlier period than for weaving, in keeping with the historical experiences of other countries.[9]

In spinning, by 1975 99.9% of the output was concentrated in the large and medium mills. If one recognises that even the small mills use technology which is more similar to the power driven shuttles and spindles in the large and medium firms, and that the non-mechanised hand spinning is scattered in remote islands then it becomes clear that the differences in technology between the two types of firms are not great. Since data for the household and cottage industries are either unavailable or unreliable and the technology compared to the modern alternative, probably inefficient, we confine our discussion to the choice of technology in the weaving sector.

Looms are the basic tools of production in weaving. It is, therefore, relatively simple to classify weaving technologies according to the type of loom used.[10] The most important functions of the loom (not necessarily separate) are:

1) warp-wise control; 2) shedding; 3) picking; and 4) beat-up.

The warp from the beam is converted to fabric and is "taken up" on a cloth roll. Warp-wise control refers to the regulation of the flow of the material along the length of the fabric. Shedding is the process of inserting the filling yarn. Beat-up is the positioning of the filling. Relatively little development of the basic design of the shuttle loom has occurred during the twentieth century though many peripheral developments such as automatic quill winding at the loom have taken place.

At present in Indonesia, at least six different types of looms can be observed. These are given below in order of increasing capital intensity.[11]

1) Alat Tenun Gedogen or backstrap loom -- very labour-intensive, uses only human energy for its operation, used mainly in the outer islands.

2) Alat Tenun Bukan Mesin or the improved handloom (hereafter HL) -- still widespread in central Java. In 1975, there were an estimated 65,000 still in use.

3) Non-automatic power loom (hereafter PL) -- The simplest type of power loom. Now manufactured in Indonesia.

4) Semi-automatic power looms (SPL) -- More capital-intensive than the previous type. Imported from several Asian countries such as Japan, South Korea and Taiwan.

5) Fully automatic power loom (APL) -- Here the weft or the cross-thread is supplied automatically. Mainly used by the foreign and large domestic firms.

6) Shuttleless looms -- used very little.

It is clear that the technologies in this industry can only be described as dualistic at the risk of being simplistic. It is however defensible to associate the APL and SPL with large and medium firms and HL and PL with the small firms and cottage industry. However, small firms have been known to use SPL's as well. Therefore the output and other trends in terms of shares of different size firms have to be interpreted with caution.

In 1975 97% of the output and 96% of the value added flowed from the large and medium scale enterprises (LME's). The LME's employed 149,021 workers, more than 6 1/2 times the 22,800 employed by small enterprises (SE's). By 1979 the SE's improved their output and value added shares by claiming 5% and 8% of the respective totals. However, this slight increase in output and value added shares of the SE's cannot necessarily be correlated with their use of more labour-intensive technologies, since SE's also could use the same capital-intensive technologies as those used by the LME's. In this situation, the employment figures might reveal more about the kind of technology in use than the output or value added per se. In 1979 the employment in LME's was 115,053, a decrease of almost 35,000 jobs. During the same period, the employment in SE's rose by almost 7000 to a total of 29,402. The employment growth of 29% in the SE's over the five years when the employment in the LME's actually declined suggests that the technique used in 1979 in the SE's may indeed be more labour intensive than that in use in the LME's. The trends in real output/worker and value added/worker tend to confirm this. For the LME's real output/worker grew from 1305 thousands of rupiahs/year to 1688 thousands of rupiahs/year. For the SE's, the figure is 272 and 341 thousands of rupiahs, respectively. The real value added per worker rose in both sizes of firms indicating decreasing labour intensity. But the LME's still remained almost five times as capital intensive as the SE's. In 1979 LME's and SE's value added per worker were 793,000 and 27,600 rupiahs, respectively.

Thus it seems that even though both types of firms are becoming more capital intensive over time, the SE's still are relatively more labour intensive than the LME's on the whole. However, it should be noted that in both output and value added per worker the SE's had a higher growth rate. Furthermore, the figures may overstate the actual difference in technology between the LME's and the SE's as the former may be more efficient than the latter in the use of the same technology.[12]

The foregoing discussion elicits two somewhat contradictory characteristics of the state of technology in the weaving industry which require further explanation. The first is the co-existence of several different types of techniques. The second is the tendency within this scenario for production to shift to the relatively capital-intensive technique, at least from 1967 to 1975. Table V.E shows that the number of modern looms (associated with capital-intensive techniques) increased from 35.3 thousands in 1967 to 57.8 thousands in 1974/75.

Table V.E

The Growth of Equipment in the Weaving Industry
REPELITA I and REPELITA II

Year(s)	HL (000's)	Other (PL, SPL, APL) (000's)
1967/70	50.0	35.3
1970/71	50.0	35.6
1971/72	50.0	43.4
1972/73	50.0	48.3
1973/74	50.0	53.7
1974/75	55.0	57.8
1975/76	60.0	60.4
1976/77	66.3	61.5
1977/78	66.3	66.9

Source: LIPI: Case Study - Textile Industry, pp. 25, 28.

From 1967 to 1978 power looms of all kinds (PL, SPL and APL) increased by almost 90% whereas the number of handlooms and backstrap looms increased by only 33% as Table V.E shows. Even after allowance for the fact that the relatively less capital-intensive non-automatic power looms also increased in number during this time, it seems likely that overall the capital labour ratio must have increased in the weaving industry.

During REPELITA I, the government set a production target of 900 million metres of clothing by the end of the planning period. In order to achieve this ambitious target, it would have been necessary to increase productivity several folds. The major emphasis was on rehabilitation and import of new equipment for spinning and finishing. In addition, the general policy of encouraging foreign investment was extended to the textiles sector as well. Between 1967 and 1978, 66 foreign-sponsored projects were approved by the government with total investment of $1.03 billion.[13] From the same BKPM (investment coordinating board) source Pitt et al. (1981) estimated that between 1969 and 1977 foreign investment in textiles was more than 50% of all the licensed investment in this sector. The typical foreign project was five times as large as the domestic one, and investment per employee was twice as large.[14] They also estimate that the foreign investment accounted for nearly 30% of the new mechanical looms over the same period.[15] The total number of foreign projects in textiles from 1967-1980 was 67 equalling a total of $1.22 billion.[16]

A reduction of the effective rate of protection from a very high percentage rate in 1971 to 217% in 1975 in non-spinning sectors of textile may also have spurred the domestic firms to adopt more capital-intensive techniques with larger scale and lower unit costs in the 1970s.

1.c) White cigarettes and clove cigarettes

Even though these are not identical products, they are substitutes to some extent. It is the clear distinction in terms of labour intensity that makes comparisons between them interesting. The output share of the clove cigarettes or Kreteks was approximately 77% of the total in 1977. However 92% of the total workers in the two sectors were employed in the production of clove cigarettes. In 1980 the output share of clove cigarettes increased to 84%. During the same period the share of employment rose to 94.3%. White cigarette manufacturing thus tends to be a much more capital intensive activity than the production of clove cigarettes.

The increased production and sales of clove cigarettes have to do with shifts in both demand and supply. However, precise information enabling one to describe causally the extent of these shifts is not available. It appears that the consumption of clove cigarettes has risen in both urban and rural areas, particularly among the lower income groups. Since clove cigarettes do not enjoy any clear price advantages relative to the white cigarettes the increase in demand may be a reflection of dominant tastes and some increase in income in the urban areas.[17] On the supply side in the absence of hard statistical evidence regarding costs and profits for either of the two products, one can only speculate. It is, however, plausible that the highly labour-intensive clove cigarette may have a cost of production advantage. This probably arises from the lower wages as indicated by the very low value added per worker in clove cigarette production. Since the wage rate in this activity is definitely lower than in white cigarette manufacturing, the added employment may not have necessarily led to an absolute increase in the income level of the workers. At the same time, it has to be admitted that in the absence of these additional jobs, entire villages which now produce clove cigarettes might have been left to seek employment elsewhere, thus exacerbating an already difficult unemployment problem for the country.

1.d) Drying and salting of fish vs. canned fish

In 1975 most of the fish (85%) in Indonesia were being preserved by drying and salting (i.e. the traditional technology). In the ensuing years, there seems to have been a slight decline in the drying and salting activity relative to canning of fish. Even so, in 1980, 83% of the total output was in the category of dried and salted fish. It is to be noted that the actual amount of fish preserved decreased for both techniques, and the share of value added for the modern technique increased almost two-fold from 6.8% to 13%. As canned fish may be an export item, it is worthwhile to investigate in the future the reasons for the absolute decline in output, but the increase in its prominence relative to the traditional technique. As of the writing of this report, very little information regarding the techniques and the market is available at the macroeconomic level.

1.e) Canning and preserving of fruits and vegetables (Traditional and Modern)

Here the available figures (the reliability is somewhat questionable, especially for the value added figures) show a drastic relative decrease for the traditional activity between 1975 and 1979. During this period the share in output of the modern activity rose from 51% to 95%. Employment, however, fell in keeping with a decline in the output, and the share of employment for the modern activity went down from 85 to 82 percent. These figures seem to imply a precipitous fall in the productivity of the traditional sector which strains credulity. It is, therefore, not very clear as to what has really happened in this sector since 1975.

1.f) Saw mills and other wood mills

Finally, we discuss a component of the wood and wood products sector. Here, too, there is a clearly discernible gradual tendency towards production by large and medium scale firms using relatively capital-intensive methods (Table V.F).

It seems that the higher value added per worker in the LME's (indicating higher productivity) can account for their increasing role in total production. This has quite significant employment implications, however. Between 1975 and 1979, the employment in the SE's increased more than 11 times as rapidly as that in the LME's. In absolute terms between these years total employment in SE's (about 3/4 of that in LME's in 1975) overtook total employment in LME's by more than 1100 workers. Even though desirable from the goal of maximising employment, it is not clear that the SE's fulfill the objective of least cost maximisation of output. Hence there may be a conflict between these two objectives in this industry. Real output/worker in the SE's seemed to have decreased from Rp. 498 thousands in 1975 to Rp. 478 thousands in 1979. Even though this is not prima facie evidence of inefficiency, it does raise the question of how efficient the SE's really are in their use of technology and other resources.

Table V.F

Output and Value Added Share, Real Value Added Per Worker and
Employment by Firm Size in Saw Mills and Other Wood Mills

		1975	1979
A.	Output Share		
	LME	79	82
	SE	21	18
B.	Value Added Share		
	LME	79	80
	SE	21	20
C.	Real Value Added/Worker (000's of rupiahs)		
	LME	552	1503
	SE	197	358
D.	Employment		
	LME	24515	25483
	SE	18336	26613

Source: BPS Sensus Industrii shows the output and value added
shares, value added/worker and employment for LME's and SE's for
the years 1975 and 1979.

The derivation of this is as follows:

Unit costs for technologies:

$$c_1 = h_1 (w_1, r_1)$$
$$c_2 = h_2 (w_2, r_2) = \frac{h_1 (w_2, r_2)}{\alpha}$$

here $h_i (\cdot)$ is a linear homogeneous function of factor prices. We assume rice to initially exceed costs of the new technology (it is sufficient to ssume $p = h_1 (w_1, r_1)$).

Instead of assuming full equilibrium, we allow the system to move towards n equilibrium. Thus

$$(\tfrac{\dot{Q}}{Q})_i = \lambda [p - h_i(w_i, r_i)] \quad \lambda > 0$$
$$Q_1 + Q_2 = Q$$

here p = product price

We assume that the expanding firms have to pay more for their factors han firms just breaking even. Ignoring the elasticities of supply of the actors, we specify the following cost equations

$$h_i (w_i, r_i) = h_i (\bar{w}, \bar{r}) + b \ [p - h_i (\bar{w}, \bar{r})] \qquad 0 < b < 1$$

here $\bar{w}$ and $\bar{r}$ are the factor prices that the firms breaking-even have to ace. Obviously, θ, λ, b can all vary across industries. Then,

$$\frac{d}{dt} \log (\frac{Q_2}{Q_1}) = (\frac{\dot{Q}_2}{Q_2}) - (\frac{\dot{Q}_1}{Q_1})$$

$$= \lambda [h_1 (r_1, w_1) - \frac{h_1 (r_2, w_2)}{\alpha}]$$

$$= \lambda [(1-b) \ h_1 (\bar{r}, \bar{w}) - (1-b) \frac{h_1(\bar{r}, \bar{w})}{\alpha}]$$

$$= \lambda [(1-b) (1 - \tfrac{1}{\alpha}) \ h_1 (\bar{r}, \bar{w})]$$

Notes to Appendix to Chapter V

1 Strictly speaking, this would be an indicator of labour intensity only if i) skill composition does not change; ii) efficiency in terms of total factor productivity remains the
   same; and iii) hours worked remian the same. All these
   factors do change over time. Nevertheless the change has not
   been nearly so drastic as to invalidate the use real value
   added/worker for our purposes.
2 C. Peter Timmer, "Choice of Technique in Rice Milling in
   Java," BIES, July 1973.
3 William Collier, Jusuf Colter, Sinarhadi and Robert d'A. Shaw:
   Choice of Technique in Rice Milling on Java, BIES, 1974, p.
   116.
4 Ibid, p. 106.
5 Leon A. Mears, The New Rice Economy of Indonesia, Gadjah Madah
   Univeristy Press, 1981, p. 5.
6 Ibid, p. 7.
7 Ibid, p. 8.
8 C.P. Timmer, op.cit., p. 72.
9 For example, Allen (1940) mentions that for decades after the
   Japanese spinning industry was virtually mechanised, hand
   looms continued to be used for weaving purposes.
10 This procedure is followed by Hill 1983, 1979 , Robson and
   Pickett 1977 , Khan 1982 , among others.
11 This classification is due to Hal Hill, "Dualism, Technology
   and Small-scale Enterprises in the Indonesian Weaving Industry", in R.G. Garnaut and P.T. McCawley, (Eds.) Indonesia:
   Dualism, Growth and Poverty, Australian National University,
   1979, p. 336.
12 See Mark M. Pitt and Lung-Fei Lee, The Measurement and Sources
   of Technical Inefficiency in the Indonesian Weaving Industry,
   Journal of Development Economics, No. 9, 1981, pp. 43-64.
13 Calculated from BKPM figures by H. Poot, op.cit., p. 93.
14 Pitt and Lee, op.cit., p. 50.
15 Ibid, p. 50.
16 Dennis Healy, The Indonesian Economy: An Early 1981 Perspective, Dept. of Economics, The University of Adelaide, p. 74,
   BKPM figures.
17 Actually the better brand clove cigarettes (usually consumed
   by upper income bracket groups), are more expensive than some
   white cigarette brands.

VI Summary, policy conclusions and new research directions

In retrospect, the major contribution of this study has been to provide a macroeconomic framework for modelling technology, the energy sector and income distribution. The framework offered for this purpose has been the Social Accounting Matrix. It has been demonstrated how the SAM can be used as a basis for simple economy-wide modelling in a fixed price setting, and how policy experiments can be carried out by using fixed price multipliers. This approach was fully operationalised in a static setting for Indonesia by incorporating a dualistic technological breakdown for six manufacturing activities, and by disaggregating the energy sector into six components, for the year 1975. The linkages between technology, production, employment, and income distribution were also examined rather minutely with the help of structural path analysis.

In addition to the (comparative) static modelling above, this study makes another contribution by extending the use of the SAM framework to include the effects of R & D on the generation and adaptation of technology. In the same vein, an attempt has also been made to incorporate the diffusion of technology by integrating a model of evolutionary technical change with the SAM framework.

The aim of this concluding chapter is to summarise the salient findings and to draw out their implications for analytical and policy purposes. At the same time some of the limitations of this study are noted along with suggestions for further research.

A. A Social Accounting Matrix for modelling technology choice and the energy sector in Indonesia

Chapter II describes in detail the procedure for the construction of the SAM-Tech for Indonesia. As shown in Table II.1, there are 23 different factors of production, 11 institutions (10 household groups and one group of companies) and 40 production activities in SAM-Tech. The major novelty is the identification of dualistic (i.e. traditional, relatively labour-intensive vs. modern, relatively capital-intensive) technologies within six of the production activities. In addition to the size of the firm (small firms and household and cottage industries typically tend to use traditional technologies), a number of other technological indicators were also used to distinguish between the two types of technologies within the relevant sectors. Indicators such as value added per worker, average expenditure propensity for energy (six different types), the capital (i.e. non-wage) share of value-added and the ratio of paid to unpaid workers were also used to characterise the technologies, and to verify if the traditional alternative could indeed be distinguished from the modern one for each of the six chosen production activities. On the basis of this limited set of indicators, it does appear that, generally speaking the traditional technological alternative was significantly different from the corresponding modern one within each pair of product-cum-technologies.[1]

Fixed price multipliers were derived in order to analyse the effects of choosing the traditional as compared to the corresponding modern technological alternative on output, employment and income distribution. Furthermore, structural path analysis was applied to the dualistic sectors by computing the direct, total and global influences, respectively. Since, in general, the global influence (here reflected by the matrix of fixed price multipliers) linking any two poles of an economic structure can be decomposed into a series of total influences, which in turn are direct influences travelling along specific elementary paths multiplied by their corresponding path multipliers, this methodology offers a very thorough way of analyzing the effect of changes in output in any of the selected twelve dualistic product-cum-technologies on the whole economic system as represented by the Indonesian SAM-Tech.[2] The results here, as in the case of the fixed price multipliers, are approximations, because of some of the guesstimates that had to be made in building the SAM-Tech. More importantly, the structural path analysis also yields the whole network of paths through which the impact of a change in output in any of the twelve dualistic sectors is propagated to the whole Indonesian SAM structure. The main results of Chapter III and their implications, obtained through the analysis of the sectoral data and SAM-Tech, are summarised below.

1) It was found through the examination of existing evidence that the modern technological alternative had been increasing in relative importance in the selected dualistic sectors between 1975 and 1979-80. There was a concomitant displacement of small industries as medium and large scale enterprises manufacturing

162

commodities similar to those produced by small, household and cottage industries, had increasingly taken over a larger share of the market. The implications of this development for employment are, of course, negative.

2) In general, it appears that the traditional technology generates greater aggregate output effects on the whole ecoomic system than the corresponding modern technology. This is true for traditional technology in four out of six activities whereas the differences between the output effects of the two techniques are negligible for the other two activities. The traditional technique shows especially strong output effects for cigarettes (total output multiplier for clove cigarettes and white cigarettes are 3.599 and 2.615 respectively), and for sugar (total output multiplier for brown sugar and refined sugar are 4.429 and 3.501 respectively). An important implication of this finding is that there is no conflict between output and employment in these sectors if ceteris paribus, the technology chosen is of the traditional variety.

3) At least within the twelve sectors included in this study, the direct and indirect linkages generated by a traditional-informal activity vis-a-vis both other traditional activities as well as modern activities were greater than those generated by the corresponding modern product-cum-technology. In addition, in four of the six production activities, the aggregate output effects on agriculture and mining (i.e. primary sectors) were greater for the traditional than for the corresponding modern technology. Needless to say, this has important employment and income distributional implications.

4) There are two interesting results in this study regarding the relationship between technology and income distribution.

a) The modern technology does not generate more capital income (including rent from land and from other agricultural capital) than the traditional alternative. This is largely explained by the fact that the traditional technology tends to generate more rent going to land and other agricultural capital than does the modern technology. On the other hand, the latter technology generates more rental for the incorporated capital than does the traditional technique.

b) The traditional technology consistently yields significantly greater labour income effects (direct and indirect) than the corresponding modern technology for the same increase in output. Moreover, as shown in Table III.6, the raising of output through the use of traditional technology has a considerably greater impact on the incomes of lower skilled workers than the corresponding modern alternative.

5) The employment effects of a change in production by alternative techniques--computed in terms of worker equivalents for the 16 labour groups in SAM-Tech--show greater employment creation through the use of traditional techniques in most cases. For

example, a million rupiahs of additional handpounded rice would yield 3.32 additional agricultural paid rural workers, as opposed to 2.23 for milled rice. In general, an equal increase in expenditure by both technologies will lead to more employment of rural and low skilled workers for the traditional alternative. As Table III.4 shows, this is certainly true for handpounded vs. milled rice activity. The methodology for computing the employment effects is, of course, applicable to any of the 40 production activities included in SAM-Tech.

6) With regards to household income distribution, it was seen (Table III.5) that for each pair of product-cum-technology, the traditional alternative yielded greater total (combined) household income than the corresponding modern activity. Making pairwise comparisons of technologies within the rice milling, sugar and cigarette activities, in each case, the traditional technology had higher multiplier values for the following household groups: agricultural employees and the three different groups of farmers defined according to amount of land owned or operated. In contrast to labour income, most of the modern technologies display higher income multipliers with respect to the income of companies than do the corresponding traditional alternative. These findings hold true for the whole set of dualistic sectors in our sample.

7) Following the methodology of structural path analysis, 13 selected examples were presented in Table III.6. These examples have in common that in each instance the pole of origin (i.e. the pole through which the exogenous injection enters the structure) is one of the 12 dualistic product-cum-technology activities. The poles of destination are, respectively, selected factors, household groups, and other production activities. Thus, the differential effects of, e.g. handpounded rice as compared to rice milling on selected factors of production, different household groups, and other production activities were ascertained quantitatively. More importantly, the various paths through which influence is transmitted were identified explicitly. Detailed graphical structural path analysis of the effects of a change in the output of a) handpounded vs. milled rice, respectively, on the income of household group consisting of agricultural employees and b) brown sugar vs. refined sugar, respectively, on the income of the household group headed by small farmers, demonstrated the usefulness of this methodology.

Even though it is impossible to analyse the total (i.e. current, capital and official settlements) balance of payments effects of choice of techniques short of modelling the international financial flows, it is possible to make a few observations regarding the balance of trade effects. The import contents of almost all traditional technology-cum-productive activities are considerably less than those of the modern techniques. The only exception is canning of fruits and vegetables. Here the total production and hence total inputs (including imports) are quite small. It may also be recalled that the available data here are quite problematic.

As far as exports are concerned the available data indicate that the export demand for milled rice, canned fish and refined sugar are higher than the comparable output produced by the traditional technique. However the total export demand as compared to the domestic demand is very low. Export of processed tea is negligible while clove cigarettes comprise almost entirely the cigarette exports from Indonesia. With the exception of the export demand for milled rice which was estimated to grow at the same rate as that of the clove cigarettes (2.7%/annum) during Repelita IV, the other dualistic sectors do not figure very prominently among the exportables. Thus, for the dualistic sectors (with the possible exception of milled rice) it is reasonable to conclude that the adoption of the traditional techniques will not lead to any more adverse balance of trade consequences than that associated with their modern counterparts.

In addition to the previous technological breakdown, SAM-Tech also was designed to include six different energy (sub)sectors. The disaggregation of the energy sector allowed us to test a modified version of the energy-labour intensity (MLE) hypothesis in Chaper IV. As information on biomass and other traditional forms of energy was not available, the disaggregated energy sector in the SAM only showed commercial, non-traditional energy (e.g. excluding firewood) as an intermediate input. The MLE-hypothesis which states that traditional technologies use more direct and indirect commercial and conventional energy than do the modern ones, had to be rejected for all but one of the six dualistic sectors. Even for the one sector where it could not be rejected, the confirmation was partial only, since the labour-intensive product-cum-technology (clove cigarettes) used more energy indirectly but less directly than did the alternative (white cigarettes).[3]

The fixed price multipliers were used to measure the impact of exogenous changes in demand for energy on household incomes and vice versa. It seems that the overall impact of a change in demand for the energy sector is more pronounced on the resulting incomes of the urban than on the rural households. Within the urban areas, the upper income households stand to gain or lose the most from an increase or a decrease in demand for energy. If the fixed price multipliers are assumed to be robust enough to be relevant for 1985 (a rather heroic assumption) then it can be shown that the recent decline in world price for petroleum and the OPEC quota for Indonesia will indeed lead to a serious fall in income, ceteris paribus, for all household groups. However, again the upper income urban households will lose the most.

A consideration of the opposite question, namely that of the effects of an increase in the incomes of various socioeconomic groups on energy consumption shows that overall the urban inactive groups spend the most on energy directly and indirectly. A relatively high proportion of the increased expenditures accrues to petroleum and natural gas. An analysis of the linkages leading to this receipt shows that most of the flow occurs indirectly, i.e. as the consumption of energy by the inputs into the other commodities consumed by the households.

In addition to the SAM analysis, the impact of the petroleum sector on the balance of payments and government revenue was also studied through the use of time-series data in the oil sector and the government budget. A look at the net contribution of the oil sector, shown as the retained values of petroleum earnings, revealed that the peak of the oil boom in this respect has already passed. Thus, without careful balancing of exports and imports, future balance of payments problems are likely to occur. With the decline in oil revenue, the expenditure side of the government budget has to grow more slowly than before unless non-oil revenues can be increased rapidly. There is thus a real prospect of belt tightening for the government of Indonesia. Leaving the static framework behind, we now highlight some conclusions reached in Chapter V which analyzed the dynamic aspects of technology choice.

B. Dynamic aspects of technology choice: R & D and diffusion of technology

As mentioned previously, this study claims to make another contribution in modelling technology choice and income distribution at a macro level by overcoming the limitations of a static SAM. Even though the present work is at the conceptual level only, the approach suggested here can be implemented if the relevant data can in fact be gathered.

In Chapter V a method for treating R & D and technology in a macroeconomic setting was outlined. The proposed strategy was to identify R & D as a separate productive activity within the SAM. This approach takes into account the dynamic effects of R & D on technology through the introduction of lags in the R & D accounts. The impact of R & D on the productivities of technologies and income distribution can be reflected quite accurately if the marginal effects on input-output and value added coefficients can be computed.

The above strategy can work quite well as a device for integrating R & D data with other macroeconomic variables, and for analyzing the implications of R & D expenditures on technology, employment and income distribution. However, a careful study of the existing data and econometric work on R & D in Indonesia revealed the impossibility of operationalising the suggested strategy without extensive collection of information on R & D expenditures in specific sectors of the economy. Further econometric work dealing with sectoral productivity changes as a result of R & D is also a necessity.

Nevertheless, a critical review of the current government R & D policies giving priority to high technology clearly confirms the propriety and indeed the desirability of a SAM approach to R & D policy analysis. Given multiple objectives of R & D policy such as growth of output, employment and 'equitable' income distribution, no ad hoc or partial equilibrium approach can be a good substitute for the SAM approach suggested here.

The second major way in which the flexibility of the SAM in modelling technology choice can be enhanced is by linking it with the microeconomic models of evolutionary technical change. This is demonstrated conceptually, in the context of SAM-Tech, by drawing on an evolutionary model of technical change incorporating technological dualism. It is seen that the estimates of relatively few parameters (diffusion index, productivity ratios of the two technologies and an adjustment parameter) can yield sufficient information on a diffusion process which then can be successfully integrated with the SAM. A synthesis of this kind shows the potential for micro-macro linkages in the area of technology diffusion.

The existing data base in Indonesia was not rich enough to permit the estimation of even the few coefficients necessary for the implementation of the above approach. However, all the available quantitative and qualitative information was used to describe and explain the diffusion pattern for four of the six dualistic sectors and three other industries as well. In most cases, the capital-intensity seems to have increased over time. This is explained by appealing to market forces such as cost, profit and demand conditions and, to some extent, by R & D expenditures. One important exception to the trend was the fall in capital-intensity for rice milling. The explanation for this phenomenon lies in the rapid diffusion of small rice milling units and the corresponding decline of large rice mills since 1975.

Our review of the microeconomic linkages between technology diffusion in rice paddy production and income distribution showed these linkages to be quite complex involving significant institutional changes. On the basis of this survey of the existing studies and our analysis of the diffusion patterns through the existing data, it seems even more urgent to pursue further the analytical approach towards integrating sectoral models of technological diffusion with multi-sectoral models based on SAM. In any event, our work highlights the crucial connection between R & D and technological change over time and their implications at both micro (sectoral) and macro (multi-sectoral) levels. The distinction drawn in Chapter V between M-diffusion (diffusion led by market forces) and R-diffusion (preceded by significant R & D expenditures) enables one to conclude--within the Indonesian context--that the former predominated. Therefore, in the absence of appropriate R & D policies, the present M-diffusion is likely to continue.

C. Limitations of this study

The present study does have limitations. A major methodological qualification is that the simple simulation exercises which were undertaken on the basis of SAM-Tech assumed the existence of excess capacity. This assumption made it possible to ignore possible supply constraints and consequent changes in prices. In the next section (VI.D) it is argued that there is some evidence of the existence of excess capacity in a number of sectors (particularly the labour intensive ones) and also excess supply of labour with the possible exception of the higher skilled workers. Therefore the comparative static exercises relying on fixed price multipliers and structural path analysis can be considered reasonably valid in the short run (say over a two-year horizon) as long as the excess supply assumption can be defended.

Another condition necessary to make the results of these exercises credible is that the SAM coefficients capture the current structure and behavior of the economy. In this respect, it cannot be maintained that a SAM built for 1975 accurately reflects the underlying structure of the economy five or even ten years later. In that sense, our analysis can be taken as a kind of retrospective and counterfactual exploration of the macroeconomic impact which different technologies would have had given the structure prevailing in the mid-seventies. Given rapid structural and other changes leading to new relative prices and coefficients, the robustness of the comparative static results over time can be questioned. It is, therefore, crucial to institutionalise the process of building new and updating existing SAMs at regular intervals to increase the operational usefulness of this tool for policy making purposes. In this connection, it bears repeating that the Central Bureau of Statistics with the help from the Institute of Social Studies is just completing a SAM for 1980 and that there is a good chance that the process will be institutionalised within the CBS.

Any serious attempt at predicting the macroeconomic effects of technology, and other, policies affecting directly the supply side and the conditions under which production takes place over the medium and long run requires a dynamic model. Such a model should be, at least partially, price endogenous, i.e. able to determine the new future set of prices. In the present state of the arts, there is a class of models, i.e. the computable general equilibrium (CGE) models which, in theory, starting from a given initial SAM--presumed to reflect the situation in the base period--can derive endogenously the SAM likely to prevail at some future date.[4] A major weakness of the present state of economic theory (and consequently CGE models) is the module dealing with the determination of investment. Typically, investment is assumed to be determined by "animal spirits" or simply be predetermined by savings. Given the sensitivity of the results of such models to the "closure" rules which are adopted, the lack of an adequate investment theory puts in question the usefulness of these models for long term planning purposes at this time.

This does not mean that less ambitious models than the pure CGE type cannot be built and prove to possess some operational usefulness at least over a planning horizon of five to seven years. In fact, models predicting the impact of investment on growth and the resulting structure of output and income distribution are a necessary complement to the use of a SAM whenever an extended planning horizon is contemplated.

168

In this connection one key question which is not addressed in this study is the impact of the adoption of traditional technologies on growth as opposed to equity (i.e. employment and income distribution). Would the choice of traditional, or even intermediate, techniques in the Indonesian context entail a conflict between these two objectives? This could be the case if the former techniques were clearly less efficient and/or led to an income distribution which reduced the supply of aggregate savings in the economy than more modern techniques.

The tentative conclusion which we reached regarding the favorable impact of traditional as compared to corresponding modern techniques on employment, poverty alleviation, energy use and the balance of payments in the short run hinges on the greater backward linkages and smaller leakages of these techniques. The main leakages in our SAM-comparative static exercises are imports and savings. Traditional production methods are generally less import-intensive both directly (in terms of intermediate import requirements) and indirectly--the resulting income distribution among socioeconomic groups is tilted more towards those groups which spend less on finished imports and import-intensive domestic goods. In contrast, these same socioeconomic groups which benefit from the adoption of traditional techniques may save relatively less than those groups which would benefit from an alternative income distribution resulting from reliance on more modern techniques. If it is assumed, furthermore, that aggregate savings are channeled into domestic investment then, a trade-off can exist between growth and equity.

This is a very important question which should be explored with the help of complementary macroeconomic models (less ambitious than the pure CGE) and sectoral models and feasibility studies for large projects. In this way, by marrying the short run comparative static SAM methodology with adjunct models, the immediate and short run effects of alternative technologies on such objectives as employment, income distribution and the balance of payments can be weighed against their more medium and longrun effects on investment and growth.

A second limitation of the study is related to the lack of certain types of data for Indonesia. Consequently, some of the conceptual advances for the SAM framework proposed here could not be demonstrated empirically. In particular, it was not possible in the present work to incorporate more sectors broken down either dualistically or according to whatever number of alternative (including possible intermediate) technologies in existence. It would have been interesting to explore the effects of alternative technologies for paddy production per se (as opposed to rice) or textiles. Similarly, it would have been useful to disaggregate the energy sector further especially by including traditional sources of energy such as biomass. Lack of data was the main reason for omitting these refinements at the present time. Likewise, it is hoped that the analytical framework of Chapter V for R & D and diffusion of technology can be applied at a later date in Indonesia or in other developing countries assuming the availability of a richer data base than currently exists. Furthermore, our theoretical results pinpoint the need for very careful data gathering in some crucial areas such as R & D expenditures, technological indicators, productivity and cost figures at the sectoral level.

In summary, it must be emphasised that at this stage of research on multisectoral general equilibrium planning models, the inadequacy of data is probably as big a handicap as inadequate conceptualisation. A number of suggested advances discussed in this study cannot be made without more and better data than are currently available for many developing countries. The present work represents what is feasible through an imaginative use of the existing data base for Indonesia. These qualifications notwithstanding the prospects for the SAM as a viable basis for comparative static and short run modelling of technology choice incorporating the disaggregated energy sectors seemed quite promising. In the next section we discuss some policy implications and further possible extensions of this study in the light of the above limitations.

D. Some policy issues and directions for future research

Is it possible to make any definite policy prescriptions on the basis of the foregoing analysis? Can the results obtained here and the methodology used be extended to other developing countries? What are the directions in which the present methodology and techniques need to be refined in the future? These are the questions addressed in the following pages.

With regard to the policy issues in choice of technology our study shows the need for very careful consideration to be given to both traditional and modern techniques in the problem of technology choice. As shown here, for a developing country such as Indonesia, the traditional technique often has more linkages with the rest of the economy, creates greater employment and benefits especially the rural and low-skilled workers more than the modern alternative. At the same time, the traditional technique is also less likely to rely on imports as most of the inputs used are produced domestically. In the case of Indonesia, unlike some other countries,[5] the traditional technique uses less energy inputs than the modern one for the same value of output. Therefore, unless the traditional alternative is clearly anachronistic and inefficient, a strong case exists for its use along with the modern technique, at least for as long as employment creation, improvement of income distribution and poverty alleviation continue to be major policy objectives together with growth and modernisation. Judicious information and studies on the supply effects of alternative technologies permitting an evaluation of their dynamic efficiency should, of course, supplement the more demand-side orientation of the SAM-approach--particularly in those sectors where bottlenecks may appear. Incidentally, structural path analysis, as discussed below, can help identify some of these supply bottlenecks.

The above policy prescription in the short or intermediate run needs to be qualified further. First of all, as mentioned before, the extent to which excess capacity prevails in specific sectors must be checked carefully. Existing information on this is very sketchy for Indonesia, but it appears that there is some excess capacity in the labour-intensive sectors. According to the survey by the Netherlands Economic Institute (the MANKAP survey), in 1980 the medium and largescale manufacturing establishments recorded a weighted average rate of 55.7% of capital utilisation.[6] Higher than average rates were recorded for sheet glass, cement, paper and chemicals and fabricated metal products. Wood products, (except plywood), clay products, basic metal, electrical machinery and transport equipment showed a lower than average rate of capital utilisation. The remaining sectors (containing many of our dualistic sectors) showed an average capital utilisation rate of 49.9%.[7] Even though disaggregated information is not available it may reasonably be guessed that the rate of capital utilisation in the dualistic sectors is not much higher than half of the existing capacity. Also given the generally low rate of capital utilisation in Indonesia by international standards, it would appear that the sectors linked to the dualistic sectors can, up to a point, respond with greater capital utilisation when demand increases.[8]

On the labour side the same survey results "suggest that under the prevailing socioeconomic circumstances attracting sufficient workers does not pose an insurmountable problem in Indonesia..."[9] Skill levels, however, need to be upgraded. In particular, engineers are in short supply. There is also a high demand for welders/fitters, designers, chemist/dispensers and product controllers without a corresponding increase in the quantity supplied at a constant wage rate. The cautious conclusion may therefore be drawn that the increase in demand for any of the products of traditional technologies will not lead to a sudden and adverse price effect in the form of an inflationary spiral, even though there may be shortages of skilled labour in some sectors and bottlenecks may indeed appear resulting in some wage increases for skilled labour in these sectors. Here structural path analysis may be used as a diagnostic device.

Indeed this method allows one to check the complete network of backward linkages resulting from a given increase (or decrease) in output in any given production activity. Thus, for example, the direct and indirect requirements for each type of labour skill consequent to a rise in any sector's output can be ascertained. By confronting these labour requirements (classified according to type and skill) with independent information about the supply (elasticity) of each corresponding type and skill-level, potential bottlenecks can be identified. This type of analysis is useful for at least two reasons, i) it allows one to forecast possible inflationary pressures (e.g. if certain higher labour skills were in short supply) which could result in the short run from increased demand for given product-cum-technology activities; and, ii) it provides signals to the policymaker that changes in its training and (vocational) education policies may be called for to increase the pool of workers possessing the required skills.

An important consideration concerning traditional technologies relates to the quality of their products. At least 31% of the respondents to the MANKAP survey admitted to "casual or frequent complaints by customers on inferior quality of their products."[10] It is, therefore, necessary to improve product quality and provide the consumer with more information about such improvements. The extent of this problem may be exagerated somewhat by sharply distinguishing only two techniques in a dualistic manner. If there exists a third (intermediate) technique which is labour-intensive relative to the modern alternative and produces similar quality product the problem of product quality can be alleviated (see also the discussion of upgrading below). We do, however, need to recognise two somewhat conflicting aspects of the products of the traditional technology. On the positive side these products may be "appropriate" for the satisfaction of basic needs, particularly in the short run. On the negative side, with economic growth the preferences of the people may shift from these to higher quality (or simply 'different') products manufactured by the modern technology. Furthermore, the small scale of production and lack of quality control makes these products unlikely candidates for export.

The foregoing discussion also shows that the short run policy issues are not always separable from long run diffusion questions. Here, lack of detailed information prevents us from being definitive. At the same time, the existing data show a tendency for the modern alternative to replace the traditional one. Since it is not clear that the traditional alternative is clearly inferior to the modern one on economic grounds, policy measures to encourage the upgrading of traditional techniques need to be considered seriously. The present trend in research and development does not seem to favor this line of attack. It is perhaps time to reconsider the emerging commitment to high technology but low employment-generating projects to the relative neglect of the traditional or intermediate techniques in the R & D allocation process.[11]

The policy of encouraging traditional/intermediate technology will also lessen the pressure that is intensifying on the energy sector. As Chapter IV shows, along with diversification of energy sources, the industrial and domestic consumption of fossil fuel energy sources will have to be curtailed. Choice of appropriate energy-saving techniques will definitely be necessary in the long run as a necessary ingredient of such an energy policy.

Our preliminary results suggest that the modern techniques in the dualistic sectors use more commercial energy than the traditional ones. These two types of techniques also use different types of energy. An up-to-date SAM with a detailed breakdown of both modern-commercial and traditional sources of energy should be prepared so that implications of technology policies for the energy sector can be determined.

Beyond technological choice Indonesia will face some serious distributional questions arising from a drop in oil revenues. Should the government continue to subsidise the urban households when its own revenues are falling? Our research raises this question, but more information than is available at present will be necessary to answer this and similar questions. If anything, this study, by raising these issues, highlights the necessity for using models based on an updated SAM as a supplement to other demand and supply side studies of the energy sector.

Perhaps even more crucial than the search for models (whether based on SAM or not) is the need to collect basic disaggregated data on the production and consumption of energy of different kinds by different user groups. Here a disaggregated SAM will serve well as a consistent data gathering framework.[12]

We conclude this section by discussing certain possible refinements and extensions of the present framework all of which can be accomplished if and when the pertinent information becomes available. The following list mentions only some key developments without claiming to be exhaustive in this respect.

1. Product disaggregation can be further extended by including an array of techniques within each of the disaggregated product categories. For example, there exist at least three technologies for rice milling quite apart from the handpounding of rice.[13] A separation of these (sub)techniques within the milled rice technology can be expected to yield much valuable information regarding the range of available technologies and their effects on output, employment and income distribution. This extension will also enrich the comparative static analysis undertaken in this study by eliminating in some cases the artificial simplifying assumption of technological dualism. Insofar as the products of these technologies are not perfect substitutes, the household consumption submatrix of SAM will capture the differences in demand for them. (See also 7. below.)

2. A related refinement is the inclusion of as many successive aspects of the production process as possible. This can be done by looking at production as a sequential process where each stage creates certain inputs for the next one. Thus technologies for paddy production yielding an input for rice processing could be included in a discussion of rice milling. It will then be possible to follow through the overall effects of a certain combination of techniques incorporating distinct processes and tasks (e.g. semi-mechanised tilling by hand held power tillers and milling by small RMU's). A second example of what can be done in this area is the combination of technologies in the spinning and weaving stages of cloth-making. As discussed in Chapter V, these stages together offer a sequential array of techniques to choose from.

3. In the modelling of energy the inclusion of traditional sources such as biomass and the further disaggregation of both

traditional and modern, commercial sources loom large as a necessary future task. Data gathering in this area should proceed hand in hand with the refinement of the present model through further disaggregation of the energy sources and their incorporation in a price endogenous model.

4. In the modelling of energy within the SAM framework a crucial advance will be to convert the monetary production and consumption figures into corresponding physical units. This will enable the researcher and the policy maker to compare the real energy-content of alternative technologies and the real energy consumption by the various household groups. Only the availability of detailed price and quantity data for the production and consumption of energy by both the households and the productive activities can enable the future researcher to accomplish this task. A second, related type of data-gathering activity can usefully supplement the present SAM. This involves the use of industrial surveys to measure the traditional and other kinds of energy used by the various technologies.

5. In studying technological diffusion it became quite apparent that more sectoral studies of R & D must be done before the proposed macroeconomic diffusion model can be tested. Further model refinements in the direction of multi-sectoral technological diffusion with external, spill-over effects (e.g. R & D in rice affecting the productivities of other food crops etc.) will be possible once the relevant data are collected for a number of sectors.

6. From the policy point of view an estimation of the supply constraints and their incorporation for all or at least the dualistic sectors is an urgent task. Clearly, if some of the constraints are binding in the short run increases in prices, wages and rentals rather than in output will be the most likely result of an increase in expenditures in these sectors. Further research in this area will either strengthen or modify the policy conclusions reached here depending on the existence or non-existence of excess capacities in the relevant sectors. In this way possible trade-offs between growth and equity objectives may be identified.

7. The accurate estimation of the marginal expenditure propensities for the commodities will make the fixed price multipliers more reliable. Once available the MEP's will provide insights as to how the consumptions of the various (imperfect) substitutes produced by different technologies vary with income.

8. Last, but not least, is the observation that the SAM framework either in its present or extended form could be applied to a number of semi-industrialised countries such as the Republic of Korea and Taiwan which are obvious candidates for further applications. But any developing country that has consciously embarked on an industrialisation program or modernisation of agriculture will benefit as well from the construction of the kind of SAM presented in this study.

The above remarks are intended to stimulate further research on relatively unexplored areas of technology choice in the developing world. As this study makes clear, theses issues range from the identification of an existing array of techniques in particular sectors to the dynamic modelling and estimation of the macro-economic effects of these techniques. The present study is best viewed as a set of results and problems in these areas organised under the rubric of a SAM. It is but a single step in unravelling the vast puzzle of technology choice and its effects on the people in LDC's in an economy-wide setting.

Notes

1 Incidentally, as is subsequently discussed in section VI.D, the classification of production activities can take any form the policymaker or researcher is interested in analyzing. Thus, for example, production activities, can be broken down according to more than two (dualistic) techniques or, alternatively according to firm size. In particular, whenever an alternative intermediate technique exists it can readily be incorporated in the SAM.

2 It should, of course, be recognised that this methodology can be applied to any other sector (not just the dualistic activities) of the SAM-Tech as well.

3 For a discussion of the limitations of this hypothesis and of the data in the Indonesian case, see pp.73-75 in Chapter IV.

4 Such a model is presently being built by a joint team of the Central Bureau of Statistics and the Institute of Social Studies relying on a basic model structure already developed by the Center for World Food Studies of the University of Amsterdam. See S.J. Keuning, "Modelling the Indonesian Social Accounting Matrix", ISS-BPS, Working Paper Series No. 5, April 1985.

5 For example, in Korea the traditional technique uses more energy than the modern technique in the textiles sector. See Khan (1982) op.cit.. Keddie and Cleghorn's findings regarding sugar processing techniques in India are similar. See James Keddie and Cleghorn in C. Baran (1980) op.cit..

6 Netherlands Economic Institute (NEI): MANKAP Project, Final Report, Rotterdam, May 1983, p. 3.

7 Ibid., p. 4.

8 The existence of excess capital in the form of plant and equipment capacity is a necesary but not sufficient condition for the firms to respond to extra demand with extra output. A second necessary condition which is discussed in the text is the existence of a pool of reserve labour, especially skilled labour. Factors such as problems of organisation, existing institutional (legal and extra-legal) framework may also prove to be relevant in this context.

9 NEI, op.cit., p. 15.

10 Ibid., p. 15.

11 The political economy of technology choice has been deliberately left out as being outside the scope of the present study. In reality, of course, politics at all levels--local, national and international will affect the choice of techniques.

12 Although a study of subsidies need not be based on SAM, the collection of disaggregated information in a SAM allows consistency checks to be made. Furthermore, once information in such a format is available, it is very easy to carry out policy experiments which can then be compared with other partial or general equilibrium results.

13 Timmer's (1973) study mentions at least four distinct techniques apart from handpounding. Mears (1981) mentions mechanical hullers and small and large rice milling units. See Timmer, op.cit. and Mears loc.cit..

Appendices

Appendix A The construction of SAM-Tech: sources of information and major assumptions

The construction of SAM-Tech involved three major steps. First, the existing CBS SAM was modified in ways described below. Next, the six sectors were extracted from the productive activities of this modified SAM (called SAM1 hereafter) for a dualistic technological breakdown. The final step involved the disaggregation of the energy sector. We describe below in detail the procedures and assumptions involved in each step.[1]

Step 1: The original CBS SAM had separate commodities and activities accounts. Imported intermediate inputs were listed for each output by separate commodities. The transactions were recorded at purchaser's prices through the inclusion of trade and transportation margins accounts. This SAM was modified in the following manner.

(1) Commodities accounts were consolidated with the activities accounts.

(2) Specifically this was done by subtracting trade and transportation margins from production accounts and adding these same margins to the trade and transportation activities.

(3) As a result of the above in the modified SAM (SAM1) production activities sectors pay net indirect taxes directly to the indirect taxes account. In CBS SAM the commodity accounts acted as intermediaries between these two sets.

(4) In a similar fashion, instead of production activities purchasing imported inputs from the imported commodities account in SAM1, imported inputs are purchased directly from the rest of the world account.

(5) Finally, it should be noted that the transactions recorded in the rest of the world account are given in c.i.f. prices plus

177

import duties and customs taxes. Insufficient information precluded their allocation to the various accounts. These taxes are assumed to be transferred directly to the government account.

Step 2: In SAM1, there were 61 rows and columns, including 22 production activities. In the second stage some of these sectors (e.g. Food, Beverage and Tobacco) were disaggregated and within these disaggregated sectors a dualistic breakdown according to the technology used was effected. The resulting SAM (hereafter called SAM2) had 34 productive activities of which six pairs were broken down dualistically. The process of compiling the Input-Output, Value-Added and Consumption submatrices of SAM2 are described below.

A. Input-output submatrix

1) Of the twelve dualistic sectors, handpounded rice, farm processed tea, dried and salted fish, brown sugar, refined sugar, canned fish and tea processing are all listed as separate production activities in the 1975 Indonesian input-output table (dimension 179 X 179). Therefore, the I/O table was used directly for these sectors.

2) For canning and processing of fruits and vegetables, the surveys of manufacturing for large, medium and small firms were used. The assumption here is that the large and medium firms in this activity use modern technology and small firms use traditional technology.

3) For clove and white cigarettes, the information came from Statistik Industri (survey of large and medium firms in manufacturing). The combined (total) output figure came from the I/O table.

4) In each case the intermediate input included domestic and imported commodities. In order to distinguish between these, the same procedure as that followed by the CBS was used by relying on import coefficients.

Import Coefficients in sector i =
Total Imports in Domestic Consumption

Imported intermediate inputs are obtained by multiplying the total intermediate inputs with the import coefficient for each sector with one exception.

5) The exception was canning and preserving of fruits and vegetables, as in this case the imports seemed to exceed domestic consumption. It was assumed that import of fruits and vegetables was for final consumption only.

B. Value added (VA) submatrix

In each of the following cases the I/O figures for VA going to capital and labor in the aggregate served as control totals.

1. Handpounded rice

Wages were obtained from the I/O table and were assumed to go to agricultural paid rural labor. Operating surplus (total VA-wages) was assumed to be received by agricultural unpaid rural workers.

2. Rice milling

The allocation between labor and capital followed the I/O table. Further allocation among various categories of labor and capital were made according to the information contained in Mears (1981) and the authors' judgements.

3. Dried and salted fish

Allocation between labor and capital in the aggregate was provided by the CBS. In the allocation between the various labor categories, the return to these in SAM1 sector of which dried and salted fish was a part fisheries and fish products was used to derive the proportions going to specific types of labor (e.g. rural agricultural workers vs. agricultural operators etc.). The share of all types of capital except agricultural capital was assumed to be zero.

4. Canned fish

For labor the procedure was the same as that followed for dried and salted fish; the relevant SAM1 column used was 'Food, Beverage and Tobacco'. For capital, the allocation followed Keuning (1981 and 1984) with one modification. It was assumed that 20% of the VA to unincorporated capital actually went to unpaid labor.

5. Brown sugar

For allocation of labor income, the proportion used came from the relevant aggregate sector in SAM1. For capital Keuning's allocations were used with the exception that 20% of the operating surplus going to the smallholders was allocated to unpaid labor.

6. Sugar

The total value added going to labor and capital from the I/O table were apportioned to the various types of labor and capital in proportion to what these factors received in the aggregate SAM productive activity of which refined sugar was a part.

179

7. Canning and preserving of fruits and vegetables (small)

Initially the same procedure as in (6) was used. Afterwards, the value added going to public capital and foreign capital were allocated to labor, as it is unlikely that these types of capital exist in this sector.

8. Canning and preserving of fruits and vegetables (large and medium)

Same procedure as in (3) initially, however, since there are no unpaid workers, their share was reallocated to the paid workers.

9. Farm processed tea

a) Same procedure as in (3) for allocationg VA to labor.

b) Keuning's 1984 ratios were used to allocate VA to capital.

c) In addition, the difference between our VA going to labor and the I/O total was allocated to unpaid labor.

10. Tea processing

a) For labor the aggregate SAM1 sector ratios were used with the following modifications:

    i) agricultural labor   0% of the VA

    ii) unpaid labor   0% of the VA

b) For capital, Keuning's figures were used to allocate the total among the various subcategories.

11. Clove cigarettes

a) For allocation of value added to the various types of labor, the procedure was the same as in (3).

b) Value added going to various types of capital was distributed according to proportions derived from Keuning.

12. White cigarettes

a) For labor, the procedure was the same as in 11a with the exception that the share going to the unpaid workers was redistributed to the paid workers, as there are no unpaid workers in this category.

b) For capital Keuning's figures were used to allocate the total VA among the various subcategories.

C. Consumption

All of the following calculations were made in producer's prices.

1. Hand Pounded Rice (HPR)

The starting point for the calculation of total consumption of HPR was the consumption of self-produced rice according to table C.2 in Downey 1984 . Since the input-output final consumpton figure is larger than Downey's figure, the difference was assumed to be consumed by the households in the same proportion as "self-produced rice".

2. Milled rice

The consumption of milled rice was computed by subtracting the HPR consumption for each household group from the total rice consumption per household group.

3. Farm processed tea

The total final consumption figure obtained from the I/O table is allocated across the household groups in proportions derived from the consumption of "Farm Non-food Crops" domestic consumption column of SAM1.

4. Tea processing

The total private final demand was taken from the 1975 I/O table and allocated among the households according to ratios derived from the 'Food, Beverage and Tobacco' domestic consumption column in SAM1.

5. Dried and salted fish

Same procedure as in 4. The ratios were derived from fisheries and fish products' column.

6. Canned fish

Same as 5. The ratios came from 'Food, Beverage and Tobacco' column in SAM1.

7. Brown sugar

The allocation followed the consumption pattern of "Brown Sugar and Coconut" in Downey Table C.36.

8. Refined sugar

This followed the consumption pattern of "Refined Sugar and Sugary Drinks" given in Downey table C.38.

9 and 10. Canning and preserving of fruits and vegetables (traditional and modern)

In each product-cum-technology the total consumption was allocated among the households according to proportions derived from "Food, Beverage and Tobacco" columns in SAM1.

11 and 12. Clove and white cigarettes

Downey Table G.46 (Tobacco Consumption) was used to calculate total private demand among the household groups for both types of cigarettes. Using well-known facts about the price differentials between the two types of products, and judgements about the income elasticities of the households, the further division of the total consumption between clove and white cigarettes was carried out.

As far as the exogenous accounts are concerned, government consumption, capital accounts consumption and exports came from the 1975 I/O table.

In case of canning and preserving of fruits and vegetables and cigarettes, the I/O table did not distinguish between the traditional and modern activities. It was therefore, assumed that there was no exogenous consumption of the products of traditional subsectors in these cases.

Step 3: Disaggregating the energy sector

In order to expand SAM2 into SAM-Tech only the energy sectors needed to be identified. The procedure followed in disaggregating the energy sector was very much the same as that used in step 2. Three productive activities sectors in SAM2 were broken down in this final step towards the construction of SAM-Tech. 'Coal' and 'Petroleum and Natural Gas' came from "Coal and Metal Ore, Petroleum and Natural Gas Mining" sector; 'Avigas and Gasoline' and 'Fuel Oil' from "Chemical Fertilizer, Clay Products, Cement and Basic Metals Manufacturing Industries"; 'Electricity' and 'Gas' from the "Electricity, Gas and Water Supply" sector. The input-output coefficients were derived mainly from the aforementioned I/O table. The value added coefficients were drawn from the aggregate SAM sectors. For consumption, in addition to the information in SAM2 and Downey, the results of the World Bank/UNDP survey were also used.

Notes

1 The careful reader will notice that the disaggregation involved in SAM-Tech could have been done all at once. That,
   however, was not what was in fact done. Our description of
   the actual procedure involves three steps and the construction of three different SAMs. Even though only the final
   SAM-Tech is used, the other two are also available. It may
   be mentioned that for some purposes these two other SAMs
   (SAM1 and SAM2 in the appendix) are quite adequate--in fact,
   preferable to SAM-Tech. For instance, if one is not interested in energy per se but only in the effects of choice
   of techniques on output, employment and income distribution,
   then SAM2 will be more appropriate than SAM-Tech. This is
   because SAM-Tech utilizes a number of additional assumptions
   in order to disaggregate the energy sectors in SAM2.

Appendix Table B: Social Accounting Matrix SAM-Tech, Indonesia, 1975, Transactions Matrix (in billion Rupiahs)

		Name	Factors of Production							
			Col 1	Col 2	Col 3	Col 4	Col 5	Col 6	Col 7	Col 8
Factors of Production	1	Ag Paid Rural								
	2	Ag Paid Urban								
	3	Ag Unpaid Rural								
	4	Ag Unpaid Urban								
	5	Prod Paid Rural								
	6	Prod Paid Urban								
	7	Prod Unpaid Rural								
	8	Prod Unpaid Urban								
	9	Cler Paid Rural								
	10	Cler Paid Urban								
	11	Cler Unpaid Rural								
	12	Cler Unpaid Urban								
	13	Prof Paid Rural								
	14	Prof Paid Urban								
	15	Prof Unpaid Rural								
	16	Prof Unpaid Urban								
	17	Uninc Capital Land								
	18	Uninc Capital Housing								
	19	Uninc Capital Rural								
	20	Uninc Capital Urban								
	21	Inc Capital Domestic								
	22	Inc Capital Government								
	23	Inc Capital Foreign								
Institutions	24	Ag Employees	323.58	11.39	18.97	0.57	21.34	3.09	19.08	0.87
	25	Farm Size 1	97.84	2.04	461.32	18.85	45.31	5.15	47.90	1.92
	26	Farm Size 2	26.10	0.68	292.61	9.08	19.20	2.53	24.21	0.92
	27	Farm Size 3	16.48	0.62	355.04	11.12	11.84	2.34	16.87	1.03
	28	Rural Lower	34.90	0.00	26.49	0.00	284.31	0.00	108.60	0.00
	29	Rural Middle	5.84	0.00	10.00	0.00	14.32	0.00	6.20	0.00
	30	Rural Higher	7.10	0.00	10.38	0.00	21.36	0.00	51.07	0.00
	31	Urban Lower	0.00	2.83	0.00	3.08	0.00	315.85	0.00	67.88
	32	Urban Middle	0.00	0.38	0.00	0.30	0.00	8.66	0.00	1.62
	33	Urban Higher	0.00	3.11	0.00	1.94	0.00	22.11	0.00	23.28
	34	Companies	0.00	0.00	0.00	0.00	0.00	0.00	0.00	0.00
Production activities	35	Food Crop								
	36	Nonfood Crop								
	37	Livestock and Products								
	38	Forestry and Hunting								
	39	Fishery								
	40	Metal Ore Mining								
	41	Other Mining								
	42	Handpounded Rice								
	43	Milled Rice								
	44	Farm Processed Tea								
	45	Processed Tea								
	46	Dried and Salted Fish								
	47	Canned Fish								
	48	Brown Sugar								
	49	Refined Sugar								
	50	Canning (s+c)								
	51	Canning (m+l)								
	52	Kretek Cigs								
	53	White Cigs								
	54	Other Fbt								
	55	Wood and Construction								
	56	Textiles, etc								
	57	Paper, Transport, Metal, etc.								
	58	Chemical, Cement, etc								
	59	Coal Mining								
	60	Petroleum Mining, etc								
	61	Gasoline								
	62	Fuel Oil								
	63	Electricity								
	64	City Gas								
	65	Water								
	66	Trade								
	67	Restaurants								
	68	Hotel, etc								
	69	Road Transport, etc								
	70	Air Transport, etc								
	71	Banking and Insurance								
	72	Real Estate								
	73	Public Services, etc								
	74	Personal Services, etc								
Exog. Accts.	75	Government	0.00	0.00	0.00	0.00	0.00	0.00	0.00	0.00
	76	Capital Accounts	0.00	0.00	0.00	0.00	0.00	0.00	0.00	0.00
	77	Net Indirect Taxes	0.00	0.00	0.00	0.00	0.00	0.00	0.00	0.00
	78	Rest of World	0.00	0.00	0.00	0.00	0.00	0.00	0.00	0.00
	79	Total Expenditure	511.84	21.05	1174.81	44.94	417.68	359.73	273.93	97.52

		Factors of Production							
	Name	Col 9	Col 10	Col 11	Col 12	Col 13	Col 14	Col 15	Col 16
Factors of Production	1 Ag Paid Rural								
	2 Ag Paid Urban								
	3 Ag Unpaid Rural								
	4 Ag Unpaid Urban								
	5 Prod Paid Rural								
	6 Prod Paid Urban								
	7 Prod Unpaid Rural								
	8 Prod Unpaid Urban								
	9 Cler Paid Rural								
	10 Cler Paid Urban								
	11 Cler Unpaid Rural								
	12 Cler Unpaid Urban								
	13 Prof Paid Rural								
	14 Prof Paid Urban								
	15 Prof Unpaid Rural								
	16 Prof Unpaid Urban								
	17 Uninc Capital Land								
	18 Uninc Capital Housing								
	19 Uninc Capital Rural								
	20 Uninc Capital Urban								
	21 Inc Capital Domestic								
	22 Inc Capital Government								
	23 Inc Capital Foreign								
Institutions	24 Ag Employees	13.37	1.27	25.57	1.40	28.26	0.60	2.31	0.18
	25 Farm Size 1	23.95	1.53	59.69	2.72	17.60	1.62	4.24	0.26
	26 Farm Size 2	9.32	0.47	26.09	0.70	11.06	0.43	1.58	0.18
	27 Farm Size 3	8.75	0.55	21.80	0.95	19.43	0.71	3.10	0.31
	28 Rural Lower	118.37	0.00	196.21	0.00	43.15	0.00	17.09	0.00
	29 Rural Middle	7.12	0.00	11.33	0.00	28.58	0.00	1.35	0.00
	30 Rural Higher	43.05	0.00	72.18	0.00	238.93	0.00	12.15	0.00
	31 Urban Lower	0.00	179.98	0.00	150.83	0.00	20.08	0.00	56.24
	32 Urban Middle	0.00	9.86	0.00	4.44	0.00	6.98	0.00	1.01
	33 Urban Higher	0.00	204.62	0.00	67.32	0.00	487.45	0.00	57.52
	34 Companies	0.00	0.00	0.00	0.00	0.00	0.00	0.00	0.00
Production activities	35 Food Crop								
	36 Nonfood Crop								
	37 Livestock and Products								
	38 Forestry and Hunting								
	39 Fishery								
	40 Metal Ore Mining								
	41 Other Mining								
	42 Handpounded Rice								
	43 Milled Rice								
	44 Farm Processed Tea								
	45 Processed Tea								
	46 Dried and Salted Fish								
	47 Canned Fish								
	48 Brown Sugar								
	49 Refined Sugar								
	50 Canning (s+c)								
	51 Canning (m+l)								
	52 Kretek Cigs								
	53 White Cigs								
	54 Other Fbt								
	55 Wood and Construction								
	56 Textiles, etc								
	57 Paper, Transport, Metal, etc.								
	58 Chemical, Cement, etc								
	59 Coal Mining								
	60 Petroleum Mining, etc								
	61 Gasoline								
	62 Fuel Oil								
	63 Electricity								
	64 City Gas								
	65 Water								
	66 Trade								
	67 Restaurants								
	68 Hotel, etc								
	69 Road Transport, etc								
	70 Air Transport, etc								
	71 Banking and Insurance								
	72 Real Estate								
	73 Public Services, etc								
	74 Personal Services, etc								
Exog. Accts.	75 Government	0.00	0.00	0.00	0.00	0.00	0.00	0.00	0.00
	76 Capital Accounts	0.00	0.00	0.00	0.00	0.00	0.00	0.00	0.00
	77 Net Indirect Taxes	0.00	0.00	0.00	0.00	0.00	0.00	0.00	0.00
	78 Rest of World	0.00	0.00	0.00	0.00	0.00	0.00	0.00	0.00
M	79 Total Expenditure	223.93	398.28	412.87	228.36	387.01	517.87	41.82	115.70

			Factors of Production							
	Name	Col 17	Col 18	Col 19	Col 20	Col 21	Col 22	Col 23	Col 24

		Name	Col 17	Col 18	Col 19	Col 20	Col 21	Col 22	Col 23	Col 24
Factors of Production	1	Ag Paid Rural								
	2	Ag Paid Urban								
	3	Ag Unpaid Rural								
	4	Ag Unpaid Urban								
	5	Prod Paid Rural								
	6	Prod Paid Urban								
	7	Prod Unpaid Rural								
	8	Prod Unpaid Urban								
	9	Cler Paid Rural								
	10	Cler Paid Urban								
	11	Cler Unpaid Rural								
	12	Cler Unpaid Urban								
	13	Prof Paid Rural								
	14	Prof Paid Urban								
	15	Prof Unpaid Rural								
	16	Prof Unpaid Urban								
	17	Uninc Capital Land								
	18	Uninc Capital Housing								
	19	Uninc Capital Rural								
	20	Uninc Capital Urban								
	21	Inc Capital Domestic								
	22	Inc Capital Government								
	23	Inc Capital Foreign								
Institutions	24	Ag Employees	35.30	21.47	73.83	0.00	0.00	0.00	0.00	0.00
	25	Farm Size 1	298.14	42.30	103.01	0.00	0.00	0.00	0.00	0.00
	26	Farm Size 2	396.76	25.70	45.31	0.00	0.00	0.00	0.00	0.00
	27	Farm Size 3	988.38	32.38	38.19	0.00	0.00	0.00	0.00	0.00
	28	Rural Lower	62.45	35.39	206.52	0.00	0.00	0.00	0.00	0.00
	29	Rural Middle	19.93	10.50	19.54	0.00	0.00	0.00	0.00	2.21
	30	Rural Higher	22.41	17.64	43.28	0.00	0.00	0.00	0.00	0.00
	31	Urban Lower	4.80	61.69	0.00	544.56	0.00	0.00	0.00	0.00
	32	Urban Middle	0.55	19.63	0.00	21.00	0.00	0.00	0.00	0.52
	33	Urban Higher	4.28	91.74	0.00	229.88	0.00	0.00	0.00	0.00
	34	Companies	0.00	0.00	0.00	0.00	1201.71	1315.30	1292.96	0.00
Production activities	35	Food Crop								111.94
	36	Nonfood Crop								5.40
	37	Livestock and Products								14.34
	38	Forestry and Hunting								2.96
	39	Fishery								9.34
	40	Metal Ore Mining								0.00
	41	Other Mining								1.05
	42	Handpounded Rice								22.20
	43	Milled Rice								152.70
	44	Farm Processed Tea								1.85
	45	Processed Tea								0.78
	46	Dried and Salted Fish								8.30
	47	Canned Fish								2.38
	48	Brown Sugar								3.66
	49	Refined Sugar								7.09
	50	Canning (s+c)								0.01
	51	Canning (m+l)								0.03
	52	Kretek Cigs								28.31
	53	White Cigs								0.00
	54	Other Fbt								9.41
	55	Wood and Construction								2.47
	56	Textiles, etc								15.86
	57	Paper, Transport, Metal, etc.								12.44
	58	Chemical, Cement, etc								8.63
	59	Coal Mining								0.00
	60	Petroleum Mining, etc								0.00
	61	Gasoline								0.42
	62	Fuel Oil								1.68
	63	Electricity								1.36
	64	City Gas								0.00
	65	Water								1.02
	66	Trade								70.26
	67	Restaurants								28.35
	68	Hotel, etc								0.17
	69	Road Transport, etc								16.56
	70	Air Transport, etc								6.15
	71	Banking and Insurance								0.47
	72	Real Estate								25.64
	73	Public Services, etc								28.32
	74	Personal Services, etc								19.35
M Exog Accts.	75	Government	0.00	0.00	0.00	0.00	0.00	59.10	0.00	1.94
	76	Capital Accounts	0.00	0.00	0.00	0.00	0.00	0.00	0.00	39.12
	77	Net Indirect Taxes	0.00	0.00	0.00	0.00	0.00	0.00	0.00	0.00
	78	Rest of World	0.00	0.00	0.00	0.00	0.00	0.00	710.92	29.18
	79	Total Expenditure	1833.00	358.44	529.68	795.44	1201.71	1374.40	2003.88	615.63

	Name	Institutions							
		Col 25	Col 26	Col 27	Col 28	Col 29	Col 30	Col 31	Col 32
Factors of Production									
1	Ag Paid Rural								
2	Ag Paid Urban								
3	Ag Unpaid Rural								
4	Ag Unpaid Urban								
5	Prod Paid Rural								
6	Prod Paid Urban								
7	Prod Unpaid Rural								
8	Prod Unpaid Urban								
9	Cler Paid Rural								
10	Cler Paid Urban								
11	Cler Unpaid Rural								
12	Cler Unpaid Urban								
13	Prof Paid Rural								
14	Prof Paid Urban								
15	Prof Unpaid Rural								
16	Prof Unpaid Urban								
17	Uninc Capital Land								
18	Uninc Capital Housing								
19	Uninc Capital Rural								
20	Uninc Capital Urban								
21	Inc Capital Domestic								
22	Inc Capital Government								
23	Inc Capital Foreign								
Institutions									
24	Ag Employees	0.00	0.00	0.00	0.00	0.00	0.00	0.00	0.00
25	Farm Size 1	0.00	0.00	0.00	0.00	0.00	0.00	0.00	0.00
26	Farm Size 2	0.00	0.00	0.00	0.00	0.00	0.00	0.00	0.00
27	Farm Size 3	0.00	0.00	0.00	0.00	0.00	0.00	0.00	0.00
28	Rural Lower	0.00	0.00	0.00	0.00	0.00	0.00	0.00	0.00
29	Rural Middle	5.18	5.87	35.00	12.92	0.27	14.18	1.71	0.00
30	Rural Higher	0.00	0.00	0.00	0.00	0.00	0.00	0.00	0.00
31	Urban Lower	0.00	0.00	0.00	0.00	0.00	0.00	0.00	0.00
32	Urban Middle	1.39	1.39	2.13	2.16	0.00	2.09	46.44	0.05
33	Urban Higher	0.00	0.00	0.00	0.00	0.00	0.00	0.00	0.00
34	Companies	0.00	0.00	0.00	0.00	0.00	0.00	0.00	0.00
Production activities									
35	Food Crop	285.15	121.07	193.39	147.79	21.18	72.66	96.99	16.55
36	Nonfood Crop	13.15	7.33	9.82	7.48	1.68	3.50	4.53	0.83
37	Livestock and Products	37.79	30.96	48.33	27.63	8.52	22.09	32.04	6.17
38	Forestry and Hunting	5.99	3.10	3.19	3.82	0.83	1.44	1.14	0.19
39	Fishery	19.29	13.37	21.48	19.23	4.96	11.70	19.30	3.35
40	Metal Ore Mining	0.00	0.00	0.00	0.00	0.00	0.00	0.00	0.00
41	Other Mining	2.10	1.14	1.93	1.46	0.31	0.73	1.10	0.19
42	Handpounded Rice	137.00	157.13	162.28	32.70	29.63	16.65	10.10	2.33
43	Milled Rice	182.66	35.04	102.66	219.03	22.16	90.63	150.45	24.17
44	Farm Processed Tea	4.70	2.57	3.39	2.62	0.94	1.31	1.56	0.28
45	Processed Tea	1.16	0.57	0.84	1.22	0.22	0.54	1.11	0.18
46	Dried and Salted Fish	17.72	12.30	19.43	17.34	4.59	10.84	17.80	2.85
47	Canned Fish	3.53	1.73	2.55	3.73	0.66	1.63	3.37	0.55
48	Brown Sugar	9.58	5.29	6.58	5.11	1.37	2.39	2.76	0.51
49	Refined Sugar	13.66	9.59	18.40	13.21	2.86	7.32	11.28	1.83
50	Canning (s+c)	0.01	0.01	0.01	0.01	0.00	0.01	0.01	0.00
51	Canning (m+l)	0.05	0.03	0.04	0.05	0.01	0.02	0.05	0.01
52	Kretek Cigs	52.59	26.42	30.98	31.50	1.75	19.07	25.89	3.02
53	White Cigs	0.00	4.10	12.79	13.06	4.32	5.05	16.04	1.88
54	Other Fbt	46.49	82.01	55.20	41.68	30.06	16.57	99.31	18.37
55	Wood and Construction	5.24	3.12	4.09	4.48	1.14	2.19	3.46	0.75
56	Textiles, etc	42.85	20.27	39.25	42.52	7.69	21.74	64.88	13.32
57	Paper, Transport, Metal, etc.	19.10	12.88	25.26	33.54	9.07	29.28	43.54	13.10
58	Chemical, Cement, etc	16.17	9.19	13.81	15.13	3.95	7.54	20.09	3.71
59	Coal Mining	0.00	0.00	0.00	0.00	0.00	0.00	0.00	0.00
60	Petroleum Mining, etc	0.00	0.00	0.00	0.00	0.00	0.00	0.00	0.00
61	Gasoline	0.53	0.38	0.90	1.63	0.43	1.61	2.07	0.65
62	Fuel Oil	2.63	1.50	2.03	2.81	0.58	1.32	3.67	0.57
63	Electricity	2.16	1.30	2.10	2.67	0.61	2.49	11.67	3.07
64	City Gas	0.00	0.00	0.00	0.00	0.00	0.00	0.14	0.05
65	Water	1.78	1.11	1.52	1.04	0.24	0.29	3.08	0.31
66	Trade	143.42	85.83	125.07	117.10	26.71	62.63	113.88	21.99
67	Restaurants	43.55	17.73	21.45	51.44	7.99	18.92	111.15	21.17
68	Hotel, etc	0.40	0.45	0.89	1.00	0.20	0.84	1.31	0.27
69	Road Transport, etc	41.10	23.74	29.34	43.79	7.01	15.86	76.61	12.59
70	Air Transport, etc	12.90	8.52	13.25	15.11	3.01	8.94	18.74	3.52
71	Banking and Insurance	1.08	1.21	2.42	2.71	0.55	2.29	3.55	0.75
72	Real Estate	52.80	31.09	39.10	43.01	12.85	23.15	80.35	23.87
73	Public Services, etc	54.11	34.52	51.02	56.45	14.52	33.82	90.62	20.06
74	Personal Services, etc	35.76	21.07	30.88	35.29	7.25	20.69	43.84	9.76
Exog Accts.									
75	Government	-5.28	5.66	28.14	4.57	1.23	4.79	23.75	2.14
76	Capital Accounts	101.08	84.85	349.53	21.30	0.38	48.63	87.76	0.35
77	Net Indirect Taxes	0.00	0.00	0.00	0.00	0.00	0.00	0.00	0.00
78	Rest of World	46.22	26.05	44.41	58.08	12.87	34.51	81.48	18.82
79	Total Expenditure	1264.46	911.47	1554.87	1157.43	254.61	641.96	1428.62	254.13

		Name	Production Activities							
			Col 33	Col 34	Col 35	Col 36	Col 37	Col 38	Col 39	Col 40
Factors of Production	1	Ag Paid Rural			337.27	76.79	12.48	14.19	24.75	0.00
	2	Ag Paid Urban			10.43	2.19	2.49	1.29	4.65	0.00
	3	Ag Unpaid Rural			944.47	46.37	40.29	26.29	21.37	0.00
	4	Ag Unpaid Urban			34.79	2.66	2.99	1.03	3.48	0.00
	5	Prod Paid Rural			0.52	1.08	0.00	2.04	0.20	7.77
	6	Prod Paid Urban			0.10	0.07	0.00	0.19	0.07	0.76
	7	Prod Unpaid Rural			2.35	0.11	0.00	2.86	0.02	0.00
	8	Prod Unpaid Urban			0.01	0.00	0.00	0.06	0.00	0.00
	9	Cler Paid Rural			0.45	1.67	0.98	1.54	0.32	1.66
	10	Cler Paid Urban			0.32	0.35	0.04	0.84	0.13	0.63
	11	Cler Unpaid Rural			0.24	0.00	1.19	0.29	0.18	0.00
	12	Cler Unpaid Urban			0.01	0.00	0.00	0.00	0.00	0.00
	13	Prof Paid Rural			0.31	3.53	0.21	0.71	0.07	0.20
	14	Prof Paid Urban			0.03	1.00	0.14	0.05	0.10	0.00
	15	Prof Unpaid Rural			2.10	0.01	0.00	0.00	0.00	0.00
	16	Prof Unpaid Urban			0.00	0.00	0.10	0.00	0.00	0.00
	17	Uninc Capital Land			1074.04	254.71	227.94	107.37	143.08	0.00
	18	Uninc Capital Housing			0.00	0.00	0.00	0.00	0.00	0.00
	19	Uninc Capital Rural			0.00	0.00	0.00	0.00	0.00	0.00
	20	Uninc Capital Urban			0.00	0.00	0.00	0.00	0.00	0.00
	21	Inc Capital Domestic			1.39	11.40	8.19	78.07	14.96	0.00
	22	Inc Capital Government			18.66	47.08	1.21	7.99	0.70	11.19
	23	Inc Capital Foreign			0.02	12.22	0.57	24.54	6.78	9.25
Institutions	24	Ag Employees	0.00	0.00						
	25	Farm Size 1	0.00	0.00						
	26	Farm Size 2	0.00	0.00						
	27	Farm Size 3	0.00	0.00						
	28	Rural Lower	0.00	0.00						
	29	Rural Middle	2.92	32.90						
	30	Rural Higher	0.00	88.03						
	31	Urban Lower	0.00	0.00						
	32	Urban Middle	74.14	42.55						
	33	Urban Higher	0.00	467.41						
	34	Companies	0.00	30.14						
Production activities	35	Food Crop	93.73	0.00	57.97	0.12	3.53	0.00	0.11	0.00
	36	Nonfood Crop	4.01	0.00	0.14	100.38	0.96	0.00	0.00	0.00
	37	Livestock and Products	51.72	0.00	2.52	0.43	105.12	0.00	0.00	0.00
	38	Forestry and Hunting	0.63	0.00	0.30	0.57	0.16	19.26	0.95	0.03
	39	Fishery	19.41	0.00	0.00	0.00	0.00	0.00	0.00	0.00
	40	Metal Ore Mining	0.00	0.00	0.00	0.06	0.00	0.00	0.00	0.01
	41	Other Mining	0.93	0.00	0.00	0.00	0.04	0.00	0.00	0.00
	42	Handpounded Rice	7.41	0.00	0.00	0.00	0.63	0.00	0.10	0.00
	43	Milled Rice	104.79	0.00	0.00	0.00	3.41	0.00	0.25	0.00
	44	Farm Processed Tea	1.41	0.00	0.00	0.00	0.00	0.00	0.00	0.00
	45	Processed Tea	0.86	0.00	0.00	0.00	0.00	0.00	0.00	0.00
	46	Dried and Salted Fish	18.03	0.00	0.00	0.00	0.06	0.00	0.00	0.00
	47	Canned Fish	2.62	0.00	0.00	0.00	0.00	0.00	0.00	0.00
	48	Brown Sugar	2.44	0.00	0.00	0.00	0.00	0.00	0.00	0.00
	49	Refined Sugar	10.80	0.00	0.00	0.00	0.00	0.00	0.00	0.00
	50	Canning (s+c)	0.01	0.00	0.00	0.00	0.00	0.00	0.00	0.00
	51	Canning (m+l)	0.03	0.00	0.00	0.00	0.00	0.00	0.00	0.00
	52	Kretek Cigs	9.29	0.00	0.00	0.00	0.00	0.00	0.00	0.00
	53	White Cigs	23.02	0.00	0.00	0.00	0.00	0.00	0.00	0.00
	54	Other Fbt	91.73	0.00	0.00	0.00	0.70	0.00	2.40	0.00
	55	Wood and Construction	2.84	0.00	12.32	8.40	2.11	6.44	3.20	1.38
	56	Textiles, etc	71.18	0.00	4.46	1.06	0.39	0.76	1.35	0.13
	57	Paper, Transport, Metal, etc.	99.80	0.00	7.03	4.38	0.81	3.86	6.66	0.05
	58	Chemical, Cement, etc	19.26	0.00	24.97	5.61	0.26	0.00	0.00	0.00
	59	Coal Mining	0.00	0.00	0.00	0.00	0.00	0.00	0.00	0.38
	60	Petroleum Mining, etc	0.00	0.00	0.00	0.94	0.00	0.00	0.00	0.54
	61	Gasoline	6.14	0.00	0.08	0.63	0.18	0.83	0.32	0.00
	62	Fuel Oil	2.38	0.00	0.47	1.37	0.21	1.24	2.76	0.00
	63	Electricity	17.89	0.00	0.01	0.43	0.16	1.28	0.00	4.54
	64	City Gas	0.27	0.00	0.00	0.00	0.00	0.00	0.00	0.01
	65	Water	1.88	0.00	0.00	0.00	0.00	0.00	0.00	0.02
	66	Trade	124.53	0.00	76.77	29.22	18.90	21.06	9.75	9.79
	67	Restaurants	74.28	0.00	0.00	1.36	0.57	0.30	0.32	0.56
	68	Hotel, etc	1.82	0.00	0.00	0.32	0.06	0.50	0.41	0.40
	69	Road Transport, etc	68.54	0.00	7.86	8.47	2.20	8.03	3.18	1.14
	70	Air Transport, etc	20.95	0.00	4.03	4.14	1.39	3.40	0.78	1.75
	71	Banking and Insurance	4.96	0.00	21.18	5.01	0.60	5.93	2.24	2.66
	72	Real Estate	117.29	0.00	0.20	0.35	0.65	1.39	0.16	1.77
	73	Public Services, etc	107.53	0.00	0.02	0.26	0.06	0.01	0.00	0.61
	74	Personal Services, etc	56.00	0.00	1.10	6.01	0.76	7.98	0.00	1.72
Exog Accts.	75	Government	39.70	1448.44	0.00	0.00	0.00	0.00	0.00	0.00
	76	Capital Accounts	228.43	1668.99	0.00	0.00	0.00	0.00	0.00	0.00
	77	Net Indirect Taxes	0.00	0.00	2.19	2.29	2.08	2.60	1.52	3.73
	78	Rest of World	98.65	79.75	37.19	17.66	1.64	5.62	6.14	0.00
	79	Total Expenditure	1684.24	3858.21	2688.32	660.70	446.47	359.84	263.43	62.67

	Name	Production Activities							
		Col 41	Col 42	Col 43	Col 44	Col 45	Col 46	Col 47	Col 48
Factors of Production									
1	Ag Paid Rural	0.00	40.40	0.00	5.97	0.00	0.00	0.00	0.00
2	Ag Paid Urban	0.00	0.00	0.00	0.00	0.00	0.00	0.00	0.00
3	Ag Unpaid Rural	0.00	87.09	0.00	8.99	0.00	0.00	0.00	0.00
4	Ag Unpaid Urban	0.00	0.00	0.00	0.00	0.00	0.00	0.00	0.00
5	Prod Paid Rural	2.69	0.00	28.16	0.08	0.38	2.22	0.13	3.19
6	Prod Paid Urban	5.05	0.00	11.12	0.00	0.18	6.54	0.06	0.00
7	Prod Unpaid Rural	5.09	0.00	30.04	0.01	0.00	6.53	0.00	3.35
8	Prod Unpaid Urban	4.68	0.00	0.00	0.00	0.00	2.18	0.00	0.00
9	Cler Paid Rural	1.72	0.00	1.88	0.13	0.04	0.07	0.01	0.37
10	Cler Paid Urban	1.11	0.00	3.75	0.00	0.07	0.02	0.02	0.00
11	Cler Unpaid Rural	1.57	0.00	0.00	0.00	0.00	0.04	0.00	0.06
12	Cler Unpaid Urban	0.57	0.00	0.00	0.00	0.00	0.00	0.00	0.00
13	Prof Paid Rural	0.08	0.00	0.75	0.27	0.02	0.01	0.01	0.11
14	Prof Paid Urban	0.70	0.00	1.13	0.00	0.03	0.02	0.01	0.00
15	Prof Unpaid Rural	0.37	0.00	0.00	0.00	0.00	0.00	0.00	0.00
16	Prof Unpaid Urban	0.06	0.00	0.00	0.00	0.00	0.00	0.00	0.00
17	Uninc Capital Land	0.00	0.00	0.00	0.21	0.00	25.63	0.00	0.00
18	Uninc Capital Housing	0.00	0.00	0.00	0.00	0.00	0.00	0.00	0.00
19	Uninc Capital Rural	19.09	0.00	93.12	0.00	0.00	0.00	4.05	16.25
20	Uninc Capital Urban	38.10	0.00	13.83	0.00	0.01	0.00	1.57	0.00
21	Inc Capital Domestic	0.69	0.00	3.28	0.82	0.08	3.16	0.74	0.08
22	Inc Capital Government	2.99	0.00	0.68	5.31	0.52	0.14	0.19	0.00
23	Inc Capital Foreign	0.04	0.00	0.00	0.31	0.03	0.00	0.43	0.04
Institutions									
24	Ag Employees								
25	Farm Size 1								
26	Farm Size 2								
27	Farm Size 3								
28	Rural Lower								
29	Rural Middle								
30	Rural Higher								
31	Urban Lower								
32	Urban Middle								
33	Urban Higher								
34	Companies								
Production activities									
35	Food Crop	0.00	482.61	785.83	0.00	0.00	0.29	0.07	0.08
36	Nonfood Crop	0.00	0.00	0.00	11.94	3.86	0.00	0.00	18.67
37	Livestock and Products	0.00	0.00	0.00	0.00	0.00	0.00	0.00	0.00
38	Forestry and Hunting	0.14	0.00	0.20	0.10	0.04	0.62	0.04	0.14
39	Fishery	0.00	0.00	0.00	0.00	0.00	58.55	8.82	0.00
40	Metal Ore Mining	0.00	0.00	0.00	0.00	0.00	0.00	0.00	0.00
41	Other Mining	0.00	0.00	0.00	0.00	0.00	0.73	0.00	0.00
42	Handpounded Rice	0.00	0.00	21.88	0.00	0.00	0.00	0.00	0.00
43	Milled Rice	0.00	0.00	10.73	0.00	0.00	0.00	0.00	0.00
44	Farm Processed Tea	0.00	0.00	0.00	0.00	0.00	0.00	0.00	0.00
45	Processed Tea	0.00	0.00	0.00	0.00	0.00	0.00	0.00	0.00
46	Dried and Salted Fish	0.00	0.00	0.00	0.00	0.00	0.00	0.00	0.00
47	Canned Fish	0.00	0.00	0.00	0.00	0.00	0.00	0.02	0.00
48	Brown Sugar	0.00	0.00	0.00	0.00	0.00	0.00	0.00	0.00
49	Refined Sugar	0.00	0.00	0.00	0.00	0.00	0.03	0.01	0.00
50	Canning (s+c)	0.00	0.00	0.00	0.00	0.00	0.00	0.00	0.00
51	Canning (m+l)	0.00	0.00	0.00	0.00	0.00	0.00	0.00	0.00
52	Kretek Cigs	0.00	0.00	0.00	0.00	0.00	0.00	0.00	0.00
53	White Cigs	0.00	0.00	0.00	0.00	0.00	0.00	0.00	0.00
54	Other Fbt	0.00	0.00	0.00	0.00	0.00	0.12	1.42	0.03
55	Wood and Construction	4.56	1.26	0.87	0.21	0.03	2.07	0.12	0.23
56	Textiles, etc	0.22	1.24	0.13	0.01	0.08	0.22	0.01	0.01
57	Paper, Transport, Metal, etc.	1.31	0.00	7.04	0.16	0.17	0.30	0.19	0.39
58	Chemical, Cement, etc	0.04	0.13	0.73	0.01	0.07	0.22	0.39	0.06
59	Coal Mining	0.00	0.00	0.00	0.00	0.00	0.00	0.00	0.00
60	Petroleum Mining, etc	0.00	0.00	0.00	0.00	0.00	0.00	0.00	0.00
61	Gasoline	0.34	0.00	0.16	0.02	0.06	0.05	0.04	0.01
62	Fuel Oil	0.12	0.02	1.17	0.07	0.10	0.10	0.04	0.20
63	Electricity	0.05	0.00	0.45	0.00	0.18	0.15	0.43	0.03
64	City Gas	0.00	0.00	0.00	0.00	0.00	0.00	0.00	0.00
65	Water	0.00	0.00	2.02	0.00	0.00	0.00	0.00	0.00
66	Trade	1.06	3.18	31.10	4.90	1.52	20.12	3.41	2.07
67	Restaurants	0.18	0.00	1.56	0.07	0.03	0.24	0.03	0.05
68	Hotel, etc	0.01	0.00	0.04	0.00	0.01	0.05	0.00	0.00
69	Road Transport, etc	0.86	0.33	6.64	0.48	0.17	1.55	0.23	0.43
70	Air Transport, etc	0.08	0.06	1.33	0.06	0.11	0.54	0.12	0.09
71	Banking and Insurance	0.11	0.00	2.48	0.09	0.08	0.71	0.09	0.06
72	Real Estate	0.30	0.00	0.58	0.00	0.02	0.05	0.01	0.17
73	Public Services, etc	0.09	0.00	0.28	0.00	0.04	0.28	0.00	0.00
74	Personal Services, etc	0.36	0.00	1.69	0.31	0.04	0.11	0.02	0.57
Exog. Accts.									
75	Government	0.00	0.00	0.00	0.00	0.00	0.00	0.00	0.00
76	Capital Accounts	0.00	0.00	0.00	0.00	0.00	0.00	0.00	0.00
77	Net Indirect Taxes	1.23	0.21	0.55	0.05	0.13	0.88	0.00	0.21
78	Rest of World	1.08	0.00	79.83	0.00	0.03	0.01	1.00	0.00
M	79 Total Expenditure	96.74	616.53	1145.044	40.58	8.13	134.56	23.75	46.95

	Name		Production Activities						
		Col 49	Col 50	Col 51	Col 52	Col 53	Col 54	Col 55	Col 56
Factors of Production									
1	Ag Paid Rural	0.00	0.00	0.00	0.00	0.00	0.00	0.00	0.00
2	Ag Paid Urban	0.00	0.00	0.00	0.00	0.00	0.00	0.00	0.00
3	Ag Unpaid Rural	0.00	0.00	0.00	0.00	0.00	0.00	0.00	0.00
4	Ag Unpaid Urban	0.00	0.00	0.00	0.00	0.00	0.00	0.00	0.00
5	Prod Paid Rural	7.88	0.03	0.03	3.60	1.43	7.04	160.78	27.15
6	Prod Paid Urban	3.70	0.01	0.01	1.69	0.67	6.91	95.82	27.67
7	Prod Unpaid Rural	5.03	0.01	0.00	1.47	0.00	16.77	77.83	12.92
8	Prod Unpaid Urban	0.64	0.00	0.00	0.19	0.00	6.39	11.48	4.33
9	Cler Paid Rural	0.91	0.00	0.00	0.42	0.17	2.20	14.34	1.65
10	Cler Paid Urban	1.48	0.00	0.00	0.68	0.27	3.46	11.94	6.01
11	Cler Unpaid Rural	0.10	0.00	0.00	0.03	0.00	0.91	1.40	0.47
12	Cler Unpaid Urban	0.12	0.00	0.00	0.03	0.00	1.14	1.03	0.81
13	Prof Paid Rural	0.39	0.00	0.00	0.18	0.07	1.07	4.99	0.93
14	Prof Paid Urban	0.56	0.00	0.00	0.26	0.10	1.63	14.35	2.73
15	Prof Unpaid Rural	0.14	0.00	0.00	0.04	0.00	1.43	3.86	0.99
16	Prof Unpaid Urban	0.31	0.00	0.00	0.09	0.00	3.13	5.32	2.00
17	Uninc Capital Land	0.00	0.00	0.00	0.00	0.00	0.00	0.00	0.00
18	Uninc Capital Housing	0.00	0.00	0.00	0.00	0.00	0.00	0.00	0.00
19	Uninc Capital Rural	16.83	0.01	0.02	1.25	2.41	0.43	33.90	23.73
20	Uninc Capital Urban	16.21	0.01	0.02	1.21	1.97	94.62	37.40	37.30
21	Inc Capital Domestic	7.63	0.00	0.01	12.59	11.78	24.67	210.02	23.46
22	Inc Capital Government	8.23	0.00	0.01	0.15	0.14	55.80	52.10	6.75
23	Inc Capital Foreign	4.48	0.00	0.00	12.61	11.80	6.36	3.97	14.47
Institutions									
24	Ag Employees								
25	Farm Size 1								
26	Farm Size 2								
27	Farm Size 3								
28	Rural Lower								
29	Rural Middle								
30	Rural Higher								
31	Urban Lower								
32	Urban Middle								
33	Urban Higher								
34	Companies								
Production activities									
35	Food Crop	1.21	0.05	0.21	0.22	0.03	118.01	4.16	0.76
36	Nonfood Crop	25.46	0.00	0.01	70.88	8.38	78.59	1.30	5.07
37	Livestock and Products	0.00	0.00	0.00	0.00	0.00	5.59	0.00	7.09
38	Forestry and Hunting	0.26	0.00	0.00	0.01	0.00	1.03	89.93	0.21
39	Fishery	0.00	0.00	0.00	0.00	0.00	0.30	0.00	0.00
40	Metal Ore Mining	0.00	0.00	0.00	0.00	0.00	0.02	0.00	0.00
41	Other Mining	0.00	0.00	0.00	0.00	0.00	0.03	75.35	0.01
42	Handpounded Rice	0.00	0.00	0.00	0.00	0.00	2.14	0.00	0.00
43	Milled Rice	0.00	0.00	0.00	0.00	0.00	11.45	0.00	0.00
44	Farm Processed Tea	0.00	0.00	0.00	0.00	0.00	0.00	0.00	0.00
45	Processed Tea	0.00	0.00	0.00	0.00	0.00	0.00	0.00	0.00
46	Dried and Salted Fish	0.00	0.00	0.00	0.00	0.00	0.06	0.00	0.00
47	Canned Fish	0.00	0.00	0.00	0.00	0.00	0.00	0.00	0.00
48	Brown Sugar	0.00	0.00	0.00	0.00	0.00	5.08	0.00	0.00
49	Refined Sugar	0.07	0.01	0.02	0.00	0.00	19.13	0.00	0.00
50	Canning (s+c)	0.00	0.00	0.00	0.00	0.00	0.04	0.00	0.00
51	Canning (m+l)	0.00	0.00	0.00	0.00	0.00	0.06	0.00	0.00
52	Kretek Cigs	0.00	0.00	0.00	0.00	0.00	0.00	0.00	0.00
53	White Cigs	0.00	0.00	0.00	0.00	0.00	0.00	0.00	0.00
54	Other Fbt	0.00	0.00	0.01	45.48	5.38	83.93	0.03	0.15
55	Wood and Construction	1.11	0.00	0.00	0.45	0.05	3.76	67.32	2.85
56	Textiles, etc	1.25	0.01	0.01	0.00	0.00	1.64	2.93	177.10
57	Paper, Transport, Metal, etc.	4.29	0.01	0.04	6.75	0.80	1.21	83.76	6.87
58	Chemical, Cement, etc	1.19	0.01	0.02	1.15	0.14	0.01	162.54	3.87
59	Coal Mining	0.14	0.00	0.00	0.00	0.00	0.00	0.00	0.00
60	Petroleum Mining, etc	0.00	0.00	0.00	0.00	0.00	0.00	0.00	0.00
61	Gasoline	0.39	0.00	0.00	0.01	0.00	0.59	3.68	1.02
62	Fuel Oil	0.35	0.00	0.00	0.01	0.00	0.95	2.58	0.69
63	Electricity	7.19	0.00	0.00	0.35	0.10	6.70	1.76	11.23
64	City Gas	0.00	0.00	0.00	0.00	0.00	0.05	0.00	0.05
65	Water	0.11	0.00	0.01	0.01	0.13	0.00	1.03	2.54
66	Trade	4.98	0.01	0.07	20.27	12.87	147.17	272.64	44.69
67	Restaurants	0.34	0.00	0.00	0.50	0.12	1.50	20.85	1.29
68	Hotel, etc	0.20	0.00	0.00	0.22	0.08	0.48	0.18	0.23
69	Road Transport, etc	1.22	0.00	0.01	2.38	0.59	17.03	75.00	5.77
70	Air Transport, etc	0.46	0.00	0.01	1.07	0.26	12.77	44.80	3.74
71	Banking and Insurance	0.72	0.00	0.00	3.21	1.09	6.72	16.10	4.05
72	Real Estate	0.05	0.00	0.00	0.08	0.03	0.64	13.21	1.12
73	Public Services, etc	0.07	0.00	0.00	0.09	0.03	0.28	1.93	0.30
74	Personal Services, etc	0.48	0.00	0.01	0.01	0.00	2.68	2.01	1.17
M Exog Accts.									
75	Government	0.00	0.00	0.00	0.00	0.00	0.00	0.00	0.00
76	Capital Accounts	0.00	0.00	0.00	0.00	0.00	0.00	0.00	0.00
77	Net Indirect Taxes	4.47	0.01	0.02	39.87	20.26	9.36	23.19	3.72
78	Rest of World	6.26	0.00	0.00	2.67	2.66	9.63	395.43	125.62
79	Total Expenditure	136.91	0.20	0.56	232.19	83.80	782.60	2102.24	604.58

Appendix Table B (cont.)

<table>
<tr><th></th><th>Name</th><th colspan="8">Production Activities</th></tr>
<tr><th></th><th></th><th>Col
57</th><th>Col
58</th><th>Col
59</th><th>Col
60</th><th>Co
61</th><th>Col
62</th><th>Col
63</th><th>Col
64</th></tr>
<tr><td>1</td><td>Ag Paid Rural</td><td>0.00</td><td>0.00</td><td>0.00</td><td>0.00</td><td>0.00</td><td>0.00</td><td>0.00</td><td>0.00</td></tr>
<tr><td>2</td><td>Ag Paid Urban</td><td>0.00</td><td>0.00</td><td>0.00</td><td>0.00</td><td>0.00</td><td>0.00</td><td>0.00</td><td>0.00</td></tr>
<tr><td>3</td><td>Ag Unpaid Rural</td><td>0.00</td><td>0.00</td><td>0.00</td><td>0.00</td><td>0.00</td><td>0.00</td><td>0.00</td><td>0.00</td></tr>
<tr><td>4</td><td>Ag Unpaid Urban</td><td>0.00</td><td>0.00</td><td>0.00</td><td>0.00</td><td>0.00</td><td>0.00</td><td>0.00</td><td>0.00</td></tr>
<tr><td>5</td><td>Prod Paid Rural</td><td>24.54</td><td>23.16</td><td>0.32</td><td>1.86</td><td>0.76</td><td>0.70</td><td>0.15</td><td>0.00</td></tr>
<tr><td>6</td><td>Prod Paid Urban</td><td>33.18</td><td>13.12</td><td>0.03</td><td>2.17</td><td>0.69</td><td>0.64</td><td>8.42</td><td>0.19</td></tr>
<tr><td>7</td><td>Prod Unpaid Rural</td><td>17.45</td><td>13.69</td><td>0.00</td><td>0.00</td><td>0.00</td><td>0.00</td><td>0.17</td><td>0.00</td></tr>
<tr><td>8</td><td>Prod Unpaid Urban</td><td>4.75</td><td>0.95</td><td>0.00</td><td>0.00</td><td>0.00</td><td>0.00</td><td>0.75</td><td>0.00</td></tr>
<tr><td>9</td><td>Cler Paid Rural</td><td>5.36</td><td>6.94</td><td>0.07</td><td>0.49</td><td>0.35</td><td>0.33</td><td>2.91</td><td>0.00</td></tr>
<tr><td>10</td><td>Cler Paid Urban</td><td>17.85</td><td>8.77</td><td>0.03</td><td>5.53</td><td>0.58</td><td>0.54</td><td>2.85</td><td>0.08</td></tr>
<tr><td>11</td><td>Cler Unpaid Rural</td><td>1.32</td><td>0.25</td><td>0.00</td><td>0.00</td><td>0.00</td><td>0.00</td><td>0.00</td><td>0.00</td></tr>
<tr><td>12</td><td>Cler Unpaid Urban</td><td>1.16</td><td>0.24</td><td>0.00</td><td>0.00</td><td>0.00</td><td>0.00</td><td>0.00</td><td>0.00</td></tr>
<tr><td>13</td><td>Prof Paid Rural</td><td>0.96</td><td>2.05</td><td>0.01</td><td>0.67</td><td>0.15</td><td>0.14</td><td>1.51</td><td>0.00</td></tr>
<tr><td>14</td><td>Prof Paid Urban</td><td>8.61</td><td>5.08</td><td>0.00</td><td>11.69</td><td>0.33</td><td>0.30</td><td>6.09</td><td>0.12</td></tr>
<tr><td>15</td><td>Prof Unpaid Rural</td><td>0.54</td><td>1.20</td><td>0.00</td><td>0.00</td><td>0.00</td><td>0.00</td><td>0.00</td><td>0.00</td></tr>
<tr><td>16</td><td>Prof Unpaid Urban</td><td>2.96</td><td>0.73</td><td>0.00</td><td>0.00</td><td>0.00</td><td>0.00</td><td>0.00</td><td>0.00</td></tr>
<tr><td>17</td><td>Uninc Capital Land</td><td>0.00</td><td>0.00</td><td>0.00</td><td>0.00</td><td>0.00</td><td>0.00</td><td>0.00</td><td>0.00</td></tr>
<tr><td>18</td><td>Uninc Capital Housing</td><td>0.00</td><td>0.00</td><td>0.00</td><td>0.00</td><td>0.00</td><td>0.00</td><td>0.00</td><td>0.00</td></tr>
<tr><td>19</td><td>Uninc Capital Rural</td><td>12.69</td><td>10.44</td><td>0.00</td><td>0.00</td><td>0.00</td><td>0.00</td><td>0.10</td><td>0.00</td></tr>
<tr><td>20</td><td>Uninc Capital Urban</td><td>23.97</td><td>14.80</td><td>0.00</td><td>0.00</td><td>0.00</td><td>0.00</td><td>1.22</td><td>0.00</td></tr>
<tr><td>21</td><td>Inc Capital Domestic</td><td>104.84</td><td>31.53</td><td>0.00</td><td>0.00</td><td>0.00</td><td>0.00</td><td>6.30</td><td>0.56</td></tr>
<tr><td>22</td><td>Inc Capital Government</td><td>32.90</td><td>79.73</td><td>0.52</td><td>487.08</td><td>21.90</td><td>20.16</td><td>39.40</td><td>0.00</td></tr>
<tr><td>23</td><td>Inc Capital Foreign</td><td>47.64</td><td>18.83</td><td>0.00</td><td>1730.82</td><td>0.00</td><td>0.00</td><td>4.99</td><td>0.00</td></tr>
<tr><td>24</td><td>Ag Employees</td><td></td><td></td><td></td><td></td><td></td><td></td><td></td><td></td></tr>
<tr><td>25</td><td>Farm Size 1</td><td></td><td></td><td></td><td></td><td></td><td></td><td></td><td></td></tr>
<tr><td>26</td><td>Farm Size 2</td><td></td><td></td><td></td><td></td><td></td><td></td><td></td><td></td></tr>
<tr><td>27</td><td>Farm Size 3</td><td></td><td></td><td></td><td></td><td></td><td></td><td></td><td></td></tr>
<tr><td>28</td><td>Rural Lower</td><td></td><td></td><td></td><td></td><td></td><td></td><td></td><td></td></tr>
<tr><td>29</td><td>Rural Middle</td><td></td><td></td><td></td><td></td><td></td><td></td><td></td><td></td></tr>
<tr><td>30</td><td>Rural Higher</td><td></td><td></td><td></td><td></td><td></td><td></td><td></td><td></td></tr>
<tr><td>31</td><td>Urban Lower</td><td></td><td></td><td></td><td></td><td></td><td></td><td></td><td></td></tr>
<tr><td>32</td><td>Urban Middle</td><td></td><td></td><td></td><td></td><td></td><td></td><td></td><td></td></tr>
<tr><td>33</td><td>Urban Higher</td><td></td><td></td><td></td><td></td><td></td><td></td><td></td><td></td></tr>
<tr><td>34</td><td>Companies</td><td></td><td></td><td></td><td></td><td></td><td></td><td></td><td></td></tr>
<tr><td>35</td><td>Food Crop</td><td>1.25</td><td>2.54</td><td>0.00</td><td>0.00</td><td>0.00</td><td>0.00</td><td>0.00</td><td>0.00</td></tr>
<tr><td>36</td><td>Nonfood Crop</td><td>0.11</td><td>7.25</td><td>0.00</td><td>0.00</td><td>0.00</td><td>0.00</td><td>0.00</td><td>0.00</td></tr>
<tr><td>37</td><td>Livestock and Products</td><td>0.69</td><td>0.00</td><td>0.00</td><td>0.00</td><td>0.00</td><td>0.00</td><td>0.00</td><td>0.00</td></tr>
<tr><td>38</td><td>Forestry and Hunting</td><td>6.82</td><td>3.47</td><td>0.00</td><td>0.00</td><td>0.00</td><td>0.00</td><td>0.00</td><td>0.00</td></tr>
<tr><td>39</td><td>Fishery</td><td>0.05</td><td>0.01</td><td>0.00</td><td>0.00</td><td>0.00</td><td>0.00</td><td>0.00</td><td>0.00</td></tr>
<tr><td>40</td><td>Metal Ore Mining</td><td>0.29</td><td>0.00</td><td>0.00</td><td>0.00</td><td>0.00</td><td>0.00</td><td>0.00</td><td>0.00</td></tr>
<tr><td>41</td><td>Other Mining</td><td>0.18</td><td>9.00</td><td>0.00</td><td>0.00</td><td>0.00</td><td>0.00</td><td>0.00</td><td>0.00</td></tr>
<tr><td>42</td><td>Handpounded Rice</td><td>0.00</td><td>0.27</td><td>0.00</td><td>0.00</td><td>0.00</td><td>0.00</td><td>0.00</td><td>0.00</td></tr>
<tr><td>43</td><td>Milled Rice</td><td>0.00</td><td>0.14</td><td>0.00</td><td>0.00</td><td>0.00</td><td>0.00</td><td>0.00</td><td>0.00</td></tr>
<tr><td>44</td><td>Farm Processed Tea</td><td>0.00</td><td>0.00</td><td>0.00</td><td>0.00</td><td>0.00</td><td>0.00</td><td>0.00</td><td>0.00</td></tr>
<tr><td>45</td><td>Processed Tea</td><td>0.00</td><td>0.00</td><td>0.00</td><td>0.00</td><td>0.00</td><td>0.00</td><td>0.00</td><td>0.00</td></tr>
<tr><td>46</td><td>Dried and Salted Fish</td><td>0.00</td><td>0.00</td><td>0.00</td><td>0.00</td><td>0.00</td><td>0.00</td><td>0.00</td><td>0.00</td></tr>
<tr><td>47</td><td>Canned Fish</td><td>0.00</td><td>0.00</td><td>0.00</td><td>0.00</td><td>0.00</td><td>0.00</td><td>0.00</td><td>0.00</td></tr>
<tr><td>48</td><td>Brown Sugar</td><td>0.00</td><td>0.01</td><td>0.00</td><td>0.00</td><td>0.00</td><td>0.00</td><td>0.00</td><td>0.00</td></tr>
<tr><td>49</td><td>Refined Sugar</td><td>0.00</td><td>1.25</td><td>0.00</td><td>0.00</td><td>0.00</td><td>0.00</td><td>0.00</td><td>0.00</td></tr>
<tr><td>50</td><td>Canning (s+c)</td><td>0.00</td><td>0.00</td><td>0.00</td><td>0.00</td><td>0.00</td><td>0.00</td><td>0.00</td><td>0.00</td></tr>
<tr><td>51</td><td>Canning (m+l)</td><td>0.00</td><td>0.00</td><td>0.00</td><td>0.00</td><td>0.00</td><td>0.00</td><td>0.00</td><td>0.00</td></tr>
<tr><td>52</td><td>Kretek Cigs</td><td>0.01</td><td>0.00</td><td>0.00</td><td>0.00</td><td>0.00</td><td>0.00</td><td>0.00</td><td>0.00</td></tr>
<tr><td>53</td><td>White Cigs</td><td>0.00</td><td>0.00</td><td>0.00</td><td>0.00</td><td>0.00</td><td>0.00</td><td>0.00</td><td>0.00</td></tr>
<tr><td>54</td><td>Other Fbt</td><td>0.01</td><td>15.34</td><td>0.00</td><td>0.00</td><td>0.00</td><td>0.00</td><td>0.00</td><td>0.00</td></tr>
<tr><td>55</td><td>Wood and Construction</td><td>21.68</td><td>7.89</td><td>0.00</td><td>3.22</td><td>0.46</td><td>0.42</td><td>3.31</td><td>0.00</td></tr>
<tr><td>56</td><td>Textiles, etc</td><td>2.35</td><td>2.88</td><td>0.00</td><td>0.25</td><td>0.00</td><td>0.00</td><td>0.04</td><td>0.00</td></tr>
<tr><td>57</td><td>Paper, Transport, Metal, etc.</td><td>37.03</td><td>11.71</td><td>0.13</td><td>11.88</td><td>1.40</td><td>1.70</td><td>2.23</td><td>0.03</td></tr>
<tr><td>58</td><td>Chemical, Cement, etc</td><td>29.77</td><td>15.78</td><td>0.01</td><td>0.55</td><td>2.03</td><td>1.87</td><td>0.59</td><td>0.03</td></tr>
<tr><td>59</td><td>Coal Mining</td><td>0.21</td><td>0.00</td><td>0.02</td><td>0.00</td><td>0.00</td><td>0.00</td><td>0.62</td><td>0.00</td></tr>
<tr><td>60</td><td>Petroleum Mining, etc</td><td>0.00</td><td>144.06</td><td>0.00</td><td>4.33</td><td>44.43</td><td>40.91</td><td>0.00</td><td>0.00</td></tr>
<tr><td>61</td><td>Gasoline</td><td>1.48</td><td>1.83</td><td>0.01</td><td>0.87</td><td>0.03</td><td>0.03</td><td>2.32</td><td>0.01</td></tr>
<tr><td>62</td><td>Fuel Oil</td><td>0.50</td><td>5.09</td><td>0.01</td><td>2.06</td><td>0.15</td><td>0.14</td><td>11.96</td><td>0.15</td></tr>
<tr><td>63</td><td>Electricity</td><td>6.36</td><td>10.01</td><td>0.12</td><td>8.77</td><td>0.93</td><td>0.81</td><td>2.63</td><td>0.03</td></tr>
<tr><td>64</td><td>City Gas</td><td>0.16</td><td>0.24</td><td>0.00</td><td>0.03</td><td>0.00</td><td>0.00</td><td>0.00</td><td>0.00</td></tr>
<tr><td>65</td><td>Water</td><td>6.22</td><td>0.00</td><td>0.00</td><td>0.07</td><td>0.00</td><td>0.00</td><td>0.04</td><td>0.00</td></tr>
<tr><td>66</td><td>Trade</td><td>93.67</td><td>47.66</td><td>0.02</td><td>0.80</td><td>0.58</td><td>0.53</td><td>3.63</td><td>0.05</td></tr>
<tr><td>67</td><td>Restaurants</td><td>2.44</td><td>1.49</td><td>0.00</td><td>0.86</td><td>0.23</td><td>0.21</td><td>0.29</td><td>0.00</td></tr>
<tr><td>68</td><td>Hotel, etc</td><td>0.19</td><td>0.19</td><td>0.00</td><td>0.86</td><td>0.01</td><td>0.01</td><td>0.15</td><td>0.00</td></tr>
<tr><td>69</td><td>Road Transport, etc</td><td>12.54</td><td>13.58</td><td>0.00</td><td>0.74</td><td>0.14</td><td>0.13</td><td>0.66</td><td>0.03</td></tr>
<tr><td>70</td><td>Air Transport, etc</td><td>8.19</td><td>8.22</td><td>0.01</td><td>2.63</td><td>0.22</td><td>0.25</td><td>1.68</td><td>0.02</td></tr>
<tr><td>71</td><td>Banking and Insurance</td><td>15.36</td><td>10.99</td><td>0.00</td><td>5.34</td><td>1.96</td><td>1.80</td><td>0.98</td><td>0.01</td></tr>
<tr><td>72</td><td>Real Estate</td><td>5.87</td><td>2.51</td><td>0.00</td><td>6.28</td><td>0.27</td><td>0.26</td><td>0.45</td><td>0.00</td></tr>
<tr><td>73</td><td>Public Services, etc</td><td>0.71</td><td>0.53</td><td>0.00</td><td>1.14</td><td>0.06</td><td>0.06</td><td>0.03</td><td>0.00</td></tr>
<tr><td>74</td><td>Personal Services, etc</td><td>3.09</td><td>2.51</td><td>0.00</td><td>2.41</td><td>0.21</td><td>0.03</td><td>0.16</td><td>0.00</td></tr>
<tr><td>75</td><td>Government</td><td>0.00</td><td>0.00</td><td>0.00</td><td>0.00</td><td>0.00</td><td>0.00</td><td>0.00</td><td>0.00</td></tr>
<tr><td>76</td><td>Capital Accounts</td><td>0.00</td><td>0.00</td><td>0.00</td><td>0.00</td><td>0.00</td><td>0.00</td><td>0.00</td><td>0.00</td></tr>
<tr><td>77</td><td>Net Indirect Taxes</td><td>9.93</td><td>8.82</td><td>0.01</td><td>88.85</td><td>0.10</td><td>0.09</td><td>1.27</td><td>0.01</td></tr>
<tr><td>78</td><td>Rest of World</td><td>337.44</td><td>74.80</td><td>0.15</td><td>21.90</td><td>14.84</td><td>14.83</td><td>24.87</td><td>0.39</td></tr>
<tr><td>79</td><td>Total Expenditure</td><td>945.32</td><td>641.59</td><td>1.49</td><td>2404.17</td><td>92.83</td><td>86.91</td><td>132.79</td><td>1.73</td></tr>
</table>

Factors of Production — rows 1–23
Institutions — rows 24–34
Production activities — rows 35–74
Exog. Accts. — rows 75–78
M — row 79

	Name		Production Activities							
			Col 65	Col 66	Col 67	Col 68	Col 69	Col 70	Col 71	Col 72
Factors of Production	1	Ag Paid Rural	0.00	0.00	0.00	0.00	0.00	0.00	0.00	0.00
	2	Ag Paid Urban	0.00	0.00	0.00	0.00	0.00	0.00	0.00	0.00
	3	Ag Unpaid Rural	0.00	0.00	0.00	0.00	0.00	0.00	0.00	0.00
	4	Ag Unpaid Urban	0.00	0.00	0.00	0.00	0.00	0.00	0.00	0.00
	5	Prod Paid Rural	0.00	5.10	0.06	0.09	49.88	6.97	0.26	1.63
	6	Prod Paid Urban	1.22	6.49	0.09	0.13	55.59	17.78	1.74	1.79
	7	Prod Unpaid Rural	0.00	0.99	0.17	0.00	46.75	4.02	0.00	0.12
	8	Prod Unpaid Urban	0.00	0.33	0.01	0.00	31.84	1.58	0.00	0.06
	9	Cler Paid Rural	0.00	41.81	3.25	2.13	7.11	2.64	3.66	4.21
	10	Cler Paid Urban	0.49	71.89	2.58	6.65	9.74	22.70	39.45	6.16
	11	Cler Unpaid Rural	0.00	358.63	28.97	0.09	0.94	0.22	0.00	0.00
	12	Cler Unpaid Urban	0.00	192.26	15.35	0.09	1.08	0.50	0.00	0.17
	13	Prof Paid Rural	0.00	1.93	0.00	0.25	0.37	1.48	1.42	0.43
	14	Prof Paid Urban	0.73	15.98	0.06	0.87	3.20	20.10	27.50	5.21
	15	Prof Unpaid Rural	0.00	19.67	2.75	0.03	0.17	0.41	0.00	0.00
	16	Prof Unpaid Urban	0.00	77.21	4.57	0.71	2.44	1.06	0.20	1.22
	17	Uninc Capital Land	0.00	0.00	0.00	0.00	0.00	0.00	0.00	0.00
	18	Uninc Capital Housing	0.00	0.00	0.00	0.00	0.00	0.00	0.00	358.42
	19	Uninc Capital Rural	0.00	174.82	45.93	1.20	51.87	7.67	0.81	1.26
	20	Uninc Capital Urban	0.00	266.55	60.42	5.45	88.55	9.69	1.56	30.65
	21	Inc Capital Domestic	0.00	458.93	5.25	0.74	60.89	8.29	13.83	62.31
	22	Inc Capital Government	3.90	134.03	0.01	4.00	6.65	144.84	130.61	5.69
	23	Inc Capital Foreign	0.00	82.97	0.33	0.90	0.00	0.00	9.36	0.00
Institutions	24	Ag Employees								
	25	Farm Size 1								
	26	Farm Size 2								
	27	Farm Size 3								
	28	Rural Lower								
	29	Rural Middle								
	30	Rural Higher								
	31	Urban Lower								
	32	Urban Middle								
	33	Urban Higher								
	34	Companies								
Production activities	35	Food Crop	0.00	2.72	41.02	0.35				
	36	Nonfood Crop	0.00	0.86	5.97	0.17	0.00	0.01	0.00	0.00
	37	Livestock and Products	0.00	0.00	36.54	0.93	0.00	1.53	0.00	0.00
	38	Forestry and Hunting	0.00	0.03	1.03	0.00	0.26	0.00	0.00	0.00
	39	Fishery	0.00	0.00	18.25	0.10	0.00	0.06	0.00	0.00
	40	Metal Ore Mining	0.00	0.00	0.00	0.00	0.00	0.00	0.00	0.00
	41	Other Mining	0.00	0.04	0.13	0.00	0.00	0.00	0.00	0.00
	42	Handpounded Rice	0.00	0.00	11.11	0.00	0.00	0.00	0.00	0.00
	43	Milled Rice	0.00	0.00	23.28	1.09	2.74	1.34	0.00	0.00
	44	Farm Processed Tea	0.00	0.00	0.81	0.00	0.00	0.00	0.00	0.00
	45	Processed Tea	0.00	0.00	0.68	0.16	0.00	0.02	0.00	0.00
	46	Dried and Salted Fish	0.00	0.00	4.06	0.01	0.00	0.06	0.00	0.00
	47	Canned Fish	0.00	0.00	0.96	0.00	0.00	0.00	0.00	0.00
	48	Brown Sugar	0.00	0.00	1.18	0.01	0.00	0.00	0.00	0.00
	49	Refined Sugar	0.00	0.00	16.19	0.56	0.00	0.30	0.00	0.00
	50	Canning (s+c)	0.00	0.00	0.07	0.02	0.00	0.00	0.00	0.00
	51	Canning (m+l)	0.00	0.00	0.16	0.02	0.00	0.00	0.00	0.00
	52	Kretek Cigs	0.00	0.00	0.00	0.04	0.00	0.09	0.00	0.01
	53	White Cigs	0.00	0.00	0.00	0.04	0.00	0.08	0.00	0.00
	54	Other Fbt	0.00	0.00	80.36	2.93	0.00	1.46	0.01	0.18
	55	Wood and Construction	2.61	12.63	3.68	1.91	3.11	10.64	4.64	54.36
	56	Textiles, etc	0.05	2.75	2.16	0.52	0.85	3.07	0.00	0.06
	57	Paper, Transport, Metal, etc.	0.01	10.69	4.17	1.14	6.24	21.22	5.26	1.66
	58	Chemical, Cement, etc	0.47	0.01	0.01	0.37	0.00	0.00	0.00	0.02
	59	Coal Mining	0.00	0.00	0.00	0.00	0.12	0.00	0.00	0.00
	60	Petroleum Mining, etc	0.00	0.00	0.00	0.00	0.00	0.00	0.00	0.00
	61	Gasoline	0.00	13.25	0.61	0.07	14.53	10.97	0.52	0.35
	62	Fuel Oil	0.00	3.08	6.44	0.41	7.90	6.02	0.00	0.32
	63	Electricity	2.06	3.74	1.40	1.01	0.84	1.81	1.05	0.53
	64	City Gas	0.01	0.00	0.44	0.12	0.01	0.00	0.00	0.00
	65	Water	0.01	0.54	0.69	0.48	0.47	0.66	0.11	0.02
	66	Trade	9.03	16.22	46.90	2.69	20.56	23.50	9.15	1.67
	67	Restaurants	0.20	21.25	1.42	0.45	2.65	6.96	1.14	2.17
	68	Hotel, etc	0.10	6.91	0.09	0.07	0.03	0.61	3.67	0.11
	69	Road Transport, etc	1.84	26.16	8.25	0.74	11.04	3.08	1.80	2.50
	70	Air Transport, etc	0.00	13.82	4.54	1.11	2.58	29.03	6.00	1.01
	71	Banking and Insurance	0.67	101.51	4.74	2.73	4.96	15.34	2.30	5.93
	72	Real Estate	0.16	31.46	4.27	0.54	0.99	5.04	4.95	2.03
	73	Public Services, etc	0.01	5.62	1.15	0.06	1.66	4.22	4.79	0.55
	74	Personal Services, etc	1.43	20.35	1.90	0.21	108.55	4.22	2.18	1.93
M **Exog Accts.**	75	Government	0.00	0.00	0.00	0.00	0.00	0.00	0.00	0.00
	76	Capital Accounts	0.00	0.00	0.00	0.00	0.00	0.00	0.00	0.00
	77	Net Indirect Taxes	0.01	22.14	6.09	0.71	8.75	1.95	0.41	0.91
	78	Rest of World	5.06	38.99	22.89	2.77	31.28	59.74	10.60	2.40
	79	Total Expenditure	30.70	2264.36	533.44	47.87	647.19	463.50	288.98	558.06

Appendix Table B (cont.)

Section	#	Name	Col 73	Col 74	Col 75	Exogenous Accounts Col 76	Col 77	Col 78	Total Income Col 79
Factors of Production	1	Ag Paid Rural	0.00	0.00	0.00	0.00	0.00	0.00	511.85
	2	Ag Paid Urban	0.00	0.00	0.00	0.00	0.00	0.00	21.05
	3	Ag Unpaid Rural	0.00	0.00	0.00	0.00	0.00	0.00	1174.87
	4	Ag Unpaid Urban	0.00	0.00	0.00	0.00	0.00	0.00	44.95
	5	Prod Paid Rural	7.55	38.22	0.00	0.00	0.00	0.00	417.66
	6	Prod Paid Urban	19.94	35.87	0.00	0.00	0.00	0.00	359.70
	7	Prod Unpaid Rural	0.37	25.80	0.00	0.00	0.00	0.00	273.92
	8	Prod Unpaid Urban	0.95	26.33	0.00	0.00	0.00	0.00	97.51
	9	Cler Paid Rural	61.73	50.41	0.00	0.00	0.00	0.00	223.94
	10	Cler Paid Urban	122.81	48.46	0.00	0.00	0.00	0.00	398.29
	11	Cler Unpaid Rural	0.75	15.24	0.00	0.00	0.00	0.00	412.89
	12	Cler Unpaid Urban	2.39	11.42	0.00	0.00	0.00	0.00	228.37
	13	Prof Paid Rural	357.49	4.22	0.00	0.00	0.00	0.00	386.99
	14	Prof Paid Urban	384.39	3.99	0.00	0.00	0.00	0.00	517.09
	15	Prof Unpaid Rural	5.59	2.51	0.00	0.00	0.00	0.00	41.82
	16	Prof Unpaid Urban	9.68	3.93	0.00	0.00	0.00	0.00	115.72
	17	Uninc Capital Land	0.00	0.00	0.00	0.00	0.00	0.00	1832.99
	18	Uninc Capital Housing	0.00	0.00	0.00	0.00	0.00	0.00	358.42
	19	Uninc Capital Rural	9.53	2.26	0.00	0.00	0.00	0.00	529.68
	20	Uninc Capital Urban	45.10	5.25	0.00	0.00	0.00	0.00	795.45
	21	Inc Capital Domestic	27.47	7.72	0.00	0.00	0.00	0.00	1201.68
	22	Inc Capital Government	42.76	0.96	0.00	0.00	0.00	0.00	1374.99
	23	Inc Capital Foreign	0.00	0.00	0.00	0.00	0.00	0.00	2003.78
Institutions	24	Ag Employees			13.15	0.00	0.00	0.00	615.60
	25	Farm Size 1			28.97	0.00	0.00	0.00	1264.36
	26	Farm Size 2			18.51	0.00	0.00	0.00	911.44
	27	Farm Size 3			25.18	0.00	0.00	0.00	1555.07
	28	Rural Lower			24.01	0.00	0.00	0.00	1157.49
	29	Rural Middle			6.72	0.00	0.00	0.00	254.59
	30	Rural Higher			14.34	0.00	0.00	0.00	641.92
	31	Urban Lower			20.79	0.00	0.00	0.00	1428.61
	32	Urban Middle			6.84	0.00	0.00	0.00	254.13
	33	Urban Higher			23.58	0.00	0.00	0.00	1684.24
	34	Companies			0.00	0.00	0.00	18.10	3858.21
Production activities	35	Food Crop			0.00	5.38	0.00	14.72	2687.84
	36	Nonfood Crop	0.08	0.00	0.00	4.51	0.00	267.38	660.68
	37	Livestock and Products	5.59	0.00	0.00	5.77	0.00	6.52	446.37
	38	Forestry and Hunting	0.02	0.10	0.00	0.00	0.00	210.83	359.83
	39	Fishery	0.94	0.00	0.00	0.00	0.00	34.86	263.37
	40	Metal Ore Mining	0.00	0.10	0.00	4.75	0.00	57.64	62.87
	41	Other Mining	0.00	0.00	0.00	0.15	0.00	0.12	96.74
	42	Handpounded Rice	2.73	0.00	0.00	0.00	0.00	0.00	616.28
	43	Milled Rice	2.77	0.00	0.00	0.00	0.00	3.08	1144.59
	44	Farm Processed Tea	0.07	0.00	0.00	0.00	0.00	19.05	40.57
	45	Processed Tea	0.03	0.00	0.05	0.29	0.00	0.00	8.12
	46	Dried and Salted Fish	0.08	0.00	0.00	0.00	0.00	0.99	134.52
	47	Canned Fish	0.00	0.00	0.00	0.03	0.00	0.00	23.74
	48	Brown Sugar	0.03	0.00	0.93	0.00	0.00	0.00	46.93
	49	Refined Sugar	0.00	0.00	0.00	0.16	0.00	3.41	136.87
	50	Canning (s+c)	0.00	0.00	0.00	0.00	0.00	0.00	0.20
	51	Canning (m+l)	0.00	0.00	0.00	0.22	0.00	0.22	0.56
	52	Kretek Cigs	0.00	0.00	0.00	3.10	0.00	0.00	232.07
	53	White Cigs	0.00	0.00	0.00	3.11	0.00	0.00	83.49
	54	Other Fbt	2.31	0.00	1.00	2.86	0.00	45.47	782.39
	55	Wood and Construction	11.00	2.10	48.29	1760.93	0.00	0.80	2102.20
	56	Textiles, etc	3.08	11.47	16.66	23.67	0.00	2.08	604.53
	57	Paper, Transport, Metal, etc.	12.14	28.12	60.57	273.55	0.00	20.18	945.16
	58	Chemical, Cement, etc	5.87	36.58	4.03	9.28	0.00	215.34	641.50
	59	Coal Mining	0.00	0.00	0.00	0.00	0.00	0.00	1.50
	60	Petroleum Mining, etc	0.00	0.00	0.00	47.73	0.00	2121.26	2404.20
	61	Gasoline	1.73	1.81	6.56	4.40	0.00	8.27	92.83
	62	Fuel Oil	0.67	1.10	1.46	1.68	0.00	9.51	86.90
	63	Electricity	4.58	1.19	4.65	0.00	0.00	0.00	132.90
	64	City Gas	0.13	0.00	0.00	0.00	0.00	0.00	1.73
	65	Water	1.30	0.40	0.90	0.00	0.00	0.00	30.07
	66	Trade	16.22	33.30	29.80	274.73	0.00	6.32	2264.00
	67	Restaurants	1.44	1.54	45.37	0.00	0.00	20.74	536.76
	68	Hotel, etc	0.32	0.12	11.95	0.00	0.00	11.96	47.88
	69	Road Transport, etc	3.04	6.72	40.43	17.78	0.00	17.10	647.01
	70	Air Transport, etc	1.99	2.69	36.61	10.92	0.00	139.83	463.43
	71	Banking and Insurance	3.82	3.96	13.48	0.00	0.00	0.00	289.00
	72	Real Estate	5.26	5.21	12.38	0.00	0.00	0.00	557.89
	73	Public Services, etc	7.17	0.40	716.42	0.00	0.00	7.83	1247.73
	74	Personal Services, etc	4.11	6.07	19.19	0.00	0.00	7.07	492.55
Exog. Accts.	75	Government	0.00	0.00	0.00	0.00	362.29	1.10	1988.13
	76	Capital Accounts	0.00	0.00	567.42	0.00	0.00	493.22	3409.94
	77	Net Indirect Taxes	5.83	2.31	0.00	0.00	0.00	85.46	362.23
	78	Rest of World	41.48	66.15	166.94	980.12	0.00	0.00	3851.06
	79	Total Expenditure	1247.95	494.03	1987.18	3409.86	362.29	3850.47	57978.40

Appendix Table C: Household Expenditure Elasticities for Indonesia, 1975*

	Name	Agricultural Employees 24	Farm 1 25	Farm 2 26	Farm 3 27	Rural Lower 28	Rural Middle 29	Rural Higher 30	Urban Lower 31
35	Farmfood	0.70	0.61	0.62	0.50	0.74	0.73	0.50	0.52
36	Fmnonfd	1.00	1.00	1.00	1.00	1.00	1.00	1.00	1.00
37	Livestoc	1.20	1.20	1.21	1.09	1.09	1.08	0.99	1.07
38	Forestry	1.00	1.00	1.00	1.00	1.00	1.00	1.00	1.00
39	Fishery	1.00	1.00	1.00	1.00	1.00	1.00	1.00	1.00
40	Metal	0.00	0.00	0.00	0.00	0.00	0.00	0.00	0.00
41	Other	1.00	1.00	1.00	1.00	1.00	1.00	1.00	1.00
42	Hprice	0.42	0.59	0.70	0.35	0.71	0.71	0.54	0.57
43	Millrice	0.71	0.70	0.70	0.50	0.72	0.76	0.51	0.57
44	Farmtea	1.00	1.00	1.00	1.00	1.00	1.00	1.00	1.00
45	Proc.tea	1.00	1.00	1.00	1.00	1.00	1.00	1.00	1.00
46	Fish (t)	1.19	1.21	1.19	1.12	1.20	1.11	1.01	1.04
47	Fish (m)	1.00	1.00	1.00	1.00	1.00	1.00	1.00	1.00
48	Sugar (t)	1.00	1.00	1.00	1.00	1.00	1.00	1.00	1.00
49	Sugar (m)	1.22	1.20	1.14	1.01	1.05	1.07	0.96	1.14
50	Can (s+c)	1.00	1.00	1.00	1.00	1.00	1.00	1.00	1.00
51	Can (m+l)	1.00	1.00	1.00	1.00	1.00	1.00	1.00	1.00
52	Kretek	1.20	1.23	1.21	1.10	1.10	0.75	3.75	1.10
53	White	0.00	0.00	1.11	1.09	1.15	1.58	0.27	1.07
54	Oth	1.18	1.20	1.10	1.07	1.11	1.09	1.05	1.05
55	Wood	1.00	1.00	1.00	1.00	1.00	1.00	1.00	1.00
56	Textiles	1.32	1.30	1.35	1.31	1.31	1.29	1.24	1.19
57	Paper	1.09	1.19	1.20	1.23	1.24	1.21	1.25	1.08
58	Chemical	1.15	1.17	1.15	1.22	1.17	1.09	1.15	1.10
59	Coal	0.00	0.00	0.00	0.00	0.00	0.00	0.00	0.00
60	Petroleu	0.00	0.00	0.00	0.00	0.00	0.00	0.00	0.00
61	Gasoline	1.17	1.19	1.21	1.21	1.21	1.01	1.16	1.11
62	Fueloil	1.13	1.20	1.16	1.23	1.15	1.10	1.17	1.09
63	Electric	1.00	1.00	1.00	1.00	1.00	1.00	1.00	1.00
64	Gas	0.00	0.00	0.00	0.00	0.00	0.00	0.00	1.00
65	Water	1.00	1.00	1.00	1.00	1.00	1.00	1.00	1.00
66	Trade	1.19	1.22	1.22	1.22	1.10	1.11	1.13	1.10
67	Restaura	1.17	1.13	1.18	1.23	1.08	1.12	1.12	1.03
68	Hotel	1.00	1.00	1.00	1.00	1.00	1.00	1.00	1.00
69	Road	1.11	1.14	1.11	1.17	1.11	1.13	1.13	0.93
70	Air	1.00	0.98	0.96	1.06	1.00	1.01	1.01	0.91
71	Banking	1.00	1.00	1.00	1.00	1.00	1.00	1.00	1.00
72	Real	1.18	1.13	1.17	1.19	1.10	1.15	1.22	1.07
73	Public	1.11	1.12	1.14	1.16	1.09	1.10	1.16	1.04
74	Personal	1.08	1.13	1.21	1.21	1.08	1.09	1.18	1.08
75	Gov't	0.95	0.96	1.61	1.22	1.01	1.03	1.34	1.20
76	Capital	0.00	0.00	1.29	1.42	2.66	1.34	1.85	1.63
77	Net ind taxes	0.00	0.00	0.00	0.00	0.00	0.00	0.00	0.00
78	World	1.05	1.09	1.05	1.05	1.00	1.01	1.12	1.05

* Guesstimated by authors. Note that all other expenditure elasticities (for commodities not shown on this Table) are assumed unitary.

	Name	Urban Middle 32.	Urban Higher 33
35	Farmfood	0.60	0.27
36	Fmnonfd	1.00	1.00
37	Livestoc	1.07	0.98
38	Forestry	1.00	1.00
39	Fishery	1.00	1.00
40	Metal	0.00	0.00
41	Other	1.00	1.00
42	Hprice	0.55	0.23
43	Millrice	0.61	0.19
44	Farmtea	1.00	1.00
45	Proc.tea	1.00	1.00
46	Fish (t)	1.07	0.84
47	Fish (m)	1.00	1.00
48	Sugar (t)	1.00	1.00
49	Sugar (m)	1.11	0.78
50	Can (s+c)	1.00	1.00
51	Can (m+l)	1.00	1.00
52	Kretek	1.10	0.73
53	White	1.08	0.73
54	Oth	1.04	0.79
55	Wood	1.00	1.00
56	Textiles	1.18	0.97
57	Paper	1.12	1.01
58	Chemical	1.08	1.15
59	Coal	0.00	0.00
60	Petroleu	0.00	0.00
61	Gasoline	1.13	1.18
62	Fueloil	1.07	1.13
63	Electric	1.00	1.00
64	Gas	1.00	1.00
65	Water	1.00	1.00
66	Trade	1.10	0.95
67	Restaura	1.15	1.09
68	Hotel	1.00	1.00
69	Road	1.07	0.88
70	Air	1.01	0.80
71	Banking	1.00	1.00
72	Real	1.09	1.01
73	Public	1.06	1.05
74	Personal	1.09	1.14
75	Gov't	0.95	1.27
76	Capital	1.45	1.69
77	Net ind taxes	0.00	0.00
78	World	1.00	1.20

Appendix Table D Household Marginal Expenditure Propensities for Indonesia, 1975*

	Name	Agricultural Employees 24	Farm 1 25	Farm 2 26	Farm 3 27	Rural Lower 28	Rural Middle 29	Rural Higher 30	Urban Lower 31
35	Farmfood	0.128	0.138	0.083	0.062	0.095	0.061	0.057	0.035
36	Fmnonfd	0.009	0.010	0.008	0.006	0.006	0.007	0.005	0.003
37	Livestoc	0.028	0.036	0.041	0.034	0.026	0.036	0.034	0.024
38	Forestry	0.005	0.005	0.003	0.002	0.003	0.003	0.002	0.001
39	Fishery	0.015	0.015	0.015	0.014	0.017	0.019	0.018	0.014
40	Metal	0.000	0.000	0.000	0.000	0.000	0.000	0.000	0.000
41	Other	0.002	0.002	0.001	0.001	0.001	0.001	0.001	0.001
42	Hprice	0.015	0.064	0.120	0.037	0.020	0.036	0.014	0.004
43	Millrice	0.175	0.101	0.027	0.033	0.136	0.116	0.072	0.060
44	Farm tea	0.003	0.004	0.003	0.002	0.002	0.004	0.002	0.001
45	Proc. tea	0.001	0.001	0.001	0.001	0.001	0.001	0.001	0.001
46	Fish (t)	0.016	0.017	0.016	0.014	0.018	0.020	0.017	0.013
47	Fish (m)	0.004	0.003	0.002	0.002	0.003	0.003	0.003	0.002
48	Sugar (t)	0.006	0.008	0.006	0.004	0.004	0.005	0.004	0.002
49	Sugar (m)	0.014	0.013	0.012	0.012	0.012	0.012	0.011	0.009
50	Can (s+c)	0.000	0.000	0.000	0.000	0.000	0.000	0.000	0.000
51	Can (m+l)	0.000	0.000	0.000	0.000	0.000	0.000	0.000	0.000
52	Kretek	0.055	0.051	0.035	0.022	0.030	0.009	0.030	0.020
53	White	0.000	0.000	0.005	0.009	0.013	0.019	0.008	0.012
54	Oth	0.018	0.044	0.099	0.038	0.040	0.129	0.027	0.073
55	Wood	0.004	0.004	0.003	0.003	0.004	0.004	0.003	0.002
56	Textiles	0.034	0.044	0.030	0.033	0.048	0.039	0.042	0.054
57	Paper	0.022	0.018	0.017	0.020	0.036	0.043	0.057	0.033
58	Chemical	0.016	0.015	0.012	0.011	0.015	0.017	0.013	0.015
59	Coal	0.000	0.000	0.000	0.000	0.000	0.000	0.000	0.000
60	Petroleu	0.000	0.000	0.000	0.000	0.000	0.000	0.000	0.000
61	Gasoline	0.001	0.000	0.000	0.001	0.002	0.002	0.003	0.002
62	Fuel oil	0.003	0.002	0.002	0.002	0.003	0.002	0.002	0.003
63	Electric	0.002	0.002	0.001	0.001	0.002	0.002	0.004	0.008
64	Gas	0.000	0.000	0.000	0.000	0.000	0.000	0.000	0.000
65	Water	0.002	0.001	0.001	0.001	0.001	0.001	0.000	0.002
66	Trade	0.136	0.138	0.115	0.098	0.111	0.116	0.110	0.088
67	Restaura	0.054	0.039	0.023	0.017	0.048	0.035	0.033	0.080
68	Hotel	0.000	0.000	0.000	0.001	0.001	0.001	0.001	0.001
69	Road	0.030	0.037	0.029	0.022	0.042	0.031	0.028	0.050
70	Air	0.010	0.010	0.009	0.009	0.013	0.012	0.014	0.012
71	Banking	0.001	0.001	0.001	0.002	0.002	0.002	0.004	0.002
72	Real	0.049	0.047	0.040	0.030	0.041	0.058	0.044	0.060
73	Public	0.051	0.048	0.043	0.038	0.053	0.063	0.061	0.066
74	Personal	0.034	0.032	0.028	0.024	0.033	0.031	0.038	0.033
75	Gov't	0.003	0.004	0.010	0.022	0.004	0.005	0.010	0.020
76	Capital	0.000	0.000	0.120	0.320	0.049	0.002	0.140	0.100
77	Net ind taxes	0.000	0.000	0.000	0.000	0.000	0.000	0.000	0.000
78	World	0.050	0.040	0.030	0.030	0.050	0.051	0.060	0.060

* Derived by multiplying the expenditure elasticity for good I in Appendix Table B (Ey,) by the
corresponding average expenditure propensity (AEP,) in Table 11.5, i.e. MEP, = Ey, AEP1.

	Name	Urban Middle 32	Urban Higher 33
35	Farmfood	0.039	0.015
36	Fmnonfd	0.003	0.002
37	Livestoc	0.026	0.030
38	Forestry	0.001	0.000
39	Fishery	0.013	0.012
40	Metal	0.000	0.000
41	Other	0.001	0.001
42	Hprice	0.005	0.001
43	Millrice	0.058	0.012
44	Farmtea	0.001	0.001
45	Proc. tea	0.001	0.001
46	Fish (t)	0.012	0.009
47	Fish (m)	0.002	0.002
48	Sugar (t)	0.002	0.001
49	Sugar (m)	0.008	0.005
50	Can (s+c)	0.000	0.000
51	Can (m+l)	0.000	0.000
52	Kretek	0.013	0.004
53	White	0.008	0.010
54	Oth	0.075	0.043
55	Wood	0.003	0.002
56	Textiles	0.062	0.041
57	Paper	0.058	0.060
58	Chemical	0.016	0.013
59	Coal	0.000	0.000
60	Petroleu	0.000	0.000
61	Gasoline	0.003	0.004
62	Fueloil	0.002	0.002
63	Electric	0.012	0.011
64	Gas	0.000	0.000
65	Water	0.001	0.001
66	Trade	0.095	0.070
67	Restaura	0.096	0.048
68	Hotel	0.001	0.001
69	Road	0.053	0.036
70	Air	0.014	0.010
71	Banking	0.003	0.003
72	Real	0.102	0.070
73	Public	0.084	0.067
74	Personal	0.042	0.038
75	Gov't	0.008	0.030
76	Capital	0.002	0.229
77	Net ind taxes	0.000	0.000
78	World	0.074	0.070

Bibliography

G.C. Allen, "Japanese Industry: Its Organization and Development to 1937," in E.B. Schumpeter (Ed.) The Industrialization of Japan and Manchukuo, 1930-40, MacMillan, New York, 1940.

Sritua Arief, "The Indonesian Petroleum Industry: A Study of Its Impact on the Indonesian Economy," Ph.D. Dissertation, 1979, University of Hull, United Kingdom.

Asian Development Bank, Energy Sector Indonesia, 1980.

Asian Development Bank, Survey of Energy Utilization, Vols. 1 and 2, 1980.

A.S. Bhalla, Technology and Employment in Industry, ILO, Geneva, 1975.

A. Wade Blackman, Jr., et al., "An Innovation Index Based on Factor Analysis", in Harold A. Linstone and Devendra Sahal (Eds.), Technological Substitution: Forecasting Techniques and Applications, Elsevier, New York, 1976.

Anne Booth and Peter McCawley, "The Indonesian Economy in the Mid-Sixties," in Anne Booth and Peter McCawley, (Eds.), The Indonesian Economy During the Soeharto Era, Kuala Lampur, Oxford University Press, 1981.

BPPT/Bechtel National Inc., Energy Planning Study for Indonesia, Jakarta, 1981.

William H. Branson, Macroeconomic Analysis of the Effects of Energy Price Decontrol in Indonesia, World Bank Report, 1982.

Central Bureau of Statistics, Input-Output Table, 1975 and 1980.

Central Bureau of Statistics, Statistik Industry, 1975, 1979, 1980.

Central Bureau of Statistics, Sensus Industri Kecil, 1975, 1979.

Central Bureau of Statistics, Sensus Industri Rumah Tangga, 1975.

Central Bureau of Statistics, Social Accounting Matrix Indonesia, 1975, Vols. 1 and 2, August 1982.

William Collier, Jusuf Colter, Sinarhadi and Robert d'A. Shaw: "Choice of Technique in Rice Milling on Java," Bulletin of Indonesian Economic Studies, 1974, p. 116.

J. Defourny and E. Thorbecke, "Structural Path Analysis and Multiplier Decomposition within a Social Accounting Matrix Framework," The Economic Journal, 94, March 1984, pp. 111-136.

Howard Dick, "The Oil Price Subsidy, Deforestation and Equity," _Bulletin of Indonesian Economic Studies_ 16(3), November 1980, pp. 32-60.

Directorate General for Power and Energy/Development International, _Energy Planning for Development in Indonesia_, Jakarta, October, 1981.

Roger A. Downey, "Indonesian Inequality: Integrated National Accounting of Who Gets What", Ph.D. Thesis, Cornell University, 1984.

Roger A. Downey and Steven J. Keuning, "Introduction to the Indonesian Social Accounting Matrix", Institute of Social Studies Working Paper Series No. 25, 1985.

Zvi Griliches, "Hybrid Corn: An Exploration in the Economics of Technological Change," _Econometrica_, October, 1957, pp. 501-522.

Prof. Dr. Ing. B.J. Habibie, "Some Thoughts Concerning a Strategy for the Industrial Transformation of a Developing Country," address delivered to the Deustsche Gesellshaft fur Luft-und Raumfabt Bonn, GDR, June 1983, p. 23.

Y. Hayami and M. Kikuchi: _Asian Village Economy at the Crossroads_, University of Tokyo Press, 1981, p. 192.

Dennis Healy, _The Indonesian Economy: An Early 1981 Perspective_, Dept. of Economics, The University of Adelaide, p. 74.

Hal Hill, "Choice of Technique in the Indonesian Weaving Industry," _Economic Development and Cultural Change_, January 1983, Vol. 31, No. 2, pp. 337-354.

Hal Hill, Survey of Recent Developments, _Bulletin for Indonesian Economic Studies_, Vol. XX, No. , August 1984.

Hal Hill, "Dualism, Technology and Small-scale Enterprises in the Indonesian Weaving Industry," in R.G. Garnaut and P.T. McCawley, (Eds.) _Indonesia: Dualism, Growth and Poverty_, Australian National University, 1979, p. 336.

International Monetary Fund, International Financial Statistics, 1984, pp. 331-333.

International Monetary Fund, Balance of Payments Yearbook, Vol. 34, Part 1, 1983, p. 266.

Faisal Kasryno: Technological Progress and Its Effects on Income Distribution and Employment in Rural Areas: A Case Study of Three Villages in West Java, Indonesia, Agro-Economic Survey-- Rural Dynamics Study, Bogor, Indonesia, 1981.

James Keddie, "More on Production Techniques in Indonesia", in Robert Stobaugh and Louis T. Wells, Jr., (Eds.) Technology Crossing Borders, Harvard Business School Press, Boston, Mass., 1984.

James Keddie and William Cleghorn, "The Choice of Technology in Food Processes: Some Case Studies", in C. Baron (Ed.) Technology, Employment and Basic Needs in Food Processing in Developing Countries, New York, Pergammon Press, 1980.

Steven J. Keuning, "Distributive Aspects of Indonesian Agriculture: With Respect to Small-holders Land and Farm Food Crops," Institute of Social Studies Working Paper Series No. 2, 1984.

Steven J. Keuning, "The Distribution of Profits in Indonesia", Institute of Social Studies Working Paper Series No. 3, 1984.

Steven J. Keuning, "Modelling the Indonesian Social Accounting Matrix", Institute of Social Studies Working Paper Series No. 1, 1984.

Haider Khan, "Technology, Energy, Employment and Basic Needs: A Study of the Korean Manufacturing Sector," Report submitted to the Technology and Employment Branch, World Employment Programme, International Labour Office, Geneva, 1982.

Haider Khan, "Technology Choice in the Energy and Textile Sectors in the Republic of Korea," (forthcoming, in A.S. Bhalla, (Ed.) Technology and Employment in Industry, 3rd edition, 1985.

LIPI, Science and Technology Policy Research: A View from the Demand Side, Supply Side and the Linkage Area, 1983, p. 3.

Edwin Mansfield, et al., The Production and Application of New Industrial Technology, W.W. Norton, New York, 1977, p. 2.

Edwin Mansfield, Industrial Research and Technologicasl Innovation: An Econometric Analysis, W.W. Norton, New York, 1968 Preface and Introduction.

Peter McCawley, "Survey of Recent Developments, Bulletin of Indonesian Economic Studies, April 1983.

Peter McCawley, "The Growth of the Industrial Sector", in Anne Booth and Peter McCawley, (Eds.), The Indonesian Economy During the Soeharto Era, Oxford University Press, Oxford, 1981.

L. Mears, The New Rice Economy of Indonesia, Gadjah Madah University Press, 1981.

Zuhayr Mikdashi, The Community of Oil Exporting Countries: A Study in Governmental Co-operations, London: George Allen & Unwin Ltd., 1972.

Raymond F. Miksell et al., Foreign Investment in the Petroleum and Mineral Industries: Case Studies of Investor-Host Country Relations, Baltimore and London: The Johns Hopkins Press, 1971.

Muhammadi and Lebdo Suwarto, "Science and Technology for Development in Indonesia," Paper presented at the ASEAN-EEC Seminar on Science and Technology Indicators and Science Policy, Royal Society, London, 1983, pp. 41-43.

R.R. Nelson, T.P. Schultz and R.L. Slighton, Structural Change in a Developing Economy, Princeton University Press, Princeton, 1971.

Netherlands Economic Institute, "Industrial Development in Indonesia, Selected Prospects and Options,", Rotterdam, 1983.

Netherlands Economic Institute, "Structural Analysis of the Indonesian Manufacturing Sector," 1983.

Netherlands Economic Institute, MANKAP Project: Final Report, 1983, 1984. Arie Kuyvenhoven and Huib Pot, Industrial Development in Indonesia--Analysis and Options.

Douglas S. Paauw, "From Colonial to Guided Economy," in Ruth T. McVey (Ed.), Indonesia, New Haven: Human Relations Area File Press, 1963.

Douglas S. Paauw, "Export Promotion and Employment Creation During REPELITA IV", Working Paper, Employment and Income Distribution Strategy Project, ILO/Dept. of Manpower, Government of Indonesia, Jakarta, 1984.

M. Parvin and H. Khan, "Technological Progress and Productivity Change with Environmental Regulations and Labor-Management Conflict," unpublished manuscript, The University of Akron, 1984.

James Pickett and Robson, "Technology and Employment in the Production of Cotton Cloth," World Development, Vol. 5, No. 3, March 1977, pp. 203-215.

Mark Pitt, "Equity, Externalities and Energy Subsidies: The Case for Kerosene in Indonesia," Center for Economic Research, Department of Economics, The University of Minnesota, Discussion Paper No. 181, August 1983.

Mark M. Pitt and Lung-Fei Lee, "The Income Distributional Implications of Increasing Energy Prices in Indonesia", mimeo, Dept. of Economics, University of Minnesota, 1983.

Mark M. Pitt and Lung-Fei Lee, "The Measurement and Sources of Technical Inefficiency in the Indonesian Weaving Industry," Journal of Development Economics, No. 9, 1981, pp. 43-64.

H. Poot, "The Development of Labour Intensive Industries in Indonesia," in Rashid, Amjad, (Ed.), The Development of Labour Intensive Industry in ASEAN Countries. ARTEP, Bangkok, 1978.

H. Poot, "The Development of Labour Intensive Industries in Indonesia," in Rashid Amjad (Ed.), The Development of Labour Intensive Industry in ASEAN Countries, Asian Employment Programme, International Labour Organization, 1981.

G. Pyatt and J.I. Round, "Accounting and fixed-price multipliers in a social accounting matrix framework," Economic Journal, 1079, Vol. 89, pp. 850-73.

G. Pyatt and E. Thorbecke, Planning Techniques for a Better Future, International Labour Office, Geneva, 1976.

V.R. Reddy, "Small Farm Equipment Technology Transfer to Developing Countries, (Experiences Gained in Indonesia)," Paper presented at the meeting of the American Society of Agricultural Engineers, Madison, Wisconsin, 1982, p. 1.

Sherman Robinson, "Multisectoral Models of Developing Countries: A Survey", California Agricultural Experiment Station, Giannini Foundation of Agricultural Economics, University of California, Working Paper No. 401, April 1986.

David Salmon, An Evaluation of Investment in Agricultural Research in Indonesia, unpublished Ph.D. dissertation, The University of Minnesota, 1984.

Merle Esmay Soedjatmiko and Robert Stevens, "Appropriate Primary Tillage Mechanization for Rice in Indonesia," Paper presented at ASAE meeting at Madison, Wisconsin, June 1982, p. 5.

Hadi Soesastro, Rural Household Energy Survey in West Jawa in Energi dan Pemerataan. Hadi Soesastro et al., (Ed.) Centre for International Studies, Jakarta, 1983, p. 240.

Stan Stavenuiter, "The Employment Effects of Indonesia's 1982/83 Development Budget," Working Paper, Employment and Income Distribution Strategy Project, Jakarta, 1984.

J. Svejnar and E. Thorbecke, "Determinants and Effects of Technological Choice," Paper presented at the annual meeting of the American Association for the Advancement of Science, 1980.

J. Svejnar and E. Thorbecke, "The Determinants and Effects of Technological Choices," in Barbara Lucas, (Ed.) Internal and External Constraints on Technological Choice in Developing Countries, Tooley-Bowker Publishing Company, London, 1982.

C.P. Timmer, "Choice of Techniques in Rice Milling on Java", Bulletin of Indonesian Economic Studies, July 1973.

C.P. Timmer and H. Alderman, "Estimating Consumption Parameters for Food Policy Analysis," American Journal of Agricultural Economics, Vol. 61, No. 5, pp. 982-87, 1979.

World Bank/UNDP, Indonesia, Issues and Options for the Energy Sector, November 1981.

World Bank/UNDP, Report No. 2788-IND. Indonesia: Long-Run Development and Short-run Adjustment, 1980.

World Bank/UNDP, Report No. 2026-IND. Recent Developments, Short-Term Prospects and Development Issues, 1978.

World Bank/UNDP, Report No. 4279-IND. Indonesia: Policies for Growth with Lower Oil Prices, 1983.

Index

A-matrix, 4, 22, 99, 107, 108
accounting multiplier matrix, 34-5
aggregate energy requirements, 5-6, 94, 96
aggregate output effects, 63-6
agriculture, 10-14, 16, 55, 64, 104-5
    mechanisation, 119, 124-8, 131
aircraft industry, 131
Alderman, H., 51
Allen, G.C., 160
alternative technologies, 174
    A-matrix, 4, 22, 99, 107, 108
    accounting multiplier matrix, 34-5
    direct effects, 1, 2, 38
    fixed price multiplier matrix, 4, 36, 38-49
    indirect effects, 1-4, 38
    marginal expenditure propensity matrix, 35, 37
    SAM methodology and, 17-20
    transaction matrix, 4, 17, 21-35, 96
analytical studies, 54
appropriate technology, 14, 120, 172
Arief, Sritua, 91, 92
Arndt, H.W., 92
average expenditure propensity, 16,36-7, 38, 71
    matrix, 4, 22, 99, 107, 108
avigas, 3, 10

backward linkage, 1-2, 85, 86, 101, 169, 171
bagasse, 110
balance of payments, 132
    Indonesia, 5, 89-94, 164, 166, 169
balance of trade, 164, 165

bawon system, 134, 136
Bhalla, A.S., 14
BIMAS programme, 124, 125, 136
biomass, 89, 94, 96, 98-9, 107, 110, 112, 116-17, 165
BKPM, 155
Blackman, A.W., 133
Booth, Anne, 87
Branson, W.H., 109
Bulletin for Indonesian Economic Studies, 54
BULOG, 149

canning industry, 16, 59, 62, 64-5, 99, 102, 157, 164
capacity utilisation, 56
capital
    income (incorporated), 17, 86
    -labour ratio, 14, 56
    -output ratio, 14
    stock, 14, 16, 17
    utilisation, 56, 171
capital account, 4, 14, 21, 22, 34, 182
capital intensity, 55-6, 101, 162
    SAM-Tech, 3, 10
    technological indicators, 14, 16
    trends, 147, 149, 153 -6, 157, 162, 167
ceblokan system, 134, 136
cement industry, 101
census information, 15
Central Bank, 149
Central Bureau of Statistics, 15, 54, 178
    SAM, 3, 7, 9-10, 67, 96, 110, 168, 176, 177

charcoal, 99
cigarette industry, 3, 17, 59, 62, 64-5, 66-7,
    76, 101-2
'circuits', 72-6, 84
Cleghorn, W., 90, 176
'closure' rules, 168
coal, 3, 10, 89-90, 94, 101, 104, 111, 112,
    115-16
Cobb-Douglas production function, 146
Collier, W., 149
Colter, J., 160
commodities, 107
    dualistic sectors, 3, 10, 14-17
    imported, 9, 177
commodity account, 9, 177
comparative advantage, 56, 125
comparative static models, 6-7, 161, 168, 169,
    173
computable general equilibrium models, 168
consumption
    energy, 6, 90, 96-8, 104-7, 111-13, 165-6
    household, see household consumption
    submatrix, 173, 181-2
costs
    comparisons, 125-8, 130
    priority areas, 128-32
    rice milling, 149, 151-2
cotton spinning process, 127, 128
credit, 125
current account deficits, 92-4
customs tax, 178

data (lack), 3, 169-70
defence industries, 132
deforestation, 98, 116
Defourny, J., 71
descriptive studies, 54
Dick, Howard, 110
diffusion index, 142, 167
direct influence, 72, 74-5, 80, 81, 84, 162
disaggregated energy requirements, 5-6, 94,
    96
Downey, R.A., 50, 96, 181-2
dualistic sectors, 21
    classification scheme, 10-14
    establishment size, 4-5, 57-62
    indirect expenditures, 101-3
    linkages, 63-6, 133-43, 161, 163, 165, 170
    selection, 3, 10, 14-17
    technology-cum-product sector, 2, 3, 5,
        15-16, 36, 39, 53, 63, 66-7, 76, 80, 123,
        128, 162-5, 171
    trends, 147-58
dynamic approach, 7, 120, 121, 168

econometric models, 54, 121, 123, 143, 166
economic growth, 169, 172, 174
economic influence, see influence (economic)
economies of scale, 50-51
economy-wide model, 119, 120-24
elasticities, 171
    expenditure, 35-7
    income, 4, 34-6, 37, 107, 182
electricity, 3, 10, 94, 96-8, 101, 102, 104,
    107, 112
'elementary paths', 72-6, 80, 81, 84
employment
    effects, 5, 54-5, 66-7, 68-9, 163-4
    firm size, 57-8, 59
    trends, 147-58
    see also labour; wages; workers
endogenous accounts, 4, 21-3, 34, 35
energy
    average expenditure propensity for, 4, 16,
        22, 99, 107, 108
    classification scheme, 10-14
    consumption, 6, 90, 96-8, 104-7, 111-13,
        165-6
    -content, 98-9, 107, 174
    -intensity, 98-102, 169
    -labour intensity hypothesis, 90, 98-9, 165
    production (patterns), 102-8
    production/reserves, 112, 114-18, 172
    requirements, 5-6, 62-3, 94, 96
    use, 101, 169
energy sector
    aggregate effects, 65
    disaggregation, 3, 10, 165-6, 169, 173-4,
        182
    macroeconomic analysis, 89-108, 111-17,
        161
equilibrium approach
    general, see general equilibrium models
    partial, 108, 166, 176
equity/growth trade-off, 169, 174
evolutionary model of technical change, 132,
    133-40, 143, 161, 167
excess capacity 2, 4, 22, 66, 167-8, 171, 174
exogenous accounts, 4, 14, 21, 23, 34, 36,
    165, 182
    leakages, 2, 22, 35
expenditure elasticities, 35-7
    see also average expenditure propensity;
    marginal expenditure propensity
exports, 4, 22, 55, 165, 182
    oil, 91-2, 105, 166
    petroleum, 90, 92, 105

factor analysis, 133
factor income, 2, 17, 21, 22, 34, 37

macroeconomic effects, 5, 66-7, 68-9
factor prices, 141, 146, 159
factors of production, 10-14, 22, 34
    fixed price multiplier matrix, 40-42
    ownership patterns, 37
farmers (income), 133-40
feasibility study, 1
feedback circuits, 74-5, 84
firewood, 99, 110, 111
firm size, 4-5
    manufacturing industries, 14, 15, 57-62
fish processing, 59, 64-5, 99, 156-7
fixed price multiplier, 161-2, 168, 174
    energy, 101, 102-5, 108
    factor income/employment, 66-7
    household income, 53, 57, 67-71, 165
    linkages, 63-6
    matrix, 4, 36, 38-49
    national/sectoral output, 62-3
    submatrix, 105-6
foreign investment, 114, 115, 155-6
forests, 98, 116-17
forward linkage, 1-2, 101
fuel oil, 3, 10, 94, 98-9, 101, 102, 104, 105,
    107, 108

Garnaut, R.G., 160
gas, 3, 10, 94, 96-8, 101-2, 104
gasoline, 3, 10, 94, 98-9, 101, 104, 107, 108,
    111
general equilibrium models, 57, 71, 176
    computable, 168
    multi-sectoral, 167-70, 174
'generalised inverse', 55
geothermal energy, 89, 111, 112, 116
Gini coefficient, 136
global influence, 74-6, 80, 81-2, 84, 85, 162
government
    exogenous accounts, 4, 14, 21
    expenditure, 22, 55, 182
    research institutions, 130-31
    revenue, 4, 5, 89-94, 95, 166
Griliches, Zvi, 133
growth, 169, 172, 174

Habibie, B.J., 128, 130
Hayami, Y., 133-4, 135
Healy, D., 160
Hill, Hal, 110, 114, 115, 160
household consumption, 2, 17, 21, 57
    energy, 90, 96-8, 104-7, 111-12, 165-6
    submatrix, 173, 181-2
household income
    energy consumption and, 90, 96-8, 104-7,
        111-12, 165-6

energy production, 102, 104-5
    fixed price multiplier, 53, 57, 67-71
    macroeconomic effects, 67, 70-71
    by socioeconomic group, 4, 17, 21, 165,
        169, 182
household and cottage industries, 15, 57-9, 62
hydroelectric power, 89, 111, 112, 116

ILO, 54
import
    coefficients, 96, 178
    duties, 178
imports, 92, 164, 166
    commodities, 9, 177
    intermediate inputs, 1, 96, 169, 177
    technology, 120, 125, 126, 130
income
    distribution, 133-40, 163, 167
    elasticities, 4, 34-6, 37, 107, 182
    factorial, *see* factor income
    growth, 169, 172, 174
    household, *see* household income
indirect expenditure, 101-3
indirect taxation, 4, 9, 14, 21, 177
Indonesia
    energy sector, 111-17
    government revenue, 5, 90-94, 95
    industrial sector (studies), 54
    macroeconomic effects, *see* macro-
        ecomic effects (analysis)
    SAM-Tech (basis), 3, 9-14, 162
    SAM-Tech (structural path analysis), 76-
        86, 168
Indonesian Institute of Sciences, 127, 128,
    130, 131, 155
industrial research institutions, 130-31
industrial sector (Indonesia), 54
industrial surveys, 174
industrialisation strategies, 56-7, 174
influence (economic), 80, 81-2, 84, 85-6, 162
    transmission of, 5, 71-6
informal sector, 16, 63-6
input-output
    coefficients, 146, 166, 182
    information, 15-16, 55, 59, 147
    matrix, 80
    methodology, 2, 4, 54-7
    submatrix, 178
    transaction matrix, 4, 17, 21-34, 35, 96
inputs, *see* intermediate inputs
Institute of Social Studies, 7, 110, 168, 176
institutions (in fixed price multiplier matrix),
    43
interinstitutional transfers, 37, 80
intermediate inputs, 10, 22, 34, 37, 57, 58, 178

imported, 1, 96, 169, 177
intermediate technology, 172, 176
International Financial Statistics, 148
International Labour Office, 54
International Monetary Fund, 148
International Rice Research Institute,124, 126
investment, 57, 125, 149, 168
  foreign, 114, 115, 155-6

Japan, 114, 115
Jatisari study, 136-40

Kasryno, F., 133, 136, 140
Keddie, J., 90, 133
kerosene, 3, 96, 98-9, 105, 111-12
Keuning, S.J., 50, 96, 176, 179, 180
Khan, H., 4, 90, 94, 128, 144, 160, 176
Kikuchi, M., 133-4, 135
Korea, 99, 174

labour
  -energy intensity, 90, 98-102, 165
  intensity, 3, 14, 54-6, 66
  skills, 14, 16, 17, 67, 171-2
  see also employment; wages; workers
land, 17, 37, 66, 81, 125, 163
land transportation, 131, 132
large/medium scale enterprises, 4, 15, 58-9, 62, 154-5, 157-8, 162-3
LDCs, 140, 141, 174-5
leakages, 2, 22, 35, 37-8, 169
Lee, Lung-Fei, 109, 110, 160
'Leontief inverse', 2, 54, 55, 57
Leontief production functions, 145
linkages, 163-5, 170
  backward, 1-2, 85, 86, 101, 169, 171
  forward, 1-2, 101
  macro level, 133, 140-43, 167
  micro level, 133-40
  nature/magnitude, 63-6
LIPI, 127, 128, 130, 131, 155
Liquified Natural Gas, 94, 115
Liquified Petroleum Gas, 115
literacy programme, 125

M-diffusion, 133, 143, 153, 167
McCawley, Peter, 54, 87, 95, 160
macroeconomic diffusion model, 174
macroeconomic effects (analysis), 162-4
  establishment size, 57-62
  factor income/employment, 66-7, 68-9
  household income, 67-70, 71
  linkages, 63-6
  national/sectoral output, 62-3

other studies, 53-7
  structural path analysis, 71-86
macroeconomic linkage, 133, 140-43, 167
MANKAP project, 171-2
Mansfield, Edwin, 133, 144
manufacturing sector, 54, 55-6, 104
  firm size, 14, 15, 57-62
  and processing, 10-14, 15, 16
marginal expenditure propensity, 36-7, 38, 71, 174
  matrix, 35, 37
  structural path analysis, 76, 81-4, 86
Mariuk study, 136-40
market-forces, 133, 143, 153, 167
Mears, L., 59, 148, 150-52, 160, 176, 179
mechanisation (agriculture), 119, 124-8, 131
microeconomic
  effects, 1
  linkages, 133-40
  technology diffusion, 140-43, 159
Mikdashi, Z., 109
mining sectors, 10-14, 15, 64, 94, 104
ministerial research institutions, 131
modern technology, 169
  cost comparisons, 125-8
  linkages, 63-6, 133-43, 161, 163-5, 170
  relative importance, 57-62, 162-3
  see also capital intensity; dualistic sectors
modified labour-energy intensity hypothesis, 99, 165
Muhammadi, Professor, 131
multi-sectoral models, 167-70, 174
multiplier analysis, 21
multiplier matrix
  accounting, 34-5
  fixed price, 4, 36, 38-49

National Centre for Research, Science and Technology, 131
national output, 5, 62-3
natural gas, 3, 10, 89, 90, 94, 96, 101-2, 104, 107-8, 111-12, 114, 165
natural resources, 56-7
Nelson, R.R., 140, 141
Netherlands Economic Institute, 54, 56, 171, 176
Nippon Sharyo, 132
North Subang study, 134-6
Norton, W.W., 144

oil
  exports, 91-2, 105, 166
  Indonesia, 89-90, 94-5, 98, 101-2, 104-5, 107, 111-12, 114-16, 166
  OPEC, 105, 165

revenue, 94, 95
output
  -capital ratio, 14
  effect (aggregate), 63-6
  national, 5, 62-3
  sectoral, 2, 5, 62-3, 162, 166
  by size class, 57-9
  trends, 147-58
ownership, 121

P.T. Industri Kereta Api (PT INKA), 132
Paauw, D.S., 54, 55, 87
partial equilibrium approach, 108, 166, 176
Parvin, M., 144
Pereira, A., 110
Pertamina, 92, 121
petrol, 3, 10, 89, 91, 94, 96, 101-2, 104, 107-8, 111-12, 114-15, 165-6
  exports, 90, 92, 105
Pickett. J., 160
Pitt, M.M., 109, 110, 155, 160
planning horizons, 168
pole of destination, 81, 84, 164
pole of origin, 76, 80, 81, 84, 164
policy issues, 170-73
political economy, 176
Poot, H., 54, 59, 62, 160
poverty, 105, 169, 170
price(s), 9, 149-50, 177, 181-2
  endogenous model, 174
  energy, 104-5
  factor, 141, 146, 159
primary sectors, 63-4, 66
priority areas (R and D), 120, 128-32
product-cum-technology, 2-3, 5, 15-16, 36, 39, 53, 63, 66-7, 76, 80, 123, 128, 162-5, 171
production
  accounts, 9, 177
  coefficients, 10, 15, 16
  of energy, 6, 102-8, 112, 114-18, 172
  functions, 125, 145-6
  scale of, 50-51, 56
  structure of, 17, 96, 98-101
production activities (sectors), 2
  classification, 3, 17, 21, 162
  fixed price multiplier matrix, 44-9
  incomes, 22-3, 34
  Indonesian SAM, 9, 10-14
  SAM-Tech construction, 177-8
productivity, 57-9
  R and D, 121-3, 125, 155, 157, 166
products, 140, 172, 173
project analysis, 1
Pyatt, G., 35, 51

R-diffusion, 133, 143, 167
Reddy, V.R., 124
rent, 66, 81, 163, 174
REPELITA I, 149, 155
REPELITA II, 127, 129, 155
REPELITA IV, 55, 128, 165
research (future directions), 170-73
research and development, 172
  agricultural, 119-20, 124-8
  current priority areas, 120, 128-32
  diffusion of technology and, 132-43, 166-7, 174
  economy-wide model, 119-24, 161, 175
research institutions, 130-31
rest of the world, 4, 14, 21, 34, 177
retained values, 91-2
rice crops, 17, 38-9, 99, 102
  establishment size, 57-62
  household income and, 67, 69-70, 71
  impact of technology, 133-40, 167
  informal sector, 64-6, 67
  milling units, 147-53, 167
  R and D, 119, 124-7
  structural path analysis, 81-2, 84-6
  wages, 134, 135, 136-40
Robson, R., 160
Round, J.I., 35, 51

Salmon, David, 125, 144
SAM (framework), 57, 174
  data/concepts, 2, 3-4, 17-49
  economic influence within, 71-6
  energy sector analysis, 5, 94-108
  Indonesian, 3, 9-14
  microeconomic technology, 140-43, 159
  modelling technology choice, 162-7
  R and D activities, 119-32
SAM-Tech, 162, 167
  basis, 3, 9-14
  construction (steps), 177-8
  selection of sectors, 3, 14-17
  structural path analysis, 5, 76-86
Sankar, T.L., 116
savings, 2, 17, 21, 169
saw mills/wood mills, 157-8
Schultz, T.P., 145
sectoral output, 2, 5, 62-3, 162, 166
sectoral studies, 54, 56, 174
Sentul study, 136-40
sequential production, 125, 126, 128
services sector, 10-14, 55, 104
sharecropping, 136
Shaw, R. d'A., 160
shipbuilding industry, 131-2
Simon, H., 146

Sinarhadi, 160
Singapore, 114
skills, 14, 16, 17, 67, 171-2
Slighton, R.L., 145
small enterprises, 4, 15, 57-9, 154-5, 157-8, 162-3
Social Accounting Matrix, *see* SAM
socioeconomic groups
consumption by, 2, 17, 21
household income, 4, 17, 21, 165, 169, 182
Soedjatmiko, M.E., 144
Soeharto, President, 94
Soesastro, Hadi, 98
South Subang study, 134-6
spill-over effects, 174
spinning, 127, 128, 153-6
Stavenuiter, S., 54
Stevens, R., 144
structural path analysis, 21, 161, 162
applied to SAM-Tech, 76-86, 168
methodology, 71-6, 164
supply bottlenecks and, 170, 171
study layout, 3-7
study limitations, 167-70
subsidies, 21, 98, 105, 173, 176
substitutes, 173, 174
sugar industry, 17, 62, 98-9, 101-2
household income and, 70, 83, 85-6
informal sector, 64-5, 66, 67
structural path analysis, 81, 83, 85
supply, 170, 171, 173
constraints, *see* excess capacity
Suwar to Lebdo, 144
Svejnar, J., 14

tea industry, 64-5, 66, 99, 102
technical change, 132-40, 143, 161, 167
technological indicators, 3, 14-17, 147, 162
technology
appropriate, 14, 120, 172
diffusion of, 132-43, 166-7, 174
energy-content, 90, 98-102, 107, 174
income distribution and, 133-40, 163
intermediate, 172, 176
R and D and, 119-32
see also alternative technologies; product-cum-technology
technology choice, 162-7
Indonesian, 53-4, 56-7
policy issues, 170-73
telecommunications sector, 131, 132
textiles, 99, 101, 107-8
R and D, 119, 124, 127-8, 129, 131
spinning, 127, 128, 153-6
weaving, 16, 127-9, 153-6

Thorbecke, E., 4, 50, 71
time-series data, 89, 142, 146, 166
Timmer, C.P., 51, 87, 148, 149, 176
total influence, 73-4, 80, 162
trade/transportation margins, 9-10, 177
traditional technology, 169
cost comparisons, 125-8
displacement 57-62, 162-3
labour-intensive, 3, 14, 54-6, 66, 162
linkages, 63-6, 133-43, 161-5, 170
see also dualistic sectors
transaction matrix, 4, 17, 21-35, 96
translog production function, 125
transportation sector, 16, 131-2

UNDP, 89, 109, 117, 182
United States, 114, 115, 124
university research, 131
USAID, 124

value added
coefficients, 96, 166, 182
distribution of, 2, 16, 17, 21
production activities, 2, 35, 37
by size class, 14, 15, 57-8
submatrix, 179-80
trends, 147-58
per worker, 14, 16, 140-41, 147-8, 154, 156, 179-80
village economies, 133-40

wages, 15-16, 67, 171, 174
rice sector, 134, 135, 136-40
weaving, 16, 127, 128, 129, 153-6
wholesale and retail trade, 9, 10
workers
paid/unpaid, 16, 17, 67, 85-6
value added per, *see* value added
see also employment; labour; wages
World Bank, 89, 109, 114, 115, 116, 117
Survey, 110, 182